Public Speaking
Choices for Effective Results

Fifth Edition

John J. Makay
Bowling Green State University

Mark J. Butland
Austin Community College

Gail E. Mason
Eastern Illinois University

KENDALL/HUNT PUBLISHING COMPANY
4050 Westmark Drive   Dubuque, Iowa 52002

Book Team
Chairman and Chief Executive Officer   Mark C. Falb
President and Chief Operating Office   Chad M. Chandlee
Vice President, Higher Education   David L. Tart
Director of National Book Program   Paul B. Carty
Editorial Development Manager   Georgia Botsford
Senior Developmental Editor   Angela Willenbring
Vice President, Operations   Timothy J. Beitzel
Assistant Vice President, Production Services   Christine E. O'Brien
Senior Production Editor   Charmayne McMurray
Permission Editor   Renae Horstman
Cover Designer   Sandy Beck
Web Project Manager   Billee Jo Hefel

This book was previously published by Harcourt Brace College Publishers

Printed in the United States of America
10 9 8 7 6 5 4 3 2 1

Dedication

To the memory of my late parents, Joseph and Olive Makay, who made my education possible and enthusiastically supported my career in education.

—John Makay

To my wife, Natalie, and son Christopher, who continue to make every day an adventure.

—Mark Butland

To my two teenagers, Sarah and Augie, and Tim, my husband and biggest fan.

—Gail Mason

Brief Contents

Contents

Chapter 4
Listening and Evaluating Speeches   54

Part 2
Preparing and Presenting Your Speech   73

Chapter 5
The Speaker and Audience Connection   74

Chapter 6
Research and Supporting Material   94

Chapter 10
Language, Style, and Humor   206

Chapter 11
Delivery   226

Part 3
Types of Public Speaking   249

Chapter 12
Speaking to Inform   250

Informative Speaking   252

Informative Versus Persuasive Intent   252

Types of Informative Speaking   253

Chapter 13
Speaking to Persuade   268

Chapter 14
Speeches for Special Occasions   296

Chapter 15
Small Group Presentations   320

Preface

By providing complete and thorough coverage for the study and practice of public speaking, the fifth edition offers students theory and practical skills, presenting public speaking as an art form for transactional communication between speaker and audience.

Our goal in writing this text is to make it one that will prepare students to become effective public speakers in any of the various speaking situations they may encounter in their lives. Whether they are presenting in a professional capacity, speaking as a community leader, offering a tribute to a retiring colleague, eulogizing a friend, delivering a commencement address, or sharing views as a concerned citizen, these and other public speaking situations will result in an effective message to the audience.

The text is comprised of three parts:
Part 1: Public Speaking in Our Lives
Part 2: Preparing and Presenting Your Speech
Part 3: Types of Public Speaking

Part 1: Public Speaking in Our Lives

Public speaking is an essential activity that begins at an early age. Part 1 explores the role of public speaking in our lives and prepares students to present, while discussing the role of ethics in speech. The importance of listening and evaluating speeches is also a key element of Part 1.

Chapter 1: Public Speaking and the Challenge of Communication

This chapter focuses on public speaking as a valuable activity that influences career and community success. The basic elements of the communication process are outlined and defined to provide the foundation for growth and understanding.

Chapter 2: Getting Started on Your First Speech

In order to prepare students to speak effectively, eight steps are presented. These include specific points such as deciding on a topic, as well as more general guidelines regarding the ethics and language used in the message. Strategies for controlling tension, a critical point for beginning speakers, are also included.

Chapter 3: The Ethics of Responsible Speech

An essential element of every speech, ethics is defined and explained through the application of nine guidelines to promote speaker credibility. Points for avoiding unethical practices are also included in this chapter.

Chapter 4: Listening and Evaluating Speeches

As crucial as the skills for speaking are to a presenter, just as important are listening skills to the audience. Understanding how you listen helps improve the process. Eight steps promote fine-tuning your listening skills. Criteria for speech evaluation are discussed as well.

Part 2: Preparing and Presenting Your Speech

The focus of Part 2 is the actual work of planning, researching, and delivering your speech. This section offers numerous strategies for the stages of preparing and presenting, from the beginning ideas of who the audience will be and what kind of message will captivate them, through to the most effective delivery techniques as you present.

Chapter 5: The Speaker and Audience Connection

The theme of this text centers on the connection between the speaker and the audience, and that is the entire focus of this chapter. In order to make a favorable impression on your audience, it is critical to understand who your audience is and how to make your message one that is most likely to make an impact.

Chapter 6: Research and Supporting Material

Research is the raw material that forms the foundation of your speech, and this chapter helps you develop an effective research strategy as well as provides guidelines for using various methods of supporting your speech.

Chapter 7: Presentational Aids

Exploring the different types available and offering criteria for their use and display, this chapter focuses on the benefits of using presentations. Your decision to include an aid should be based on the extent to which it enhances your audience's interest and understanding. Guidelines are presented for determining what to incorporate and how to use it. Extensive information on PowerPoint presentations is also included.

Chapter 8: Organizing and Outlining Your Ideas

Organizing your speech helps your audience follow your points and understand your message. This chapter concentrates on developing the body of your speech, including selecting, supporting, and organizing your main points. This chapter also discusses how to create effective outlines and speaker's notes to best serve you as you present.

Chapter 9: Introducing and Concluding Your Speech

This chapter approaches introductions and conclusions in relation to how your speech can make a lasting impression. It discusses both how to engage your audience at the beginning of the speech so they will want to listen, and then how to remind your audience at the end of what you said and why it was relevant. Techniques and suggestions for introductions and conclusions are offered.

Chapter 10: Language, Style, and Humor

It is important to remember to consider how words affect your listeners.
In this chapter, we identify characteristics of spoken language and provide guidelines for using it more effectively. We also address pitfalls, which are aspects of language that a speaker should avoid. The use of humor is also discussed.

Chapter 11: Delivery

Your ability to communicate information, persuade, and entertain is influenced by the manner in which you present yourself to your audience. Chapter 11 discusses methods of delivery and offers specific strategies for vocal delivery and physical delivery so your message is favorably enhanced by the way you convey it.

Part 3: Types of Public Speaking

In Part 3, we discuss specifically the kinds of different speeches intended to inform, persuade, and entertain or inspire your audience. Another common scenario is speaking in a small group situation, and this section offers suggestions for all types of public speaking environments.

Chapter 12: Speaking to Inform

The intent of an informative speech is to communicate information and ideas in a way that your audience will understand and remember. The different types of informative speeches are identified, and goals and strategies for informative speaking are presented.

Chapter 13: Speaking to Persuade

Persuasion is intended to influence choice through appeals to your audience's sense of ethics, reasoning, and emotion. This chapter explores the goals of persuasive speaking and discusses reasoning, appeals, and arguments as well as the ethics of persuasive messages.

Chapter 14: Speeches for Special Occasions

Beginning with general guidelines for special occasion speeches, this chapter discusses how to present effectively in the most common situations wherein a brief speech is appropriate. This chapter addresses topics such as speeches of introduction, speeches of presentation, speeches of acceptance, commemorative speeches, the keynote speech, and after-dinner speeches.

Chapter 15: Small Group Presentations

Small groups are a part of life and you may have opportunities to speak in a variety of professional, academic, and community situations in a small group setting. This chapter discusses role responsibilities, working and presenting in a small group, and small group formats.

This text offers a comprehensive view of public speaking by exploring thoroughly all its elements and offering practical suggestions and guidelines for students to apply in their speaking efforts in any situation.

Student Oriented Pedagogy

Because we recognize the importance of assessing student learning, we have included features in each chapter that facilitate student learning and help instructors measure learning outcomes.

- **Chapter Outlines** serve as a map to guide students through the content of the chapter and focus on key points.
- **Bold-faced Key Terms** throughout the chapter include clear definitions for each term.
- **Real-world Examples and Strategies** illustrate chapter theories and concepts, as well as help students apply those concepts in their own work.
- **Questions for Study and Discussion** encourage students to further explore the concepts they learned in the chapter.
- **Activities** provide additional opportunities to apply students' knowledge of chapter material.
- **Glossary of Terms** serves as a helpful reference tool at the end of the text.

Instructional Online Enhancements

Both students and instructors have access to online content that is integrated chapter by chapter with the text to enrich student learning. The web access code is included on the inside front cover of the textbook.

 Look for the web icon in the text margins to direct you to various interactive tools.

Student Web Content

- **Poll Questions** draw students into the subject matter of the chapter by asking questions relevant to students and the chapter theme.
- **Video** brings the chapter content to life, clearly illustrating theory by showcasing actual student speeches.
- **Interactive Video Exercises** reinforce chapter concepts by incorporating chapter content with an actual speech example to illustrate the application of the concept.
- **Applications** offer real-world scenarios to key terms so students can apply them effectively.
- **Interactive Flashcards** reinforce definitions of key terms.

Instructor Web Content

- **Chapter Outlines** highlight central ideas for each chapter and can serve as lecture notes.
- **Activities and Worksheets** further explore chapter content and can be made accessible to students.
- **Extensive Teaching Tips** enhance the textbook content to aid student understanding.
- **Comprehensive Test Bank** offers several different types of questions to better assess student comprehension.

Acknowledgements

I wish to thank Thomas Gantz for initially encouraging us to undertake a fifth edition of this book and to the editorial and production staff at Kendall/Hunt Publishing Company, especially Paul Carty and Angela Willenbring. I want to thank my friend and former advisee Dr. Jennifer Walton for her support of our text and my countless students in public speaking classes for providing me with knowledge and motivation to write about public speaking.   —John Makay

I wish to thank the Kendall/Hunt and Great River Technologies people, including Paul Carty, Angela Willenbring, Billee Jo Hefel, Keith Kropp, Tom Gantz and others, who made this project a wonderful experience. I also want to express my heartfelt gratitude for the encouragement, guidance and mentorship I have received from Diana K. Ivy, Steven A. Beebe, and Mark L. Knapp. Special thanks to my students, particularly those who provided feedback on early editions of this text. Finally, thanks to my entire family for their unending encouragement.   —Mark Butland

I echo John's comments regarding Paul Carty and Angela Willenbring at Kendall/Hunt. I couldn't ask for better editors! I would like to acknowledge three professional role models and mentors whose unique insight and dedication influenced me immeasurably: Tim Hopf, Joe Ayres, and Dennis Gouran. Thanks also to my husband Tim and my good friend Therese for all their love and encouragement. My deepest appreciation goes to my students who energized me and who provided me with countless examples that appear throughout this text.   —Gail Mason

We gratefully acknowledge the constructive comments of the colleagues who provided reviews for individual chapters of this text. They include:

Kenneth Albone
Rowan University

Tim Anderson
Elgin Community College

Christa Brown
Minnesota State University–Mankato

Sabrina Caine
Erie Community College–City

Eric Carlson
Collin County Community College

Scott Christen
Tennessee Technical University–Cookville

Kathryn Dederichs
Minneapolis Community & Technical College

Linda Desjardins
Northern Essex Community College

Sally Deuermeyer
Blinn College

Anie Dubosse
Norwalk Community College

John Edwards
Fayetteville Technical Institute

Steven Epstein
Suffork County Community College–Brentwood

Barbara Franzen
Central Community College–Hastings

Karrie Gavin
Temple University

Steven Ginley
Morton College

Debbi Hatton
Sam Houston State University

Kim Higgs
University of North Dakota

Karen Huck
Central Oregon Community College

Mark Johnson
Rhodes State College

Bernadette Kapocias
Southwestern Oregon Community College

Michele King
College of William & Mary

Kara Laskowski
Shippensburg University

John Luecke
University of Wisconsin–Whitewater

Edie MacPherson
Suffolk County Community College–Selden

Diane Matuschka
University of North Florida

Jamie McKown
College of Charleston

Shawn Miklaucic
Pace University–New York

Mike Milford
Tarleton State University

Emma Moore
Santa Barbara City College

Beverly Neville
Central New Mexico Community College

Tushar Oza
Oakland University

Joyce Pauley
Moberly Area Community College

Matthew Petrunia
University of New Mexico

Kelly Rocca
St. John's University

Marybeth Ruscica
St. John's University

Nick Russell
California State University–Long Beach

Cindy Stout
Midlands Technical College

Darren Sweeney
Manchester Community College

Charles Tichy
Creighton University

Mike Wartman
Normandale Community College

Sharon Waters
Tidewater Community College

Trent Webb
Nassau Community College

Richard West
University of Texas–San Antonio

John J. Makay, Ph.D., is currently Professor Emeritus in the Department of Interpersonal Communication and the School of Communication Studies at Bowling Green State University. His teaching experience includes courses and seminars at the graduate and undergraduate levels. He has served as a department chair and as director of the School of Communication Studies at BGSU. He was the director of the basic course in public speaking at the Ohio State University for 16 years, and he has taught public speaking at Purdue University, The Pontifical College Josephinum, The State University of New York at Geneseo, Bowling Green State University, and Owens Community College in Toledo, Ohio. Dr. Makay has authored, edited, and co-authored a number of books in communication and his work has appeared in national, regional, and state communication journals and at international, national, regional, and state conventions. He currently resides in Maumee, Ohio.

Mark Butland, M.A., has taught public speaking at Texas State University, Baylor University, McLennan County Community College, and Austin Community College, where he currently serves as Professor of Speech Communication. In addition to his 20 years of teaching experience, Mark is a professional speaker and workshop trainer. Mark is an active member of the National Speakers Association, a professional speakers association that focuses on the art and business of speaking, and the American Society of Training and Development, a professional trainers association. Insights and lessons from the trenches enliven and inform his academic perspectives on public communication. While on faculty at Austin Community College, Mark served as founder and coordinator of the college Honor's Program from 1997-1999, was a pioneer in distance learning and has received recognition and awards for his excellent teaching. He has published scholarly research in instructional communication and has written instructor's manuals in interpersonal communication and public speaking. Mark received his B.A. and M.A. at Texas State University.

Gail Mason, Ph.D., is a professor in the Department of Communication Studies at her undergraduate alma mater, Eastern Illinois University. In addition to serving as Basic Course Director and Graduate Teaching Assistant Supervisor, Gail teaches a variety of undergraduate and graduate courses, including public speaking, small groups, conflict management, organizational communication, communication research, intercultural communication, and women's studies. After receiving her master's degree from Washington State University, Gail worked for the extension program at the University of Missouri-Columbia and taught public speaking on-campus. After finishing her Ph.D. at Indiana University, she taught graduate and undergraduate courses at Central Michigan University, the University of Arkansas at Little Rock, and the University of Maryland European Division. Her publications and conference presentations reflect on ongoing interest in pedagogy as well as a life-long love of international travel.

PART 1

Public Speaking in Our Lives

© JupierImages Corporation.

CHAPTER 1

"There is an elemental power in having a living, breathing human being—right here, right now—interacting with other human beings. And when that living, breathing human being is a skilled communicator, he or she possesses real power. The power to change the way people feel, to change the way they think, and even to change the way they act."

Rex Kelly, General Manager,
Corporate Communications,
Mississippi Power Company

Public Speaking and the Challenge of Communication

Public Speaking in Your Life

Reflect for a moment about the first time you stood before a group of people. How old were you? Were you in kindergarten doing "show and tell?" Maybe you participated in "sharing" in first grade. Before you engaged in this activity, you had many decisions to make: What is it that I most want to show my class? What will my parents allow me to bring? What do I want to "share" about what I bring? Will my classmates think it is "awesome"? Perhaps you had some foreign coins to show your class. Maybe you wanted them to see your live bug collection, or the snake your parent captured recently. Maybe your parents would let you bring in your Dalmatian puppy, creatively named "Spot." You had a message to convey to your classmates: "Spot does tricks." You used a presentational aid: "Spot." You were hoping for some response from your listeners: "Awesome!"

However "elementary" the above example may seem, the point is this: We start speaking in public at a young age. We may not know that it is called public speaking. We may not receive public speaking training, but our teachers get us started at an early age. Why? Because public speaking is very important as a communication skill. And, at the same time, speaking in front of a group of listeners can be difficult. However, speaking effectively with an audience can be a *powerful process.* An impassioned eulogy may bring us to tears. An inflammatory speech may arouse anger, and an entertaining speech may lead to a good belly laugh. Through public speaking, we can take part in our democratic tradition by expressing our thoughts and ideas. At the local level, concerned citizens have the opportunity to exercise one of their First Amendment rights at open meetings of the city council and school board, where they may inform, persuade, or chastise their elected officials. In organizational settings, presentations and public speeches are common as spokespersons and audiences gather daily to manage the businesses and services in which their professional lives are centered. At the national level, public speaking skills may further someone's political career. For example, after his speech at the Democratic National Convention in 2004, Barack Obama went from being an unknown U. S. Senator from Illinois to being a regular presence on newscasts. Now we see him making a bid for the White House.

The impact a speaker has before an audience may be known immediately. For example, students generally clap to show approval or appreciation for what pleases them and they find ways to show dissent or disagreement for what does not. Recently, conservative spokesperson David Horowitz visited the college campus of one of your authors and found it a challenge to complete his speech amidst vocal protests by members of the Communist Party in America. Liberal journalist, the late Molly Ivans, however, visited several years earlier, and opponents stood quietly at the side of the room holding a banner, letting her know that there were those who did not want her to appear. These examples show that

Was your first experience as a speaker when you were in Kindergarten?
© *Andrey Stratilatov, 2008. Under license from Shutterstock, Inc.*

public speaking has the power to influence our behavior in some way, but not always in the way the speaker intended.

The way we live as American citizens has dramatically changed since the destruction of lives and the twin towers in New York City on September 11, 2001. As we write this book, the United States is engaged in military action in the Middle East. In the midst of national and international tensions and military actions, public speaking serves as a powerful force for taking action, resolving disagreements, persuading adversaries, and keeping audiences informed. Power is inherent in effective public speaking—power to communicate facts and emotions, convictions and attitudes, and values and beliefs—in a way that leaves a lasting, and often unequalled, impression on the audience.

Public speaking is also a *creative activity* that includes both mental and physical aspects. The mental aspect involves connecting thoughts and ideas in an original or innovative manner while centering on the audience's needs and interests. Delivering the speech is the physical aspect of the creative process, which includes knowing when to look at the audience, where to pause, where to place emphasis, being able to use appropriate gestures and body movement, communicating ethically, and expressing self-confidence.

Effective speakers have learned the art of public speaking and are able to design and deliver a speech that resonates with listeners through careful word-choice, organization, supporting material, appropriate eye-contact, and meaningful gestures. This art is audience-centered, and its core is the message.

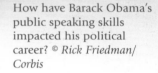

How have Barack Obama's public speaking skills impacted his political career? © *Rick Friedman/ Corbis*

Truly creative inventions such as post-it notes, the "It," and the Iphone may seem magical; the creative process, involving innumerable decisions, is often unseen by the user. Similarly, good public speaking requires a level of creativity. Developing an introduction that captures the attention of the audience, organizing the body of the speech to include relevant and interesting information, and creating a conclusion that is memorable are all tasks that are inspired by the individual.

Clearly, creativity requires important decision-making. While taking your public speaking class, you will have to determine your interests, analyze your audience, decide where to look for information, figure out the best way to organize your information, make decisions about word-choice, and decide how to deliver your speech most effectively. Public speaking is also a *decision-making process*.

Nancy Pelosi demonstrates one of her awkward gestures. © *ShawnThew/epa/ Corbis.*

As viewers watch speakers on television, it is easy to find examples of poor decision-making. Some star athletes who make millions of dollars for their knowledge and ability in a particular sport may come across poorly when speaking before an audience because they did not think about being interviewed in advance and were unprepared to comment on their performance. Politicians are fodder for late night television comedians, such as when John Stewart of the Daily Show lampooned newly-elected Speaker of the House Nancy Pelosi for her awkward gestures. On the television program *Dancing with the Stars*, one of the three critics slipped and referred to country singer Billy Ray Cyrus' dancing efforts as "crap." This was a public embarrassment and the singer responded defensively to the critic's poor choice of words. As authors, our task is to help you think about all the decisions you make when developing and delivering a speech and to guide you to be effective as a speaker and critical as a listener.

Public Speaking Is a Valuable Activity

It is fair to ask what value successful public speaking has in your life. Gaining self- confidence in front of an audience, learning how to make the best use of the time allowed to speak, and being active when given an opportunity to express what you know and how you feel are genuine benefits to be gained from success as a public speaker. Consider these two real-life examples:

- A student proudly announced to her class that what she was learning in her public speaking course had been instrumental in raising her level of personal achievement. She had been asked to help obtain corporate sponsors for her sorority's fundraiser to aid a nearby children's hospital. Her speech to an audience of executives at a local corporation persuaded them to make a contribution of $1,000. A company spokesperson told the student that she gave the best presentation the executives had heard from a college student. Her announcement moved her classmates to applause.
- A young, talented, and ambitious woman on a fast track for advancement in her career at a Washington, DC-based trade association was approached by her supervisor, who had given her a glowing job rating. After praising the woman for her performance during the past year, the supervisor explained that he wanted her to begin speaking about the industry to consumer groups across the country. The more specific he became about her future public speaking responsibilities, the more uneasy the woman grew. After several minutes, she said she had rarely given speeches before and that she wanted to avoid this responsibility—even if it meant changing her job. However, after a productive conversation with her boss, she agreed to enroll in a public speaking course taught in the evenings at a nearby college and to join one of the Toastmasters groups in the area. (Toastmasters International is an important self-improvement organization for busy adults who have a need to improve their public speaking skills.)

Public speaking skills are important for success in school, career advancement, and for increasing self-confidence. In the first example, a student reached her fundraising goals and the feedback from the executives and classmates raised, or at least reinforced, her self-confidence. In the second example, we are shown how a lack of skills may hinder career growth. Learning to communicate in a public setting is valuable for many reasons, including the six identified below.

Public Speaking Influences Success in College

Since you are currently in a higher-education classroom, it makes sense to note that the first reason to learn and practice the essentials of public speaking is because they may influence your success in college. Oral presentations in English, philosophy, political science, or environmental science are all considered public speaking events. Normally, part of your grade is based on your presentation skills. In addition to making presentations in your classes, any involvement in extracurricular activities may also be influenced by your ability to speak in public. If you are comfortable and possess the skills to address an audience, it will be possible to run for student body president, to present your point during an organizational meeting, or to be part of a film criticism workshop or a participant in a forensic program.

Public Speaking Teaches Critical Thinking Skills

A second reason for studying public speaking is that it teaches critical thinking. Generally, teachers of any subject are concerned that students learn to think critically. Some argue that of all the skills you will learn in college, and thereafter, none is more important than critical thinking—the application of the principles of reasoning to your ideas and the ideas of others. *Critical thinking enables you to evaluate your world and make choices based upon what you have learned.* It is the intellectual tool necessary to make critical decisions at work ("Do I recommend or discourage a new product line?"), at home ("Should I encourage my children to learn to read before entering kindergarten?"), and in your roles as a consumer and citizen ("Should I believe what the auto sales representative tells me or do my own independent research?"). The critical thinking skills required to answer these questions can be developed, in part, through public speaking. Here are five ways you use critical thinking every time you prepare a speech.

> **Use Critical Thinking Skill to:**
>
> 1. Choose appropriate speech topics
> 2. Research your topic
> 3. Organize your presentation
> 4. Build, advance, and assess arguments
> 5. Choose appropriate language and style of expression

Choose Appropriate Speech Topics

Evaluate different subjects based on their significance to you and your audience. For example, you may decide that although a speech describing how to fix a car's transmission would be right for a group of auto mechanics, it would be too technical for your public speaking classmates. Because gas prices have risen so high, you may decide to persuade your classmates to trade in their old cars for newer, hybrid cars. As everyone in your audience is probably a driver, this topic would be quite appropriate.

Research Your Topic

You must decide what kinds of supporting material, or evidence, best enables you to express your views and develop your arguments. Questions to ask include: What evidence is available and necessary? Should I use quotations, examples, statistics, analogies, or a combination of these, as well as other forms of support? What and how should I present visually?

Organize Your Presentation

The order in which you present your ideas reflects the clarity of your thinking. Your audience is more likely to comprehend what you say and give importance to your message if you have organized your information in a way that best serves your specific purpose for speaking.

Build, Advance, and Assess Arguments

You must know how to construct lines of reasoning for both informative and persuasive purposes. **Reasoning** *is the process of using known and believed information to explain or prove other statements less well understood or accepted.* Thinking critically requires thinking about arguments in active, organized, and purposeful ways.

Choose Appropriate Language and Style of Expression

Language choices are based on an analysis of how much your audience already knows about your subject and its specialized vocabulary as well as on the needs of the occasion. It would be inappropriate, for example, to use slang while accepting a prestigious academic award.

Think about how you would respond to your classmate who started her speech with the following:

> Most of us have experienced "it" at school or the doctor's office. We have to get a shot. It may be a flu shot or a vaccine. The shot is given in your arm, your rear-end, or your leg. Some of us do not flinch. Others are slightly anxious; and still others confess this is one of their worst moments in life.
>
> So, how often do you get a shot? Once a year? Less than that? More? How many shots do you think you've had over the last 10 years? 10? 20? 30?
>
> Well, I've had around 11—11,000 that is. I'm an insulin dependent diabetic. I take three or four shots a day. I also draw blood from my fingers to test my sugar levels at least twice a day. I get bruises on my belly from time to time from poorly placed shots, and if you look closely at my fingertips, you'll see lots of little marks from some 9000 needle sticks. Welcome to my world.

The way she addressed the class, her language, the use of emphasis, pauses, and her reference to numbers had an impact on her listeners. After reading this introduction, you might think, "Wow! It would be awful to take shots so often," or "I could NEVER take shots," or "Yeah. I have asthma. I can relate to someone dealing with a chronic illness." Some students may reflect on their own experiences with injections. Others may think of friends or relatives they know who are insulin-dependent. Still others may focus more on the speaker and wonder how it must be to live with a life-threatening disease. If the student had started her speech by explaining what insulin-dependent diabetes is without providing a personal example and engaging the audience, there would be less of an effect on the audience.

As you can see, critical thinking is necessary when choosing your topic and developing your speech. Critical thinking is also important in your role as **listener.** *A listener perceives through sensory levels and interprets, evaluates, and responds to what he or she hears.* Critical thinking skills are essential as you listen to and evaluate the messages of other speakers. As an audience member, your analysis will focus on several factors, including the purpose and organization of the speech; whether the speaker has accomplished his/her goal to persuade, inform, or speak appropriately on a special occasion; whether he/she has satisfied your needs as an audience member; and so on. As your critical thinking skills develop, you will be able to say effectively exactly what you mean and be able to assess another speaker's effectiveness. Our attention to listening is blended within our treatment of public speaking, for we firmly believe you can improve your listening skills considerably while you are working at developing your speaking skills.

Public Speaking Skills Influence Career and Community Success

A third reason to study public speaking is that your public speaking skills may influence your success in career and community settings. Upward movement in the corporate hierarchy may depend on your ability to speak to groups at business conferences and at public presentations. Public speaking skills are an essential part of most professional interactions, including sales presentations, campaigns for public office, teaching and training programs, the presentation of research findings at conventions, regulatory and consumer meetings, annual stockholders' meetings, employee recruitment campaigns, and award ceremonies. People who can speak on their feet, are articulate in meetings, or just engage in good conversation have clear advantages. People involved in business, politics, and community activities, and members of the clergy who promote their ideas also promote themselves and who or what they represent, whether this is their intention or not. Few professionals can avoid public speaking. Even top administrators in higher education lose important positions because their constituencies have disapproved of their public speaking.

In your community, unexpected events may move you into the public arena. For example, in a largely rural region of the Midwest, an international company attempted to acquire scenic land for use as a place to deposit waste materials. Many residents believed this would threaten—if not destroy—much of their rural setting. Citizens left their homes to rally and form a grassroots organization. Through the power of its most effective spokespersons, the organization provided enough resistance to persuade the company to cease its effort to acquire and use the land. A second example is one that makes teachers of public speaking classes proud. One of our students attended a community meeting to speak against an institution moving into the quiet suburb where she lived with her husband and children. Speakers were allowed five minutes to speak. After she expressed her views in public, her neighbor told her, "I have known you for fifteen years and I have never heard you say so much in five minutes." Our student told her neighbor she was taking a course in public speaking where organizing ideas and expressing them concisely and with confidence were keys to success.

Public Speaking Skills Are Key to Leadership

A fourth reason public speaking is valuable is that it is a key to leadership. In his book, *The Articulate Executive*, corporate communication consultant Granville Toogood discusses the relationship between effective speaking and coming across as a leader. He advises, "You've got to be able to share your knowledge and information (perhaps even your vision) with other people. It is not in any job description, but you've got to be a translator (explaining the law or technology to neophytes, for example), a teacher, and, eventually, a leader. The only way you can ever be a leader is to learn to speak effectively" (Toogood 1996, 10). Barbara Boxer emerged as a leading spokesperson in the U.S. Senate, Condoleeza Rice became Secretary of State for the United States, and Donald Trump is an important leader in American business. Steve Jobs has made Apple Computers profitable, and after leaving Hewlett-Packard, Carly Fiorina has been traveling around the globe giving speeches on leadership from her corporate perspective. Each of these individuals is a leader who demonstrates considerable public speaking skills. A skill all of these leaders possess is the ability to appear before audiences with well-prepared speeches and deliver them with authority, sincerity, enthusiasm, and self-confidence.

As Secretary of State, Condoleeza Rice's position requires considerable public speaking skills.
© *CHIP EAST/Reuters/Corbis.*

Public Speaking Skills Complement Technology

A fifth reason we find public speaking skills important is that they complement technology. While a speaker may receive compliments on his or her multi-media presentation, when we use the term *complement* we are referring to the fact that technology "goes with," or provides support, for the speaker. The "mega churches" in Protestant Christianity rely greatly on graphics and other technology to put forth their message (Wolf 2003, 76). Upon entering a large room that can seat approximately 1,000 people, individuals may find themselves facing up to six large video screens and a stage with a half dozen musicians in place. The main speakers have microphones clipped on, replacing the traditional microphone at the pulpit. In the midst of this multi–media and technologically supported stage the audience is addressed by the main speaker.

Through Internet access, we can access millions of facts, but those facts may not be as impressive without the added human element. Speeches are supported by computer-generated graphics, supporting material is discovered on electronic databases, and images can easily be projected while a speech is being delivered.

Peggy Noonan, successful author, political commentator, and former presidential speechwriter notes that, "the biggest problem in America, the biggest problem in any modern industrialized society, is loneliness. A great speech from a leader to the people eases our isolation, breaks down the walls, includes people: It takes them inside a spinning thing and makes them part of the gravity" (Noonan 1990). Technology has changed our lives, but it cannot bring to us the depth of human emotion nor the caring, concern, hope, and trust that spring from it.

Public Speaking Is Part of Our Democratic Tradition

The last, but certainly not the least, important reason public speaking is valuable is that it is part of our democratic tradition. The drive for change often begins with the spoken word. Indeed, since the colonial period of America when the First Amendment to the U.S. Constitution guaranteed certain freedoms, public speaking has served an important purpose in our democratic processes and procedures. Citizens have gathered at our nation's capital to listen to abolitionists, suffragettes, and individuals who support the civil rights movement, the women's movement, and gay rights. We have witnessed peace marches, Million Dollar Man marches, and anti-war protests.

As you speak to your classmates, keep in mind that your speeches are rhetorical opportunities to show your understanding of and commitment to an idea and your ability to communicate your thoughts and feelings to others. If you use your public speaking class as a training ground to develop and refine your skills as a communicator, these learning experiences will serve you well throughout your life.

Public Speaking and the Communication Process

Communication can be defined as *the creation of shared meaning through symbolic processes*. You communicate your thoughts and feelings to your audience with the intent of generating knowledge and influencing values, beliefs, attitudes, and actions. Often, your purpose is to reach mutual understanding (Makay and Brown 1972). As you speak in public, you will use the shared symbols of communication to achieve a specific purpose. The speeches you deliver will fall into three general categories: *to inform, to persuade, and to entertain*. Sometimes, you may want to share information and create a clear understanding with an audience. Other times, you may want your audience to change their attitudes and/or follow a different course of action. On special occasions, your task may be to entertain, inspire, or celebrate. Each of these main categories is treated in separate chapters to explain fully what is required for success and effectiveness. No matter what type of speech you deliver, your speaking objective is to elicit a response from your audience—a response further defined by the specific purpose of your speech.

Elements of the Communication Process

At least eight elements affect the creation of meaning in a public speaking setting: the speaker, the message, the channel, the occasion, the cultural context, the audience, feedback, and noise. We will briefly discuss these elements here and they will be explored in more detail throughout the book.

1. Speaker

The speaker is the person who initiates the message. The impact of the speech is affected by whether or not the audience finds the speaker to be believable, trustworthy, competent, sincere, and confident. Each speaker brings something unique to the occasion. As the speaker, you may have an interesting perception of an issue because of static and dynamic variables. **Static variables** are those things that remain stable from speaking situation to speaking situation. These include biological aspects such as race, gender, and age. Experience and knowledge are also considered static, since you do not change your experience, knowledge, health, and personality based on the speaking situation. Health may change, such as before and after surgery, but again, it is not something that changes with the speaking situations. **Dynamic variables** are variables that are subject to change. They would include decisions you make about a particular speech, word-choice, the structure you choose to support your points, and aspects of appearance that are easily changed (clothing, hair, accessories). In your role as a speaker, remember two things:

First, your image makes a statement. Always keep this in mind. The image your audience has of you will be shaped with each comment you make. If you are a member of an athletic team or a frequent performer in plays on campus, your reputation may precede you to the lectern and determine, in part, how your audience responds. However, speaking in front of the class or from your seat as a member of the audience will also play a role in the construction of an image of you and, as a public speaker, you must deal with your audience's preconceived notions. When you speak, your words and style of delivery communicate your involvement with your topic, and your listeners will need only a few moments to pass judgment on your confidence, knowledge, integrity, and skill. Your image in the eyes of the audience will play an important role in the meaning of your speech.

As a speaker, your words and style of delivery communicate your involvement with your topic. © *Chris Anderson, 2008. Under license from Shutterstock, Inc.*

Second, the speaker and the audience both have needs. The speech is about you AND your audience. Through the communication exchange, speakers seek from their audience a response that can satisfy certain needs. Depending upon their goal, speakers need to be understood, to have influence, to bring about action, to be liked, and to be respected. A common practice among financial advisers is to invite clients and potential clients to evening seminars where informative sales presentations are made. The needs of the speakers are to produce results in the sale of their financial products and services. Once the speaker is finished speaking, she or he hopes for success in showing how both the immediate and long-term financial needs of members of the audience can be met.

2. Message

The message is what is communicated by the speaker and perceived by the audience. Public speaking is a meaning-centered process. Theorists have long recognized that *the essence of the message lies not only in what the speaker intends, but also in the meaning ascribed to the message by the listeners.* A speaker may intend to send a certain message, such as knowledge about a movie, but may also send an unintentional message, such as superiority or a faulty memory.

Though one hundred people may listen to the same speech, each will come away with his or her own interpretation of what the speaker said. While we may share the same language, we do not share identical experiences. Consider the following example:

> Angry students have gathered in a residence hall lounge to hear their protest leader. A meeting was called to express frustrations over a new college ruling declaring two freshmen residence halls off-limits to persons of the opposite sex after 9:00 p.m. Violators are to be expelled from the dorm. Most of the residents are in attendance, and the primary spokesperson in opposition to the ruling is one of the residence hall presidents, who is about to learn what it is like to be at the center of a conflict. She stated initially:

> *We are here today as responsible adults, although the administration insists on treating us like children; we are here today because we do not want an anonymous college official behaving like our parent. As a matter of fact, our parents never asked for this either. We are old enough and smart enough to know when others have stepped over the line that divides guidance from interference.*

As the hall president continued, she called upon her fellow students to respect the privacy and personal values of their roommates. Some listeners perceived her remarks as too authoritative, while others questioned why she labeled the school's decision as too parental. The process is one of give-and-take between a speaker and the audience. While the residence hall president spoke, members of her audience listened to her remarks, attributed meaning to them, and responded based upon their own attitudes, values, and beliefs. Near the end of the meeting, a petition was placed on a table in the back of the room, and members of the audience lined up and began signing their names.

The need to speak, listen, and respond was considerably important to the speaker and her audience. She responded to the feedback from her audience. *A fundamental task of the speaker's message is to minimize misunderstanding—clarity is imperative.* You are challenged to make your speech as clear as possible—through your words, lines of reason, and delivery. The message is constructed from your knowledge, feelings, and additional research.

3. Channel

The channel is the medium through which the message is sent. Every message is communicated through a channel. In the previous example, the message was sent from speaker to audience through face-to-face communication. Students could respond nonverbally, displaying disagreement or agreement and understanding or confusion through their facial expressions and body movement. In our wired and wireless society, a speaker's message can be sent by a variety of channels, including a public address system, radio, television, the Internet, recordings, the use of land lines and numerous configurations of cell-phones.

However, when you are in the same room with a speaker, you have the advantage of experiencing the speaker firsthand. You react to a person rather than a televised image or a disembodied voice and make judgments that might not be possible in other circumstances. You are in a better position to judge the intangible qualities, including the speaker's honesty, ethical stance, commitment to the topic, trustworthiness, and sincerity. Those qualities can be communicated through eye contact, gestures, and the speaker's voice. When you listen to a speech through a less direct channel, your ability to judge these qualities is diminished.

4. Occasion

Every speech occurs within the context of an occasion—the time, place, event, and traditions that define the moment. Before a speech begins, we often have expectations of what we would like to hear. At a recent college commencement ceremony, the usual speakers gave their speeches in the five-to-seven minute range. Then it was time for the invited speaker to present. She spoke for twenty-five minutes about her background and experience. After about ten minutes, audience members started shifting in their chairs. After twenty minutes, the audience's annoyance was clear to everyone but the speaker. The invited speaker failed to recognize that the commencement ceremony is an occasion designed to focus on the students graduating. She violated their expectations and lost the listening audience.

A sense of occasion is critical to your success as a speaker. In the earlier residence hall example, students who came to listen expected a course of action. It is important to understand what the audience wants and needs. Physical surroundings help define the speaking occasion. As a speaker, you should know in advance whether you are speaking to five people or several hundred and whether you will be speaking from an elevated platform or from an easy chair surrounded by an audience of listeners also seated in easy chairs. You must also be aware of the order of your speech in the day's events. Are you the first or last speaker? Is your speech scheduled right before or after lunch? Knowing the circumstances surrounding your speech, you will be better prepared to meet the needs of the occasion with an appropriate presentation. For example, if your speech is scheduled at the end of the day, a short speech is more appropriate than a long one. As the final speaker for a three-day seminar of executive public accountants, one of your authors knew that a lively, brief, but pertinent, message was best suited to this group because the audience was heading home after his speech. So to have some meaning and impact, an informative but animated message was necessary.

5. Cultural Context

Every speaking occasion operates within a broader cultural context affecting the entire experience. Culture *is defined in terms of norms, the rules people follow in their relationships with one another; values, the feelings people share about what is right or wrong, good or bad, desirable or undesirable; customs accepted by the community of institutional practices and expressions; institutions; and language.* Culture often determines the common ground between speaker and audience.

Cultural similarities and differences exist not only between nations, but also between subcultures within our own population. Therefore, adaptation is necessary. A university hired a new president who was familiar with the corporate culture of a large business organization. When he sought to impose standards mostly from the culture from which he had come, there was considerable opposition to his efforts. Finally, at a faculty meeting, one department chair stood up, faced the new president, and declared: "With all due respect for your new position, you need to understand that this is a different culture than the one you have worked in, and what you found to be successful rules there are not going to work here."

As a speaker, it is important to realize that cultural differences exist between audiences. As U.S. markets expand throughout the world, Americans need to understand that different countries view speaking situations differently. For example, China is a hierarchical society, and the senior member of delegation meeting with Chinese contacts should do the talking. According to their book about business customs around the world, Morrison, Conaway, and Douress (2001) state that senior executives in a delegation often do the talking, "junior members do not interrupt and only speak when spoken to" (75). Russians, they claim, "*expect* walkouts (during negotiations) and dire proclamations that the deal if off" (319). Regarding Japanese culture, the authors purport that, "A persuasive, positive presentation is compatible with Japanese culture—a high-pressure, confrontational approach is not" (229).

An effective speaking style in the United States may not be viewed as such by members of a different culture. If we want to be successful speakers, knowledge of our audience's cultural norms is crucial. Failure to adapt can result in a loss of credibility, and prevent you from achieving the purpose of your speech.

6. Audience

While we consider the audience as the sixth element, we underscore the primary importance of the audience in any public speaking situation. As speakers, our purpose is centered on having some meaningful impact on our listeners. Listeners bring their own frames of reference, which are influenced by the same variables found in the speaker: race, gender, age, health, personality, knowledge, experience, and so on. These variables influence how the audience responds to a speaker's message.

An audience hopes to learn something from your presentation, so it is important to make your message meaningful. © *Dmitriy Shironosov, 2008. Under license from Shutterstock, Inc.*

Although audience members may hear every word a speaker says, they can miss shades of meaning or may attribute meanings that have little or nothing to do with the speaker's intent. Because the potential for misunderstanding always exists, it is critical to plan every speech with your audience in mind. In the classroom, use terms your classmates can understand and use examples that touch their lives. Use language that they understand and find engaging but not offensive. Both the speaker and members of the audience share the responsibility of achieving mutual understanding. As such, listening as a necessary skill is mentioned frequently in this book. The audience arrives to listen to someone speak, so the speaker has a primary responsibility to do everything she/he can to be meaningful. Ron Hoff, a consultant and author on making speeches explains: "By coming to your presentation, by simply showing up, your audience is expressing a need for help, counsel, wisdom, inspiration—maybe even something that can change its life… If truth be told, the audience arrives on the scene with the ardent hope that the presenter knows something that it does not" (1998, 9).

Although you may not think your classmates need something from you, they actually seek your counsel on two levels. First, they hope to learn something from your presentation that may improve their own public speaking skills. Second, although they are required to be there, they can be open to your message—if it relates to or touches their lives.

7. Feedback

In the public speaking transaction, feedback refers to the messages the audience sends back to the speaker. Feedback may be immediate or delayed. **Immediate feedback** may range from applause, yawns, laughter, verbal comments, and even to boos. A speaker may choose to ignore the feedback or he may change his message in response to the feedback. For example, if the audience looks confused, you may want to slow down, elaborate more fully, or give additional examples. Immediate feedback may be difficult to interpret accurately. Audience members rarely stop a speech to ask questions or express differences. However, once a member of the clergy was building a Christmas message around his family's traditions when suddenly a member of the audience stood up and indicated that he and his family came to the service to hear about the biblical story of the first Christmas and not about the speaker's family activities. Of course, this type of immediate feedback seldom happens.

Delayed feedback may come in the form of letters, emails, phone calls, formal evaluation, or votes. For example, it was discovered that a politician had plagiarized much of a speech delivered in a local campaign. A report of the incident was noted in the local newspaper, and the politician lightly dismissed using someone else's words without acknowledgement. Subsequently, a letter was written and sent by an irate citizen to the editor of the newspaper. The published letter was a form of delayed feedback.

8. Noise

In an ideal world, the eighth element would not exist. The seven previous elements are all critical aspects of the communication process. Noise is not a necessary element of the process, but it exists, and speakers should not ignore it. Noise is anything that interferes with the communication process and can be physical, psychological, or semantic.

Physical noise includes anything within the environment that distracts the speaker or listeners. Examples include: cell phones going off, the microphone not working well, people talking in class, students kicking chairs or clicking pens, people talking outside the classroom, thunder, noisy cars, heating that kicks on and off, lights that make buzzing sounds. Physical noise does not actually have to be heard to be considered noise. The classroom may be too cold, the lights may too dim, the listener may be seated too far from the speaker, or the room may have distracting artwork. Generally, both speaker and listeners are aware of physical noise.

Semantic noise refers to a disconnect between the speaker's words and the listener's interpretation. The disconnect may result from the use of inappropriate or offensive words, misunderstanding or misinterpretation, or disagreement on the meaning of words. If you look at the very first paragraph of this chapter, you will note the word "awesome" was used. Another possibility was "wicked," but it was decided that "awesome" is more universal. Your professor may use words you do not know, or you may experience cultural differences. Even though Australians, British, and Americans have English as their native tongue, many words cause confusion.

Psychological noise occurs within the individual. The speaker could be having a bad day and is not happy to be there; it may be near lunch time and the listeners are thinking about how hungry they are. One listener may be thinking about a fight she just had with her boyfriend, and another listener may be thinking about the project that is due next period. Or, the listener may not like the speaker. Understanding psychological noise is more difficult than understanding physical or semantic noise. It is easy to tell that the auditorium is cold or that there is too much noise in the hallway. While a speaker concerned about semantic noise will choose words effectively, it is not possible to see or hear what affects people psychologically. Sitting in the same row may be a person who is happy to be there, another who is distracted by relationship problems, and a third who is worried about his or her future career.

As speakers, we need to be aware of those aspects of public speaking we have some influence over, and those we do not. It is in the speaker's best interest to address the issue of noise. This may include closing doors, not allowing cell phones, making sure the equipment works, being aware of cultural differences, choosing words carefully and thoughtfully, and possibly providing examples for concepts that might be difficult for the audience. While we cannot change things like hunger or imminent verbal conflicts, effective delivery may help minimize some of the psychological noise.

Summary

If we had to choose one thing for you to remember from this chapter, well, we could not do it. But perhaps we could boil it down to two. First, the spoken word can be very powerful. Second, public speaking is audience-centered. At the beginning of this chapter, we presented six reasons for studying public speaking. Public speaking is an art that involves creativity, decision-making, and critical thinking skills. We define communication for you, and identify the general speaking categories. As a result of our discussion of the eight elements of communication, we hope you understand that communication is a complex process. This book will discuss the elements of communication and help you develop and then present your speeches. The next chapter is designed to get you started in your public speaking class.

Questions for Study and Discussion

1. Considering your personal career goals, how are public speaking skills likely to help you in achieving your goals for the future?
2. Think of some of the major institutions in society including, among others, government, schools, the judicial system, and organized religion. What role do public speakers play in each of these settings and what do you see as their strengths and their weaknesses?

Activities

1. Think of someone in the public eye who you admire as a public speaker and write an essay describing why you have chosen to write about this person as a speaker.
2. Prepare, in detail, a written statement about how you think public speaking will benefit you personally and professionally.
3. Design and detail a model of communication as you understand the key elements.

References

Cowan, A. L. 1989. Meek and mumblers learn the ways of getting a word in. *New York Times,* May 29, 1989, 1.

Hoff, R. 1988. *I can see you naked: A guide to making fearless presentations.* Kansas City, MO: Andrews and McMeel.

Makay, J. J., and W. R. Brown. 1972. *The rhetoric dialogue: Contemporary concepts and cases.* Dubuque, IA: Wm. C. Brown Company.

Morrison, T., W. A. Conaway, and J. J. Douress. 2001. *Dun & Bradstreet's guide to doing business around the world.* Paramus, NJ: Prentice Hall Press.

Noonan, P. 1990. *What I saw at the revolution: A political life in the Reagan era.* New York: Random House.

Toogood, G. N. 1996. *The articulate executive.* New York: McGraw-Hill, Inc.

Wolf, A. 2003. *The transformation of American religion: How we actually live our faith.* New York: Free Press.

"Speech is a mirror of the soul: as a man speaks, so is he."

Publilius Syrus (c. 42 B.C.)

Getting Started on Your First Speech

For some, speaking in public can be an exciting, adrenalin-producing activity, but for others, it is a dreaded experience to be feared. Whereas some will jump at the chance to perform in public, others will do just about anything to avoid standing, let alone speaking, before a group of people. A few years ago, there was a community fundraiser at a local restaurant. People gathered for a meal, a silent auction, and some entertainment. Those in charge of entertainment thought it would be fun to select some community members to provide the group with a rendition of the song "YMCA." Wendell, an enormously successful businessman, was chosen to participate. He stood up, opened his wallet, and took out $50, stating, "I won't do it, but I'll pay my way out." His money was welcomed, and Wendell was allowed to choose the person to replace him. He chose John, another successful businessman. John stood up, opened his wallet, and shelled out $50. John then selected Bob, a restaurant owner, who opened his wallet, frowned, showed the crowd he only had $2, and said, "I guess I'm in!"

Think about your response to this situation. Some of you may have jumped at the idea of performing "YMCA." After all, most of the people knew each other, and the atmosphere was festive. But for those of you with real apprehension, the comfort of a friendly group is not good enough.

Lack of preparation time may have influenced Wendell and John's apprehension. Wendell confesses his dislike of public speaking, no matter what the circumstances. He admits that not having a college education, combined with his own poor perception of his speaking skills make public speaking one of the worst possible situations for him to endure.

Whether you embrace the opportunity for public speaking or feel the urge to run away, there are many things you can do to enhance your potential for success. Following is an overview of eight key steps you should follow when preparing and presenting a speech. This overview is particularly important for your first speech. Keep in mind that you will most likely move back and forth among the steps. The chapters ahead are designed to provide more detail so you may increase your knowledge about public speaking and your skill as a speaker and as a listener.

Eight Steps for Preparing to Speak

1. Decide on a topic.
2. Demonstrate ethical behavior throughout the process.
3. Determine the general purpose, specific purpose, and thesis statement.
4. Define your audience.
5. Document your ideas through firm support and sound reasoning.
6. Draft the beginning, middle, and end.
7. Develop the language of your speech with care.
8. Deliver your speech while making your tension work for you.

1. Decide on a Topic

A difficult task for students beginning the study and practice of public speaking is to select a topic. Some instructors will give you a topic and others will provide strict limits. If you can choose, however, often the best place to begin your search for a speech topic is yourself. When the topic springs from your own interests, you bring to it personal involvement, motivation, and the information necessary for a good speech.

For example, Courtney found herself preoccupied with choosing the topic for her informative speech. As she reflected on her possibilities, she thought about her two years' experience at a local day care center before college. She realized she could speak to her classmates about how working at a day care led to her decision to work with children as her vocation. She felt earning a degree in education would open more doors, and she stressed the notion of getting some experience through work or internship in one's area of interest before completing a major. Her speech was full of informative anecdotes and her enthusiasm made the speech highly effective.

Perhaps you have some interesting work experience to share with your class, or an amazing travel story, or maybe a life-changing service learning experience. In any case, if at all possible, choose your first speech topic from what you know best.

If no ideas come to you when thinking about a speech topic, try the following. Write down two or three broad categories representing subjects of interest to you, and divide the categories into parts. You might begin, for example, with the broad areas of politics and sports. From these general topics useful lists will emerge.

If you choose a speech topic that you're interested in, the audience will share in your enthusiasm.
© *PhotoCreate, 2008. Under license from Shutterstock, Inc.*

Politics
1. Campus politics
2. Political corruption
3. Contemporary political campaign tactics

Sports
1. Learning from participation in sports
2. The challenges facing student athletes
3. Why NASCAR races are increasingly popular

As your list of choices grows, you will probably find yourself coming back to the same topic or a variation of it. For example, "Football after college" could be added to "The challenges facing student athletes." Perhaps your brother played college football, and then attempted to join a professional football league. You could talk about his experiences, including successes and failures. Now you have your topic.

Do not assume, however, that *any* topic is relevant. Before choosing a topic, make sure you know the amount of time you have to speak, your level of knowledge about the topic, and the needs of your audience. A five-minute speech is not supposed to last ten minutes; it is not even supposed to last six. In some public situations, you may be in danger of getting cut off if your speech is too long. If you have a wealth of information, you need to determine what must be left out. If you do not have much knowledge about the topic, recognize where you need to do research, or choose another topic. If you know about the background of your audience, you can decide what information is most relevant and how much time should be spent on each point.

2. Demonstrate Ethical Behavior Throughout the Process

A consideration of ethics is important in virtually all aspects of speech development, including, but certainly not limited to, how you approach a topic, where you get information, how you edit or interpret information, word choice, and distinguishing between your own ideas and those which need to be cited. **Plagiarism,** which involves using other's work, words, or ideas without adequate acknowledgement, has never been easier than it is today, according to Plagiarism.org (p.1). Add the ability to send files and share information via computers to the overwhelming amount of information available through the Internet, and the potential for engaging in unethical behavior is enormous.

Ethics are being discussed within the context of many disciplines, including medicine, psychology, business, and communication. It is relatively easy to find stories in the newspaper concerning ethical issues. According to communication professor Bert Bradley, "Speakers have ethical responsibilities which must be accepted if rhetoric is to play its most meaningful role in communication" (Bradley 1998, 47). That said, government officials have failed to speak truthfully until forced to do so, deception continues to be uncovered in the nation's business practices, and students, when questioned anonymously, admit to what can be described as wide-spread cheating.

On August 24, 2006, the Associated Press reported that "Allegations of criminal wrongdoing and ethical lapses among lawmakers are coloring a handful of competitive House and Senate races across the country this midterm election year." In October 2004, pop culture's Ashlee Simpson was derided for using a pre-recorded vocal track for a performance on *Saturday Night Live.* Certainly, politicians and pop stars are not the only ones engaging in unethical behavior. During the early months of 2006, Oprah Winfrey brought to task James Frey, author of the book *A Million Little Pieces.* On national television, Frey admitted to making up part of his "memoir," and his publisher discussed how the firm was duped. More than 3.5 million people bought Frey's book assuming it was non-fiction.

These abuses have heightened our sensitivity to the need for honesty from all sources, including public speakers. Speakers may have different values and beliefs based on family, cultural, and educational backgrounds, but many ethical standards are considered universal.

Freedom of speech is a fundamental right in our democracy, and implied in this freedom is the speaker's responsibility to avoid deceiving others. As you think critically about your topic, your audience, supporting material, and so on, remain concerned for the welfare of others. Use accurate and current information, rely on sound reasoning, and present a speech that is your own, based on your independent research and views. Remember to cite sources and to quote and paraphrase correctly when you present information or ideas that are not your own.

Ashlee Simpson's pre-recorded vocals were accidentally exposed in a performance on Saturday Night Live. © *Fred Prouser/ Reuters/Corbis.*

3. Determine the General Purpose, Specific Purpose, and Thesis Statement

The time you spend preparing your speech may be of little value if you do not determine what you want your speech to accomplish. At the beginning, you should clarify the general and specific purposes of your speech. Then determine which statement will be the expression of your main idea; that is the thesis statement for your speech.

General Purpose

There are three general purposes for speeches: to inform, to persuade, and to entertain or inspire. If you want to explain the differences between a scooter and a motorcycle, the general purpose of your speech would be "to inform." If you hope to make people laugh after eating a good meal, your general purpose is "to entertain." If you want people to choose a hybrid for their next car, you are attempting "to persuade."

Keep in mind, however, that it is difficult to deliver a speech that is *just* informative or *just* persuasive or *just* entertaining. Often, in the perception of listeners, the purposes may converge or overlap. For example, as a speaker informs her audience about various options for eating a healthy breakfast each day, some audience members may interpret her speech as an attempt to persuade them to change their daily behavior.

Specific Purpose

Once the general purpose is set for your speech, determine the specific purpose. This is the precise response you want from your audience. Specific purpose statements should be expressed as an infinitive phrase that includes the general purpose as well as the main thrust of your speech. The specific purpose also identifies who the audience will be. Here are two examples of specific purposes:

1. To inform the class of differences between the operations of an on-campus political club and an off-campus political party
2. To persuade the class that requiring all college students to participate in service-learning projects benefits the student, college, and community

Because the specific purpose identifies the audience who will hear your speech, it guides you in speech preparation. A speech on health care reform given before a group of college students would be different than a speech on the same topic given before an audience of retirees. Obviously, the second audience has a much more immediate need for reform than the first group of listeners. The speech would be different because the older listeners usually feel a greater overall need to deal with health issues.

Thesis Statement

While the general and specific purpose statements set the goals for your speech, the thesis statement, or your core idea, focuses on what you want to say. The thesis statement distills your speech to one sentence, summarizing your main idea. According to James Humes, a corporate speech consultant, Great Britain's Prime

Minister Winston Churchill once sent back a pudding because he said it had no theme. (Kleinfield 1990). A well-defined theme is critical to your speech's success. The thesis statement is the central message you want listeners to take with them. The following examples show how one moves from a topic to the thesis statement.

Topic: Study abroad
General purpose: To inform
Specific purpose: To explain to my class what is involved in the study abroad options available to them at our university
Thesis statement: Students interested in earning college credit while studying abroad have several options that differ in terms of academic content, location, length of stay, potential number of credit hours, and cost.

Topic: Study abroad
General purpose: To persuade
Specific purpose: To convince my class that studying abroad will be a life-changing experience
Thesis statement: Studying abroad can be a life-changing experience because students gain knowledge in an academic area, face the unfamiliar, and interact with individuals from a different culture.

As you can see, although the topic is "study abroad," there are different aspects of studying abroad that one could address. The above example shows choices for an informative speech and persuasive speech. A speech with the general purpose to entertain could include humorous examples and illustrations of the trials and tribulations of studying abroad.

4. Define the Audience

As stated throughout our book, public speaking is an audience-centered activity. Your reason for presenting a speech is to communicate your message to others in the clearest and most convincing way. When preparing your specific purpose you must define your audience. *An effective speaker analyzes and adapts to the audience.* This involves finding out as much as possible about your audience. What are their demographics (age, race, gender, religious affiliation, political affiliation, etc.)? What is their level of knowledge about your topic? Is the audience there because they want to be? Do they lean toward your point of view, or away from it? Critical thinking skills are valuable here as you determine these parameters.

The initial way to approach your responsibility as an audience-centered speaker is to find answers to the following six pertinent questions.

What Does the Audience Know About Me?

Outside of the classroom, you may become a spokesperson for an issue, a cause, or an organization. Generally speaking, your audience will have some basic information about you. In college, characteristics such as age, gender, race, and level of education are easily known, but you may need to include relevant background information at the beginning of your speech. For example, if you wanted to talk about the problems associated with children of state and federal prisoners and your father worked in the prison system, it would be helpful to note this as you begin your speech.

What Does the Audience Know About My Specific Purpose?

The amount of supporting material you include and the extent to which you explain or elaborate are influenced by the expertise of your audience. If you are speaking to a group of cardiologists on the need to convince pregnant women to stop smoking, you can assume far greater audience knowledge than if you were to deliver the same message to a group of concerned citizens.

What Are the Audience's Views on My Topic and Purpose?

Attitudes can be more important than information in determining how your audience responds to a message. It is natural to expect some preconceived attitudes about what you are hoping to accomplish. The views of your audience should influence your choice of main points, the supporting material, and the way you develop your speech.

How Do Audience Members Define Themselves as an Audience?

Individuals who come together to listen to speeches often assume the cultural or organizational identity they share with the body of listeners. Is this a general group of college students? Conservatives? Music majors? At a city council meeting that addresses housing regulations in your community, you might be with several college students attending as tenants of rental property. At another city council meeting, you might gather with other college students because the council is discussing changing the bar-entry age in the city. Though the same people might be in the audience, how you identify or define your-selves differs from situation to situation. In one instance, you and the other college students identify yourselves as renters. In the second situation, you are with college students who are interested in expanded entertainment options.

How Does the Setting and Occasion Influence My Audience?

The setting may be an indoor gymnasium or an out-door stadium. The occasion may be a graduation cer-emony or a funeral service. It helps a speaker to plan carefully when she or he learns in advance what the general feeling is about the setting and the occasion for the presentation. We recall when a member of the clergy drifted off from his main message and began talking about his old family gatherings during a Christmas Eve service when his audience was expecting to hear about the story of the birthday of Jesus and what this event means in our present day. The congregation grew very restless. Remember that it is harder to reach a **captive**

It's important to consider the setting and the occa-sion when preparing to speak to better prepare.
© *Andresr, 2008. Under license from Shutterstock, Inc.*

audience (those who are required to attend) than a **voluntary audience** (those who choose to attend). Students who attend a guest lecture on campus simply to obtain extra credit to boost their grade in a class may feel somewhat indifferent, if not bored, while those who chose to attend because of a keen interest in the speech and speaker will feel much differently. As a speaker, you need to obtain some helpful information about audience attitudes toward the setting and occasion that will bring everyone together for the speech.

What Other Factors Might Affect How the Audience Responds?

Are you the first speaker of the day? The last speaker? Are you speaking at a convention in Las Vegas at 8:00 a.m.? Were the participants out late? Are you one of six students to give a speech during graduation ceremony? Are you the school board representative giving a speech at graduation? If you have knowledge of any factor that may influence your listeners' attentiveness, you can plan in advance ways to increase the likelihood that they will listen carefully. You can shorten the speech, include more vivid examples, and/or work to make your speech even more engaging.

As time goes by, you get to know your classmates and their concerns. Use that information to create interest and engage their attention. Reflect on the six questions identified above and then adapt your topic, language, support, and delivery based on what you decide.

5. Document Ideas Through Support and Sound Reasoning

Each point made before an audience should be backed up with reliable supporting information and sound reasoning. For example, if you want to persuade your audience that sales tax instead of real estate tax should be used to fund education, concrete evidence will be necessary to support your specific purpose. Later in the book we devote an entire chapter to research and supporting materials, but briefly, we want to point out five different ways that you can provide support.

Use Facts

Facts are verifiable. They hold more weight than opinions. If your specific purpose was to demonstrate how political campaigns have changed dramatically over the last several decades, you might include the following facts:

- In 1960 John Kennedy became the first presidential candidate to use his own polling specialist.
- In 1972 George McGovern pioneered mass direct-mail fundraising.
- In 1980 Jimmy Carter campaigned by conference phone calls to voters in Iowa and New Hampshire.
- In 1984 Ronald Reagan used satellite transmissions to appear at fundraisers and rallies.
- In 1988 a number of presidential hopefuls used videotapes to deliver their message to voters in the early primary states.

- In 1992 California Governor Jerry Brown introduced a 1-800 number for fundraising and answering questions.
- In 1996 candidates and prominent party supporters recorded one-minute phone calls that focused on issues believed to be important to voters.
- In 2007 Hillary Clinton established a website that included video snippets, news reports, an opportunity for blogging, and numerous ways to contribute to her presidential campaign.

These facts support the speaker's claim, and show how candidates have attempted to reach the masses over time. Keep in mind that you need to cite your sources as you provide the facts.

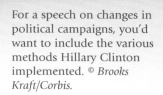

Provide Statistics

Providing statistics can offer strong support to your speech. Statistics inform, startle, and convince. In trying to convince his audience about the dramatic increase in the use of the Internet in political campaigns, one student cited the work of Bruce Bimber and Richard Davis:

For a speech on changes in political campaigns, you'd want to include the various methods Hillary Clinton implemented. © *Brooks Kraft/Corbis.*

> The number of Internet sites is in the tens of millions. A 2001 survey of Internet usage found that the top ten sites together attracted just under 17 percent of all Internet traffic. Despite the undeniable clout of some key businesses in delivering content on the Internet, this is a far different media environment than when Kennedy and Nixon squared off on the three networks in 1960 (2003).

Recognizing that Internet usage is increasing every day, a student giving a similar speech today could use statistics posted May 24, 2006 from "The Bivings Report." Survey results show that "ninety-six percent of this year's Senate candidates have active websites, while only fifty-five percent of candidates had websites in 2002" (www.bivingsreport.com). Statistics updated on June 30, 2006 reveal Internet users in the United States to be around 227,000,000, which reflects approximately seventy percent of the population (www.internetworldstats.com). These statistics provide useful support to the claim that technology has changed how candidates campaign. Keep in mind, however, that your speech should not be a laundry list of statistics.

Illustrate Using Examples

A third form of support is the use of examples to help illustrate a point or claim. Illustrations, especially detailed and current ones, help to clarify points and they may leave a lasting impression on your audience. If the purpose of your speech was "to convince the class that voters are influenced by information provided on the Internet," you might use the following illustration:

> The use of computers by members of the general public has increased considerably in recent years. For example, my brother-in-law, Tom, and his friends purchased personal computers at some point before the last national campaign.

Tom meets regularly with a group of friends who have retired after years of working in a nearby automobile plant. As they developed basic computer skills and surfed the Internet, they also began to pay attention to political news and advertisements. The information they gathered as individuals became subjects for their informal get-togethers leading up to the election. They reported to their friends and family members that the information from the Internet served as a strong influence on how they voted.

This example, along with other forms of support such as facts and statistics, can demonstrate to the audience the increasing use and effectiveness of the Internet in political campaigns. As an audience-centered speaker, you want to think of the best way to keep the attention of your audience, and provide support that is best suited to them. Chapter 6 will elaborate on the use of examples.

Include Testimony

A fourth form of support is the use of testimony, which involves quoting someone's experience or opinion. Testimony can be a powerful form of support because everyone pays attention to an expert. Courts of law frequently call on the testimony of expert witnesses; televised news programs broadcast the observations of experts on newsworthy stories; and, from time to time, even commercials provide the endorsement of experts rather than celebrities to confirm the reliability of a product or service. So to prove, reinforce, or clarify a point, a public or presentational speaker often links his/her contention with a statement of a recognized expert on a subject.

Construct Analogies

Using analogies is a fifth form of support. This involves making comparisons to clarify or prove a point. They lend support by encouraging listeners to think in a novel way. Figurative analogies compare different kinds of things, and literal analogies compare similar categories. If you compare an argument with a sporting event, you are using a figurative analogy, but if you compare one college with another college, you are using a literal analogy. For example, in a speech about studying abroad, a student could use the following figurative analogy.

Studying abroad is like your first week in college. You're unfamiliar with the environment, you don't know the people who are around you, and you're not quite sure what to expect. But as the week goes on, you start to make friendships, your environment becomes more comfortable, and you start to get into some kind of predictable routine. Keep in mind, anytime you have a new experience, you'll experience some uncertainty.

Then, the literal analogy:

Studying abroad is similar to studying at this or any other university. You attend classes and take exams. You have a place to live, and dining options. You have to study, and you also have free time. The difference is, you're far from home, you aren't familiar with your environment, and people speak a different language.

6. Draft the Introduction, Body, and Conclusion

If you spend days researching your first speech but only a few hours organizing your ideas, the result is likely to be a speech that fails to present your message in a focused way. To be effective, speeches require an easy-to-follow organizational plan that makes it possible for others to receive and understand your message. As you will see in Chapters Eight and Nine, the logical way to organize your speech is to divide it into three parts: the introduction, body, and conclusion.

As you draft your speech, lay it out into the three parts. Construct a comprehensive, full-sentence outline and work to tie the sentences into a coherent whole. Then, reduce these sentences to key words and phrases and transfer them onto speaker's notes, which will serve as your guide when you deliver your speech. A well-thought out, clearly constructed outline and speaker's notes will greatly increase the potential for success. The following paragraphs highlight important aspects to consider as you develop your first speech.

Introduction

The introduction should capture the attention and interest of your audience, establish your credibility as a speaker, and preview your speech. You can accomplish these aims in many ways, such as humorous anecdotes or a dramatic or startling statement. Jonathan Esslinger, a student at the University of Wisconsin, introduced the following remarks when he spoke about the conditions and trends of the U.S. national parks:

> Imagine yourself viewing a film showing the most beautiful landscape on earth. Surrounded by trees, you look ahead and see a deep blue lake shining. In it the reflection of beautiful, white-capped mountains—with only the chattering of the squirrels and the music of the birds to keep you company—you feel you could sit back and stay forever. The darkness and credits start to roll. What you have been watching, according to the Audubon…is a film promoting our nation's parks. But if the current trends continue, this film is all that will be left of the beauty our national parks have to offer. With all these benefits being lost, we must examine the destruction of our nation's parks. In my effort to convince you that there is something you can do to stop this, I will first describe the destruction, then explore the causes of this destruction, and finally, explore some solutions to save our national treasures (1992, 133).

In his introduction, Jonathan captures our attention through his vivid description of the landscape. He establishes credibility by using *Audubon* as supporting material, showing us he has done research. Finally, in his last sentence, he presents a preview statement, which lets his audience know what he intends to cover in the body of his speech. He accomplishes the three goals of an effective introduction.

Body

The body of your speech contains your key ideas and relevant supporting material. It is the most time-consuming aspect of speech development. Frequently, speakers work on the body before the introduction, because gaps in logic or information may be discovered as the body is developed. Main points should flow from the thesis statement. To be effective, the speech needs to follow some logical pattern. Chapter Eight discusses organizing and outlining your ideas. You have at least five patterns of organization to consider: chronological, topical, spatial, cause and effect, and problem-solution.

Conclusion

Your concluding remarks have three purposes: (1) to reinforce the message, (2) to summarize the main points, and (3) to provide closure in some way that relates your message to your listeners' lives. Main ideas will be summarized. Your final thought may take the form of a quotation, a statement, or a question that reinforces or even broadens the purpose of your speech. The conclusion of a persuasive speech may also describe the specific actions you want your listeners to take. Esslinger accomplished the goals of a conclusion this way:

> Every flower picked, every piece of paper thrown carelessly in the bushes debilitates our parks. National parks exist to remind us of the beauty and complexity of nature. Realizing how parks are being ravaged for their resources, polluted, and enveloped by concrete, 'civilization' has illustrated the frailty and vulnerability of our national parks. National legislation, local development of buffer zones, and our personal involvement can save them. Perhaps in the future it won't be a matter of walking down the movie theatre aisle to see the beauty and benefits of our parks. It will simply be a matter of walking through the park gates (1992, 135).

Choose your words with care to convey your message in the best way possible. © *Stephen VanHorn, 2008. Under license from Shutterstock, Inc.*

7. Develop the Language of the Speech with Care

An enthusiastic young woman looked out into the audience of almost 1,500 people on her graduation day and was overwhelmed with the spirit that marked this important occasion. A hush fell over the crowd as she began her address as president of the senior class: "You guys are all terrific! Awesome! This has been an awesome four years for us, right? Like, we have really made it! Wow!" As she proceeded, reflecting on the events of the past four years, her comments were laced with slang that may have been suitable for the coffee shop or gatherings with friends, but not for such a special occasion.

The words you choose to convey your message reflect your personality, your attitude toward your subject, occasion, and audience, and your concern for communicating effectively. Words are your primary vehicle for creating meaning. They set forth ideas, spark visions, arouse concerns, elicit emotions, but if not used carefully, produce confusion. The following four guidelines will help you choose your words with care.

Use Plain English

Let simple, direct language convey your message. Your audience should not need an interpreter. You could say "contusion" or "ecchymosis," but most audiences would find the word "bruise" clearer. Also, it is generally best to avoid the use of slang.

Remember That Writing and Speaking Are Different Activities

While in a written report the terms "edifice," "regulations," and "in the eventuality of," may be acceptable; in public speaking the words, "building," "rules," and "if," are far more effective.

Relate Your Language to Your Audience's Level of Knowledge

If you are describing drug testing in professional sports, do not assume your audience understands such terms as "false positives," "chain of custody," and "legal and individual safeguards." If you use these terms in your speech, you should define them in order to keep the message clear.

Use Language for Specific Effect

If your goal is to sensitize your audience to the plight of America's working poor, the following statement is not incorrect, but it may be ineffective: *"Although millions of Americans work a full day, they cannot pay their bills or provide for their families."*

For a more powerful effect, you might try the following alternative: *"Millions of Americans come home each day, exhausted and covered with a layer of factory filth or kitchen grease. Their backbreaking labor has given them few rewards: They cannot pay their rent, buy shoes for their children, or eat meat more than once a week."* Clearly, the second version paints memorable word pictures. We explain more about the power of language to create meaning in Chapter Ten. Keep your audience in mind as you choose effective language for communicating your ideas.

8. Deliver Your Speech While Making Your Tension Work for You

As we noted earlier, you are not alone if you have some tension or anxiety about speaking in front of an audience. Most likely, you will engage in some in-class activities to help you feel more comfortable speaking in class. In the next several paragraphs, we first focus on delivery and then discuss how to make tension work for you.

Verbal and Nonverbal Delivery

Vocal elements of delivery include, but are certainly not limited to: volume, articulation and pronunciation, pacing, and avoiding "fillers." Nonverbal aspects include: eye contact, gestures, and movement. Your audience is not expecting perfection, but you do not want to create a situation where your lack of effective vocal and/or physical delivery keeps you from achieving your goals.

Your audience must hear you. No matter how convincing or eloquent your speech is designed to be, if you speak too softly your audience cannot hear your message and will not be able to respond. Be aware that your pace (rate of speech) may be slower in the comfort of your dorm room than it is in front of your class. Some nervous speakers unconsciously race through their speech. Normally rapid speakers should try to slow down. Varying your pace can aid in maintaining audience interest and draw attention to certain parts of your speech.

Proper **articulation,** the verbalization of distinct sounds, is important in formal speaking situations. Saying "hafta," "gonna," and "wanna" is discouraged. Also, if you have any question about the correct pronunciation of a word, check on it before your speech. When speakers mispronounce words, the audience may infer a lack of knowledge, interest, or preparation.

We also encourage you to avoid **vocal fillers.** In casual conversation, it is common to hear people say "you know," or "like," or "you know what I mean?" In front of a public audience, these pauses may be filled with "ah," or "um," or "er." Fillers can be awkward or distracting and should be reduced and, if possible, eliminated.

In addition to working on the verbal aspects of your speech, you need to tune in to the nonverbal aspects of your speech. Even if your verbal message is well developed and solidly researched, remaining frozen or slouching in front of your audience is likely to distract from what you intend to communicate. Look at your audience. Through eye contact a speaker can establish a connection with the audience. Your facial expression should match the tone of your voice. Speak conversationally, and use movement, nonverbal gestures, and appropriate facial expressions to provide meaning to your words as well as to gain and maintain your audience's attention. And do not forget, enthusiasm is contagious! For some, this is difficult, but choosing a topic that truly interests you and practicing your speech repeatedly can help greatly.

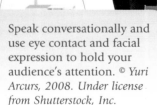

Speak conversationally and use eye contact and facial expression to hold your audience's attention. © *Yuri Arcurs, 2008. Under license from Shutterstock, Inc.*

Strategies for Controlling Tension

The chances are slim of being "cured" of communication apprehension, to use an academic term. However, we can provide some help. One thing to consider is that a major symptom of "speech tension" is a physiological reaction. Most people experience three stages of physiological arousal immediately before and during the first few moments of a speech. The *anticipatory stage* takes place in the minutes before the speech—heart rates zoom from a normal testing rate of about 70 beats per minute to between 95 and 140. The *confrontational stage* is typically at the beginning of the speech, when heart rates jump to between 110 and 190 beats per minute. This stage usually lasts no more than thirty seconds and gives way to the *post-confrontational stage*. This final stage is when the pulse returns to anticipation levels or lower. Confrontation experienced in stage two is so strong that speakers may not perceive the decrease. As a nervous speaker, you may stop feeling nervous without realizing it. (Motley 1988).

Most fearful speakers experience the symptoms of a dry mouth and sweaty palms, and sometimes even heavy breathing. These symptoms are the body's "fight or flight" response. People who experience speech tension often feel the urge to withdraw (Run away! Run away!). We are not always aware of this desire. Even as we convince ourselves that we are not nervous, our nonverbal behavior may reveal our unconscious discomfort. Below are several strategies for controlling tension.

Many strategies are available for reducing anxiety. Ultimately, your goal is to channel this nervous energy into public speaking with self-confidence.

1. *Focus on your message and your audience, not yourself.* Keep your mind on your message and the best way to convey it to your audience. Always think of your audience as being on your side.
2. *Prepare!* Preparation sharpens your presentation and builds confidence. Start with a sound speech plan and then rehearse the speech aloud by yourself. Then practice in front of others to get the feel and response of an audience.
3. *Take several deep breaths.* Deep breathing has a calming effect on the body and mind. We have used this technique ourselves and find our students have used it with success as well. You can do this as you are waiting to speak. It also helps to take a final deep breath after you get in front of the audience and just before you speak. Try it!
4. *Realize that you may be your own worst critic.* Studies have shown that the amount of tension a speaker reports has little relationship to the amount of nervousness an audience detects. Even listeners trained to detect tension often fail to perceive it (Motley 1988, 47).
5. *Gain proficiency and confidence by choosing to speak.* Find opportunities to speak. Give "mini speeches" at meetings or in classes when discussion is invited. A colleague of ours conquered his considerable fear of public speaking before an audience and became a successful speaker in large lecture classes by volunteering to speak whenever a situation was convenient and available.
6. *Visualize your success as a speaker.* Creating powerful mental images of skillful performances and winning competitions is a technique that has been used for years by athletes who use visualization to help them succeed. This technique can also be used in public speaking. Visualize yourself speaking with confidence and self-assurance and imagine the sound of applause after your presentation (Ayers, Hopf, and Myers 1997).
7. *Release tension through assertive and animated delivery.* Here is where a nervous speaker may be caught between a rock and a hard place. Being nervous can inhibit your delivery, but assertive and animated delivery can provide a release from pent-up tension. So, if you are prepared to speak, you have practiced speaking out loud, and you focus on your audience, you will be able to gesture, use eye contact, and move—all means for releasing nervous energy.

We encourage you to try several of these suggestions during your first speech. You may not overcome your fear of speaking, but you may reduce it, and you may use your nervous energy productively. Keep in mind, nothing substitutes for preparation and practice. Just like when getting ready for a piano recital, choral concert, or a competitive sports activity, the more you practice, the more you learn, and the greater the likelihood of success.

Summary

As public speaking instructors, we would prefer to cover everything in this text *before* you give a graded speech. However, we know that is not possible. That said, this chapter was designed to help you with your first speech as well as to provide a preview of the text. We have outlined eight steps for preparing to speak; each step involves reflection and decision-making. Remember to choose a topic you care about, engage in ethical behavior, determine the purpose of your speech and, as you develop your speech, use language that is appropriate and relevant to your audience. Focus on your audience. As you practice your speech, work on nonverbal aspects of delivery, such as eye contact, gestures, and movement. Find strategies to reduce tension and project enthusiasm and self-confidence.

Questions for Study and Discussion

1. What factors should you keep in mind when choosing a topic and framing a purpose for speaking?
2. Discuss with member of your class what is understood to be the relationships between a speaker's link to a topic, choice of a purpose, amount of information available, and the needs of the audience.
3. Although degrees of speech tension vary from speaker to speaker, most inexperienced speakers share common feelings of discomfort. What can you do to minimize your feelings of apprehension and make your nervous energy work *for* you rather than against you?

Activities

1. Take an inventory of what you believe to be your own strengths and weaknesses as a public speaker and establish goals as well as expectations you intend to pursue as you participate in this course.
2. Make a list of the basic steps in preparing your first speech for class. Study your list to see how it relates to the steps featured in this chapter.
3. Prepare and deliver a five- to six-minute informative speech. Draw the topic from your own experiences or interests and not from one of your college courses.

References

Ayers, J., T. Hopf, and D. M. Myers. 1997. Visualization and performance visualization: Application, evidence, and speculation. In J.A. Daly, J. C. McCroskey, J. Ayers, T. Hopf, and D.M. Ayers (Eds.), *Avoiding communication* (305–330). Cresskill, NJ: Hampton Press.

Bimber, B., and R. Davis. 2003. *Campaigning online: The Internet in U.S. elections.* New York: Oxford.

Bradley, B. 1988. *Fundamentals of speech communication, (5th ed.)* Dubuque, IA: Wm. C. Brown.

Esslinger, J.J. 1992. "National parks: A scenery of destruction and degradation." In *Winning orations of the interstate oratorical association.* WI: Mankato State University.

Motley, M. T. 1988. Taking the terror out of talk. *Psychology Today*, 46–49.

CHAPTER 3

"A speaker's honesty is intimately connected with his personal commitment. Neither one can be faked. If a speaker doesn't really believe what he is saying, the audience will sense it.... It is foolish, even dangerous, to think we can fool very many people even some of the time. Honesty is not only the best policy, it is the only policy."

Rex Kelly, General Manager,
Corporate Communications,
Mississippi Power Company

© Corbis.

The Ethics of Responsible Speech

Our Freedom of Speech

Since the First Amendment to the U.S. Constitution was passed in 1791, American citizens have had a constitutional guarantee of freedom of speech. As a student, you are allowed to interact with your teachers, and you have opportunities to speak before your class about issues that concern you. You have the right to publicly support the political party of your choice, and you can engage in activities that reflect your social values. As a community resident, you have the right to speak before city council or the local school board to express agreement or disagreement with their policies. You can write a letter to an editor that supports or opposes the President of our nation. With access to the Internet, you have numerous and highly varied means of communication. Ultimately, limitations to our freedom of speech are decided by the U.S. Supreme Court. While we live with wide boundaries for speaking, periodically attempts are made to censor both our public and private lives. Since the terrorist attacks of 9/11, First Amendment rights have been challenged as the government figures out how to secure the country and fight terrorism. And as First Amendment lawyer Robert Corn-Revere notes, the "seemingly simple command" of the First Amendment becomes "exceedingly complex" when applied to electronic media (2007). The difficulty of monitoring the use/abuse of free speech is especially true in this age of "blogging," where every second a "citizen journalist" creates a new blog site, adding to the already 37 million existing sites, according to David Sifri, founder of the Technorati weblog dataset and link tracker/search engine (2006).

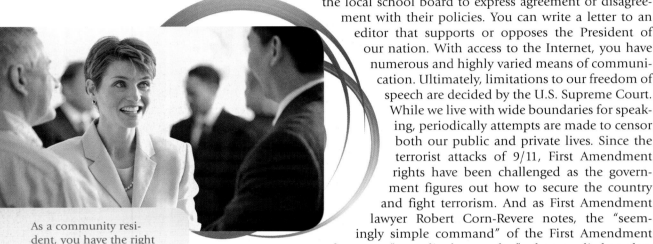

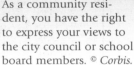

As a community resident, you have the right to express your views to the city council or school board members. © *Corbis*.

Freedom of expression comes with responsibility. In class, each speaker has the ethical responsibility to communicate accurately with sound reasoning and to decide what is said and best not said, based upon individual values. This responsibility requires a speaker to be truthful without hesitation. As listeners we are also given a responsibility: to respect the opinions of others, some of which will be different from ours.

This chapter emphasizes the importance of meeting your ethical responsibilities in any speech you give, whether it is informative, persuasive, or to entertain. We begin by discussing the connection between ethics and public speaking and then turn to guidelines for incorporating ethical standards in your speeches.

Ethics and Public Speaking

Ethics involve the rules we use to determine good and evil, right and wrong. These rules may be grounded in religious principles, democratic values, codes of conduct, and bases of values derived from a variety of sources. Without an ethical roadmap based on socially accepted values to guide you, you could disregard your audience's need for truth, and engage in self-serving deceit, ambiguity, intellectual sloppiness, and emotional manipulation. If you do, your credibility as a speaker is lost as your listeners turn elsewhere for a message—and a speaker—they can trust. Because public speaking is a reciprocal process, audience mistrust can stand in the way of communication.

As citizens and consumers, we are bombarded by messages each day through various print and electronic media. Intense competition exists among these outlets as they strive to be the most-watched or most-read. Walter Cronkite, who served for nearly two decades as top news anchor on CBS News (1962–1980), was once called, "the most trusted man in America." People welcomed him nightly into their homes and believed what he said. Since Cronkite, however, no media person has attained such status as a trustworthy source. On the contrary, much has happened to diminish the public's trust in the media and those affiliated with it. During the same period Walter Cronkite delivered the nightly news on CBS, Jim Bakker was achieving success on a different channel as a television evangelist. An articulate public speaker, he abused the trust of millions of people for decades as he asked for money to do the work of God and used it to build a personal fortune instead. After serving about five years in prison, Bakker returned to participate in a far less visible inner-city ministry, and authored the book *"I was wrong."*

As media outlets look for bottom-line profits, ethical standards are occasionally bent. Such was the case in 1993, when *Dateline NBC* alleged that some General Motors pickup trucks had a tendency to explode during collisions. It was later revealed that those trucks had been rigged with incendiary devices to assure footage of an explosion. General Motors Corporation threatened litigation, which resulted in the on-air admission by journalist Stone Phillips that NBC used the devices without informing the viewers.

Ethical violations are not limited to those in the media. Politics continues to mix profit, power, and public service to create ethical breaches by people in powerful positions. One of your authors has lived in Ohio most of his adult life and in 2005 he began following a scandal reported in the news that provided details of unethical and unlawful activities by public officials. Ohio has proven to be a key state in national elections and Tom Noe, a key Republican fundraiser now serving time in prison for violating federal campaign law, was the initial subject in a series of stories that reported questionable investments of state funds, the loss of millions of dollars, and a web of cover-up activities. Accused with Noe were other Republican supporters and officials, and even the governor of the state pleaded no contest to charges that he failed to report gifts he received while in office. After hearing and reading about the charges, counter-charges, admitted mistakes, and denials, the general public was left with disappointment and cynicism because of public reports of ethical violations.

Unfortunately, scandalous behavior is not limited to either political party's leaders as power, status, and money, have led to unethical behavior and deceptive speeches throughout our history. And political public speaking is often a key form of communication when this sort of action occurs. During local, state, and national campaigns, the media provides the public with

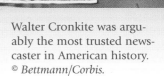

Walter Cronkite was arguably the most trusted newscaster in American history.
© *Bettmann/Corbis.*

details of sexual misconduct, bribery, poor parenting, and unimpressive military service. No candidate is immune, which leaves the public faced with the dilemma over who is really telling the truth. In fact, as we are preparing this edition of our book, President Bush's approval rating is at an all-time low, and the approval rating of the U.S. Congress is even lower. A war in Iraq continues and leaders in public speeches attack the president's conduct of the war while the chief executive and commander-in-chief defends his policy and asks for patience from the general public. The leadership in Washington was unwilling to pass immigration reform and no effective energy policy was enacted either. Meanwhile, surfacing in campaign rhetoric for the 2008 presidential elections are questions and ethical implications about truth and deception and right versus wrong.

Ethical violations seem commonplace in media reports, but this does not suggest that ethics are unimportant. On the contrary, it is important to recognize that every time you speak, you are risking your reputation. Listeners will forgive many things--stumbling over words, awkward gestures, lack of examples--but if you lie or mislead them, they may never trust you again. For some, maintaining strong ethical standards is second nature. For others, a little deliberation is needed. Some speakers rationalize their unethical behaviors so they can continue to misguide their audiences.

The Link Between Ethics and Values

Inherent to a discussion about ethics in public speaking is the concept of values and how they ground us. **Values,** which are *socially shared ideas about what is good, right, and desirable,* propel us to speak and act. They determine what we consider important and what we ignore, how we regard our listeners, and how we research and develop a speech. Values are communicated through what speakers say—and fail to say—through delivery, and through responsiveness to audience feedback.

You can speak out against anti-Semitism or remain silent. You can support, through public discourse, the university's right to displace poor families from their university-owned apartments to build another office tower or you can plead for a more humane solution. In a public speaking class, you have a forum to talk about those things you feel are right or wrong, desirable or undesirable. Though you may be hesitant to speak out, you may be surprised by how many others agree with you.

"Ethos" and Speaker Credibility

Although ethics seems to be a "hot button" topic in academic courses as well as governmental and organizational activities, it has been under consideration for over 2000 years. In references to rhetoric, Aristotle discussed the term **"ethos,"** meaning "ethical appeal." In a translation by Lane Cooper (1960), we find that **Aristotle** defined ethos in terms of the intelligence, character, and goodwill a speaker communicates during a speech:

> Speakers are untrustworthy in what they say or advise from one or more of the following causes. Either through want of intelligence they form wrong opinions; or, while they form

correct opinions, their rascality leads them to say what they do not think; or, while intelligent and honest enough, they are not well disposed [to the hearer, audience], and so perchance will fail to advise the best course, though they see it.

Aristotle believed speakers can abuse their ethical relationship with their listeners when they misinterpret information or fail to collect all the information needed to give a complete and fair presentation, and when self-interest leads them to dishonesty and lack of goodwill. For example, a developer comes into a community in the hopes of building a large super-store and, in a public forum, explains how many jobs and how much revenue will be brought to the community. The developer's self-interest in this project may result in his leaving out information, such as the negative impact the super-store will have on employees and owners of the community's smaller businesses.

Since Aristotle, scholars have made the distinction between intrinsic ethos and extrinsic ethos. Whereas **intrinsic ethos** is the ethical appeal found in the actual speech, including such aspects as supporting material, argument flow, and source citation, **extrinsic ethos** is a speaker's image in the mind of the audience. Extrinsic aspects include perceived knowledge and expertise as well as speaker confidence and enthusiasm. Both elements contribute to a speaker's credibility. Communication theorists James C. McCroskey and Thomas J. Young (1981) tie credibility to the audience's perception of the speaker as an expert, as a person to trust, and as a person with positive and honest intent. If you are too casual, unprepared, and have ignored the necessity to provide support for your claims, your credibility will be limited and you will have a negative reputation to overcome. An ethical speaker takes credit for his or her own ideas and, through source citation, credits others for their ideas. An ethical speaker will not mislead others through omission or confusion.

Engage in Dialogue with the Audience

According to Richard L. Johannesen (1974), a scholar in rhetorical and communication studies, there are clear signs that indicate speaker sensitivity to ethical responsibility. The least sensitive speakers, says Johannesen, engage in what he describes as **monologic** communication. From this perspective, the audience is viewed as an object to be manipulated and, in the process, the speaker displays such qualities as deception, superiority, exploitation, dogmatism, domination, insincerity, pretense, coercion, distrust, and defensiveness—qualities Johannesen considers unethical. About such communication, he has written:

> Focus is on the speaker's message, not on the audience's real needs…Audience feedback is used only to further the speaker's purpose; an honest response from receiver is not wanted or is precluded…In contrast, sensitive speakers engage in **dialogic communication** that demonstrates an honest concern for the welfare of their listeners. Their speech communicates trust, mutual respect and acceptance, open-mindedness, equality, empathy, directness, lack of pretense, and non-manipulative intent. Although the speaker in dialogue may offer advice or express disagreement, he does not aim to psychologically

coerce an audience into accepting his view. The speaker's aim is one of assisting the audience in making independent, self-determined decisions (1974).

Public speaking is a listener-centered activity, so all decisions made in the development process should take the audience into consideration. Recognizing the importance of speaker credibility and projecting firm ethical standards, we encourage you to reflect on the following habits and guidelines as you develop your speeches.

Promoting Ethical Speaking

Rhetorical theorist Karl Wallace (1955) identified four habits that promote ethical communication. Following descriptions of these habits are specific guidelines to help you address them.

Habit of Search

The habit of search refers to putting forth effort to learn enough about your topic so you are able to speak knowledgeably and confidently. As you speak before your class, try to realize that, at that moment, you are the primary source of information about your chosen topic. You are responsible for presenting a message that reflects thorough knowledge of the subject, sensitivity to relevant issues and implications, and awareness that many issues are multi-faceted.

Habit of Justice

This habit reminds us to select and present facts and opinions openly and fairly. According to Karl Wallace (1955), the speaker should not distort or conceal evidence (1-9). The speaker should avoid substituting emotionally loaded language for sound argument. Be sure supporting material offers the audience the opportunity to make fair judgments. The Food and Drug Administration makes sure the pharmaceutical industry puts all its cards on the table, leading to disclaimers such as "side-effects may include nausea, vomiting, dizziness, stroke or heart attack, and should not be taken by children under twelve, women who are pregnant, or people who have heart problems, liver problems, kidney disease or diabetes." As a result, the consumer has the opportunity to make a judgment based on known information rather than taking a risk when information is withheld or unavailable. Similarly, if someone is considering cosmetic surgery, it is important that the potential risks are addressed in addition to identifying the benefits.

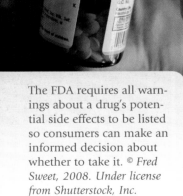

The FDA requires all warnings about a drug's potential side effects to be listed so consumers can make an informed decision about whether to take it. © *Fred Sweet, 2008. Under license from Shutterstock, Inc.*

Habit of Preferring Public to Private Motivation

As a speaker, you need to determine whether your motives for speaking are purely personal or whether they go beyond your own concerns. Ethical speakers reveal the sources of their information and opinion, which assists

the audience in weighing any special bias, prejudices, and self-centered motivations in source materials. Avoid concealing information about your source materials or your own motives because, if revealed, the effectiveness of your message will be weakened.

A person may be motivated to give an informative speech on the warning signs of methamphetamine (meth) abuse because of the rise in the number of meth users and meth-related deaths in her community. Clearly, her specific purpose meets the habit of preferring public to private motivation, assuming she has reliable information on meth use and meth-related deaths. In contrast to public motivation is private motivation. If a teacher tries to convince students to sign up for internships in his department, not because it is a beneficial academic experience, but because as internship coordinator, he gets paid per student, his motivation is private.

Habit of Respect for Dissent

This habit addresses the necessity for accepting views that differ from our own. As stated earlier, freedom of expression is a guiding principle of our democracy, and is constitutionally protected. The respect for dissent allows for and encourages diversity of argument and opinion. It involves seeing a different point of view as a challenge rather than as a threat. It does not mean we have to give in. We can still advocate our convictions while acknowledging that others may be as firm in their opposition to us.

Guidelines for Meeting Ethical Habits

In order to ensure these four habits are incorporated into your speech development, the following nine guidelines are provided.

1. Understand the Power of the Podium

Have you ever watched a commercial and decided you *had* to have that product? Have you been in church when a minister tells about a needy homeless shelter, and you were compelled to donate at that moment? Have you heard a message about environmental hazards created by plastic bottles and tossed your next bottle of water in the recycle bin? These examples indicate that speaking is a powerful activity.

Do public service announcements cause you to be more conscientious about recycling? © *Marilyn Barbone, 2008. Under license from Shutterstock, Inc.*

Speakers travel to campuses across the country to address a wide range of issues related to race, ethnicity, poverty, public health, alcoholism, immigration, and national security, to name a few. Some speakers are recruited by organizations on campus; others advertise their expertise in the hopes of being allowed to speak. These people understand the power of the podium. They know they can inform audiences, they can move them emotionally, or they can move students to act.

Speakers may have national forums through the media or through their positions, such as members of Congress. Some speakers abuse the power. An historical example is the "witch hunt" that occurred in the 1950s. The "witches" in this case were communists, communist sympathizers, or anyone who had a direct or indirect association with someone in the Communist Party in the United States. Heading up this hunt was U.S. Senator Joseph R. McCarthy, who used the podium to attack government employees, educators, individuals in the entertainment industry, and union activists, claiming they were directly contributing to the rise in communism in the U.S. and were being disloyal and un-American. In his heyday, McCarthy had the support of more than half of the American people. He took advantage of the power of the podium, by playing up to people's fears, using dramatic oratory, manipulating facts, and accusing critics of disloyalty. Examples of abuses by other speakers are easy to find. As speakers, we need to be aware that we may have the power to persuade and the power to pass on information to others—powers that must be used for the common good.

Senator Joseph McCarthy took advantage of the power of the podium in his communist witch-hunt.
© *Bettmann/Corbis.*

2. Speak Truthfully and Know Your Facts

Whenever you speak before an audience, it is your ethical responsibility to be certain of your facts. If you present material as being true when it is not, you mislead your listeners and diminish your credibility. When your listeners realize your facts are wrong, they will trust you less. If, for example, during a speech on campus thefts you blame students for the majority of crimes, when, in fact, most thefts are committed by city residents, you will lose credibility with listeners who know the facts.

Even well-known speakers present inaccurate statements. President George W. Bush received national as well as international criticism for stating that weapons of mass destruction (WMD) existed in Iraq. An exhaustive search for such weapons failed to uncover any WMD. The U.S. intelligence community apparently lacked accurate information and the president's credibility suffered considerably.

On a more commonplace level, a couple bought a home that developed plumbing problems within a few months of ownership. The plumber determined the septic tank was filled and needed cleaning. "But the real estate agent told us we are connected to the sewer," the homeowner told the plumber. The plumber answered, "No matter, the septic tank is in the backyard and you are responsible for the problem." When the homeowner confronted the sales representative for not telling the truth, she attempted to justify her position by saying, "I did not tell you that the home was *connected* to the sewers;

President Bush's credibility suffered because of his statements asserting that Iraq possessed weapons of mass destruction.
© *Brooks Kraft/Corbis.*

I told you the sewers were *available.*" This statement was simply not true, and the homeowners believe they were victims of the ethic that "the end justifies the means" or "do what it takes to get the sale."

3. Use Credible Sources

When collecting supporting material for a speech, it is your ethical responsibility to determine whether you are quoting a professional who has conducted research or someone who is simply writing a story. Often you can answer this question by digging a little deeper in the library or by checking key websites.

Certain sources have more credibility than others. If you are researching the need for college students to update vaccinations with booster shots, an article in *The New England Journal of Medicine* or *Science* would be preferable to an article in *Newsweek* or *Time.* Although the latter publications are generally reliable, scientific journals are the better choice for this specific type of information. Wikipedia may be very informative, but is generally not considered a reliable source.

4. Use Current and Reliable Information

An ethical speaker will expend effort to find current and reliable information on multiple sides of an issue. Note the terms "current" and "reliable." If your specific purpose is to inform your class on the latest technology for diabetes management, a simple search may lead you to the insulin pump. However, by probing a little further and finding more recent information, you should find articles about the insulin inhaler, which has just recently hit the market.

Reliability is related to the credibility, or believability, of the source. Certainly, outdated information will not be as reliable as current information. Also, the speaker needs to determine whether or not the information makes sense, especially in light of where it was found. For example, recent research has shown that there are health benefits to eating chocolate and drinking a glass of red wine each day. Now, if the wine or cocoa industries commissioned those studies, one might question the reliability of the findings. If the science community came to these conclusions after independent tests, the information would have greater credibility. An ethical speaker will look for the most recent, authentic and unbiased information.

Occasionally, there are situations when information may not be current but remains an appropriate illustration to show your audience what you mean. For example, if you are informing your audience about criteria for critiquing film acting, you may find what you want in a dated review of *Man with a Golden Arm*, starring Frank Sinatra as a heroin addict who sweats out his addiction "cold turkey." On the other hand, if you are trying to prove that heroin addiction is dramatically increasing in our country, you need to rely on the most recent facts available.

Our world is changing rapidly. Old facts are often wrong facts, especially in such volatile areas as public safety and civil liberties. As you prepare your speech, take into consideration the need for currency in matters and issues that are relevant now. If you find credible evidence that appears to undermine your position, be honest enough to evaluate it fairly and change your position if you must. Throughout this process, keep in mind your ethical obligation to present accurate information to your listeners.

5. Avoid Purposeful Ambiguity

If you are preparing a speech on how men's home and child care responsibilities have increased over the decades, you might say:

> Men are doing more today than ever before. Today's husband is in the kitchen along with his wife preparing meals and keeping house. He is changing more diapers, doing more laundry, and reading more bedtime stories to the children. And in most homes, he still takes out the garbage.

If you left it at this, the audience is left with many questions, since you have not addressed the reasons for this phenomenon. Essential details have been omitted. To be less ambiguous and more specific, you might add:

> Despite this transformation, research has shown that the average American working woman puts in roughly fifteen more hours of work each week than her husband. According to Arlie Hochschild, a sociologist at the University of California at Berkley, women still do far more housework and child care than men. In a survey of couples in the San Francisco area, Hochschild found that only eighteen percent of the men share housework equally with their wives, while more than three out of five say they do little or nothing at home.

Adding the above information shows that women are still doing more work in the home, it is just that men are now doing more than they used to do. Clarification is provided. Sometimes speakers eliminate details from their speeches, supposedly to make it easier for their listeners to understand their messages. But they may be attempting to control audience opinion. When details can make a difference in audience perception, it is your responsibility to present as complete a picture as possible.

Choose words carefully to communicate your point. Realize, for example, that references to "hazing abuses" may conjure images of death and bodily injury to some, while others may think of harmless fraternity pranks. Ambiguities often stem from inadequate or sloppy research.

6. Avoid Rumors and Innuendo

It is unethical to base your speeches on rumors, which, of course, are everywhere. We may be guilty of listening to them, and perhaps passing them along. Rumors are unproven charges, usually about an individual, that are often untrue. By using them as facts, you can tarnish—or ruin—a reputation and convey misleading information to your audience.

Pop culture is ripe with rumors. Weekly entertainment magazines are filled with stories about the lives of Hollywood celebrities, many which are based on rumors. We find out that stars are battling drug and alcohol abuse, or that they are gaining or losing weight. We read that Jennifer is dating Michael. Oh, no, they just broke up. Wait…they are back together. Now they are married. Oops, they are divorced. She is pregnant. Is it his? Or does it belong to old boyfriend, Jason? Every aspect of their lives is reported, frequently without any reliance on facts.

It is also ethically unacceptable to use innuendo to support a point. **Innuendo** includes hints or remarks that something is what it is not. Essentially, they are veiled lies. Innuendo frequently surfaces in the heat of a strongly contested political race. The exaggerated rhetoric of opponents results in observations ranging from misstatements about events to hints about improprieties in the alleged behavior of the political opponent. Just before Barack Obama announced his bid for the presidency, stories surfaced about his early childhood education. As a young child, he spent several years in Indonesia, where he attended school. In an attempt to discredit him, Obama's opponents reported that he was taught a radical form of Islam during this time. These remarks were proved to be untrue. An ethical speaker avoids any use of rumor or innuendo when preparing a speech.

7. Be Willing to Rock the Boat

Speaking in support of the public good implies a willingness to air a diversity of opinions, even when these opinions are unpopular. According to Roderick Hart (1985), professor of communication, we must "accept boat rocking, protests, and free speech as a necessary and desirable part of [our] tradition" (162). Your goal as a speaker can be to encourage the "ideal of the best ideas rising to the surface of debate" (46).

Despite the statute of free speech in Western society, taking an unpopular stand at the podium is not easy, especially when the speaker faces the threat of repercussions.

In the United States, a debate continues over Intelligent Design Theory as a challenge to Darwin's Theory of Evolution. Dr. Richard Sternberg, editor of a highly respected scientific journal, was harassed and treated punitively after he published a paper on intelligent design by Steven Myer of Cambridge University. Myer argued that intelligent design should be taken seriously. Having allowed the article to be published, Sternberg was the recipient of harsh criticism by officials of the Smithsonian Institute and the National Center for Scientific Education. Sternberg indicated false charges were made against him. Some charged that he had not sought peer reviews of Myer's essay. Some charged him with taking money under the table, and others called for his resignation as editor. Sternberg believes these accusations were all attempts to prevent scientific dissent. The message to him, in other words, was to be a gatekeeper of *acceptable* scientific ideas or "Don't rock the boat," which can be viewed as an unethical proposition.

8. Be Clear in Your Motives

Suppose you are a real estate agent with a home for sale in a suburban community that is in the grip of a severe real estate recession. There are many homes for sale but few buyers. You are among dozens of agents who will find it difficult to make a satisfactory living unless conditions improve. In order to attract potential homebuyers to your commu-

Bending facts to make a sale is not ethical. © *Stephen Coburn, 2008. Under license from Shutterstock, Inc.*

nity, you give a series of speeches in a nearby city, extolling the virtues of suburban life. Although much of what you say is true, you bend some facts to make your community seem the most attractive and affordable. For example, you tell your listeners there are jobs available, when in fact, the job market is slight (the rosy employment figures you use are a decade old). You mention that the community schools are among the top in the state, when, in fact, only one in five is ranked above the state average. With your goal of restoring your community to its former economic health, you feel justified in this manipulation.

Do the ends justify the means? While your intentions were good, your ethics were faulty. As a speaker, you have only one ethical choice: to present the strongest possible legitimate argument and let each listener decide whether or not to support your position.

9. Avoid Excessive and Inappropriate Emotional Appeals

As listeners, we expect speakers to make assertions that are supported by sound reasoning. We expect the speech to flow logically, and to include relevant supporting material. However, some speakers prey on our fears or ignorance and rely heavily on the use of excessive and inappropriate appeals to emotion. To be ethical, emotional appeals must be built on a firm foundation of good reasoning and should never be used to take advantage of susceptible listeners. In our chapter on persuasive speaking, we examine further the nature of emotional appeals. However, following are four circumstances that create particularly troublesome ethical concerns.

Your speech creates a need in your audience through deception and requires an action that will primarily benefit you. It is manipulative and unethical to try to convince a group of parents that the *only way* their children will succeed in school is to purchase an educational program that is comprehensive in detail, according to the company *you* represent.

 The emotional appeal is aimed at taking advantage of those particularly susceptible to manipulation. A bit of channel surfing late at night will bring the viewer to quite a number of infomercials full of emotional appeals to persuade the viewer to purchase expensive programs that are supposed to lead them to considerable wealth, health, or both.

Emotional appeals are part of a sustained plan to confuse an audience and make them feel insecure and helpless. If, as a community leader, you oppose the effort to establish group homes for the developmentally handicapped by referring repeatedly to the threat these residents pose to the neighborhood children, you leave your listeners feeling vulnerable and frightened. Fear can become so intense that homeowners may dismiss facts and expert opinions that demonstrate developmentally disabled persons are neither violent nor emotionally disadvantaged.

You realize your logic will not hold up under scrutiny, so you appeal to audience emotions to disguise the deficit. Instead of relying on facts to convince your listeners, you appeal to their emotional needs. There are many ways unethical speakers disguise and deceive in order to achieve their specific purpose. Among them are the following: name calling, glittering generalities, testimonials, plainfolks, and bandwagoning.

Name calling involves linking a person or group with a negative symbol. In a persuasive speech, if your purpose is to convince your audience that abortion is morally wrong, you would be engaging in name calling if you referred to individuals who support a woman's right to choose as "murderers" and "baby-killers." You may believe these labels are truthful, but they are emotionally charged names that will arouse emotions in your audience, and many listeners may tune you out.

Glittering generalities rely on audience's emotional responses to values such as home, country, and freedom. Suppose the real issues of a campaign are problems associated with the growing budget deficit, illegal immigration, and being dependent on foreign oil. If a candidate avoids these issues and argues for keeping the Ten Commandments in front of court houses, reciting the pledge of allegiance more often, and amending the constitution to prevent flag-burning, that candidate is likely to rely considerably on glittering generalities. Although acceptable to talk about these latter concerns, manipulating the audience's response so that critical judgments about major issues are clouded in other areas is unethical.

Testimonials can be both helpful and destructive. People who have had their cholesterol levels improve because of a particular prescription medicine may lead others to success. People who love their hybrid cars may help others make the decision to buy one. However, we are bombarded by celebrities touting countless products including shampoo, sports drinks, and phone service because they are paid to do so, not because they have expert knowledge of those products. In most cases no damage is done. However, Suzanne Somers created an uproar in the scientific community when she promoted her own diet plan. In addition to the fact that she lacks professional qualifications, her diet plan de-emphasizes exercise and she suggests a daily caloric threshold that is very dangerous. Since it is well-known that any diet or new exercise regimen should be discussed with a medical professional, her testimonial can be damaging.

A candidate that speaks more about good old-fashioned values such as respect for the flag, rather than real issues, is relying on glittering generalities.
© Paul B. Moore, 2008. *Under license from Shutterstock, Inc.*

Plain folks is an effort to identify with the audience. Be cautious when a speaker tells an audience, "Believe me, because I'm just like you." Speakers who present themselves as *"plain folks"* may be building an identification with their audience appropriately (something speakers often want to do), or they may be manipulating their listeners. One of your authors recalls an incident where an investment adviser conducting a seminar for senior citizens told his audience: "One main reason I chose this career path is because my own parents, not unlike you gathered here tonight, did not have the opportunities I am offering you. I discovered that they are struggling in their retirement years to make ends meet on a monthly basis. Like you, they worked hard throughout their careers. However, what was available to them to live on when they left their work was modest." This speaker appeared believable, but in fact, his parents retired with considerable funds acquired from owning a successful business for thirty years. The emotional tactic of using plain folks as an emotional appeal was simply to gain sales.

Bandwagoning is another unethical method of deception. Often listeners are uncomfortable taking a position no one else supports. Realizing this reluctance, unethical speakers may convince their listeners to support their point of view by telling them that "everyone else" is already involved. For example, you may live in a residence hall on a campus where your school's mascot is being threatened with extinction. A rally will be held, and someone on your floor is going door-to-door telling all the residents that "everybody" on campus will be at the rally to support the mascot. Chances are, this is an exaggeration.

As a speaker, you should try to convince others of the weight of your evidence—not the popularity of your opinion. In the case above, the resident should not be asking everyone to jump on the bandwagon, but should be explaining to people why keeping the mascot is a positive thing.

Avoiding Unethical Practices

In his text *Ethics in Communication*, Richard Johannesen (1990) provides a number of ways speakers can avoid engaging in unethical speaking practices. The following suggestions relate to developing and presenting your ideas.

When developing your speech:

- Do not use false, fabricated, misrepresented, distorted, or irrelevant evidence to support arguments or claims.
- Do not intentionally use unsupported, misleading, or illogical reasoning.
- Do not oversimplify complex situations into simplistic two-valued, either-or, bi-polar views or choices.

When giving your speech:

- Do not represent yourself as informed or as being an "expert" on a subject when you are not.
- Do not deceive your audience by concealing your real purpose, self-interest, the group you represent, or your position as an advocate of a viewpoint.
- Do not distort, hide, or misrepresent the number, scope, intensity, or undesirable aspects, consequences, or effects.
- Do not use "emotional appeals" that lack a supporting basis of evidence or reasoning or that would not be accepted if the audience had time to examine the subject themselves.
- Do not pretend certainty where tentativeness and degrees of probability would be more accurate.
- Do not advocate something in which you do not believe yourself (254).

Summary

Because of the many ethical abuses that have taken place in recent years, audiences have become skeptical about the ethics of public speakers. Ethical public speaking is anchored in the values of the speaker, his or her audience, and the larger society. Heed the advice of Richard Johannesen (1974), who reminds us that ethical speakers engage in a "dialogue" with their audience, communicating qualities such as trust and directness, while unethical speakers engage in a "monologue" as they manipulate their audience to their own end (95).

Once you have chosen your speech topic, recognize that ethics are part of every step of speech development and remember these guidelines: understand the power of the podium, speak truthfully and know your facts, use credible sources, use current and reliable information, avoid purposeful ambiguity, avoid rumors and innuendo, be willing to rock the boat, be clear in your motives, and avoid excessive and inappropriate emotional appeals.

Questions for Study and Discussion

1. How would you define the ethical responsibilities for a public speaker?
2. Who are public speakers you can think of who are not mentioned in this chapter but who you believe have spoken ethically and/ or unethically?
3. What do to believe is an appropriate ethical relationship between self-interest and the needs of the audience?

Activities

1. Locate and select a speech either in print or recorded and critically analyze it in terms of the ethics of responsible speech.
2. Select a speaker and one of his or her speeches that you believe possesses considerable ethical appeal and write a brief paper on what you believe to be the speaker's intrinsic and extrinsic ethos.
3. Write a short paper or prepare a speech for delivery on the proposition that "through public speaking we wield enormous power for good and for evil." Then meet in small groups in class to discuss and explore each other's points of view.

References

Corn-Revere, R. 2006. Internet and the first amendment. Retrieved from www.firstamendementcenter.org.

Hart, R. 1985. "The politics of communication studies: An address to undergraduates," *Communication Education*, 34, 162.

Johannesen, R. C. 1990. *Ethics in communication.* Prospect Heights, IL: Waveland Press.

McCroskey, J.C., and T. J. Young. 1981. "Ethos and Credibility: The Construct and Its Measurement after Three Decades," *The Central States Speech Journal* 22, 24–34.

Sifri, D. 2006. "Chinese bloggers top 17 million," Retrieved May 26, 2006, from www.vnunet.com.

Wallace, K. 1987. "An ethical basis of communication," *The Speech Teacher*, 4, 1–9.

"It is the disease of not listening,
the malady of not marking,
that I am troubled withal."

William Shakespeare

Listening and Evaluating Speeches

The Importance of Good Listening Skills

As discussed in previous chapters, public speaking is an audience-centered process. Decisions made throughout this process, from topic selection to delivery, should focus on your listeners. One way to improve your chances of success is to approach the process from the listening side—that is, to work at developing better listening skills. These skills are essential for two different, but complementary, reasons:

1. By understanding the needs of your listening audience, you will be able to develop and deliver speeches that have the greatest chance of communicating your intended meaning.

2. By understanding the factors affecting listening, you will be able to monitor your own listening habits and more effectively evaluate and criticize the speeches of others, including those of your classmates. There is a direct relationship between the quality of your listening and the quality of your speaking. *Good speakers use what they hear to analyze and respond to the needs of their audience, and to present information in a way that promotes communication.*

Despite the amount of time we spend listening, our ability to retain what we hear is limited. According to communication professor Ralph G. Nichols, a pioneer in listening research, immediately after listening to a speech, we can recall only half of what was said. After several days, only about twenty-five percent of the speech stays with us (Nichols 1961).

We can illustrate Nichols' findings by examining what people remember about John F. Kennedy's 1960 inaugural address. Although all who heard it when it was first delivered (or later on tape) remember these words, "And so, my fellow Americans, ask not what your country can do for you—ask what you can do for your country," few recalled the militant nature of Kennedy's remarks: "Let all our neighbors know that we shall join with them to oppose aggression or subversion anywhere in the Americas. And let every other power know that this hemisphere intends to remain master of its own house."

Few who heard Kennedy's inaugural address recall the militant nature of his remarks; they focused on the inspirational message.
© *Bettmann/Corbis.*

Reflect on How You Listen

Many people think of listening as a simple task that involves sitting back and giving the speaker your attention. As the following interchange suggests, listening is more complicated than it appears. As public speakers, we hope our message and meaning will be understood. As audience members, we may have other things on our minds—distractions, preconceived notions, prejudices, misunderstandings, and stress— and the message we receive may be much different from the message sent. The speaker (left-hand column) is an activist from the 1960s. The listener (right-hand column) is a student in the new century.

Speaker

Around forty years ago, at about this time of year, I—and a whole lot of other committed students—spent a solid week—day and night—in the offices of our college president. Needless to say, we hadn't been invited.

We were protesters and proud of it. We were there because we believed the Vietnam War was wrong. We were there because we believed racism was wrong. We were there because we believed that women should be given the same opportunities as men.

Were we victorious? For about ten years, I thought so. Then something happened. The signs were subtle at first. Haircuts got shorter. The preppie look replaced torn jeans. Business became the major of choice.

In a flash—it happened that quickly— these subtle changes became a way of life. Campus life, as I knew it, disappeared. Revolution and concern for the oppressed were out, and conservatism and concern for the self were in.

From the point of view of someone who has seen both sides—the radical, tumultuous sixties and the calm, money-oriented eighties, nineties, and the new century— students of today are really forty-year-olds in twenty-year-old bodies. They are conservative to the core at the only time of life when they can choose to live free. I am here to help you see how wrong you are.

Listener

Here I am again—listening to another speaker who says he stormed his college administration building in the 60s. This must be a popular topic on the college speaking circuit. Maybe this guy will be different from the other three middle-aged radicals I heard, but I doubt it… The least they could do is turn up the air conditioning. It's so hot I can hardly breathe, let alone listen.

These guys keep talking about how they know the way and how we're all wrong… I wonder what he does for a living. I'll bet he hasn't saved any lives lately or helped the poor. He probably earns big bucks giving speeches on campus telling us how horrible we are… He looks like he spends a lot of time cultivating his hippie look. He must have slept in those clothes for a week. These guys all look the same.

He's harping on the same old issues. Doesn't he know the Vietnam War is ancient history; that African Americans have more opportunities than they ever had—I wish I could earn as much as Denzel Washington; that women are on the job along with men—I wish I could earn as much as Katie Couric … I guess I'll have a pizza for dinner. I should have eaten before I came. I'm really hungry.

Of course we're interested in business. Maybe he had a rich father who paid his tuition, but I don't. I need to earn money when I graduate so I can pay back my student loans.

Who does he think he is—calling us conservatives. I'm not a bigot. When I believe something is wrong, I fight to change it—like when I protested against ethnic cleansing overseas and flag burning right here.

I wonder when he'll finish. I've got to get back to the dorm to study for my marketing exam. He just goes on and on about the same old things.

Reasons Audiences Stop Listening

You may see a bit of yourself in the speaker-listener example. Maybe you do not have this internal dialogue frequently, but most of us experience this occasionally. Based on the listening facts from Rankin and Nichols, it is clear that we spend much of our time listening. We can probably agree that listening is important, but research has shown that we do not retain much of what a speaker says. So, the question remains, why do we stop listening? There is no single answer to this question, but the six reasons listed below may strike a familiar chord. We stop listening:

- *When our attention drifts*
  Listeners drift in and out of a speech, thinking about the heat, their next meal, or an impending exam. Studies have shown that few of us can pay attention to a single stimulus for more than twenty seconds without focusing, at least momentarily, on something else.

- *When we are distracted*
  Our environment determines how well we can listen. In the speaker-listener example, the heat made it difficult to pay attention. Internal stresses—hunger, unresolved conflict, and concern about exams—are also distractions.

How often do you feel your attention drifting away from the speaker when you're in a meeting? *© Marcin Balcerzak, 2008. Under license from Shutterstock, Inc.*

- *When we have preconceived notions*
  Before the speaker in the example above opened his mouth, the listener had already decided what the speaker stood for based on the speaker's appearance and on a stereotype of what sixties radicals stood for. Although in this case he was right—the speaker's views conformed to the listener's preconceived notions—he may be wrong about other speakers.

- *When we disagree*
  Although the speaker identified continuing social ills, the listener did not share his concerns. From his point of view, much more was right with the world than the speaker admitted—a perspective that reduced the listener's willingness and ability to consider the speaker's message.

- *When we are prejudiced or inflexible*
  Few African Americans are as famous or financially successful as Denzel Washington; few women earn as much as Katie Couric. Yet the listener based his reaction to the speaker's message on the premise that if one member of a group can succeed, all can. His prejudice prevented him from seeing the truth in the speaker's words.

- *When we are faced with abstractions and form our own opinions*
  The speaker never defined the term "conservative." As a result, the listener brought his own meaning to the term, equating it with bigotry. This meaning may or may not have coincided with the speaker's intent.

As audience members, we know our purpose is to listen, think critically, and retain the central idea of the message. But think about what *you* do as you listen and why you stop listening. You may consciously or unconsciously tune the speaker out. You may focus on minor details at the expense of the main point. You may prejudge the speaker based on appearance. You may allow your own emotional needs and responses to distort the message, and so on. Later, we will provide specific tips for improving your listening skills, but first, we will discuss the elements of listening.

The Four Stages of Listening

Think back to a time when, in an argument with one of your parents, you responded with, "I hear you!" You may have been correct. You *heard* your parent. It is possible, though, that you did not *listen* to your parent. American musical icon Paul Simon points to this problem in his song "The Sound of Silence," and if you listen to the lyrics, you will hear a reference to people "hearing without listening."

While hearing is the physical ability to receive sound, listening is a more complex process. Although listening seems to be instantaneous, it consists of several identifiable stages. Researcher Lyman Steil (1983) analyzes and explains listening in terms of four progressive stages: sensing, interpreting, evaluating, and responding (see figure 4.1). We move through these stages every time we listen, regardless of the situation. We may be part of a formal audience listening to a paid speaker, we might be engaged in conversation with a friend, or we might be home alone, listening to "things that go bump in the night." Listening can take place on several different levels which are characterized by different degrees of attention and emotional and intellectual involvement. At times, we only partially listen as we think about or do other things; other times we listen with complete commitment. The following is an elaboration of the four stages of listening.

REACTION:
What is the reaction or response of the receiver(s)? How does it match with the sender's objective?

EVALUATION:
How is the message evaluated or judged by the receiver(s): Acceptance or rejection, liking or disliking, agreement or disagreement, etc., on the part(s) of the receiver(s)? Is evaluation similar to sender's objective?

INTERPRETATION:
How is the message interpreted by the receiver(s)? What meaning is placed on the message? How close (similar) is the interpreted message's meaning to the intended message's meaning?

SENSING:
Is the message received and sensed by the intended receiver(s)? Does the message get into the stream-of-consciousness of the intended receiver(s)?

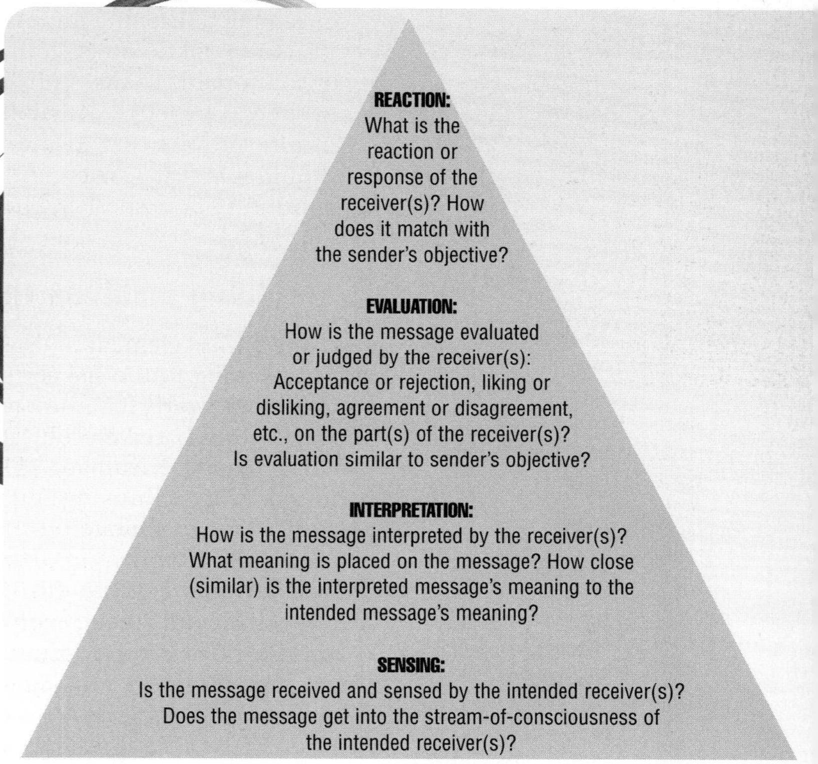

FIGURE 4.1
Four-stage communication model.

1. Listening Starts When You Sense the Information from Its Source

Listening begins with sensation, which requires the ability to hear what is said. Sight is also a factor, since the speaker's gestures, facial expressions, and the use of presentational aids communicate intent. Normally, the speaking voice is in the range of fifty-five to eighty decibels, a level that comfortably enables us to hear a speaker's words. Figure 4.2 shows how this level of sound compares with others in the environment.

As anyone who has tried to listen to a speech over the din of a car siren will realize, obstacles can—and often do—interfere with reception. These obstacles are known to communication theorists as "noise," which was discussed in Chapter One as part of the communication model. When your neighbor in the seat to your left starts coughing or when you are forced to sit at the back of a large, nonamplified auditorium, hearing is difficult, making concentrated listening impossible.

Noise takes other forms, such as environmental annoyances like uncomfortable chairs, stuffy rooms, or struggling air-conditioning systems. At times a remedy is possible. The speaker, for example, can ask the audience to move closer to the front and audience members can find more comfortable seats. When nothing can be done about noise, put yourself in the position of the speaker. Then work hard to listen to the message.

2. Listening Involves the Interpretation of Messages

A second critical element in listening is interpretation, the phase in which you attach meaning to the speaker's words. As a listener, it is important to keep in mind that words have different meanings to different people and that we interpret words based on subjective experiences. According to communication professor Paul G. Friedman, "When listening we can only *hope* to know what a speaker actually is thinking and trying to convey. Often, our attempts at 'mind reading' … are inaccurate" (1986, 12)

Our ability to interpret what we hear is influenced by emotional and intellectual barriers that get in the way of the speaker's intended message. We may hear specific words that offend us, or we find a statement or message repugnant. These barriers are forms of semantic or psychological noise. Novelist David Leavitt (1989) explains how emotional barriers prevented him from dealing with the topic of AIDS many years ago. A gay man, Leavitt found any mention of AIDS so threatening that he shut off his ability to listen:

The truth was that AIDS scared me so much I wanted to block it out of my mind. When AIDS came up in a conversation, I'd change the subject. When a frightening headline leaped out at me from the pages of the newspaper, I'd hurriedly skim the article, and, once assured that it described no symptoms I could claim to be suffering from myself, turn the page. Only later … did I recognize the extent to which I was masking denial with self-righteousness (30).

In this case, the psychological mechanism of denial caused the listening obstruction. A college student who is $40,000 in debt due to loans and maxing out credit cards may consciously "tune out" a classmate's persuasive speech on credit card debt in order to avoid thinking about the future. A zoning board member might unconsciously stop listening after two of five citizens have spoken in favor of a petition. An expert on public health can hardly sit still as he listens to a lecture on asbestos removal. After a few minutes he realizes that he and the speaker have completely different views on removal

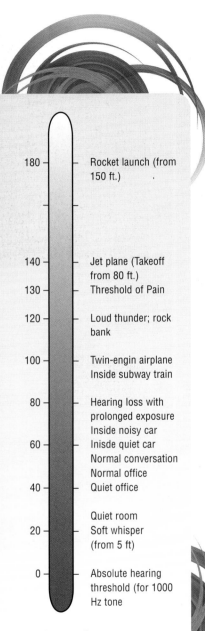

FIGURE 4.2

How loud are the sounds around us?

180	Rocket launch (from 150 ft.)
140	Jet plane (Takeoff from 80 ft.)
130	Threshold of Pain
120	Loud thunder; rock bank
100	Twin-engin airplane Inside subway train
80	Hearing loss with prolonged exposure Inside noisy car
60	Inisde quiet car Normal conversation Normal office
40	Quiet office
20	Quiet room Soft whisper (from 5 ft)
0	Absolute hearing threshold (for 1000 Hz tone

procedure safety. Instead of listening to the rest of the information, he fumes over this difference of opinion.

Whether emotional and intellectual barriers are the result of an unwilling-ness to deal with real-world problems, a refusal to take advice, or a difference of opinion, the result is the same: Listening is obstructed, interpretation skewed, and communication prevented.

3. Listening Involves Evaluating the Message

Evaluation requires that you assess the worth of the speaker's ideas and deter-mine their importance to you, particularly when listening to a persuasive message. You must decide whether you share the speaker's point of view and, if not, why not? Research has shown that when we perceive speakers as trustworthy, compe-

tent, reliable, highly regarded by others, dynamic, sociable, and simi-lar to ourselves, we are more likely to evaluate them positively than when we see them in negative or less acceptable ways. (Berlo, Lemert, and Mertz 1969)

When you're in a large audience, there are many distractions that make it difficult to concentrate on the speaker. © *Corbis.*

It is a mistake to assume that we judge these messages solely on their own merits. Research shows that our assessment is influenced by how the message fits into our value system. According to Friedman (1986) "This results from the human preference for maintaining internal consistency among personal beliefs, feelings, and actions" (13). We agree with messages that are consistent with other beliefs we have, and we disagree with messages that conflict with our beliefs.

This tendency was first described by psychologist Leon Festinger (1957) in his theory of cognitive dissonance. Essentially, the theory argues that we seek internal consistency between attitudes and behaviors. If we do not like a col-league and that person acts badly, we experience consistency between attitude and behavior. If someone we do not like acts in a sincere, friendly manner, we experience inconsistency.

When inconsistency exists, we experience mental stress. To reduce the stress, we are forced to change one or more of our attitudes or behaviors so that the inconsistency is reduced or eliminated. For example, assume you are a school board member who holds a high opinion of the school superintendent, until he angrily tells you to "Shut up!" during a meeting with administrators and other board members. You may experience dissonance because you cannot reconcile your previous esteem for this person with your new feelings of being disrespected. Dissonance disappears when your overall impression is consistent. In this case, you have a choice. You either rationalize the inappropriate behavior and go back to having a high opinion of the school superintendent ("He was under a lot of stress; he didn't mean it."). Or, you change your opinion of the person ("Someone who behaves this way in a formal meeting should not be leading our district."). Thus, as listeners, we seek information consistent with what we already know; we accept ideas more readily if they are linked to our values and commitments.

To preserve psychological balance, we often reject conflicting ideas and retain our original point of view. According to Friedman (1986, 13) this rejection can take many forms, including the following.

Shoot the messenger. If you are a member of a college fraternity, you may reject the notion that any fraternity found guilty of a hazing violation should be banned from campus. You may criticize the speaker as uninformed or as someone who was never able to get into a fraternity himself.

Rally 'round the flag. Listeners who disagree with a speaker's message may seek the support of others who share their point of view—in this case, other fraternity members. Shared support provides comfort and reassurance. However, it does not necessarily mean that you are right.

What the speaker says is not what you hear. Although the speaker may focus on hazing violations that put pledges in physical jeopardy, you hear him say that all violations—even minor infractions—should result in the fraternity being banned.

Convince yourself that the speaker's message has nothing to do with you. Even when opinions collide, you may convince yourself that you and the speaker are talking about two different things.

Don't think about it and it will go away. If, as a fraternity member, you took part in several unpleasant hazing incidents, listening to the speech may force you to question what you have done. To avoid the emotional discomfort that goes with this soul-searching, you may unconsciously block messages with which you do not agree.

Although these methods may seem extreme, we all rely on one or more of them at one time or another. Those who use them excessively—individuals who are threatened by any difference of opinion—are considered dogmatic and authoritarian (Ehrlich and Lee 1969).

4. Listening Involves Responding to the Speaker's Message

Feedback is also part of the listening process. In a conversation, the roles of listener and speaker change regularly. As the listener, you can interrupt the speaker, ask questions, engage in nonverbal behavior such as maintaining eye contact, touching, or hugging. At the mass media level, you may respond positively to a television series by watching it weekly or by purchasing a product that is advertised during the commercial. Listeners in a public speaking setting provide feedback in a variety of ways: laughing, smiling, nodding in agreement, cheering or booing, clapping, and questioning the speaker after the presentation is over. Listeners also provide feedback on a less conscious level, such as yawning, looking around the room, or whispering to the person next to you.

Effective speakers rely on and encourage feedback from their audience. They watch carefully for messages of approval or disapproval and adjust their presentations accordingly. We discuss audience feedback in detail in our chapter on the connection between the speaker and the audience.

A smiling and clapping audience provides good feedback to the speaker. *© Dmitriy Shironosov, 2008. Under license from Shutterstock, Inc.*

Eight Steps to Fine-tune Your Listening Skills

As a skill, listening is notoriously undervalued. Philosopher Mortimer Adler (1983) uses the following sports analogy to describe why the act of listening is as important as the act of speaking: "Catching is as much an activity as throwing and requires as much skill, though it is a skill of a different kind. Without the complementary efforts of both players, properly attuned to each other, the play cannot be completed." The players involved in the act of communication are speakers and listeners, all of whom have a role in the interaction. In this section, we explain how you can improve your listening skills—and, therefore, the chances of meaningful communication—by becoming conscious of your habits and, when necessary, redirecting your efforts. Listening is a multi-stage process that can be improved in many different ways (Pudy 1989).

1. Get Ready to Listen

Preparation is critical, especially when you have other things on your mind. Plan to make the effort to listen even before the speech begins, deliberately clearing your mind of distractions so you are able to concentrate on the speech.

2. Minimize Listening Barriers

This step is more difficult than it sounds, for it often involves overcoming emotional and intellectual barriers to listening that we identified in preceding passages. Often, we need help in recognizing our listening "blind spots." As you talk with your classmates about each other's speeches, try to determine whether the message you received from a speaker was the same message they heard. If it was not, think about what the topic means to you; try to identify any reasons for your misunderstanding. It may be possible that you are the only one who accurately understood the speaker's message. Sometimes an entire audience misses the point. If a question-and-answer period follows the speech, you can question the speaker directly to make sure you have the right meaning.

3. Leave Distractions Behind

Some distractions are more easily dealt with than others. You can change your seat to get away from the smell of perfume but you cannot make a head cold disappear. You can close the door to your classroom, but you cannot stop the speaker from rattling change in his pocket. Although dealing with distractions is never easy, you can try to put them aside so you can focus on the speaker and the speech. This task will become easier if you view listening as a responsibility—and as work. By considering listening as more than a casual interaction, you will be more likely to hear the message being sent.

4. Don't Rush to Judgment

Resist the temptation to prejudge speakers. You may think about dismissing someone because "she's old," "he's conservative," or "he always dresses like a dork." As a listener, you have the responsibility to evaluate the content of the speech and not to jump to conclusions based on impressions of what you know about the speaker or how he or she looks.

Listeners have the tendency to prejudge topics as well as speakers. You may yawn at the thought of listening to one of your classmates deliver an informative speech about the "pickling process" or "stage make-up" until you realize that the topic is more interesting than you expected. You may not have an inherent interest in the topic, but that does not mean the speaker cannot be interesting or thought-provoking.

Some speakers save their best for last. They may start slowly and build a momentum of ideas and language. Your job is to listen and be patient.

5. Listen First for Content, Second for Delivery

Both words and delivery impart meaning, and your public speaking class is designed to help you develop appropriate content and to deliver your speech in a meaningful way. But most of you have never participated in a speech tournament. Few of you have acted before. Your speaking engagements, for the most part, have been limited. Your job as a listener is to separate content from delivery, and focus first on the message.

Confronted with poor delivery, it is difficult to separate content from presentation. The natural tendency is simply to stop listening when speakers drone on in a monotone, deliver speeches with their heads in their notes, or sway back and forth. Delivery often has little to do with the quality of the speaker's ideas. Many of the speakers you will hear over the years will be in the position to address you because of their accomplishments, not their speaking ability. While a Nobel prize-winning scientist may be able to explain a breakthrough in cancer therapy, he or she may have no idea how to make eye contact with an audience. To avoid missing these speakers' points, look past poor delivery and focus on content.

6. Become an Effective Note Taker

Each time a professor lectures or conducts a class discussion, you and your fellow students are expected to take notes. After years of note taking, this activity probably seems as natural as breathing; it is something you do to survive. Ironically, though you worked hard to develop this skill, it often disappears at graduation. Most people do not pull out a pad and pen when listening to a speech in the world outside the classroom. But note taking is as appropriate and necessary for nonstudents as it is for students. When you listen to a speech at a public event, a political rally, or on television, taking notes will help you listen more effectively. The following suggestions will help you improve your note-taking—and listening—skills:

- Create two columns for your notes. Write ``Facts'' at the top of the left-hand column and "Personal reactions/questions" at the top of the right-hand column. If the speaker does not answer your questions during the course of the speech, ask for clarification at the end. This is particularly important when someone is talking about something complex, such as a change in insurance coverage, taxes, or city development.

A speaker's presentation may be lacking, but try to concentrate on the content rather than the delivery. © *Marcin Balcerzak, 2008. Under license from Shutterstock, Inc.*

- Use a key-word outline instead of full sentences to document the speaker's essential points. If you get bogged down trying to write full sentences, you may miss a huge chunk of the message. At the end of the speech, the key-word outline also gives you a quick picture of the speaker's main points.
- Use your own abbreviations or shorthand symbols to save time. If you know that "comm" means communication, then use that. If you are not sure whether it means "communication," "communism" or "community," then the abbreviation is not working for you. We have seen students use up and down arrows instead of writing "increase" or "decrease." Use a system that works for you.
- Use diagrams, charts, scales, and quick-sketch images to summarize thematic concepts or theories. Smiley faces may seem trite, but they can express succinctly how you feel about a concept. A scale may be useful as someone presents the pros and cons of some issue.
- Use a numbering system to get down procedural, directional, or structural units of information. Numbering helps organize information, especially if the speaker did not organize the units of information for you.
- If, no matter how quickly you write, you cannot keep up, ask the speaker—verbally or nonverbally—to slow down. Be somewhat cautious with this last suggestion. Do not ask the speaker to slow down so that you might write full sentences. You are just asking the person to slow down for purposes of general understanding. If you are the only person who is experiencing difficulty, you may want to ask questions at the end, or make an appointment to fill in any gaps in understanding.

Try to use a key-word outline in your notes to get the speaker's essential points quickly. © *Corbis.*

7. Be an Active Listener

One of the worst things about lecturing to 200 or more students is that some of them believe they cannot be seen because there are so many in the audience. So they talk to their neighbors, toss notes to their friends, slouch low in the seat, put their heads on their desks, or tuck into the cover of the hood on their sweatshirt. What these students do not know (surely you are not one of them!) is that we can see you and we want you to be engaged in the listening process.

As listeners, we have the ability to process information at the rate of about 400 words per minute. However, as most people talk at only about 150 words per minute, we have a considerable amount of unused thinking time to spare (Wolf et al. 1983, 154). This "extra time" often gets in the way of listening because we have the opportunity to take mental excursions away from the speaker's topic. It is natural to take brief trips ("I wonder what's for lunch?") but it can be problematic when they become major vacations ("Wow. Last night when I was talking to Suzy on the phone…and she said….. and then I said….and I couldn't believe it when she said….so I said…") To minimize the potential for taking a lengthy vacation while listening, experts suggest the following techniques:

Do you tend to take "mental vacations" during class lectures? © *Dmitriy Shironosov, 2008. Under license from Shutterstock, Inc.*

- Take notes to keep your focus on the speech.
- Before the speech begins, write down any questions you have about the topic. As the speech progresses, determine whether the speaker has answered them.
- Apply the speaker's comments to your own experience and knowledge. This makes the message more memorable.
- Define the speech's thesis statement and main supporting points. This helps you focus on the critical parts of the speech.
- Decide whether you agree with the speaker's point of view and evaluate the general performance. This keeps you engaged by focusing on the message and the speaker.

8. Provide Feedback

Let speakers know what you think. Even in a large lecture hall, the speaker is aware of the audience and will establish eye-contact with members of the audience. Lean forward in your chair, nod your head, smile, frown. This kind of participation will force you to focus your attention on the speaker and the speech. Providing feedback at the various stages of a speech can be hard work, requiring total involvement and a commitment to fighting distractions.

Evaluating Public Speeches

When you evaluate speeches, you engage in a form of feedback, a process that makes you a speech critic. As you consider the elements included in a speech and note the speech's strengths and weaknesses, you are taking part in a formal process of analysis and appraisal.

This formal process is not limited to the public speaking class. After virtually every speech the United States president gives, including the inaugural speech and the yearly State of the Union speech, politicians, rhetoricians, and media critics provide analyses. Over a decade ago, President Clinton received a grade in a syndicated column written by William Safire, a political columnist and former speechwriter. Safire is the author of numerous books and has distinguished himself as an expert on language.

Safire gave the president's speech good marks in terms of its theme (simple, direct, fitting); use of metaphor ("a season of service," "we force the spring"); hint of policy information; anaphora (communications and commerce are global; investment is mobile; technology is almost magical; and ambition for a better life universal); length (blessedly brief—fourteen minutes); historic resonance (echoes of Jefferson, Wilson, Roosevelt, Kennedy); turn of phrase ("anyone who has ever watched a child's eyes wander into sleep"); and delivery (his strong voice, confidence, demeanor, lack of flubs). The weaknesses he identified were with what he called "cheap shots" (The old "people are working harder for less"); ``fuzzy sacrifice'' ("We must invest more in our own people [i.e., raise taxes] … and at the same time cut our massive debt"); "applause lines" ("There is nothing wrong with America that can't be cured by what is right with America"); and ``lift'' (it never soared). Safire wrote: "I give it a B. Maybe he'll have another chance" (1993).

Outside of the classroom, chances are slim that you would receive a graded critique. Regardless, the point to keep in mind is that criteria are applied each time someone in an audience thinks about a speech, what it means, and what its value may be. As a participant in a public speaking course, you will be expected to criticize constructively your classmate's speeches. It is important that you note the constructive nature of this process.

As you criticize the strengths and weaknesses of speeches, keep in mind that your comments will help your classmates develop as speakers. Your remarks will help to focus their attention on areas that work effectively as well as areas that need improvement. All speakers need this feedback to improve the quality of their performance.

Unfortunately, many students feel reluctant to criticize their classmates' speeches. They may feel they are not experienced enough, they do not like the idea of having people critique *their* speeches, or they are simply unwilling to work at listening. These students do not view criticism

President Clinton delivers his State of the Union address with a thumbs-up.
© *Reuters/Corbis.*

as a skill in the same way they do public speaking. They do not realize that their public speaking success is measured by their ability to listen, speak, and critique.

Criteria for Evaluating Public Speeches

While it is easy to say whether or not we enjoyed a speech or found it engaging, providing constructive criticism involves more work. The same criteria can be applied to a special occasion speech, an informative speech, or a persuasive speech. The following guidelines take the form of ten separate questions that analyze speeches in terms of their components. For our purposes, we examine content and delivery separately. However, these elements are parts of a unified whole that makes up the dynamic process of communication.

1. Was the topic appropriate for the assignment/audience?
2. Were the general and specific purposes clear?
3. Did the speaker make an effort to analyze the audience and adapt the speech to its needs?
4. Did the speaker use effective and relevant material to support the thesis statement?
5. Was the speech effectively organized?
6. Did the speaker use clear, interesting, and accurate language?
7. Did the speaker appear confident and self-controlled?
8. Was the quality of the speaker's voice acceptable?
9. Were the speaker's movement and gestures meaningful?
10. Did the speaker look for and respond to feedback?

Use these ten questions as a guide to evaluate your classmates' speeches. When you begin to offer criticism, try to be as substantive and concrete as possible. Instead of saying, "She was great," or "I certainly did not like his topic," say, "I liked the way she linked her own experiences as a lifeguard to the need for greater water safety," or "His discussion of the way accounting students are trained was irrelevant for an audience of nonaccounting majors."

Because student speakers are likely to feel vulnerable and defensive in the face of their classmates' criticism, it is important to put them at ease by pointing out first what was right with their speech. Then you can offer suggestions for improving their presentation. Instead of saying, "Your views on the link between electromagnetic fields and cancer were completely unsupported," you might say: "Your examples were clear and crisp when you talked about how common electric appliances, including coffee makers, emit potentially dangerous fields." Then you can add, "I don't think you were as clear when you started talking about how these fields can produce changes in body cells. More concrete examples would be helpful." Rather than saying, "Delivery needs work," you could write something more concrete, such as, "You had so much written on your note cards, you didn't look up. Perhaps having less on your note cards would make it easier to look at the class."

To encourage this type of criticism, many instructors ask students to use a speech evaluation form, similar to that shown in figure 4.3. This gives feedback to the speaker on a sliding scale and also gives listeners the opportunity to provide constructive comments. Try to provide as much written commentary as possible, for your explanations help speakers improve.

Public Speaking Evaluation Form

Speaker _____   Date _____

Topic _____

Purpose (general or specific)

_____

Speech Critic _____

5 — excellent   4 — very good   3 — satisfactory   2— fair   1 — unsatisfactory

1. Was the topic appropriate for the assignment?   5   4   3   2   1

2. Was the general and specific purpose of the speech clear?   5   4   3   2   1

3. Did the speaker use strong supporting material to present
    the speech's core idea?   5   4   3   2   1

4. Did the speaker use clear, interesting, and accurate language?   5   4   3   2   1

5. Did the speaker make an effort to analyze the audience and
    adopt the speech to its needs?   5   4   3   2   1

6. Was the speech effectively organized?   5   4   3   2   1

7. Did the speaker appear confident and self-controlled?   5   4   3   2   1

8. Was the quality of the speaker's voice acceptable?   5   4   3   2   1

9. Did the speaker's body language create meaning?   5   4   3   2   1

10. Did the speaker look for and respond to feedback?   5   4   3   2   1

Comments

FIGURE 4.3
Using a public speaking evaluation form like this one can help you give a speaker constructive and valuable criticism.

Summary

Good listening skills are important for two reasons. First, by understanding the listening needs of your audience, you have a better chance of developing and delivering successful speeches. Second, an understanding of the factors affecting listening will enable you to monitor your own listening habits and help you to evaluate the speeches of others. Studies have shown that although we spend a great deal of time listening, most of us are not good listeners.

Listening is a complex activity that involves four separate stages: you sense the information from its source through the physiological process of hearing; you interpret the message by attaching your own meaning to the speaker's words; you evaluate what your hear by judging the worth of the speaker's message and deciding its importance to you; and you respond to the speaker's message through feedback.

You can improve your listening skills by preparing yourself to listen, minimizing listening barriers and leaving distractions behind, by not making snap judgments, listening first for content and second for delivery, becoming an effective note taker, being an active listener, and by providing feedback.

In speech class, you will use your listening skills to evaluate the speeches of your classmates. It is important to learn the art of constructive criticism in order to encourage the speaker.

Questions for Study and Discussion

1. What role do our emotions play in listening, and how are they related to our ability to think about and analyze a message? Can we suspend our feelings while listening to a speaker? Why or why not?

2. Why is preparation important in listening? How would you prepare to listen to:
   a. a speech on a topic about which you have strong, negative feelings?
   b. a political campaign speech delivered by a candidate you support?
   c. a speech on a crisis that affects your life?
   d. a lecture on a topic that interests but does not excite you?

3. From a listener's point of view, what is the relationship between the content and delivery of a speech? How does a dynamic delivery influence your opinion of the speaker's message? Compare this to your reaction to a flat, uninspired delivery.

4. Discuss the art of criticism as it pertains to public speaking. Why do so many people define criticism only in negative terms? Think of several well-known public speakers and evaluate the content and delivery of their messages.

Activities

1. Attend a lecture, political event, or religious service with the intent of monitoring your own listening behavior. What barriers to listening do you notice as you attempt to follow the speaker's message?

2. Listen to a controversial speech in person or on a video cassette. Then, with the stages of listening in mind, jot down your thoughts and feelings at different times in the speech.

3. Write a brief paper (one to three pages) about a successful listening experience. Be certain to explain what made the experience successful for you.

References

Adlet, M. J. 1983. *How to speak, how to listen*. New York: Macmillan.

Berlo, D. K., J.B. Lemert, and R. Mertz. 1969. Dimensions for evaluating the acceptability of message sources, *Public Opinion Quarterly* 33, 563–76.

Ehrlich, H. J., and L .D. Lee. 1969. Dogmatism, learning, and resistance to change: A review and new paradigm, *Psychological Bulletin, 71*, 249–60.

Festinger, L. 1957. *A theory of cognitive dissonance*. CA: Stanford University Press.

Friedman, P. G. 1986. *Listening processes: Attention, understanding, evalaution*, (2nd ed.), 6–15. Washington, DC: National Education Association.

Leavitt, D. 1989. "The Way I Live Now," *The New York Times Magazine*, July 9, 30.

Nichols, R. G. 1961. Do we know how to listen? Practical helps in a modern age, *Speech Teacher*, March, 118–24.

Pudy, M. 1989. Why listen? Speaking creates community. Doesn't it? The role of listening in community formation. *New York State Communication Association: New Dimensions in Communication: Proceedings of the 47th Annual New York State Speech Communication Association, III* (October 13–15) 71–76.

Rankin, P. T. 1926. "The Measurement of the Ability to Understand Spoken Language," unpublished Ph.D. dissertation, University of Michigan. *Dissertation Abstracts* 12 (1952), 847–48.

Safire, W. January 22, 1993. No spot on dean's list for Mr. Clinton, *The Toledo Blade*, 13.

Steil, L. K. 1983. *Listening:Key to your success*. New York: Random House.

Wolf, F. L., N. C. Marsnik, W. S. Taceuy, and R. G. Nichols. 1983. *Perceptive listening*. New York: Holt, Rinehart and Winston.

Preparing and Presenting Your Speech

© JupierImages Corporation.

"Like hungry guests, a sitting audience looks."

George Farquhar

The Speaker and Audience Connection

Listeners want to know what they can learn from you that will somehow enhance their lives. © *Corbis*.

"Hey professor, why don't you use some examples about cars?" This question was shouted from the back of the room during a workshop for supervisers at a large General Motors manufacturing plant. With frustration in his voice, the young critic was indicating that the speaker should link his ideas to the cultural context of his audience in order to connect with them; in this case, the automobile industry. Fortunately, the speaker had been raised in a family centered in the automobile industry. He himself had worked summers in a plant that produced parts for cars and trucks. The speaker was able to draw from his experiences and could share a considerable number of illustrations with his audience.

Whether in a large auditorium, a corporate boardroom, or a classroom, audiences are usually self-centered. Listeners want to know what they can learn from your speech or how they can take action that will, in some way, enhance their lives. If you solve listeners' problems, show that you understand what their needs are, and help them to achieve their goals, they will listen.

How do you prepare and deliver a speech that will mean enough to your audience to capture their attention and convince them to listen? Begin by learning as much as you can about your listeners so you can identify and focus on their concerns.

Who Are My Listeners?

Peggy Noonan is well known for crafting the speeches of presidents and presidential candidates. When George H. W. Bush was about to accept the nomination of the Republican National Party, Noonan wrote the speech he delivered, and when he accepted the Republican nomination for president in 1988, she drafted that speech as well. As a top writer for Ronald Reagan, Noonan prepared the speech the president delivered after the 1986 *Challenger* disaster, in which American astronauts were tragically lost after a dramatic launch toward outer space. She also prepared the speech President Reagan delivered on the fortieth anniversary of D-Day. Noonan's writing was effective because she made sure her speeches and the men who delivered them were deliberately connected to the audiences she envisioned. She explains:

President Ronald Reagan speaks about the explosion of the space shuttle Challenger. © *Corbis*.

I strived to make each [speech] special. I thought about the audience. I would think how happy they were to be near the president and how each deserved something special, something personal... . I did not endear myself to the researchers when I asked them to go back again and again to find out who the leader of such and such an organization was and what his nickname was and has he ever met the President. And in the town where he's speaking, what are the people talking about, is there a local problem like a garbage scow nobody wants, does the local school have a winning team, what's the big local department store and are they hiring? Anything to make it seem as if someone had thought about this speech and these people (1989).

Finding out about the audience enabled Peggy Noonan to write speeches that were especially meaningful. You need not be a presidential speechwriter to understand your audiences in this way. All speakers can create a profile of their listeners by analyzing them in terms of key demographic and psychological characteristics: age, sex, level of knowledge, group membership, and shared values and lifestyles. The information that emerges from this analysis is the raw material for a successful speaker-audience connection. (Woodwad and Denton 2004)

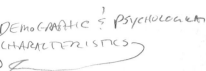

DEMOGRAPHIC & PSYCHOLOGICAL CHARACTERISTICS

Avoid the Age Gap

Is your audience filled with senior citizens or high school students, middle-aged executives or newly hired corporate recruits? By finding out the average age of your listeners, you can avoid being patronizing and condescending.

Avoid assumptions about the average age of your audience. If you are speaking to a group of students, do not assume they will all be in your age bracket. Today, millions of nontraditional students are enrolled in four-year colleges. On any campus, you will meet forty-year-old sophomores seeking a new career or returning to school after their children are grown and sixty-year-old freshmen returning because they love learning.

Focus on your speech, not your age. Business consultant Edith Weiner started to deliver speeches to senior-level executives at the age of twenty-three. "I was much younger than people thought I was going to be," said Weiner. "When I got up to speak, they didn't know what to make of me." Weiner's response was to focus on her message. "If I did well in the first three minutes, not only did I surprise the audience, I created fans. Expectations were so low that when I came across as confident and funny and comfortable, the audience was hooked into the rest of my speech" (1989).

Avoid dating yourself with references or language. If you are addressing a group of teenagers on the topic of popular culture, talk about their current favorite rock group, not the New Kids on the Block. If you are addressing a group of middle-aged executives, do not assume that they know what college students are thinking.

Jettison the Gender Stereotypes

Today, a speaker must be inclusive to avoid unfairly categorizing or stereotyping members of the audience. Airlines no longer have "stewardesses," for example, but instead, use "flight attendants." "Car salesmen" have been replaced by "sales associates." Departments on college and university campuses are no longer headed by a "chairman" but rather by a "chair" or a "chairperson." For the most part, speakers should also avoid relying on the masculine pronoun and find ways to include men *and* women in their audiences.

Gender role differences do exist, however, and generalizations based on these differences are not necessarily wrong. Therefore, if you are addressing a group of young men who you know are likely to enjoy professional sports, it is fair to use a sports analogy to make your point—not because you are a fan but because talking about the Cleveland Browns or the Dallas Cowboys will help you connect with your listeners.

Determine How Much Your Audience Knows

Are the members of your audience high school or college graduates, experts with doctorates in the field, or freshmen taking their first course? Use this information to gear the level of your remarks to listeners' knowledge.

Do not assume that expertise in one area necessarily means expertise in others. For example, if you are a stockbroker delivering a speech to a group of scientists about investment opportunities, you may have to define the rules that govern even simple stock trades. Although the more educated your audience, the more sophisticated these explanations can be, explanations must be included for your speech to make sense.

Be careful about assuming what your audience knows—and does not know—about technical topics. Mention a server to people who know nothing about computers and they may be baffled. Define it for a group of computer experts and they will wonder why you were asked to speak to them. In both cases, you run the risk of losing your audience; people who are confused or who know much more about a subject may simply stop listening.

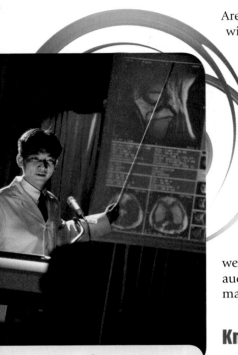

To avoid losing your audience's attention, be aware of their level of knowledge regarding your topic.
© *Corbis.*

Know the Group

Are the members of your audience members of labor organizations or service clubs? Are they volunteers for a local or national organization? Are they politically liberal or conservative? Are they members of the Young Republicans Association? Are they active members of the Chinese Student and Scholar's Association on your campus? If the answer is yes to any of these questions, then the listeners belong to organized groups or party affiliations that may very well affect choices they make.

Listeners may identify themselves as members of formal and informal interest groups. An informal interest group may include YouTube watchers, Starbucks customers, and residents of an inner city neighborhood. A formal interest group may be those persons who belong to and are active with the Future Farmers of America or members of a LISTSERV on alternative treatments for Alzheimer's.

If you are addressing members of the Sierra Club, you can be sure the group has a keen awareness of environmental issues. Similarly, if you are addressing an exercise class at the local Y, you can be sure that physical fitness is a priority of everyone in the room. It is important to know something about the group you are speaking before so you can adapt your message to their knowledge level or interests.

Some people identify themselves by their occupational group. It is important to know the types of jobs your listeners hold. The speaking occasion often makes this clear. You may be invited by a group of home builders to speak about the dangers of radon, or a group of insurance agents may ask you to talk about the weather conditions associated with hurricanes.

Occupational information can often tell you a great deal about listeners' attitudes. An audience of physicians may be unwilling to accept proposed legislation that would strengthen a patient's right to choose a personal physician if it also makes it easier for patients to sue for malpractice. A legislative speaker might need to find creative ways to convince the doctors that the new law would be in the best interests of both doctors and patients.

Knowledge of what your listeners do for a living may also tell you the type of vocabulary appropriate for the occasion. If you are addressing a group of newspaper editors, you can use terms common to the newspaper business without bothering to define them. Do not use job-related words indiscriminately, but rather, use them to your advantage.

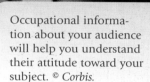

Occupational information about your audience will help you understand their attitude toward your subject. © *Corbis*.

Groups are often defined by socio-economic status. Do your listeners earn more than $100,000 a year or less than $30,000? The answer to this question may influence the nature of your speech and help you create common ground with your audience. When Rabbi Harold S. Kushner talks to groups about his book, *When All You've Ever Wanted Isn't Enough,* he learns the group's socioeconomic status in advance. He explains:

> Generally, if I'm addressing affluent business executives, I concentrate on the downside of economic success and on the spiritual nature of affluence. When the group is less affluent, I talk about learning to cope with economic failure and with the feeling of being left behind.

Religious background of the group may be a consideration. According to the article, "Where we Stand on Faith," many people in the United States consider themselves spiritual and religious (*Newsweek*, September 6, 2005, 48–49). Suppose your topic is in vitro fertilization, one of medicine's generally effective techniques to help infertile couples have children. Your presentation goes well, but the faces of your listeners suggest you hit a nerve. Without realizing it, you may have offended your audience by failing to deal with the religious implications of this procedure. Speakers rarely intend to offend their audiences, especially about religion. But when speakers fail to realize that religious beliefs may also define moral attitudes about issues like abortion, premarital sex, homosexuality, and birth control, they risk alienating their audience. Failing to acknowledge and address the religious beliefs of your listeners when your speech concerns a sensitive topic sets up barriers to communication that may be difficult to surmount.

Groups may identify themselves in terms of race and ethnicity. Long ago, the image of the United States as a melting pot gave way to the image of a rainbow of diversity—an image in which African Americans, Hispanics, Asians, Greeks, Arabs, and Europeans define themselves by their racial and ethnic ties as well as by their ties to the United States. Within this diversity are cultural beliefs and traditions that may be different from your own.

Even now, more than four decades after the most sweeping civil rights legislation in American history was passed by Congress and signed into law by the President, racial issues and differences spawn controversy. In 2005, Hurricane Katrina devastated much of the southeastern shoreline of America. Charges were made by a variety of leaders, essentially declaring that if the majority of the population of New Orleans had been white, there would have been much greater and quicker efforts to move citizens to safe places with ample food and water. If you deliver a speech on the topic of communication failures and the devastation of Hurricane Katrina, you need take into account the considerable problems faced by black citizens in New Orleans and along the southeastern shoreline. If you do not, you are likely to fail in achieving your specific purpose for your speech and you will make your presentation unacceptable to some of your listeners. This is not to suggest that you change your views if they are carefully conceived and supported. However, if your topic includes racial and ethnic issues that you fail to acknowledge during your speech, you can expect members of your audience to be offended.

A speech about the devastation of Hurricane Katrina would require explanation of racial and ethnic issues. © *Michael Ainsworth/ Dallas Morning News/Corbis.*

Political affiliation of the group may be relevant. If you are fundraising for the homeless, you will probably give a different speech to a group with liberal beliefs than to a group of conservatives. Following are some variations.

To a group of political liberals:

We are a nation of plenty—a nation in which begging seems as out of place as snow in July. Yet our cities are filled with poor citizens who have no food or lodging. They are the have-nots in a nation of haves. I ask for your help tonight because we are a nation built on helping one another escape from poverty. No matter how hard you work to cement your own success, you will never achieve the American Dream if one person is left on the streets without a home.

To a group of political conservatives:

> It is in your best interest to give money to homeless causes. I'm not talking about handouts on the street but money that goes into putting a roof over people's heads and into job training. In the long run, giving people dignity by giving them a home and training them for productive work will mean fewer people on welfare and lower taxes. Is it a leap of faith to see this connection or just plain common business sense?

Acknowledging political differences has been important in America since its founding. You will not compromise your values when you accept the fact that political differences exist. Rather, you will take the first step in using these differences as the starting point for communication.

Recognize the Importance of Lifestyle Choices and Values

Your lifestyle choices say a lot about you. If you choose to be a city dweller, living in a studio apartment twenty-two stories up, you probably have less inclination to experience nature than if you opt to live on a fifty-acre farm in Vermont. If you put in twelve-hour days at the office, your career is probably more important to you than if you choose to work only part-time. Lifestyle choices are linked to the attitudes, beliefs, and values of your listeners.

Attitudes are predispositions to act in a particular way that influence our response to objects, events, and situations. Attitudes tend to be long-lasting, but can change under pressure. They are often, but not always, related to behavior.

Beliefs represent a mental and emotional acceptance of information. *They are judgments about the truth or the probability that a statement is correct.* Beliefs are formed from experience and learning; they are based on what we perceive to be accurate. To be an effective speaker, you must analyze the beliefs of your audience in the context of your message. For example, if you are dealing with people who believe that working hard is the only way to get ahead, you will have trouble convincing them to take time off between semesters. Your best hope is to persuade them that time off will make them more productive and goal-directed when they return. By citing authorities and providing examples of other students who have successfully followed this course, you have a chance of changing their mind-set.

Having an understanding of your listeners' attitudes, beliefs, and values will help you express your message effectively. © *Corbis.*

Values are deep-seated abstract judgments about what is important to us. Values separate the worthwhile from the worthless and determine what we consider moral, desirable, important, beautiful, and worth living or dying for. Free enterprise, free speech, hard work, and being part of a stable family are a few of the most important American values.

An audience of concerned students that values the importance of education might express this value in the belief that "a college education should be available to all qualified students" and with the attitude that "the state legislature should pass a tuition-reduction plan for every state college." If you address this audience, you can use this attitude as the basis for your plea that students picket the state capitol in support of the tuition-reduction plan. Understanding your listeners' attitudes, beliefs, and values will help you put your message in the most effective terms.

Determine Why Your Audience *IS* an Audience

Although an analysis of demographic characteristics, the first stage of audience analysis, will give you some clue as to how your listeners are likely to respond to your speech, it will not tell you anything about the speaking occasion, why people have come together as an audience, how they feel about your topic, or about you as a speaker. This information emerges from the second stage of audience analysis, which centers on the speaking situation.

Audiences are made of individuals drawn together in ways that create unity and a shared identity. This identity may be centered in roles, interests, group membership, ethnicity, or a combination of factors. For example, at the political conventions are held every four years. The audience comes together because of a shared commitment to a political perspective. Those in attendance represent their state, and they gather to vote for the presidential candidate they feel will best represent their interests and will conduct the most successful campaign against the other political party. They come into the convention with a shared political identity (Democrat or Republican), and the outcome of the convention is to create support (unity) for one candidate.

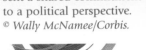

Political conventions represent a shared commitment to a political perspective.
© *Wally McNamee/Corbis.*

Are They Interested?

Interest level often determines audience response. High school seniors are more likely than high school freshmen to listen to someone from the financial aid office at the local college discuss scholarship, grant, and financial aid possibilities. People who fly frequently are less likely to pay attention to the flight attendant's description of safety procedures than individuals who have seldom flown. We tend to pay attention to things that are timely and that we know will affect us.

Many topics do not guarantee the same degree of audience interest, especially if they have been used by other speakers. Jenny Clanton, a student at Southeastern Illinois College, skirted this pitfall when she chose to speak on the *Challenger* disaster. She involved her audience through an unconventional approach (1989):

On January 28, 1986, the American space program suffered the worst disaster in its more than thirty-year history. The entire world was shocked when the space shuttle *Challenger* exploded seconds after lift-off, claiming the lives of seven brave astronauts and crippling our ... space agenda. I suppose the oldest cliche in our culture, spoken on battlegrounds and indeed virtually anywhere Americans die, is, "We must press forward so we can say they did not die in vain." Rest assured: They didn't. The deaths of our seven astronauts probably saved the lives of untold thousands of Americans.

For, you see, if the O-rings had not failed on January 28, 1986, but rather on May 20, 1987, the next scheduled shuttle launch, in the words of Dr. John Gofman, Professor Emeritus at the University of California at Berkeley, you could have "kissed Florida good-bye." Because the next shuttle, the one that was to have explored the atmosphere of Jupiter, was to carry forty-seven pounds of Plutonium 238, which is, according to Dr. Gofman, the most toxic substance on the face of the earth (24–25).

What Are They Thinking? — *QUESTIONAIRES OBSERVAFTIONS*

Experienced and successful professionals who frequently speak to audiences around the country collect information that will tell them who their listeners are and what they want and expect from their presentations. For example, Stew Leonard Jr. has delivered hundreds of speeches to corporate audiences about what makes his family's unusual supermarket (with petting zoo, entertainment, and employees in costume) in Norwalk, Connecticut a success. Leonard says he focuses on what the audience needs: "If I don't give them what they need, I am not doing my job. That's why I spend so much time learning about an audience before I speak. I start by sending out a questionnaire that asks the goals and objectives of the meetings and the challenges facing the company. I also like to learn as much as I can about the audience—the age of the people attending, how many males, how many females, their educational backgrounds, and so on." (1989)

Robert Waterman Jr., coauthor of the very successful book *In Search of Excellence*, indicates he spends a day or two before a speech observing his corporate audience at work. What he learns helps him address the specific concerns of his listeners (Kiechel 1987). Both Waterman and Leonard have achieved success as professional speakers, and both assume very little about the characteristics of their prospective audiences. Often, to analyze their audiences, they use questionnaires and observation—techniques that can be used successfully in the classroom.

Using a Questionnaire

Public opinion polls are an American tradition, especially around election time. Pollsters Gallup, Harris, and Zogby ask Americans for their views on the candidates and issues. And when elections are over, pollsters try to find out

what Americans think about such varied topics as U.S. foreign policy, church attendance, illegal drugs, and ice cream preferences. Their tool in these investigations is the questionnaire. Questionnaires also are used by market research companies to learn how the public might respond to a product and, every ten years, by the Census Bureau.

For audience analysis, a questionnaire can determine the specific demographic characteristics of your listeners as well as their perceptions of you and your topic. It can also tell you how much knowledge your listeners have about your topic and the focus they would prefer in your speech.

By surveying all your classmates, by sampling every fourth person in your dorm, or by calling selected members of your audience and asking them questions, you can find out information about your audience in advance. These methods are simple and effective. In addition—and depending upon the age of your intended audience—online survey creation and response tabulation companies like SurveyMonkey.com now make it easier to poll a group of people via the Internet.

The first step in using a questionnaire is designing specific questions that are likely to get you the information you need. Three basic types of questions are most helpful to public speakers: fixed-alternative questions, scale questions, and open-ended questions (Churchill 1983).

If you send a questionnaire to audience members, you can determine their demographics and perceptions to help you focus your message. © *Stephen Coburn, 2008. Under license from Shutterstock, Inc.*

Questions w/ fixed choices.

Fixed-alternative questions. Fixed-alternative questions limit responses to several choices, yielding valuable information about such demographic factors as age, education, and income. Fixed-alternative questions can offer many different responses, or they can offer only two alternatives (yes/no questions fit into this category). These questions can help you analyze the attitudes and knowledge of your prospective listeners. Here is an example of a fixed-alternative question focusing on attitudes:

> *Do you think all professional athletes should be carefully tested for drugs and steroids? (Choose one)*

> Professionals should be carefully tested for drugs and steroids.

> Professional athletes should be tested for the use of drugs and steroids in selected sports.

> Professional athletes should never be required to test for drugs and steroids.

> No opinion.

This type of question is easy to tabulate and analyze and, from the point of view of your audience, easy to answer. In addition, you can be fairly sure that if you asked the same question a second time, you would get the same answer (assuming, of course, that attitudes had not changed). These questions also give you standardized responses. That is, for everyone answering the question, the frame of reference is the same. If you ask people, "How many times a week do you eat out?" and do not supply possible responses, you may receive answers like "regularly," "rarely," "every day," and "twice a day." Answers like these are more difficult to interpret than answers guided by a fixed set of alternatives.

Fixed alternative questions help avoid confusion. Ask people to describe their marital status and they may reply "unhappy." If you want to know whether they are single, married, widowed, or divorced, ask them the question and provide choices.

> *What is your marital status?*
>
> Single
>
> Widowed
>
> Married
>
> Divorced

However, using fixed-alternative questions does have disadvantages. It may force people to respond to a question when they have no opinion or strong feelings, especially if you fail to include "no opinion" as a possible response.

Scale questions. Scale questions are a type of fixed-alternative question that ask people to respond to questions set up along a continuum. For example:

> *How often do you vote?*
>
> Always   Sometimes   Occasionally   Never

Although these responses could have been asked in the form of an ordinary fixed-alternative question, this format, placed at the top of a page, allows you to list different variables along the left margin. For example, you can ask people to use the scale to tell you how frequently they vote in presidential elections, congressional elections, state elections, and local elections.

Open-ended questions. In an open-ended question, audience members can respond however they wish. For example:

> *How do you feel about a twelve-month school year?*
>
> *Why do you think the Japanese sell so many cars in the United States?*

A variety of answers is possible for these questions. In response to your question about extending the school year, one respondent may write, "Keep the school year as it is," while another may suggest a workable plan for extending the year. Because the responses to open-ended questions are so different, they can be difficult to analyze. The advantage to these questions is that they allow you to probe for details; you give respondents the opportunity to tell you what is on their minds. Following are a few guidelines for constructing usable questions.

Avoid leading questions. Try not to lead people to the response you desire through the wording of your question. Here are two examples of leading questions:

> *Do you feel stricter handgun legislation would stop the wanton killing of innocent people?*

*Do you believe able-bodied men who are too lazy to work should be
eligible for welfare?*

These questions should be reworded. For example, "Do you support
stricter handgun legislation?" is no longer a leading question.

Avoid ambiguity. When you use words that can be interpreted in different
ways, you reduce the value of a question. For example:

How often do you drink alcohol?

Frequently

Occasionally

Sometimes

Never

In this case one person's "sometimes" may be another person's "occasionally." To avoid ambiguity, rephrase the possible responses:

How often do you drink alcohol?

More than once a week

At least once a month

Not more than once every six months

Never

Ask everyone the same questions. Because variations in the wording of
questions can change responses, always ask questions in the same way. Do not
ask one person, "Under what circumstances would you consider enlisting in
the army?" and another, "If the United State were attacked by a foreign nation,
would you consider joining the army?" Both of these questions relate to enlisting in the military, but the first one is an open question while the second is a
closed question. The answers you receive to the first question have much more
information value than the second, which could be answered "yes" or "no." If
you do not ask people the same questions, your results may be inaccurate.

Be aware of time constraints. Although the results can help you determine interest, attitudes, and knowledge level, you do not want it to take too
much time or be too complex. If your instructor allows you to pass out a
questionnaire in class, make sure it takes only a few minutes to complete. You
do not want to take too much time. Ask only what is necessary. Make sure the
format fits your purpose.

Observe and Interview

You may find that the best way to gather information about a prospective
audience is to assume the role of an observer. If you are to deliver a speech on
weight control to a former smokers' support group, attend a meeting to determine how many members believe they are overweight and how much weight
they have to lose. Then ask several people whether their weight problem is the
result of their efforts to stop smoking or if they were overweight at other times
in their lives. Similarly, if you are delivering a speech to corporate executives

on ways to improve their written communication, ask for samples of letters, memos, and reports they have written in order to be personally familiar with their writing skills and styles.

The interviews you conduct during this process are likely to be less formal than the style of interview you use to gather information about your speech topic. When questions occur as you watch a group in action, ask people their thoughts and feelings. Their responses will help you analyze audience need.

Create the Link Between Speaker and Audience

Unless they determine you have something relevant to say, it takes your listeners only seconds to tune out your message. You convince an audience your message has value by centering your message on your listeners and not locking into a prepared script. The following suggestions will help you build the type of audience connection that defines the reciprocal nature of public speaking.

Get to the Point Quickly

First impressions count. What you say in the first few minutes is critical. Tell your listeners how you can help them first, not last. If you save your suggestions to the end, it may be that no one is listening. Experienced speakers try to make connections with their listeners as they open their speeches. And, more importantly, they try to convey to their listeners the idea that the speech will be important to them.

Center your message on your listeners rather than concentrating on a prepared script. © *Corbis*.

Have Confidence: They Want to Hear Your Speech

It happens all the time. Speakers with relatively little knowledge about a subject are asked to speak to a group of experts on the subject. An educator may talk to a group of athletes about intercollegiate sports. A lawyer may talk to a group of doctors about the doctor-patient relationship. A politician may talk to a group of drug counselors about the problem of crack cocaine. When you feel your listeners know more than you do about your topic, realize they have invited you for a reason. In most cases, they want your opinions. Despite their knowledge, you have a perspective they find interesting. Athletes may want to learn how the college sports program is viewed by a professor; doctors want to hear a lawyer's opinion about malpractice; and drug counselors want to know what a politician will do, if elected, to relieve the drug problem.

Be of the People, Not Above the People

No one wants to listen to speakers who consider themselves more accomplished, smarter, or more sophisticated than their audience. If you convey even a hint of superiority, your listeners will tune you out. As a speaker, you will learn that modesty inspires confidence. James D. Griffin endeared himself to his audience with his self-effacing modesty during a commencement speech at Moorpark College in California:

When I received the call several months ago that Moorpark College would like to have me as this year's commencement speaker, I was told that the school likes to choose a past graduate for this address, one who has gone on after graduation to achieve, perhaps, something great.

I was also told at that time that I was in fact a world-famous professor of Medieval Literature at the University of California, Berkeley. That I was chosen for this address, as I said before, struck me as a very great honor. That I was a professor, however, struck me only as a very great surprise. I had studied at Berkeley; was admitted to the Ph.D. program in classical and medieval languages; I even taught for a while, as a graduate student. But the sad truth is I am not now and never was a professor of anything, let alone world famous. From across the miles, it would seem, rumor had made me greater and more successful that I actually was.

No problem! There was an alternate story floating around. According to this view, I had become a multi-millionaire and now gave generously to various charitable organizations. Ladies and gentlemen, I am indeed very sorry to report that this rumor is also false. In fact, only two things are definitely true. The first is that I did graduate in 1976 from this very school. The second is that I moved away (1989, 735).

Later in his speech Griffin talked honestly about his accomplishments, but his earlier self-effacing remarks made it clear that he was not bragging. He mentioned his own success only in the context of the success of others.

Humor can help you make this connection with your audience. Opening your speech with something that makes people smile or laugh can put both you and your listeners at ease. Humor encourages people to think of you as approachable rather than remote. Effective humor should be related in some way to the subject of your speech, your audience, or the occasion.

Connect with Your Listeners — You & we

Before management consultant Edith Weiner gives a speech, she learns the names of several members of her audience as well as their roles in the company. During her speech, she refers to these people and the conversations she had with them, thereby creating a personal bond with her audience. Connections can be made by linking yourself directly to the group you are addressing and by referring to your audience with the pronoun "you" rather than the third-person "they." The word "you" inserts your listeners into the middle of your presentation and makes it clear that you are focusing attention on them. Here is an example in a speech delivered by Jeffrey R. Holland, as president of Brigham Young University, to a group of early childhood educators:

You are offering more than technical expertise or professional advice when you meet with parents. You are demonstrating that you are an ally in their task of rearing the next generation. In all that you do … however good your work, and whatever the quality of life parents provide, there is no comparable substitute for families. Your best opportunity to act in children's best interests is to strengthen parents, rather than think you can or will replace them (1988, 559).

Make It a Participatory Event

When a speaker invites the listeners to participate in her or his speech, they become partners in an event. One of the author's friends, a first-degree black belt in karate, gave a motivational speech to a group of college women at a state university in Michigan. At the beginning of her speech, and to the excitement of the crowd, she broke several boards successfully. She talked about her childhood, her lack of self-esteem, and her struggle to become a well-adjusted business woman. She used the phrase, "I can succeed" several times during her speech, and encouraged her audience to join in with her. By the end of her speech, the group, standing, invigorated and excited, shouted with her, "I can succeed!"

Another way to involve your listeners is to choose a member of your audience to take part in your talk—have the volunteer help you with a demonstration, do some role playing—and the rest of the group will feel like one of its own is up there at the podium. Involve the entire audience and they will hang on your every word.

Examine Other Situational Characteristics

When planning your speech, other situational characteristics need to be considered, including time of day, size of audience, and size of room. When speechwriter Robert B. Rackleff (1987) addressed his colleagues about the "art of speech writing," he offered this advice:

> The time of day affects the speech. In the morning, people are relatively fresh and can listen attentively. You can explain things more carefully. But in the late afternoon, after lunch …, the audience needs something more stimulating. And after dinner, you had better keep it short and have some fireworks handy (311–12).

Rackleff was reminding his listeners about the intimate connection between time of day and audience response. The relationship between physical surroundings and audience response is so strong that you should plan every speech with your surroundings in mind.

Plan every speech with your surroundings in mind. © *Corbis.*

Management consultant Edith Weiner says there is a vast difference between an audience of six people and an audience of dozens or even hundreds of people: In the first case, says Weiner, "I'm speaking with the

Practice proper microphone technique, preferably in the actual setting.
© *Corbis*.

audience," but in the second, "I'm speaking to the audience." The intimacy of a small group allows for a speaker-audience interchange not possible in larger groups. Small groups provide almost instantaneous feedback; large groups are more difficult to read.

Room size is important because it influences how loudly you must speak and determines whether you need a microphone. As a student, you will probably be speaking in a classroom. But in other speaking situations, you may find yourself in a convention hall, a small office, or an outdoor setting where only the lineup of chairs determines the size of the speaking space.

If you are delivering an after-dinner speech in your own dining room to ten members of your Great Books club, you do not have to worry about projecting your voice to the back row of a large room. If, on the other hand, you are delivering a commencement address in your college auditorium to a thousand graduates, you will need to use a microphone. And keep in mind, proper microphone technique takes practice, preferably in the auditorium in which you will speak.

Post-speech Analysis

As you know from your classroom experience, hearing what your audience thought of your speech can help you give a better speech the next time around. Realizing the importance of feedback, some professional speakers hand out post-speech questionnaires, designed to find out where they succeeded and where they failed to meet audience needs. At workshops, a feedback sheet is often provided that can be turned in at the end of the specific workshop or at any time during the day. As the speaker, you may choose to distribute questionnaires randomly to a dozen people or you may ask the entire audience to provide feedback. Valuable information often emerges from these responses, which enables speakers to adjust their presentation for the next occasion. Hypothetically, let us assume you delivered a speech to a civic organization on the increasing problem of drunk boating. You handed out questionnaires to the entire audience. From this procedure, you learn that your audience would have preferred a speech with fewer statistics and more concrete advice on combatting the problem. In addition, one listener suggested a good way to make current laws more effective, a suggestion you may incorporate into your next presentation.

Finding out what your audience thought may be simple. In your public speaking class, your fellow classmates may give you immediate, written feedback. In other situations, especially if you are running a workshop or seminar, you may want to hand out a written questionnaire at the end of your speech and ask listeners to return it at a later time. (A self-addressed stamped envelope will encourage a large response.) Here are some questions you can ask:

1. Did the speech answer your questions about the topic? If not, what questions remain?
2. How can you apply the information you learned in the presentation to your own situation?

3. What part of the presentation was most helpful? Least helpful?
4. How could the presentation have better met your needs?

To encourage an honest and complete response, indicate that people do not have to sign their names to the questionnaire.

Summary

The most important relationship in public speaking is the relationship between speaker and audience. Learn everything you can about your audience, so you can meet its needs in your topic and your approach. Start by developing a profile of your listeners based on demographic and psychological evaluations. Learn the average age of your listeners, whether they are predominantly male or female, their educational level, and how much they know about your subject. Try to identify members of your audience in terms of their membership in religious, racial and ethnic, occupational, socioeconomic, and political groups. Lifestyle choices can tell you a great deal about audience attitudes, beliefs, and values.

Successful speakers define the expectations that surround the speaking occasion. They learn how much interest their audience has in their topic and how much their audience knows about it before they get up to speak. Audience analysis is accomplished through the use of questionnaires based on fixed-alternative questions, scale questions, and open-ended questions. Audience analysis can also be conducted through observation and interviews.

To ensure a speaker-audience connection, show your listeners at the start of your speech how you will help them; have confidence your audience wants to hear you, even if they are more knowledgeable than you are. Present yourself as fitting into the group, rather than as being superior to the group. Refer to people in your audience and involve your listeners in your speech. When your speech is over, try to determine your audience's response through a post-speech evaluation-questionnaire.

Questions for Study and Discussion

1. Why will a speech fail in the absence of audience analysis?
2. Can speakers be ethical and adapt to their audiences at the same time?
3. Does adaptation imply audience manipulation or meeting the audience's needs?
4. What underlying principles should you use to conduct an effective audience analysis?
5. From what you have learned in the chapter about listening, what steps can you take to ensure a positive speaker-audience connection?

Activities

1. Focusing on the specific purpose of your next speech, analyze the students in your public speaking class who will be your audience. Conduct several in-depth interviews with your classmates. Circulate a questionnaire. Based on the information you gather, develop an audience profile. Write a three- to four-page paper describing the attitudes, values, interests, and knowledge of your listeners as they relate to your topic and you. Finally, outline a strategy of audience adaptation that will serve your interests and the interests of your listeners.

2. Before delivering another speech, give every member of your class, including your instructor, an index card on which a seven-point scale is drawn, with 1 being the most negative point on the scale and 7 being the most positive. Ask your classmates to register the degree to which your speech was relevant to them. If most of the responses fall below the scale midpoint, analyze how you could have prepared a more successful speech.

3. Select a recent speech you have attended or a famous speech about which you have read that exemplifies a successful audience adaptation. In a written paper, analyze the factors that contributed to the audience's positive response and present findings to your class. Conduct the same analysis for a speech that failed to meet the audience's needs.

References

Churchill Jr., G. A. 1983. *Marketing research: Methodological foundations*, 3rd ed., (168–231). Chicago, IL: the Dryden Press.

Clanton, J. 1988. "Title unknown," *Winning orations of the interstate oratorical association*. Mankato, MN: Interstate Oratorical Association.

Griffin, J. D. "To Snare the Feet of Greatness: The American Dream Is Alive," speech delivered at Moorpark College, Moorpark, California, July 16, 1989. Reprinted in *Vital Speeches of the Day*. September 15, 1989, 735–36.

Holland, J. "Whose Children Are These? The Family Connection," speech delivered at the 1988 Conference for the Association of Childhood Education International, April 23, 1988. Reprinted in *Vital Speeches of the Day*, July 1, 1988, 559.

Kiechel III, W. "How to give a speech," *Fortune*, June 8, 1987, 179.

Kushner, H. S. October 13, 1989.

Leonard, S. October 3, 1989.

Noonan, P. October 15, 1989. "Confessions of a White House Speechwriter," *New York Times*, 72.

Rackleff, R. B. "The art of speechwriting: A dramatic event," delivered to the national Association of Bar Executives Section on Communications and Public Relations, September 26, 1987. Reprinted in *Vital Speeches of the Day*, March 1, 1988.

Weiner, E. October 10, 1989.

Woodwad, G. C., and R. E. Denton Jr. 2004. *Persuasion and influence in American life,* 5th ed. (173–174). Long Grove, IL: Waveland Press, Inc.

When you need help, consult your librarian.

Research and Supporting Material

Each speaker faces multiple decisions during the speech development process. Sometimes beginning speakers find selecting a topic to be the most difficult aspect of the process. You may feel relief when your instructor approves the topic you have chosen, but your work has just begun. After choosing a topic and developing the general and specific purposes of your speech, it is time for research and to develop appropriate supporting material. Credibility is crucial. To a large extent, your listeners will evaluate your speech on the amount and relevance of research conducted and the types of supporting material used. The extent to which a speaker is perceived as a competent spokesperson is considered **speaker credibility.** A person's background, set of ethics, and delivery are all part of speaker credibility. **Message credibility,** on the other hand, is the extent to which the speech is considered to be factual and well supported through documentation (Fleshler, Ilardo, and Demoretcky 1974). It is this second type of credibility that is the focus of this chapter. Through research, one can find sufficient, relevant, and timely supporting material which will enhance a speaker's message credibility.

We live in an information society that produces far more information than we can use. Books are added to library collections on a regular basis, new information is found quarterly in journals, weekly in magazines, and daily in newspapers. Computers give us access to innumerable websites and ever larger databases. As a result of this galaxy of available information, one of your most important jobs will be to decide what is relevant and what is not, what you should incorporate into your speech and what you should discard. Setting limits on your own research requires that you stay focused on your specific purpose. Do what is required to give an effective presentation; do not allow yourself to be led down an interesting, but unrelated, path.

With all the information available on the computer, it's a big job to decide what material to use and what to discard. © *Laurence Gough, 2008. Under license from Shutterstock, Inc.*

Research is the raw material that forms the foundation of your speech. It gives you the tools you need to expand your specific purpose into a full-length presentation. The raw material may include interviewing experts on your topic and locating print and web-based information. The result of this process is your knowledge of the topic.

Often, research can lead you to deliver a slightly different type of speech than you expected. As facts emerge, you may expand your speech in one place, streamline it in another, and take it apart to accommodate new information. Ultimately, you will piece it together in its final form.

The research process alone is not sufficient. You must determine how to use it most effectively. **Supporting material** is the information used in a particular way to make your case. For example, if you were preparing a speech to inform your class on services available in your community for individuals who are categorized as low income, your *research process* may lead you to an organization that specializes in debt consolidation, another that offers free or low-cost medical care, an agency that gives out food for low-income individuals, and a organization that supplies children with free school supplies. As you develop your speech, one of your points might be that "a variety of services are available in our community." For *supporting material*, these agencies provide *examples* of available services. As the types of supporting material can be quite varied, you must determine what is most suited to the topic and to your listeners.

Develop a Research Strategy

Instructors rarely say, "Go! Prepare an informative speech." Instead, they establish parameters regarding topics, length of speech, minimum number of sources, and types of sources. What is the minimum number of sources required? How many different sources do you need? If you use three different issues of *Newsweek*, do they count as one source or as three? Can you use information from 1980 or 1990, or did your instructor say all material needs to be no more than five years old? Do you need both print and online sources? Does online access to a magazine count as a print source? Can you use all types of print sources? Does your instructor allow you to count an interview as a source? Can you use your family or yourself as a source? Before you begin to research your topic, make sure you know the constraints of the assignment as specified by your instructor.

The outline at the beginning of this chapter identifies aspects of the research strategy. Supporting material will be discussed later in the chapter. Specifically, in developing your research strategy, you need to address the following aspects.

1. Analyze the audience
   (What are the needs, interests, and knowledge level of my audience?)
2. Assess your knowledge/skill
   (What knowledge or skill do I have in relation to this topic?)
3. Search print and online resources
   (Based on available resources, where and what will I find the most useful?)
4. Interview, if appropriate
   (Will this speech be helped by interviewing someone with personal knowledge or expertise about this topic?)

Each of these aspects can be viewed as stages. The following section provides a look at each of these stages in greater detail.

Before you begin your topic research, make sure you know the parameters of the speech assignment. © *Brandon Blinkenberg, 2008. Under license from Shutterstock, Inc.*

1. Start (and End) with an Audience Analysis

Throughout this book we stress the importance of connecting with your audience. Before you determine the general or specific purpose for your speech, consider your audience's needs. As explained in the previous chapter, a careful audience analysis gives you information about who they are and what they value. Understanding your audience helps you develop specific questions that can be answered as you follow your search strategy. For example, suppose you were planning an informative speech explaining prenuptial agreements. You may have some general questions about the topic, such as the following:

When do most people get married?
What are the statistics on the number of marriages and divorces each year?
Who benefits financially and who suffers as a result of a divorce?

What happens to property in divorce?
How expensive is an agreement?
Can people draw up the agreement without legal counsel?

To construct an effective speech that achieves its specific purpose, whether it is informative or persuasive, think about your specific audience. So, if you are working on a speech about prenuptial agreements, consider additional questions such as:

Considering the age of my audience, how much do they know about prenuptial agreements?
What do most people think about prenuptial agreements?
What might be this audience's greatest areas of concern or interest regarding the topic?

Answering the more specific questions related to your audience helps you to determine the depth and breadth of information needed to answer your more general questions. By developing questions based on your understanding of the needs of your audience, you can increase the likelihood of establishing an effective speaker-audience connection. Reflect again on your audience *after* you have gathered information to determine whether or not you have collected enough material and if it is the right type of material to meet your audience's needs and interests.

2. Assess Your Own Knowledge and Skills

Some students find topic selection difficult because they think they have nothing to offer or the class will not be interested. Upon reflection, however, you may find you have unique experiences or you have knowledge that others do not. Perhaps you were an exchange student, so you have had firsthand experience of another culture. Maybe you were raised by parents who spoke a different language, and you know what it is like to be bilingual. Maybe you live with an unusual disease.

Start your research process by assessing your own knowledge and skills. Most likely, you have direct knowledge or experience related to several topics. Your family may own a monument shop or a restaurant, and you grew up exposed to issues related to these professions. Maybe by the time you started college, you held one or more jobs, joined a political club, pursued hobbies like video games, or played sports such as soccer or rugby. You may know more about Jackie Chan movies than anyone on campus, or you may play disk golf. Examining your unique experiences or varied interests is a logical starting point for developing a speech.

Do you have unique knowledge that would make an interesting speech topic? © *Simone van den Berg, 2008. Under license from Shutterstock, Inc.*

Having personal knowledge or experience can make an impact on your audience. A student with Type I diabetes can speak credibly on what it is like to take daily injections and deal with the consequences of both low and high blood sugar. A student who works as a barista at the local coffee shop can

demonstrate how to make a good shot of espresso. CAUTION: Remember the phrase, "Too much knowledge may be dangerous." Sometimes students want to share every detail with the audience, and that information can become tedious or overwhelming.

3. Search Print and Online Resources

Once you have assessed your own knowledge or skills, it is time to search print and online resources for other supporting material. The computer provides a rich playing field that also complicates our lives. We have more choices, but we have to work harder to sift through them.

Your search may result in more questions, including the following: What information is most essential to this topic? What will have the greatest impact? How much background do I need to give? Utilizing a variety of sources is advantageous for a variety of reasons; different sources focus on research, philosophy, or current events. They may be part of a daily publication, or are contained within a one-time publication. Sources target different audiences. We suggest you examine and evaluate materials from various sources to select materials that will help you most.

Avoid wasting valuable time floating aimlessly in cyberspace or walking around the library. Instead, if you need direction, *ask a librarian*. Librarians are experts in finding both print and online information efficiently, and they can show you how to use the library's newest search engines and databases. With new online and print resources being added daily, using the expertise of a librarian can make your job as a researcher much easier.

If you are new to campus, and your instructor has not arranged a library tour for your class, consider taking a workshop on using the library. Your library's home page is helpful. Most college libraries belong to a "live chat" consortium on the web, where students may contact a librarian twenty-four hours a day. Also, you can try the Library of Congress online Ask-a-Librarian Service at www.loc.gov and click on "Ask a librarian."

Librarians are experts in finding information efficiently to help save research time. © *Alan Egginton, 2008. Under license from Shutterstock, Inc.*

Narrow Your Focus

It is natural to start with a broad topic. But as you search, the information you find will help you move to a more focused topic, enabling you to define—and refine—the approach you take to your speech. Say you are interested in giving an informative speech about the use of performance enhancement drugs in sports. You need to narrow your topic, but you are not quite sure what aspects to consider. Choose a search engine, such as Google, Yahoo!, AltaVista, or Excite.

Try conducting a **key-word search** on Google for "drugs in sports." This is very general. The key-word search leads you to a list of records which are weighted in order of amount of user access. You may have more than a million records or "hits" from which to choose. Look for valid subject headings, and search more deeply than the first three or four records listed.

Results of the key-word search lead you to many possibilities, including "anabolic steroids." You find a website that addresses topics such as what they are, how they work, who uses them, how prevalent they are, the different types, drugs banned by the NCAA, and medical uses. Now you have other areas to pursue. Decide what aspects you want to cover that are relevant to the audience and can be discussed effectively within the given time constraints. Perhaps you are interested in who uses them, so you enter "Who uses anabolic steroids?" This leads you to a website on uses and abuses of steroids. You know you need to define what anabolic steroids are and to find out how they are used and abused. You can continue your research by examining both print and online resources for these specific aspects of performance enhancement drugs. Now you can develop a specific purpose statement and search for information to support it.

As you search for information, keep three aspects of research in mind: First, recognize the distinction between primary and secondary sources. **Primary sources** include firsthand accounts such as diaries, journals, and letters, as well as statistics, speeches, and interviews. They are records of events as they are first described. **Secondary sources** generally provide an analysis, an explanation, or a restatement of a primary source. If the U.S. Surgeon General issues a report on the dangers of smoking, the report itself (available from the U.S. Surgeon General's Office) is the primary source; newspaper and magazine articles about the report are secondary source material.

Second, there is a relationship between the length of your speech and the amount of time you must spend in research. Many students learn the hard way that five minutes of research will not suffice for a five-minute speech. Conventional wisdom suggests that for every one minute of speaking time, there is an hour of preparation needed. Whatever the length of the speech, you have to spend time uncovering facts and building a strong foundation of support.

Third, finding information is not enough; you must also be able to evaluate it (relevance, reliability, and so on), and utilize it in the most appropriate way in order to achieve your specific purpose. For example, your audience analysis may suggest that specific statistics are necessary to convince your audience. On the other hand, perhaps personal or expert testimony will be most persuasive. Overall, developing a research strategy is one of the most useful things you will learn in college.

Evaluating and using information appropriately is as important as finding it.
© *Jaimie Duplass, 2008. Under license from Shutterstock, Inc.*

Specific Library Resources

In addition to providing access to computers for online searches, each library houses a variety of research materials, including books, reference materials, newspapers, magazines, journals, and government documents. Microfilm, specifically for archived newspapers may still be available, but the government has stopped producing microfiche. If information is not housed in your library, you can electronically extend your search far beyond your campus or community library through interlibrary loan. It may take two weeks or longer to process requests, so planning is especially important when relying on interlibrary loan.

Each library is different. One may not have the same databases or reference materials as another. Some libraries are depositories for your state, and it may be one of a few that receives state documents automatically.

Books. Historically, libraries have been most noted for their collection of books. Many universities have several libraries so students may access the large volume of books in general collections, archived collections, and specific collections. Using the library catalog is essential. Most libraries today have online computer catalogs, which contain records of all materials the library owns. In addition to identifying what books are available and where to find them, an online catalog will also indicate whether a particular book is checked out and when it is due back. Keep in mind that the library groups books by subject, so as you look in the stacks for a particular book, it makes sense to peruse surrounding books for additional resources.

General reference materials. At the beginning of your search, it may be helpful to start with one or more general reference resources, including encyclopedias, dictionaries, biographical sources, and statistical sources. Most likely, your time spent with these materials will be short, but these resources can provide you with basic facts and definitions.

Unlike some of our experiences in primary school, seldom does a student's research start and end with the encyclopedia. The *World Book Encyclopedia* is helpful if you are unfamiliar with a topic or concept. It can provide facts that are concise as well as easy to read and understand. Encyclopedias are either general or specialized. **General encyclopedias** (e.g., *The Encyclopedia Americana* and *Encyclopedia Britannica*) cover a wide range of topics in a broad manner. In contrast, **specialized encyclopedias,** such as the *Encyclopedia of Religion*, and the *International Encyclopedia of the Social Sciences*, focus on particular areas of knowledge in more detail. Over the last decade, there has been an explosion of discipline-specific encyclopedias. Articles in both general and specialized encyclopedias often contain bibliographies that lead you to additional sources.

Although encyclopedias are helpful as a basic resource, they generally are not accepted as main sources for class speeches. Use them to lead to other information. CAUTION: Do not fall into Wikipedia's web of easy access and understanding. Its legitimacy is questionable. Stephen Colbert, host of the TV show *The Colbert Report*, asked his viewers to log on to the entry "elephants" on Wikipedia.com to report that the elephant population in Africa "has tripled in the last six months." This online encyclopedia noted a spike in inaccurate entries shortly after the show aired. Most instructors discourage use of this online resource.

During your research, you may consult a dictionary when you encounter an unfamiliar word or term. They also provide information on pronunciation, spelling, word division, usage, and etymology (the origins and development of words). As with encyclopedias, dictionaries are classified as either general or specialized. It is likely you have used some general dictionaries such as the *American Heritage Dictionary* or the *Random House College Dictionary*. The

General reference resources may be helpful as you begin your search for material. © *Laurence Gough, 2008. Under license from Shutterstock, Inc.*

dictionary is also just a click away. You might try Merriam-Webster Online (www.m-w.com). Specialized dictionaries cover words associated with a specific subject or discipline, as in the following: *The American Political Dictionary, Black's Law Dictionary, Harvard Dictionary of Scientific and Technical Terms*, and *Webster's Sports Dictionary*. Many disciplines use their own specialized terminology that is more extensive and focused, and those definitions are found in their journals and books. CAUTION: Check with your instructor before beginning your speech with, "According to Webster's dictionary, the word _____ means..." As Harris (2002) notes in his book, *Using Sources Effectively*, "Generally speaking, starting with a dictionary definition not only lacks creativity but it may not be helpful if the definition is too general or vague" (35).

Biographical sources. Biographical sources, which are international, national, or specialized, provide information on an individual's education, accomplishments, and professional activities. This information is useful when evaluating someone's credibility and reliability. A biographical index indicates sources of biographical information in books and journals whereas a biographical dictionary lists and describes the accomplishments of notable people. If you are looking for a brief background of a well-known person, consult the biographical dictionary first. If you need an in-depth profile of a lesser-known person, the biographical index is the better source. Some examples of these sources are Author Biographies Master Index, Biography Index, the New York Times Index, Dictionary of American Biography, European Authors, World Authors, and Dictionary of American Scholars.

Statistical sources. When used correctly, statistics can provide powerful support. Facts and statistics give authority and credibility to research. Many federal agencies produce and distribute information electronically. The *American Statistics Index* (ASI) includes both an index and abstracts of statistical information published by the federal government. Try also the *Index to International Statistics* (IIS) and the *Statistical Abstract of the United States.* The online source LexisNexis touts itself as providing "authoritative legal, news, public records and business information" (www.lexisnexis.com).

Magazines, newspapers, and journals. Magazines (also known as periodicals) and newspapers provide the most recent print information. Once you identify ideas that connect with the needs of your audience, you can look for specific information in magazines and newspapers. General indexes cover such popular magazines and newspapers such as *Time, Newsweek, U.S. News & World Report*, the *New York Times*, and the *Chicago Tribune*. The *Readers' Guide to Periodical Literature* is an index available online as well as in print form. Other popular indexes include: the *New York Times Index, Wall Street Journal, Christian Science Monitor, Los Angeles Times, The Education Index, Humanities Index, Public Affairs Information Service Bulletin, Social Sciences and Humanities Index*, and *Social Sciences Index*.

Newspapers and magazines can be distinguished from journals in many ways. First, the frequency of distribution is different. While newspapers can be accessed daily, and magazines are either weekly or monthly, journals are usually quarterly publications. Second, authors of articles in newspapers and magazines are generally paid by their publisher, whereas authors of journal articles (usually referred to as "researchers" rather than "authors") are generally experts in their particular fields, and have submitted their article(s) on a competitive, reviewed basis. In general, the more prestigious the journal, the more difficult it is to get an article printed in it. Journals may have editorials or book reviews, but they generally focus on qualitative and quantitative research conducted by professionals—doctors, professors, lawyers, and so on. Third, magazines and newspapers are written for general audiences, whereas journal articles are written for a specific audience; an example would be faculty or graduate students interested in communication apprehension. Many journals can be accessed online, but not all are available electronically.

Fourth, and very importantly, journals focus on original, qualitative, and quantitative research. Much of the content in a journal is considered to be a primary source because it reports findings from research conducted by the author.

Government documents. Government documents are prepared by agencies, bureaus, and departments that monitor the affairs and activities of the nation. Documents are issued by the Office of the President, the U.S. Congress, the departments of Commerce, Agriculture, Education, Navy and Army, Indian Affairs, the Veterans' Administration, the Food and Drug Administration, and the FBI.

Through the U.S. Government Printing Office (GPO) one can find unique, authoritative, and timely materials, including detailed census data, vital statistics, congressional papers and reports, presidential documents, military reports, and impact statements on energy, the environment, and pollution. Consult the Monthly Catalog of United States Government Publications, which is available online.

Online Research

As stated earlier, your librarian can lead you to a variety of material. An enormous amount of databases exist, and one can approach web research in many ways. Without help of some kind, looking for information on the web is like upending the library in a football field and being given a pen light to search for information. The librarian can at least provide you with stadium lights.

Consider using online databases such as InfoTrac and EBSCO. According to InfoTrac College Edition's website (infotrac.thomsonlearning.com), more than 20 million articles from nearly 6,000 sources are available to you. The advantage of using this resource is that you may access cross-disciplinary, reliable, full-length articles. It is free of advertising and available twenty-four hours a day. EBSCO (www.ebsco.com) offers a similar service, and claims to be the most widely used online resource, with access to over 100 databases, and thousands of e-journals. By the time this book is printed, it is a sure bet that even more databases will be available.

If you're unfamiliar with online databases, ask the librarian for assistance.
© *Lisa F. Young, 2008. Under license from Shutterstock, Inc.*

Web Evaluation Criteria

Many students will start their research online. Computers are in dorm rooms, dorm halls, academic buildings, and the library. It may take only a few steps to access one. While there is nothing inherently wrong with this, we urge you to proceed with caution. Evaluating the credibility of your online resources is critical. The quantity of information available via the Internet is colossal, and includes highly respected research as well as pure fiction presented as fact. Seek information from competent, qualified sources and avoid information from uninformed individuals with little or no credentials. Ultimately, you are held accountable for the quality and credibility of the sources you use.

As you access each website, it is important to evaluate its legitimacy as a source for your speech. Radford and his colleagues (2006) identify five web evaluation criteria that serve as useful standards for evaluating online information.

1. **Authority.** Authority relates to the concept of credibility. As we know, virtually anyone can become a web publisher. A website that passes this first test contains information provided by an individual, group, or organization known to have expertise in the area.

Questions to guide evaluation include the following:

- What type of group put up the site? (Educational institution? Government agency? Individual? Commercial business? Organization?)
- Can you identify the author(s)? (What is the organization or who is the person responsible for the information?)
- What are the credentials of those responsible?

2. **Accuracy.** A website that is accurate is reliable and error-free. One aspect of accuracy is timeliness. If the last time the site was updated was two years ago and the site is discussing a bill before the legislature, then it is no longer accurate. One assumes more accuracy when it is clear that information is scrutinized in some way before being placed on the web. Accuracy is clearly related to authority, since the sites with greater authority are most likely to have mechanisms for determining how something becomes "site-worthy."

Questions to guide evaluation include the following:

- Is the information accurate?
- Does the information confirm or contradict what is found in printed sources?
- Are references given to the sources of information?

3. **Objectivity.** The extent to which website material is presented without bias or distortion relates to objectivity. As you examine the material, you want to determine if it is presented as opinion or fact.

Questions to guide evaluation include the following:

- What is the age level of the intended audience? (Adults? Teenagers? Children?)
- Is the information on the site factual or an expression of opinion?
- Is the author controversial? A known conservative? A known liberal?
- What are the author's credentials?

4. **Coverage.** Coverage refers to the depth and breadth of the material. It may be difficult to determine who the site is targeting. As a result, material may be too general or too specific. Determine if it meets your needs or if critical information is missing.

Questions to guide evaluation include the following:

- What is the intended purpose of the site? (Educational? Informational? Commercial? Recreational?)
- Who is the intended audience (General public? Scholars? Students? Professionals?)
- Is information common knowledge? Too basic? Too technical?
- Does information include multiple aspects of the issue or concern?

5. **Currency.** Currency refers to the timeliness of the material. Some websites exist that have never been updated. Information may be no longer valid or useful. If you look for "Most popular books of the year," and find a site from 2003, that information is no longer current or relevant. Looking at birth rates or literacy rates from the past would not produce relevant information if you are looking for the most recent information.

It's easy to access computer resources, but make sure you carefully evaluate the material you find. © *Stephen Coburn, 2008. Under license from Shutterstock, Inc.*

Questions to guide evaluation include the following:

- When was the site created?
- Is the material recent?
- Is the website updated?

When using these five criteria to evaluate your online information, remember that *all* criteria should be met, not just one or two of the above. Accurate and current information must also be objective. If critical information is missing (coverage), no matter how accurate and current the information is, it should be eliminated as a source.

4. Interview, If Appropriate

Interviews are useful if you want information too new to be found in published sources or if you want to give your listeners the views of an expert. By talking to an expert, you can clarify questions and fill in knowledge gaps, and you may learn more about a subject than you expected. In the process, you also gather opinions based on years of experience.

Look around your campus and community. You will find experts who can tell you as much as you need to know about thousands of subjects. You can get opinions about the stock market, the effect of different types of running shoes on the development of shin splints, race relations, No Child Left Behind legislation, ethanol, water or air pollution, or curbside recycling.

If you decide to interview one or more people, we offer the following four suggestions:

Contact the person well in advance. Remember, *you* are the one who needs the information. Do not think that leaving one voice message is the extent of your responsibility. You may have to make several attempts to contact the person. Schedule a date and time to interview that leaves you with ample time to prepare your speech.

Prepare questions in advance. Make sure you know what topics need to be covered and what information needs to be clarified.

Develop questions in a logical order. One question should lead naturally to another. Place the most important questions at the top to guarantee that they will be answered before your time is up.

Stay within the agreed time frame. If you promise the interview will take no longer than a half hour, keep your word, if at all possible. Do not say, "It'll just take a minute," when you need at least fifteen minutes. Build in a little time to ask unplanned questions, questions based on the interviewee's answers or for clarification.

After reading this section on research, hopefully you are aware that it involves a significant time commitment. It is never too early to start thinking about your next speech topic and where you might find sources. Explore a variety of resources. Ask for help from your instructor or the librarian. Make sure you know the constraints of the assignment.

When you conduct an interview, make sure your questions develop in a logical order to get the information you need.
© *ArrowStudio, 2008. Under license from Shutterstock, Inc.*

Citing Sources in Your Speech

Any research included in your speech needs to be cited appropriately in order to give due credit. If you interviewed someone, your audience should know the person's name, credentials, and when and where you spoke with him or her. If you use information from a website, the audience should know the name of the website and when you accessed it. For print information, the audience generally needs to know the author, date, and type of publication. Your credibility is connected to your source citation. Expert sources and timely information add to your credibility. Essentially, all research used in your speech needs to be cited. Otherwise, you have committed an act of plagiarism. Following are ways to cite sources in your speech. *Consult with your instructor*, however, as he or she may have specific concerns.

Example 1

Correct source citation. In their 1995 book on family communication, researchers Yerby, Buerkel-Rothfuss and Bochner argue that it is difficult to understand family behavior "without an adequate description of the historical, physical, emotional, and relational context in which it occurs."

Incorrect source citation. Researchers on family communication argue that it is difficult to understand family behavior without an adequate description of the historical, physical, emotional, and relational context in which it occurs.

Explanation. We need the date to evaluate the timeliness of the material. We need to know that this information was found in a book, as opposed to a television show, a newspaper, magazine, or other source. We need the authors' names so we know who wrote the information, and so we can find the book.

Example 2

Correct source citation. According to a personal interview last week with Diane Ruyle, principal of Danube High School, fewer students are choosing vocational classes than they were ten years ago.

Incorrect source citation. According to Diane Ruyle, fewer students are choosing vocational classes.

Explanation. We need to know why the person cited Diane Ruyle. As a principal, she ought to be able to provide accurate information regarding course selection. Adding "than they were ten years ago" gives the listener a comparison basis.

Example 3

Correct source citation. According to an Associated Press article published in the *New York Times* on August 9, 2007, "unlike in South Carolina, state laws in Iowa and New Hampshire require officials there to hold the first caucus and primary in the nation, respectively. "

Incorrect source citation. "Unlike in South Carolina, state laws in Iowa and New Hampshire require officials there to hold the first caucus and primary in the nation, respectively."

Explanation. First, if this is published information, it should be cited. Second, most of us do not know these facts, a citation is necessary. Otherwise, the speaker could be making this up. The date provided allows us to look up the source and shows us that the information is timely. No author was identified, and since Associated Press articles can be found in many newspapers, it is important to note this was found in the *New York Times*.

Example 4

Correct source citation. According to the current American Diabetes Association website, "Cholesterol is carried through the body in two kinds of bundles called lipoproteins—low-density lipoproteins and high-density lipoproteins. It's important to have healthy levels of both."

Incorrect source citation. Cholesterol is carried through the body in two kinds of bundles called lipoproteins—low-density lipoproteins and high-density lipoproteins. It's important to have healthy levels of both.

Explanation. This information is not common knowledge, so it should be cited. Many different organizations might include such information on their website, so it is important to note that it came from the American Diabetes Association (ADA). An audience would infer that the ADA is a credible organization regarding this topic. Using the word "current" suggests that one could find that information today on the ADA website, which reinforces the timeliness of the material.

In summary, remember that you *do not* need to cite sources when you are reporting your own original ideas or discussing ideas that are commonly held. You *must* cite sources when you are quoting directly or paraphrasing (restating or summarizing a source's ideas in your own words). You must also cite the source of an illustration, diagram, or graph. Providing the date of publication, date of website access, credentials of the source, and/or type of publication where applicable will allow the listener to evaluate the credibility of the information.

Supporting Your Speech

Imagine a chef with a piece of steak, some cauliflower, and rice, the main ingredients for a dinner special. What the chef does with these raw materials will influence the response of the consumers. The chef decides whether to grill, broil, bake, steam, or fry. Different spices can be used for different results. Numerous possibilities exist.

The research you have gathered for your speech can be viewed as the raw material. Now you need to figure out how to organize and present the material in the most effective way for your audience. This is where the concept of supporting material applies.

Supporting material gives substance to your assertions. If you say that *Casablanca* is the best movie ever produced in Hollywood, you are stating your opinion. If you cite a film critic's essay that notes it is the best movie ever, then your statement has more weight. You may also be able to find data that indicates how well the movie did, and a public opinion poll that had it ranked as the top movie. These different resources provide support. Just about anything that supports a speaker's idea can be considered supporting material.

When developing your speech, you also have many decisions to make. Consider the following example:

Your public speaking professor has just given your class an assignment to deliver an informative speech on the problem of shoplifting. These two versions are among those presented:

Version 1:
Shoplifting is an enormous problem for American retailers, who lose billions of dollars each year to customer theft. Not unexpectedly, retailers pass the cost of shoplifting onto consumers, which means that people like you and me pay dearly for the crimes of others.

Shoplifting is increasingly becoming a middle-class crime. Experts tell us that many people shoplift just for kicks—for the thrill of defying authority and for the excitement of getting away with something that is against the law. Whatever the reason, one in fifteen Americans is guilty of this crime.

Version 2:
Imagine walking up to a store owner once a year and giving that person $300 without getting anything in return. Could you afford that? Would you want to do that? Yet that's what happens. Every year, the average American family of four forks over $300 to make amends for the crimes of shoplifters.

Shoplifting is a big cost to big business. According to recent statistics from the National Association for the Prevention of Shoplifting, people who walk out of stores without first stopping at the cash register take with them more than $13 billion annually. That's more than $25 million per day. Their website claims that one out of eleven of us is guilty of this crime. To bring this figure uncomfortably close to home, that's at least two students in each of your classes.

Interestingly, shoplifting is no longer a poor person's crime. Hard as it is to imagine, many shoplifters can well afford to buy what they steal. Wynona Ryder received a great deal of unwanted press when she shoplifted $5,000 worth of merchandise at a Beverly Hills store in 2001.

Why do middle- and upper-income people steal? According to psychiatrist James Spikes, quoted in a recent *Ms.* magazine, shoplifters are "defying authority. They're saying, `The hell with them. I'll do it anyway … . I can get away with it … .'" Psychologist Stanton Samenow, quoted in the July issue of *Life* magazine, agrees:

> ``Shoplifters will not accept life as it is; they want to take short-cuts. They do it for kicks" (Sawyer, Glenn Dowling 1988).

Although both versions say essentially the same thing, they are not equally effective. The difference is in the supporting materials.

Five Functions of Support

Support should strengthen your speech in five ways. Comparing Version 1 with Version 2 will help illustrate the value of supporting material.

1. *Support is specific.*
   Version 2 gives listeners more details than Version 1. We learn, for example, how much shoplifting costs each of us as well as the financial burden retailers must carry.
2. *Support helps to clarify ideas.*
   We learn much more about the reasons for shoplifting from Version 2. This clarification—from the mouths of experts—reduces the risk of mis-understanding.
3. *Support adds weight.*
   The use of credible statistics and expert opinion adds support to the second version's main points. This type of support convinces listeners by building a body of evidence that may be difficult to deny. The testimonies of Drs. Spikes and Samenow are convincing because they are authoritative. We believe what they say far more than we do unattributed facts.
4. *Support is appropriate to your audience.*
   Perhaps the most important difference between these two versions is Version 2's attempt to gear the supporting material to the audience. It is a rare college student who would not care about a $300 overcharge or who cannot relate to the presence of two possible shoplifters in each class. Also, movie star Wynona Ryder's shoplifting is noted in Version 2. Students are familiar with her name, but college students would not be as familiar with an older famous person who has shoplifted, such as Bess Myerson, winner of Miss America in 1945 and actress on several television shows in the 1960s.
5. *Support creates interest.*
   Although Version 1 provides information, it arouses little or no inter-est. Listeners have a hard time caring about the problem or becoming emotionally or intellectually involved. Version 2, on the other hand, cre-ates interest through the use of meaningful statistics, quotations, and an example. When used properly, supporting materials can transform ordi-nary details into a memorable presentation.

Effective support is used to develop the message you send to your listeners. It is through this message that communication takes place between speaker and audience. In public speaking, you cannot separate the act of speaking from the message the speaker delivers. Supporting your message is one of your most important tasks as you develop your speech.

Forms of Support

Effective speeches generally rely on multiple forms of support. To give your speech greater weight and authority, at least five forms of support can be used. These include facts, statistics, examples, testimony, and analogies. Each of these forms of support will be discussed, and guidelines for using them will be presented.

Facts

Nothing undermines a presentation faster than too few facts. **Facts** are pieces of information that are verifiable and irrefutable. **Opinions** are points of view that may or may not be supported in fact. Too often, speakers confuse fact and opinion when adding supporting material to a speech. For example, while it is a fact that Forest Whitaker won the 2007 Academy Award for Best Actor, it is opinion to state that he is the best actor in Hollywood.

Include facts that will clarify the concepts you are describing in your speech.
© *Peter Hansen, 2008. Under license from Shutterstock, Inc.*

Facts serve at least three different purposes:

1. *Facts clarify your main point.*
   They remove ambiguity, making it more likely that the message you send is the message your audience will receive.

2. *Facts indicate your knowledge of the subject.*
   Rather than say, "The League of Women Voters has been around for a long time," report, "The League of Women Voters was founded in 1919." Your audience wants to know that you have researched the topic and can discuss specifics about your topic.

3. *Facts define.*
   Facts provide needed definitions that may explain new concepts. If you are delivering a speech on "functional illiteracy," you may define the term in the following way:

> While an illiterate adult has no ability to read, write, or compute, relatively few Americans fall into this category. However, some 27 million Americans can't read, write, compute, speak, or listen effectively enough to function in society. They cannot read street signs, write out a check, apply for a job or ask a government bureaucrat about a Social Security check they never received. Although they may have minimal communications skills, for all intents and purposes, they are isolated from the rest of society. These people are considered functionally illiterate.

In the above example, you anticipated the potential confusion between the terms "illiteracy" and "functional illiteracy," and you differentiated between these terms. While you defined this term for your public speaking class, if your audience was comprised of literacy coaches, this would not be necessary.

Guidelines for Using Facts

Carefully determine the number of facts to use. Too few facts will reveal that you spent little time researching, while too many may overwhelm your listeners. Sometimes, students want to impress their audience, or at least their instructor, with the amount of research completed for a particular speech. The desire to include *all* information may result in a "data dump," where facts are given in a steady stream with little or no connection to the speech or to each other. This results in an overload of information that is difficult to process.

To be effective, the number and complexity of your facts must be closely tied to the needs of your listeners. A speech to a group of hikers on poison ivy prevention may include practical issues such as identifying the plant and recognizing, treating, and avoiding the rash. However, if you are delivering a speech on the same subject to a group of medical students, a detailed explanation of the body's biochemical response to the plant is probably more relevant.

Make sure your meanings are clear. If you use words or phrases that have different meanings to you than they do to members of your audience, the impact of your speech is lessened. Misunderstandings occur when your audience attributes meanings to terms you did not intend. Think about the following words: success, liberal, conservative, patriot, happiness, good, bad, and smart. Collectively, we do not agree on the meanings of these words. One person may define success in terms of material wealth, while another may think of it in terms of family relationships, job satisfaction, and good health. When it is essential that your audience understand the meaning you intend, take the time to define it carefully as you speak.

Define terms when they are first introduced. The first time you use a term that requires an explanation, define it so that your meaning is clear. If you are talking about the advantages of belonging to a health maintenance organization, define the term the first time it is used.

Statistics

The second form of supporting material is **statistics**: the collection, analysis, interpretation, and presentation of information in numerical form. Statistics give us the information necessary to understand the magnitude of issues and to compare and contrast different points. Basic measures include the mean, median, and mode, which are generally referred to as descriptive statistics, because they allow us to discuss a set of numbers easily. The **mean** is calculated by adding all the numbers in a group and dividing by the number of items. It is the most widely used statistical measure. The **median** measures the middle score in the group. That is, half the values fall above it and half fall below. The **mode** is the value that occurs most frequently.

But statistics can be misleading. For example, if one were to examine the National League Baseball (NLB) salaries for 2005, one would find the average, or mean, salary for those players was $2,585,804 (http://asp.usatoday.com/sports/baseball/salaries). However, the highest salary went to San Francisco Giant's Barry Bonds who earned $22 million. Meanwhile, the median salary for all NLB players was $800,000. This means that half of the 439 players received more than $800,000 and half received less than that. In addition, the mode was $316,000. Twenty-six players received this amount. In this case, simply discussing these three statistical measures is not helpful, unless you want to make the point that salaries are not consistent. It might make more sense to discuss the range of salaries or look at a particular group of players' salaries. When using statistics in your speech, it is important to understand what they mean.

Guidelines for Using Statistics

Be precise. Make sure you understand the statistics before including them in your speech. Consider the difference between the following statements.

> A 2-percent decrease was shown in the rate of economic growth, as measured by the gross national product, compared to the same period last year.
> The gross national product dropped by 2 percent compared to the same period last year.

In the first case, the statistic refers to a drop in the rate of growth—it tells us that the economy is growing at a slower pace but that it is still ahead of last year—while in the second, it refers to an actual drop in the gross national product in comparison to the previous year. These statements say two very different things.

It is critical that you not misinterpret statistics when analyzing the data. If you have questions, refer to a basic statistics text or another source that further explains the data.

Avoid using too many statistics. Too many statistics will confuse and bore your audience and blunt the impact of your most important statistical points. Save your statistics for the places in your speech where they will make the most impact.

Round off your numbers. Is it important for your audience to know that, according to the Census Bureau's daily population projection on March 3, 2006, the U.S. population reached 298,228,575? The figure will have greater impact—and your audience will be more likely to remember it—if you round it off to "more than 298,000,000."

Cite your sources. Because statistics are rarely remembered for very long, it is easy for speakers to misquote and misuse them—often in a calculated way for their own ends. As an ethical speaker, you need to make sure your statistics are correct and you need to quote your sources. For example, if you were talking about the history of Girl Scout cookies, you could mention that during peak production of Girl Scout cookies, according to the Little Brownie Bakery website (www.littlebrowniebakers.com), one of two bakers for the Girl Scouts, 1,050,000 pounds of flour a week are used in production.

Use visual aids to express statistics. Statistics become especially meaningful to listeners when they are presented in visual form. Visual presentations of statistics free you from the need to repeat a litany of numbers that listeners will probably never remember. Instead, by transforming these numbers into visual presentations, you can highlight only the most important points, allowing your listeners to refer to the remaining statistics at any time. For example, in a speech extolling the virtues of graduate school, a graph displaying average salaries by degrees earned would be helpful. (See Figure 6.1).

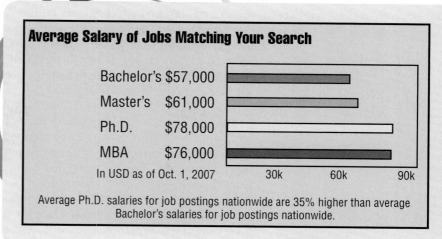

Average Salary of Jobs Matching Your Search

Bachelor's $57,000
Master's $61,000
Ph.D. $78,000
MBA $76,000

In USD as of Oct. 1, 2007   30k   60k   90k

Average Ph.D. salaries for job postings nationwide are 35% higher than average Bachelor's salaries for job postings nationwide.

FIGURE 6.1
A bar graph can be used to clearly illustrate differences in values.

Examples

Examples enliven speeches in a way that no other form of supporting material can. Grounding material in the specifics of everyday life has the power to create an empathic bond between speaker and audience, a bond strong enough to tie listeners to a speech and the speaker even after the example is complete.

Examples can be brief or extended, real or hypothetical, and narrative. Although examples differ in length, factual base, and source, their effectiveness lies in the extent to which they support the speaker's core idea.

Examples are brief or extended. Brief examples are short illustrations that clarify a general statement. If you made the following assertion: "Americans are more modest than Europeans," you could support it by using brief examples, such as, "If you take a walk on the beach in Italy or France, you should not be surprised to find women sunbathing topless. Also, many European countries, such as Sweden and Germany, have public saunas that are enjoyed by men and women—who are in the same sauna, sitting naked on their towels." Brief examples can be used effectively throughout a speech. Your decision to use them will depend on many factors, including the needs of your audience, the nature of your material, and your approach.

Extended examples are longer and richer in detail than brief examples. They are used most effectively to build images and to create a lasting impression on the audience, as can been seen in the following excerpt from a speech in 2006 given by Steven Darimont, candidate for sheriff in Coles County, Illinois. When making the point that money is spent unnecessarily on jail food, he stated:

> "Our food budget alone is at $140,000 and we will go over that by $12–15,000 this year. The sheriff has requested that (amount) be raised (an additional) $20,000, to $160,000 next year. The inmates currently get three hot meals a day. An example of this is breakfast: scrambled eggs, toast with butter and jelly, cold cereal with milk, hash browns, fruit, and juice. The Department of Corrections mandates only one hot meal per day, yet we feed three hot meals."

Providing more detail about the budget and the ample food choices creates a greater impact on the listener rather than saying, "We provide three hot meals a day, and we're going over budget."

Because of their impact, extended examples should not be overused or used at inappropriate points. As with other forms of support, they should be reserved for the points at which they will have the greatest effect: in clarifying the message, persuading listeners to your point of view, or establishing a speaker-audience relationship.

Examples are real or hypothetical. Sometimes the best examples are real, and come from your personal experience. By revealing parts of your life that relate to your speech topic, you provide convincing evidence and, at the same time, potentially create a powerful bond between you and your audience. Consider the student who has watched her mother die from lung cancer. The experience of hearing about the diagnosis, discussing treatment possibilities, and making final arrangements while her mother was alive can have a powerful effect on the audience. The words and emotion have great impact because the situation is real, not hypothetical, and the speaker provides a sense of reality to the topic.

At times, it suits the speaker's purpose to create a fictional example, rather than a real example, to make a point. Although these examples are not based on facts, the circumstances they describe are often realistic and thus effective. Robert J. Aaronson (1989), president of the Air Transport Association, spoke hypothetically to the American Bar Association Forum on Air and Space Law:

> It is not often that someone outside the legal profession has a chance to tell an audience of lawyers what he thinks about their line of work. So I will seize this opportunity, using the case study method to describe, in layman's terms, what legal practice is all about.
>
> The case I have chosen is that of an airport construction worker named Charlie. He is finishing work for the day on [an] airport expansion project... . He is aware of the OSHA [Occupational Safety and Health Administration] rule against leaving loose materials on a scaffold overnight. So when he notices some loose bricks on his scaffold, he grabs an empty barrel, hoists it up on the scaffold with a rope and pulley and puts the bricks inside of it.
>
> Back on the ground, Charlie proceeds to lower the load. He has no trouble swinging the barrel free of the scaffolding. But the barrel, filled with bricks, is heavier than he is. So the barrel goes down, Charlie goes up, and along the way they collide, giving Charlie a severe bump on the head. Charlie somehow manages to hold on, but when he reaches the top, his fingers get mangled in the pulley, just as the barrel crashes to the ground and breaks open... he goes down, the barrel goes up. Again they collide. This time Charlie breaks a few ribs. He hits the ground. He's stunned, and he lets go of the rope.
>
> You probably can guess how this sorry tale ends. The barrel, no longer connected to Charlie, falls a second time. It lands on Charlie, and it breaks his leg. We all have our ups and

downs in life, but certainly his falls in the category of a very bad day at the office.

I am sure all of you have identified the central legal question here: Does Charlie sue the airport, the construction firm, the brick company or the barrel maker? The answer, of course, is all four, PLUS the first grade teacher who made it possible for Charlie to read the OSHA handbook in the first place! (592)

Hypothetical examples are useful when you want to exaggerate a point as Aaronson did. They are also useful when you cannot find a factual illustration for your speech. To be effective, they must be tied in some way to the point you are trying to illustrate.

It is important that your listeners know when you are using a hypothetical example and when you are not. Avoid confusion by introducing these examples in a direct way. You might start out by saying, "Imagine that you live next door to a college professor we'll call Dr. Supple," or "Let's talk about a hypothetical mother on welfare named Alice."

Examples can be in narrative form. Narratives are stories within a speech, anecdotes that create visual images in listeners' minds. In many ways, they take extended examples a step further by involving listeners in a tale that captures attention and makes a point—a story connected to the speaker's core idea. Many listeners love a good story, and when the speech is over, the narrative is what they remember.

Imagine Laura, a person who has traveled significantly, giving an informative speech on "The art of shopping outside the United States: Bartering made simple." She might include the following:

My husband and I were in Morocco shopping with my mother and my aunt. They stopped to speak with a shop owner about carpets and my husband and I went on. About forty-five minutes later, we walked by to see them STILL speaking with the shop owner. Now, though, all three were seated, and they were drinking hot, mint tea. We approached the shopkeeper and introduced ourselves. He proceeded to tell us how different my mother and aunt were from most American women. He said that American women will ask the price of something, and he'll throw out some high price. Then the women will offer a significantly lower price. He rejects that but comes down on his original high price. The American women, usually, will accept his second price, no matter how high! Not these women! My mom and aunt bartered back and forth with the shopkeeper about the price, never giving in! The shopkeeper said he really enjoyed negotiating with them; that they were both friendly **and** insistent. They didn't back down easily, and, according to the shopkeeper, they ended up paying a reasonable price for their carpet.

By their nature, narratives demand that listeners take an active part in linking the story to the speaker's main point. The story moves from beginning to middle, to end. Even if the speaker supplies the link after the narrative, audience members still make the connections themselves as they listen.

A narrative can be used anywhere in a speech. No matter where it is placed, it assumes great importance to listeners as they become involved with the details. Through the narrative, speakers can establish a closeness with the audience that may continue even after the story is over.

Guidelines for Using Examples

Examples add interest and impact. They should be representative because examples support your core idea only when they accurately represent the situation. No matter the type of example you use as supporting material, the following three guidelines will help you choose examples for your speeches:

Use examples frequently. Examples are often the lifeblood of a speech. Use them to make your points—but only in appropriate places. When using examples to prove a point, more than one example generally is needed.

Use only the amount of detail necessary. To make your examples work, you want to use only the amount of detail necessary for your audience and no more. The detail you provide in examples should be based on the needs of your audience. If your listeners are familiar with a topic, you can simply mention what the audience already knows. Interspersing long examples with short ones varies the pace and detail of your discussion.

Use examples to explain new concepts. Difficult concepts become easier to handle when you clarify them with examples. Keep in mind that although you may be comfortable with the complexities of a topic, your listeners might be hearing these complexities for the first time. Appropriate examples can mean the difference between communicating with or losing your audience.

Testimony

The word testimony may conjure a vision of witnesses in a court of law giving sworn statements to a judge and jury, adding credibility to a case. In public speaking, testimony has nothing to do with the law, but it has everything to do with credibility. When you cite the words of others, either directly or through paraphrasing, you are attempting, in effect, to strengthen your position by telling your audience that people with special knowledge support your position or take your side. Testimony can cite either experience or opinion. Also, short quotations may be an effective way to provide testimony.

In order to be effective, however, testimony needs to be used in its proper context. Purposefully distorting the testimony of an expert to suit the needs of your speech is misleading and unethical. Be honest to your source as well as your audience.

Experience as testimony. Experience may be the most credible choice in some cases because someone was "on the scene." For example, hundreds of thousands of individuals were directly affected by hurricane Katrina. A student writer for the University of Texas at Austin newspaper interviewed Lorraine Brown about her personal experience during hurricane Katrina. The following account was printed in the September 6, 2005 issue of *The Daily Texan*.

At 5 a.m. on Monday, after floodwaters breached the New Orleans levees, Brown awoke to find water seeping into her house. 'I saw the water on my kitchen floor, and I picked up a mop and started mopping. But then I looked out the window and saw that the water was already up to here,' she said, holding her hand at her waist. 'It's lucky that I woke up at five, because by six the water would've been too high to get out.' She explained that the doors of her house swung outward and that she couldn't have pushed hard enough to overcome the weight of the water. 'I think about what if we woke up, and the water was already up over the house. Then it's just like a monster is outside, and there's nowhere to go.'

September 6, 2005 by Delaney Hall. Copyright © 2005 by Daily Texan. Reprinted by permission.

Lorraine Brown's experience as one of the survivors of the hurricane provides vivid imagery that helps the listener recognize the terror that many experienced.

It is possible to use your own testimony when you are an expert. If you are writing a speech on what it is like to recover from a spinal cord injury, use your own expert testimony if you have suffered this injury. Similarly, if you are talking about the advantages and problems of being a female lifeguard, cite your own testimony if you are female and have spent summers saving lives at the beach. When you do not have the background necessary to convince your audience, use the testimony of those who do.

Opinion as testimony. In some circumstances, the opinion of a recognized authority may provide the credibility needed to strengthen your argument or prove a point. Jimmy Carter, former president and winner of the Nobel Peace Prize in 2002, is an outspoken critic of the Iraqi War. At a news conference in July 2005, CBS News quoted him as saying, "I thought then, and I think now, that the invasion of Iraq was unnecessary and unjust. And I think the premises on which it was launched were false" (www. cbsnews.com). While he is clearly stating an opinion, Carter carries a certain amount of credibility because of his previous position as president of the United States and as a Nobel Peace Prize winner.

Shown here making a statement after receiving the Nobel Peace Prize, Jimmy Carter's opinions carry credibility because of his past accomplishments. © *Reuters/Corbis.*

Short quotations. A short quotation is a form of testimony, but its purpose is often different. Frequently, short quotations are used to set the tone for a speech, to provide humor, or to make important points more memorable. If you were receiving the MVP award for football at your high school or college, you might start out with something like this:

"Wow. I'm reminded of John Madden's words when he was inducted into the Pro Football Hall of Fame in 2006, 'And right now, I don't have, I got like numb, you know, a tingle from the bottom of my toes to the top of my head.' Yep. That's exactly how I feel."

Madden's quote is not the most articulate or insightful comment, but it certainly expressed the emotion the football player was feeling, and this quote would set an engaging tone for an acceptance speech.

Sometimes quotations are too long or too complicated to present verbatim. You can choose to cite the source but paraphrase the message. Instead of quoting the following description of the effect crack cocaine has on the body, it might be more effective to paraphrase.

Quote:

> According to Dr. Mark S. Gold, nationally known expert on cocaine abuse, founder of the 800-COCAINE helpline, and author of *The Facts About Drugs and Alcohol*, "as an anesthetic, cocaine blocks the conduction of electrical impulses within the nerve cells involved in sensory transmissions, primarily pain. The body's motor impulses, those that control muscle function, for example, are not affected by low-dose use of cocaine. In this way cocaine creates a deadening blockage (known as a differential block) of pain, without interfering with body movement" (Gold 1986, 36).

Paraphrase: According to Dr. Mark S. Gold, nationally known expert on cocaine abuse,

> founder of the 800-COCAINE helpline and author of *The Facts About Drugs and Alcohol*, cocaine blocks pain without interfering with body movement.

The second version is more effective when speaking to a lay audience who knows little about medicine, while the former is appropriate for an audience of science students or physicians.

Guidelines for Using Testimony

Use only recognizable or credible testimony and quotations. At a time when media exposure is so pervasive, it is easy to find someone who will support your point of view. Before citing a person as an authoritative source, be sure that he or she is an expert. If you are giving a speech on the greatest movies ever produced, it would make sense to quote Roger Ebert, film critic and author of numerous books on the subject of film. However, he would not be the proper choice for a speech on the joys of collecting and trading baseball cards.

As you review expert testimony, keep in mind that the more research you do, the more opinions you will find. Ultimately, your choice should be guided by relevance and credibility of the source. The fact that you quote Supreme Court Justice Sandra Day O'Connor in a speech on affirmative action is as important as the quote itself.

Choose unbiased experts. How effective is the following testimony if its source is the *owner* of the Oakland Athletics?

> There is no team in baseball as complete as the Athletics. The team has better pitching, fielding, hitting, and base running than any of its competitors in the National or American League.

If the same quote came from a baseball writer for *Sports Illustrated* you would probably believe it more. Thus, when choosing expert testimony, bear in mind that opinions shaped by self-interest are less valuable, from the point of view of your audience, than those motivated by the merits of the issues.

Identify the source. Not all names of your experts will be recognizable, so it is important to tell your audience why they are qualified to give testimony. If you are cautioning overseas travelers to avoid tourist scams, the following expert testimony provides support:

> According to Rick Steves, travelers should be wary of "The 'helpful' local: Thieves posing as concerned locals will warn you to store your wallet safely—and then steal it after they see where you stash it. Some thieves put out tacks and ambush drivers with their "assistance" in changing the tire. Others hang out at subway ticket machines eager to "help" the bewildered tourist buy tickets with a pile of quickly disappearing foreign cash" (www.ricksteves.com).

Without knowing anything about Rick Steves, your readers will have no reason to trust this advice. However, if you state his credentials first, you can establish the credibility of your expert. So instead, the speaker could start begin with, "According to Rick Steves, host and producer of the popular public television series *Rick Steves' Europe* and best-selling author of thirty European travel books, travelers should be wary of…"

Develop techniques to signal the beginning and ending of each quotation. Your audience may not know when a quote begins or ends. Some speakers prefer to preface quotations with the words, "And I quote" and to end quotations with the phrase, "end quote." Other speakers indicate the presence of quotations through pauses immediately before and immediately after the quotation or through a slight change of pace or inflection. It may be a good idea to use both techniques in your speech to satisfy your listeners' need for variety. Just do not make quotation signs with your fingers!

Analogies

At times, the most effective form of supporting material is the analogy, which points out similarities between what we know and understand and what we do not know or cannot accept. Analogies fall into two separate categories: figurative and literal. **Figurative analogies** draw comparisons between things that are distinctly different in an attempt to clarify a concept or persuade. Biology professor and world-renowned environmentalist Paul Erlich uses an analogy of a globe holding and draining water to explain the problem of the world population explosion. The following is an excerpt from a speech delivered to the First National Congress on Optimum Population and Environment, June 9, 1970:

> As a model of the world demographic situation, think of the world as a globe, and think of a faucet being turned on into that globe as being the equivalent of the birth rate, the input into the population. Think of that drain at the base of that globe—water pouring out—as being the equivalent to the output, the death rate of the population. At the time of the

Agricultural Revolution, the faucet was turned on full blast; there was a very high birth rate. The drain was wide open; there was a high death rate. There was very little water in the globe, very few people in the population—only above five million. When the Agricultural Revolution took place, we began to plug the drain, cut down the death rate, and the globe began to fill up.

This analogy is effective because it helps the audience understand the population explosion. It explains the nature of the problem in a clear, graphic way. Listener understanding comes not from the presentation of new facts (these facts were presented elsewhere in the speech) but from a simple comparison. When dealing with difficult or emotionally charged concepts, listeners benefit from this type of comparative supporting material.

Keep in mind that although figurative analogies may be helpful, they usually do not serve as sufficient proof in a persuasive argument. Erlich, for example, must back his analogy with facts, statistics, examples, and quotations to persuade his listeners that his analogy is accurate—that we are indeed in the midst of a population crisis.

A **literal analogy** compares like things from similar classes, such as a game of professional football with a game of college football. If, for example, you are delivering a speech to inform your classmates about Russia's involvement in the war in Afghanistan, the following literal analogy might be helpful:

The war in Afghanistan was the former Soviet Union's Vietnam. Both wars were unwinnable from the start. Neither the Vietnamese nor the Afghans would tolerate foreign domination. Acting with the determination of the Biblical David, they waged a struggle against the Goliaths of Russia and the United States. In large part, the winning weapon in both wars was the collective might of village peasants who were determined to rid their countries of the Superpowers—no matter the odds.

Literal analogies serve as proof when the aspects or concepts compared are similar. When similarities are weak, the proof fails. The analogy, "As Rome fell because of moral decay, so will the United States," is valid only if the United States and Rome have similar economic and social systems, types of governments, and so on. The fewer the similarities between the United States and Rome, the weaker the proof.

Guidelines for Using Analogies

Use analogies to build the power of your argument. Analogies convince through comparison to something the audience already knows. It is psychologically comforting to your listeners to hear new ideas expressed in a familiar context. The result is greater understanding and possible acceptance of your point of view.

Be certain the analogy is clear. Even when the concept of your analogy is solid, if the points of comparison are not effectively carried through from beginning to end, the analogy will fail. Your analogy must be as consistent and complete as in the following example:

In political campaigns, opponents square off against one another in an attempt to land the winning blow. Although after a close and grueling campaign that resembles a ten-round bout, one candidate may succeed by finding a soft spot in his opponent's record, the fight is hardly over. Even while the downed opponent is flat against the mat, the victor turns to the public and tells yet another distortion of the truth. "My opponent," he says, "never had a chance." Clearly, politicians and prize fighters share one goal in common: to knock their opponents senseless and to make the public believe that they did it with ease.

Avoid using too many analogies. A single effective analogy can communicate your point. Do not diminish its force by including several in a short presentation.

Summary

Research gives you the tools you need to support your thesis statement. A solid research base increases your credibility. To begin your research strategy, assess your personal knowledge and skills. Then look for print and online resources. The librarian can lead you to valuable sources within the physical library as well as online. You may need to look up information in encyclopedias, dictionaries, books, newspapers, magazines, journal articles, and government documents. When using online resources, it is important to use website evaluation criteria and to question accuracy, authority, objectivity, coverage, and currency.

Supporting materials buttress the main points of your speech and make you a more credible speaker. Among the most important forms of support are facts—verifiable information. Facts clarify your main points, indicate knowledge of your subject, and serve as definitions. Opinions differ from facts in that they cannot be verified. Statistical support involves the presentation of information in numerical form. Because statistics are easily manipulated, it is important to analyze carefully the data you present.

Five different types of examples are commonly used as forms of support. Brief examples are short illustrations that clarify a general statement. Extended examples are used to create lasting images. Narratives are stories within a speech that are linked to the speaker's main idea. Hypothetical examples are fictional examples used to make a point. Personal examples are anecdotes related to your topic that come from your own life.

When you use testimony quotations, you cite the words of others to increase the credibility of your message. Your sources gain expertise through experience and authority. Analogies focus on the similarities between the familiar and unfamiliar. Figurative analogies compare things that are different, while liberal analogies compare things from similar classes. Literal analogies can often be used as proof.

Questions for Study and Discussion

1. How important is research in the preparation of most speeches? How can an audience tell whether a speech lacks a sound research base?
2. Why is it important that you conduct both an audience analysis and reflect on your own knowledge and skills when it comes to developing your topic?
3. When you are considering information you found on a website, how do you evaluate whether or not the information you found is appropriate to include as supporting material?
4. How can you best use the services of a librarian?
5. With the idea of a research strategy in mind, how will you determine the types and amount of support you will need to meet the specific purpose of your next speech?
6. Which supporting materials are most effective for clarifying a point and which are most appropriate for proof? Can some forms of support serve both aims? How?
7. In the hands of an unethical speaker, how can statistics and analogies mislead an audience? What is your ethical responsibility in choosing supporting materials?

Activities

1. Tour the libraries at school and in your community. In a written report, compare the facilities and use your findings as a guide when you research your next speech.
2. For your next speech assignment, develop and follow a search strategy that includes both interviews and library research.
3. Analyze the connection between your choice of topic and your choice of support.
4. Select three different forms of support and assess the strengths and weaknesses of each as evidence in public speeches.
5. Include in your next persuasive speech as many different forms of support as possible. After your speech, hand out a questionnaire to determine which form of support had the most effect.

References

Aaronson, R.J. "Air transportation: What is safe and needed." *Vital Speeches of the Day,* July 15, 1989.

Erlich, P. June 9, 1970. Speech delivered to First National Congress on Optimum Population and Environment.

Fleshler, H., J. Ilardo, and J. Demoretcky. "The influence of field dependence, speaker credibility set and message documentation on evaluations of speaker and message credibility," *The Southern Speech Communication Journal* (Summer 1974): 389–402.

Glenn Dowling, C. "Shoplifting," *Life,* August 1, 1988, 33.

Gold, M.S. 1986. *The facts about drugs and alcohol.* New York: Bantam Books.

Sawyer, S. "Psychology of a middle-aged shoplifter," *Ms.,* September 1988, 46.

"We will draw the curtain and show you the picture."

William Shakespeare

© *Corbis.*

Presentational Aids

Suppose an assignment in your class is one that really excites you, and makes you think of a speech topic that your audience will find provocative and controversial. Unlike many of the speeches you have heard, this one will tell a story your classmates will find difficult to ignore-or so it seems.

The topic is concerned with how so few of the college football and basketball program athletes ever graduate—a scandal that looms large in your own school. Recent articles in the student newspaper have criticized your school's athletic department for emphasizing winning over education. An editorial in last week's edition asked, "How can student-athletes practice forty hours a week and still go to class, study, and complete their assignments?" The answer is, they cannot. As you collect supporting material for your speech, you find statistics that tell a story of athletes not equipped to go professional, and not prepared for anything more than menial work. Here is part of the speech your classmates hear:

> According to a study by the federal Governmental Accountancy Office, of the 97 colleges with Division 1-A basketball programs, considered the best in intercollegiate sports, 35—that's more than one third—graduate no more than 1 in 5 athletes; 33 graduate between 21 percent and 40 percent; 11 graduate between 41 percent and 60 percent; 10 graduate between 61 percent and 80 percent; and only 8 graduate between 81 percent and 100 percent.

> The graduation rates for football players on Division 1-A teams is little better. Of the 103 teams in this division, 14 graduate no more than 1 out of 5 players; 39 graduate between 21 and 40 percent; 31 graduate between 41 and 60 percent; 13 between 61 and 80 percent; and only 6 between 81 and 100 percent (Molotsky, *New York Times*, September 10, 1989).

Instead of startling your listeners, these statistics numb them. You may see several people yawning, many doodling, a few whispering. You have no idea why until your classmates comment during the post-speech evaluation. The complaints are all the same: Your "can't miss" speech was boring and difficult to follow. Instead of stimulating your listeners, your long list of statistics put them to sleep.

Few of us think of speech making in visual terms—or find ways to reach our speaking goals by turning to presentational aids. In this example, an appropriately constructed visual aid could have helped you avoid saying so much in words. Despite the interest your listeners had in your topic before your speech began, the number and complexity of your statistics made it difficult for them to pay attention. By presenting some of your data in visual form, you could communicate the same message more effectively. Consider the difference when the following speech text is substituted for the text above and combined with figure 7.1.

> A study by the U.S. Governmental Accountancy Office, an arm of the federal government, shows that at some Division 1-A colleges, including those with the best intercollegiate athletic programs, no more than 1 out of 5 basketball and football players graduate. As you can see, [*speaker points to*

the figure] there are far fewer colleges with an 80 percent graduation rate than colleges graduating athletes at a rate of 20 percent or less. Although only 8 out of 97 colleges fit into the former group, 35 fit into the latter—and our college is one of them.

GRADUATION RATE FOR BASKETBALL PLAYERS FROM 97 COLLEGES					
0 to 20%	21–40%		41–60%	61–80%	81–100%
35 colleges	33		11	10	8

FOR FOOTBALL PLAYERS FROM 103 COLLEGES					
0 to 20%	21–40%		41–60%	61–80%	81–100%
14	39		31	13	6

FIGURE 7.1
A visual aid can be an effective way to present statistics.

Numbers are still used, but not as many, and with the presentational aid, the audience gets a visual feel for the information and they are able to process the information for a little longer than if you just said the numbers.

This chapter focuses on the benefits of using presentational aids (frequently called visual aids). The different types of presentational aids are explored and criteria are given for their use and display. Based on the increasing use of PowerPoint for classroom presentations, a specific section on the creation/use of computer generated slides is included.

Functions of Presentational Aids

A decade ago, no one expected to see professional quality presentational aids for a class speech. As technology becomes more accessible, however, expectations have increased. Regardless of our advances in technology, we all expect to see effective presentations that communicate a message in a clear, direct manner.

Presentational aids function in a variety of ways. They are more than "add-ons." Your instructor may require you to use presentational aids not only to enhance the effectiveness of your speech, but also to learn how to work with them as you speak. Following are five functions of presentational aids.

Presentational Aids Create Interest and Attraction

Have you ever seen a lotto billboard along side an interstate? As you approach it, you can see the jackpot amount increasing as the digital numbers change constantly. When a presentational aid is well prepared, little can compete with it to capture—and hold—audience interest. We live in a visual age. The images that surround us in the mass media make us more receptive, on conscious and unconscious levels, to visual presentations of all kinds. We are attuned to these presentations simply because they are visual— a phenomenon you can use to your advantage during a speech.

Regardless of the presentation, an audience expects your message to be communicated clearly. © *Corbis.*

A student wanted to emphasize how fast the world's population is growing. During her speech, she accessed a website that keeps a digital tally of births, and kept the digital counter on the screen for about a minute. Then she made reference to the number of births that had occurred during that time frame. It kept the interest of the class.

A well-placed, professional-looking presentational aid will draw attention to the point you are trying to make or to the statistics you want the audience to process.

Our suggestions: In an effort to maintain interest and attention, try to limit each visual to one main point. Leave details out. Use as few words as possible. Be aware of spacing, and do not crowd the images. If there is too much information or the slide looks too "busy," you will lose attention and interest.

Presentational Aids Make Complex Ideas Clear

Presentational aids have the power to clarify complex ideas. They are invaluable tools when explaining mechanical functions such as how a hot air balloon rises or how a computer stores information. They can help clarify complex interrelationships involving people, groups, and institutions. They can show, for example, the stages a bill must go through before it becomes a law and the role Congress and the president play in this process. Visuals reduce, but do not eliminate, the need to explain verbally the complex details of a process.

Presentational aids take the place of many words and, therefore, shorten the length of a speech. They do not replace words, and one or two statements are insufficient verbal support for a series of visual displays. But presentational aids and words *in combination* can reduce the amount of time you spend creating word pictures.

Remember, however, to keep your visuals simple. Speech consultants Karen Berg and Andrew Gilman (1989) explain, "When in doubt, simplify; eliminate extraneous material. If necessary, use an additional visual rather than burdening one with more information than it can efficiently transmit" (73).

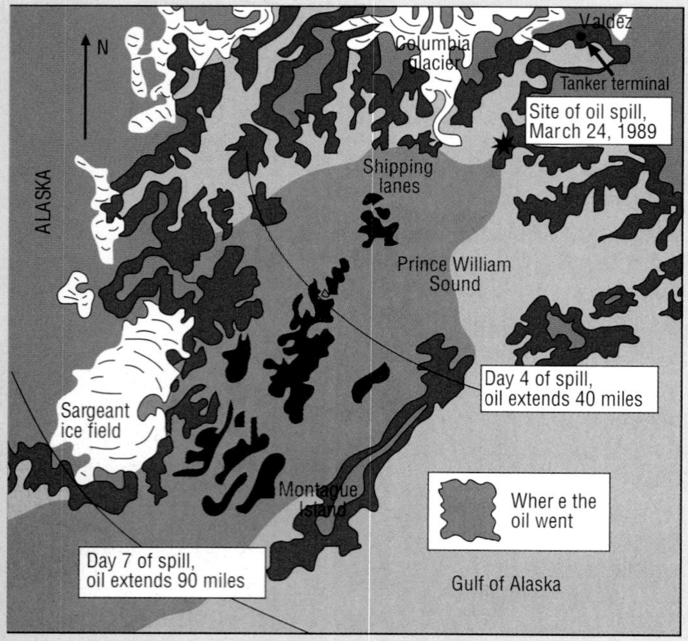

FIGURE 7.2
The audience listening to a speech that includes explanations of where the oil spills took place needs to view a map with necessary detail included. In this figure, the words and the illustration work together to create meaning.

Presentational Aids Make Abstract Ideas Concrete

Few of us enjoy abstractions. If you are delivering a speech on the effects of the 11 million gallon oil spill from the Exxon tanker on Alaska's Prince William Sound, it may not be enough to tell your audience that the spill was allowed to drift 470 miles in a period of 56 days. It is far more effective to refer to a map of the drifting spill that illustrates the extent of the spread on different days. Figure 7.2 shows the enormity of the disaster and eliminates any confusion audience members may have about its impact on the Alaskan coast.

Along with this visual, you explain:

> For three days after the Exxon tanker rammed into a reef on Alaska's Prince William Sound, the spill miraculously lingered near the ruptured hull. But officials were unable to take action. Instead they wasted this time—this precious time—arguing what to do. On day four, a powerful storm made their arguments academic as it spread the oil down the Alaskan coast where it drifted uncontrollably for 56 days and stained 470 miles of Alaska's pristine shore (Newsweek, September 18, 1989).

The image of the spill's movement provides us with a visual picture that makes the situation much more easily understood. Sometimes we need to see something in order to process it effectively.

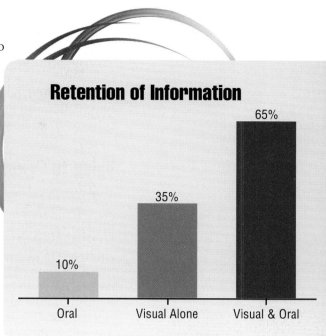

FIGURE 7.3
A simple bar graph can display information clearly so it is easier to understand.

Presentational Aids Make Messages Memorable

Did you read the newspaper this morning? What do you remember from it? Chances are, a photo comes to mind—the picture of a fireman rescuing a child from a burning building or the president of your university getting a pie in the face at the end of a fundraiser. You may have read the articles that accompanied these pictures, but the images are likely to have had the greatest impact.

The tendency for an audience to recall pictures longer than words gives speakers an important advantage. Research has shown, for example, that three days after an event, people retain 10 percent of what they heard from an oral presentation, 35 percent from a visual presentation, and 65 percent from a visual and oral presentation (www.osha.gov 2007). Using a simple bar graph to display this information makes it easier to understand these significant differences (see figure 7.3).

Presentational aids have persuasive power. Business speakers, especially those in sales, have long realized that they can close a deal faster if they use visual aids. A study by the University of Minnesota and the 3M Corporation found that speakers who integrate visuals into their talks are 43 percent more likely to persuade their audiences than speakers who rely solely on verbal images (Vogel, Dickson, and Lehman 1986).

Presentational Aids Serve to Organize Ideas

As with every other aspect of your speech, presentational aids should be audience-centered. They may be eye-catching and visually stimulating, but they do serve a more practical purpose. The flow and connection of a speaker's ideas are not always apparent to an audience, especially if the topic is complicated or involves many steps. Flow charts, diagrams, graphs, and tables can help listeners follow a speaker's ideas.

Keep your audience's needs in mind as you plan the presentational aids you use in your speech. © Corbis.

General Criteria for Using Presentational Aids

Your decision to include an aid should be based on the extent to which it enhances your audience's interest and understanding. The type of aid you choose should relate directly to the specific purpose of your speech and information you intend to convey. As you consider using a presentational aid, consider the following four general criteria.

Value to Presentation

Your instructor may require you to use a presentational aid for one or more of your speeches, but it does not mean that *any* aid is better than no aid. First and foremost, the aid must add value to your presentation. If you are bringing in a presentational aid just to meet the constraints of the assignment, it may not be effective. For example, if a student is giving a speech about the "cola wars," and brings in a can of Pepsi and a can of Coke, there is not much value to the presentation. We all know what they look like. But if the same student was giving a speech on the history of Coca-Cola, it would be interesting to see past Coke can designs or a lineup of all the various flavors available internationally.

So ask yourself, what is the purpose of the aid? To surprise? To entertain? To illustrate? To make some concept concrete? If you think your presentational aid will make your speech better, then it has value. If you think the audience will benefit from the visual aid, then it has value.

Value of an Item

If the item is precious to you, think twice about bringing it to class. Maybe there will be a rain or snow storm. You might drop it. Someone might take it. You are taking a chance by bringing in an item that has either a high financial or sentimental value.

Ease of Transportation

Think about what may happen to your object during transportation. Is it a large poster you are trying to carry on a subway? Does it weigh forty pounds? Do you have to carry it with you all day? Is it bigger than a breadbox? Is it alive? You want to consider how difficult your aid will be to transport, as well as what you are going to do with it before and after your speech.

Size of Object and Audience

Imagine spending hours preparing a series of graphs and charts for a speech on low-impact aerobics. However, no one beyond the third row saw them. This violates the cardinal rule of presentational aids: To be valuable, they need to be visible. Whether you use a flip-chart or bring in an object of some kind, people in the back of the room need to see it. If they cannot read what is on the table or cannot see the pie chart clearly, the aid does not serve its purpose.

Consider both object and audience size. Showing an 8″ x 10″ picture of Joseph Smith, founder of the Church of Latter Day Saints, would be appropriate in a small class but not in an auditorium. Bringing a coin to show the class is not helpful, unless the coin has little value, and each student can examine it. Students are better served by viewing an enlarged picture of the coin on a slide or poster. And, even if you bring in enough objects for everyone, you may lose their attention as they examine the object, drop it, or otherwise play with it during your speech.

Types of Presentational Aids

Presentational aids fall into four general categories or types: actual objects, three-dimensional models, two-dimensional reproductions, and technology-based. Each of these will be described in greater detail.

Actual Objects

Actual objects are just that—actual. Students have unlimited options. A student who had been stricken with bone cancer as a child, a condition that required the amputation of her leg, demonstrated to her classmates how her prosthetic leg functioned and how she wore it. Not one of her listeners lost interest in her demonstration.

Another student, seeking to persuade her audience to pressure their members of Congress to support stricter toy safety regulations, brought to class a box filled with toys that could injure, maim, or even kill young children. Her demonstration was so persuasive that everyone signed the speaker's petition to encourage Congress to pass stronger toy safety legislation.

Yet another student, concerned about the vast amount of disposable diapers that linger in our landfills, brought to class a (heavy) week's worth of dirty diapers from one infant. In addition to having some shock value (students being grossed out), it left a powerful image to accompany her statistics about the "shelf life" of a dirty diaper, and the average amount of space diapers consume in a community landfill.

As these examples demonstrate, actual objects can be effective visual aids. Because you are showing your audience exactly what you are talking about, they have the power to inform or convince unlike any other presentational aid.

In addition to the general criteria, when thinking about bringing an object to class, you need to be concerned with safety. Make sure the object you intend to use will not pose a safety risk to you or to your audience. Animals certainly fall into this category as well as chemicals and weapons. You may feel safe with your object(s), but that does not mean your classmates will feel safe. You think your little pet scorpion is adorable. It may terrify your classmates.

If your speech is about learning to play the violin, it would be good to bring your instrument along to demonstrate its features. *© Nicholas Sutcliffe, 2008. Under license from Shutterstock, Inc.*

Three-dimensional Models

If you decide that an actual object is too risky, a three-dimensional model may be your best choice. Models are commonly used to show the structure of a complex object. For example, a student who watched his father almost die of a heart attack used a model of the heart to demonstrate what physically happened during the attack. Using a three-dimensional replica about five times the size of a human heart, he showed how the major blood vessels leading to his father's heart became clogged and how this blockage precipitated the attack.

Models are useful when explaining various steps in a sequence. A scale model of the space shuttle, the shuttle launch pad, and its booster rockets will help you describe what happens during the first few minutes after blast-off.

Some replicas are easier to find, build, and afford than others. If you are delivering a speech on antique cars, inexpensive plastic models are available at a hobby shop and take little time to assemble. But if you want to show how proper city planning can untangle the daily downtown traffic snarl, you would have to build your own scaled-down version of downtown roads as they are now, and as you would like them to be—a model that would be too time-consuming and expensive to be feasible.

When considering using a three-dimensional model, you need to take into account the construction time and availability. It is possible you already have the model or you know where you can borrow one, so no construction time is needed. If, however, you need to create the three-dimensional model from a kit or your own imagination, you need to consider how much time it will take you to put it together. You do not want your construction time to take longer than your speech preparation.

If the three-dimensional model is in your possession, availability is not an issue. If it is in your bedroom, attic, or garage in your hometown, you need to take travel time into account. If you have to sign your life away to borrow it, or if you have to plan six weeks or more ahead to access the model, it may not be worth your trouble. If the model is sold at the local Wal-Mart, then availability is not an issue.

Two-dimensional Reproductions

Two-dimensional reproductions are the most common visual aids used by speakers. Among these are photographs, diagrams and drawings, maps, tables, and graphs.

Photographs

CAUTION

Although photographs are effective aids, avoid the negative impact. If a photograph truly offends or disgusts your audience, you have reduced the impact of your message.

Photographs are the most realistic of your two-dimensional visual choices and can have the greatest impact. For a speech on animal rights, a photo of a fox struggling to free his leg from a trap will deliver your message more effectively than words. If you are speaking about forest fire prevention, a photo of a forest destroyed by fire is your most persuasive evidence.

To be effective, photos must be large enough for your audience to see and using magazine or newspaper photos will not be as clear as a photo. If a photo is important to your presentation, consider enlarging it so the entire audience can see.

Drawings and Diagrams

When you cannot illustrate your point with a photograph—or would rather not use one—a drawing is an adequate alternative. A drawing is your own representation of what you are describing. If you are demonstrating the difference between a kettledrum and a snare drum, a simple drawing may be all you need. If you want to extend your explanation to show how musicians are able to control the pitch of the sound made by a drum, your drawing must include more detail. The location of the screws used to tighten the skin of the drum must be shown as well as the relation between the size of the drum and the pitch of the sound.

A detailed drawing showing the arrangement and relation of the parts to the whole is considered a diagram. Figure 7.4 is a simple diagram of a kettledrum. Labels are often used to pinpoint critical parts.

Avoid attempting a complex drawing or diagram if you have little or no artistic ability. Do not attempt to produce these drawings while your audience is watching. Prepare sketches in advance that are suitable for presentation. Keep your audience's needs—and limitations—in mind when choosing sketches. Too much detail will frustrate your audience as they strain to see the tiniest parts and labels. And when people are frustrated, they often stop listening. Imagine the glazed look in the audience's eyes in a basic speech course as they listen to someone using figure 7.5 to discuss the dimensions of the UH-60 Black Hawk helicopter.

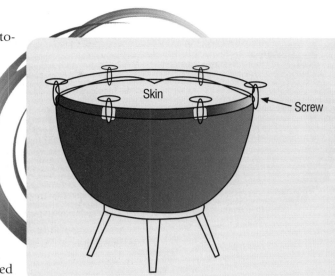

FIGURE 7.4

A simple diagram can show how the parts of objects such as this drum interact.

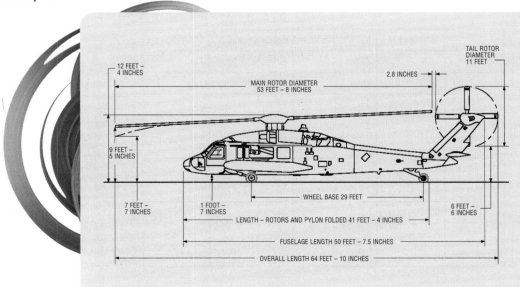

FIGURE 7.5

An intricate line drawing will only serve to frustrate your audience as they strain to see the details. Keep illustrations simple.

Maps

Weather reports on TV news have made maps a familiar visual aid. Instead of merely talking about the weather, reporters show us the shifting patterns that turn sunshine into storms. The next time you watch a national weather report, pay attention to the kind of map being used. Notice that details have been omitted because they distract viewers from what the reporter is explaining.

When talking about Europe's shrinking population, do not include the location of the Acropolis or the Eiffel Tower. Too much detail will confuse your audience. Because your map must be designed for a specific rhetorical purpose, you may have to draw it yourself. Start with a broad outline of the geographic area and add to it only those details that are necessary for your presentation.

On election night 2004, many news programs showed a map of the United States that was divided into "blue states" and "red states." Blue states were those where the majority of voters chose John F. Kerry, and red states were those where the majority of voters chose George W. Bush. The map (see figure 7.6) gave a quick update on where the candidates stood. This map was so successful as a visual aid, that the concept of "blue states" and "red states" has become part of our political vernacular.

FIGURE 7.6

This map shows "blue states" and "red states", making it easier to get a quick update on each candidate.

Tables

Tables focus on words and numbers presented in columns and rows. Tables are used most frequently to display statistical data. When delivering a speech on the fat content of food where you note the types and percentage of fat in nuts, you could refer to a table similar to that shown in figure 7.7) This single table should be divided into two parts because it contains too much information to present in one visual. Keep in mind the audience's **information absorption threshold**—the point at which a visual will cease to be useful because it says too much.

	Saturated	Monosaturated	Polyunsaturated	Other
Chestnuts	18%	35%	40%	7%
Brazil Nuts	15%	35%	36%	14%
Cashews	13	59	17	11
Pine Nuts	13	37	41	9
Peanuts	12	49	38	6
Pistachios	12	68	15	5
Walnuts	8	23	63	6
Almonds	8	65	21	6
Pecans	6	62	25	7
Hazelnuts	6	79	9	6

FIGURE 7.7

The fat content of food is measured in a single table.

Charts

Charts help the speaker display detailed information quickly and effectively. Charts can summarize data in an easy-to-read format, they can illustrate a process, or they can show relationships among things. **Flow charts** are used to display the steps, or stages, in a process. Each step is illustrated by an image or label. If you are an amateur cartoonist, you might give a talk on the steps involved in producing an animated cartoon. Figure 7.8 displays a simple flowchart of the process one goes through when a lamp does not light. This visual shows your audience that there is a sequence, and one is dependent on the other.

Pictorial flow charts are also effective. You can draw the pictures yourself or, if your artistic ability is limited, you can use a series of carefully selected photographs from a variety of sources. Flow charts that depend on words alone should use short, simple labels that move the audience through the stages of a process. Figure 7.9 shows how authority and responsibility are delegated in a corporation to meet organizational objectives.

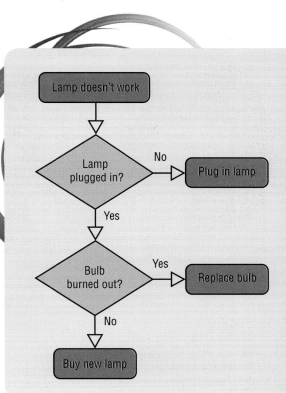

FIGURE 7.8
A simple flow chart of what to do if a lamp doesn't work.

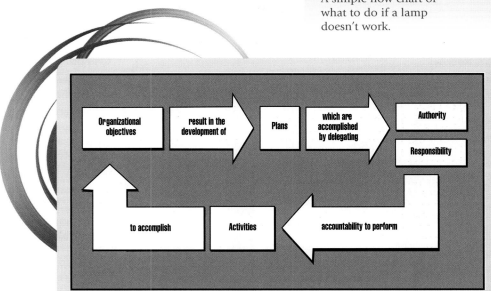

FIGURE 7.9
Flow charts can use blocked boxes and words to show how a corporation delegates authority and responsibility to achieve its objectives.

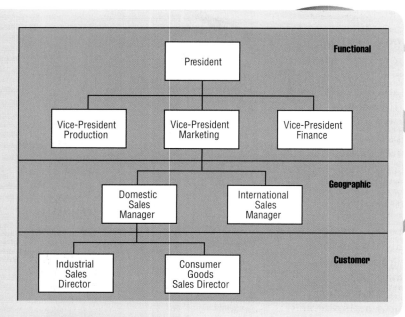

FIGURE 7.10

Almost every large group or company has an organization chart to illustrate the official hierarchy and lines of access.

Organizational charts reflect our highly structured world. Corporations, government institutions, schools, associations, religious organizations, and so on, are organized according to official hierarchies that determine the relationships of people as they work. You may want to refer to an organizational hierarchy in a speech if you are trying to show the positions of people involved in a project. By looking at a chart like that shown in figure 7.10, for example, your audience will know who reports to whom.

Graphs

When referring to statistics or when presenting complex statistical information, a visual representation can be extremely effective because it has the ability to simplify and clarify. Statistics may be presented in numerous ways, including bar graphs, pictographs, line graphs, and pie graphs.

In a speech urging students to consider teaching the social sciences and humanities in college, you want to show, graphically, that our universities will face a serious shortfall of liberal arts professors well into the twenty-first century. As part of your speech, you tell your audience:

There were days back in the 1980s when having a Ph.D. in history or sociology or English literature or philosophy guaranteed little or nothing. Indeed, many people who aspired to teach the humanities and social sciences were forced into menial jobs just to survive. So great was the supply of potential faculty over the demand that a new phenomenon was created: the taxi-driving Ph.D.

Today, the story is different. As you can see in this graph, by 1997 three out of ten faculty jobs in the humanities remained unfilled and it hasn't been until now that the situation gets any better.

The visual referred to is shown in figure 7.11, a bar graph of supply and demand projects for faculty members into the early part of the twenty-first century. The graph compares supply and demand figures for five-year periods and measures these figures in thousands. This type of graph is especially helpful when you are comparing two or more items. In

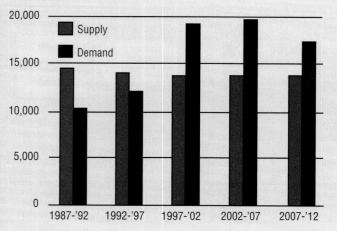

FIGURE 7.11

A speech to outline the projected need for new faculty as we face the next centurey can be enhanced by a bar graph such as this.

this case, one bar represents the supply of potential faculty while the other represents the potential demand for faculty. To make the trend clear, you may want to color code the bars.

Pictographs are most commonly used as a variation of the bar graph. Instead of showing bars of various lengths comparing items on the graph, the bars are replaced by pictorial representations of the graph's subject. For example, if you are giving a speech on the effects of television on book sales, you can use a pictograph like that shown in figure 7.12 to demonstrate the sales trend. The pictograph must include a scale explaining what each symbol means. In this case, each book represents 200 million books sold.

When you want to show a trend over time, the **line graph** may be your best choice. When two or more lines are used in one graph, comparisons are also possible. Figure 7.13 is a startling visual representation of the number of Irish immigrants entering the United States between 1820 and 1990. The tall peak in the graph represents the period of time when the potato famine was affecting the majority of Ireland. This simple graph could be used in a variety of speeches about Ireland and immigration.

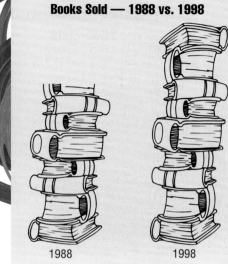

Books Sold — 1988 vs. 1998

1988   1998

FIGURE 7.12
Pictographs prove a twist on the traditional bar graph by using pictures or the items discussed to illustrate the "bar". The pictography should include an explanatory scale to explain what each symbol means, such as each book represents 200 million sold.

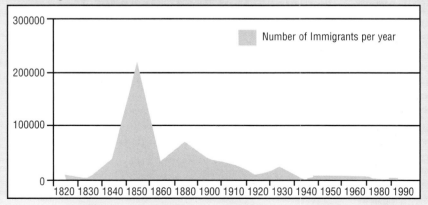

Irish Immigration to the United States (1820–1990)

Number of Immigrants per year

FIGURE 7.13
This is a graph of the number of Irish immigrants that entered the United States from 1820 to 1990. The climax of the migration was in 1851 when 221,253 Irish immigrants entered the United States. This was around the time when the potato famine was infesting the majority of Ireland. As the famine faded, the number of Irish immigrants decreased. It has gone up and down over time and is low today. This is because of the laws on European immigration. It takes many years before a citizen of Ireland can enter the U.S.

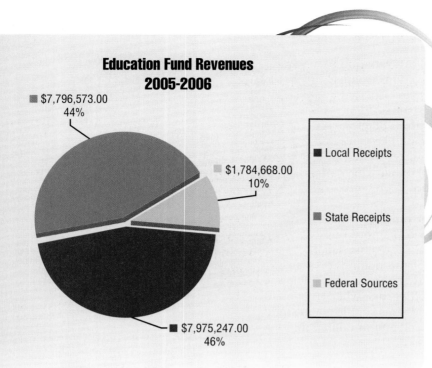

**Education Fund Revenues
2005-2006**

■ $7,796,573.00
44%

$1,784,668.00
10%

■ Local Receipts

■ State Receipts

Federal Sources

■ $7,975,247.00
46%

FIGURE 7.14

The pie chart effectively
illustrates how parts of a
whole are divided.

Pie graphs, also known as circle graphs, show your audience how the parts of an item relate to the whole. The pie chart is one of the most popular and effective ways to show how parts of a whole are divided. The pie is used frequently to display the division of expenses or resources a speaker wants an audience to see. The most simple and direct way to demonstrate percentages graphically is with an accurate pie graph. In a budget presentation to the local school board, the chief financial officer displayed a series of pie graphs. He explained that revenue comes from three levels, federal, state, and local. Figure 7.14 shows that taxes from local communities provide approximately half of the total revenue generated for the district. The federal government provides only ten percent, thus illustrating how dependent the school district is on local funding.

No matter what type of two-dimensional aid you choose, clarity is essential. It may happen that you create a two-dimensional aid that makes your audience think, "What does it *mean*?" Any presentational aid you use must clarify rather than confuse. If the aid contains too much information, your audience will be unable to process easily, and you may lose their attention. If you use graphs, pie charts, maps or tables, information must be understandable. For example, if you have an x-axis and a y-axis, they should be clearly labeled so your audience knows what you are referring to quickly and easily.

Displaying Two-dimensional Presentational Aids

When you decide to use a line graph to illustrate the volatility of the market place, your next decision involves how to display the graph. Speakers have numerous options for displaying two-dimensional presentational aids. The amount of time used and money does not necessarily indicate the effectiveness of a presentational aid. Sometimes emphasizing important points on a flip chart or using prepared overhead transparencies will be perfectly acceptable. This next section focuses on how to display the two-dimensional aid. In particular, we discuss the benefits and disadvantages of using blackboards, large post-its, posters, and flip charts.

Blackboard

It is a rare classroom that does not have some type of board to write on, be it black, green, or white. The blackboard is the universal presentational aid. One advantage is that you know it is already in the classroom, so you cannot lose or damage it. A second advantage is that it involves no preparation time (other than the day of presentation). It is the easiest visual aid to use and involves the least amount of preparation time.

For the most part, however, the blackboard should be limited to serving as the back-up plan. If your poster is ruined, you cannot find an easel for your flip chart, or the computer is not available or is malfunctioning, then the blackboard may become Plan B.

The blackboard requires neat, legible handwriting. Seldom is it acceptable to write on the blackboard *during the speech*, but if you must, try to write as little as possible. Use key terms only. If possible, arrive early and complete most, or all, of your visual presentation in advance. If the board has a screen above it, and you write on the board before your speech, pull the screen down until time for your presentation.

In terms of disadvantages, the blackboard is generally viewed as less professional than other presentational aids and your audience may interpret your use of it as indicating you have not prepared sufficiently. Also, when writing on the blackboard during your speech, you must turn your back to your audience as you write. Turning from your audience is never a good idea, and writing on the board cuts into your valuable speaking time.

Poster Board

Even posters have changed over the years. We used to be limited to a white background, and they were somewhat flimsy. Then colors were introduced, then vibrant colors were added as possible options, and now we can use poster-sized foam board in different colors.

When your parents were in school, the clarity of a poster was dependent on the art skills of the student since posters were made by hand. If your university has an instructional materials office of some kind, you can make your own posters, using die-cuts (generally, Ellison die-cuts). These allow you to cut out letters and shapes to make the poster look more professional. Even better, a computer lab on campus or a photocopying facility will allow access to poster-sized computer-generated graphics.

One primary advantage to using a poster board is that it is relatively inexpensive, and most students have used them before. A second advantage is that poster boards are useful in a classroom where computer-generated technology is not available or difficult to access, and third, they can display any type of two-dimensional information.

Three specific disadvantages of using poster boards are first, not everyone has the time, talent, or patience to create a professional-looking poster. Second, displaying the poster may be a problem if you do not have an easel or a chalkboard with a chalk tray, and third, they may get damaged during transportation.

Many of you have already abandoned poster board because you have the opportunity to use computer-generated graphics in the classroom. For those who do not, posters are still a viable way to display two-dimensional information.

Flip Chart

Flip charts are still a popular method for displaying two-dimensional information. According to Laskowski (2006), since most presentations are delivered before small groups of thirty-five people or less, the flip

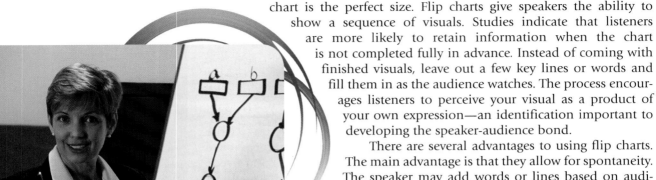

chart is the perfect size. Flip charts give speakers the ability to show a sequence of visuals. Studies indicate that listeners are more likely to retain information when the chart is not completed fully in advance. Instead of coming with finished visuals, leave out a few key lines or words and fill them in as the audience watches. The process encourages listeners to perceive your visual as a product of your own expression—an identification important to developing the speaker-audience bond.

There are several advantages to using flip charts. The main advantage is that they allow for spontaneity. The speaker may add words or lines based on audience response. A flip chart can be prepared in advance *or* during your speech. Other advantages are that they do not require electricity, they are economical, and one can add color to them easily (Laskowski 2006).

Disadvantages to using flip charts are they may not be seen by all, and they may be distracting. Laskowski (2006) suggests avoiding yellow, pink, or orange markers, and sticking to one dark color and one lighter color for highlighting. Also, less expensive paper may lead to the marker bleeding through to the following page.

A flip chart is most effective if you fill in a key point to help draw the audience in as you speak. © *Corbis*.

Repositional Note Pad

The large repositional note pad, most commonly known as a poster-sized Post-It, is a new breed of flip chart. Speakers can stick their presentational aid on a board or wall. These large sticky notes have useful application in group meetings where members brainstorm and then display the results on multiple pages around the walls. In your speech, you may want to have some pre-designed "Post-Its" that you stick on the board at different intervals for emphasis. These are most useful in classrooms lacking technology.

The two advantages to using poster-sized sticky notes are that you do not have to worry about chalk, tape, push pins, or staples, and you have tremendous flexibility. In addition to being able to stick just about anywhere, the speaker can write on it before or during the speech. The main disadvantage is that, as they are most likely hand-written, they may not look as professional as some other display techniques.

CAUTION

In general, a flip chart belongs on an easel. It looks more professional than leaning it on a blackboard, pages can be turned with little difficulty, and it provides needed support. Be sure an easel or similar stand is available. Many speakers come prepared with elaborate poster-board-mounted visuals only to find that they have no place to display them. If you place the flip chart on the blackboard, make sure it is stabilized, and that pages can be turned without dropping the chart.

General Suggestions for Using Presentational Aids

Do not let your presentational aid leave the lectern. When you pass things around the room, you compete with them as you speak. Your listeners read your handouts, play with the foreign coins, eat the cookies you baked, and analyze your models instead of listening to you. If handouts are necessary, distribute them at the end of the speech. When appropriate, invite people to take a close look at your displays after your speech.

Be aware of timing and pauses. Timing is important. Display each visual only as you talk about it. Do not force people to choose between paying attention to you and paying attention to your aid. If you prepare your flip chart in advance, leave a blank sheet between each page and turn the page when you are finished with the point. Cover your models with a sheet. Turn the projector off. Erase your diagram from the blackboard. Turn your poster board around. These actions tell your audience that you are ready to go on to another point.

Display your presentational aid, then pause two or three seconds before talking. This moment of silence gives your audience time to look at the display. You do not want to compete with your own visual aid. Try to avoid long pauses as you demonstrate the steps in a process. To demonstrate to his class how to truss a turkey, a student brought in everything he needed including a turkey, string, and poultry pins. He began by explaining the procedure but stopped talking for about five minutes while he worked. Although many members of the class paid attention to his technique, several lost interest. Without a verbal presentation to accompany the visual, their attention drifted to other things. Long periods of silence are not a good idea. Because most audiences need help in maintaining their focus, keep talking.

Make sure the equipment is working but be prepared for failure. Set up in advance. Make sure equipment is working *before* class, and know how to operate the equipment. Instructors are frustrated when time is wasted, and students will be bored if each speaker wastes valuable class time trying to figure out how the equipment works. Find out if the computer is equipped for a jump drive or zip disk. When things go wrong, you have to take responsibility for not being prepared.

Also, be prepared for equipment failure. What is Plan B? How much time are you willing to waste before you acknowledge that you cannot use the computer? Your audience may be sympathetic to your troubles, but we really do not want to hear you complain. Your presentation may be acceptable without the slide show. Perhaps you need to bring in a jump drive *and* a floppy disk. Maybe you want to use handouts or, as a back-up plan, write on the blackboard. The key here is the old Boy Scout motto, "Be prepared."

Use multimedia presentations only with careful planning and practice. Multimedia presentations can be effective, but they can be challenging. Gracefully moving from a flip chart to the computer to an overhead

Always be sure to test the equipment and know how to use it before your presentation. © *iofoto, 2008. Under license from Shutterstock, Inc.*

projector while maintaining audience interest requires skill that comes from practice and experience. Mixing media increases your chance that something will go wrong. You can mix media successfully, but careful planning and preparation is essential.

Technology-based Presentational Aids

Often, speakers must communicate statistics, trends, and abstract information in a clear manner. Thirty years ago, teacher education programs stressed the importance of being proficient at changing light bulbs in all machines, threading a film projector, using a tape recorder, putting slides in the slide projector, and operating the overhead projector. My, how things have changed!

Virtually all classrooms have black or white boards, and an overhead projector. As funds become available and technology costs decrease, more and more classrooms will be technology-enhanced. Students will bring their jump drives to class and incorporate PowerPoint presentations into their speeches. This does not mean, however, that *all* previous technology is rendered useless. Instances still exist where a tape-recording or slide projector may make more sense than a computer-generated slide presentation. This next section discusses audio and projected images.

Audio and Projected Images

Seldom will the blackboard be your only option for a presentational aid. Depending upon the needs of your audience, the content of your speech, and the speaking situation, you may choose a presentational aid requiring the use of other equipment.

Audiotape/CD

Not all presentational aids are visual, and incorporating some audio clip into your speech is a simple task. If you are trying to describe the messages babies send through their different cries, using an audiotape or CD may be appropriate, just as it would for a discussion of contemporary music. Of course, in a technology-enhanced room, students can access music and many sounds on the computer.

Take care when using an audio clip. Time is an issue, and the clip can overshadow the oral presentation if it consumes too much time. The inexperienced speaker may not have the audiotape or CD set up at the right spot or the right volume, and recording quality may be an issue. Getting set up on the computer may take too much time. Students need to check the equipment to make sure it is working, the volume is set correctly, and that it is properly queued.

Traditional Slides

A slide projector is no longer easy to find because digital cameras allow us to put pictures into a PowerPoint slide presentation. However, slides may be available that show historical sites, art from a particular collection, or plant biology. Rather than convert existing slides, a speaker may use a slide projector on occasion. The advantages to using traditional slides are that the slides already exist, and your library may have an extensive slide collection. Clearly, the primary disadvantage is not knowing how to operate the slide projector. Another disadvantage is that slide projectors may be more difficult to find.

Overhead Projector

Using an overhead projector allows you to face your listeners and talk as you project images onto a surface. They may be used in normal lighting, which is an important advantage to the speaker. You can face your listeners and use a pointer, just as you would if you were using any other visual. If you choose to remain near the projector instead, you run the risk of talking down to the transparency you are showing rather than looking up at your audience. Unlike slides, transparencies can be altered as you speak, such as underlining a phrase for emphasis or adding a key word.

Marjorie Brody (2006), president of Brody Communications Ltd., provides several suggestions for using transparencies during your presentation, including: using 18- point font or larger so the audience can read the information, numbering the sheets so you stay organized, using color to add appeal, and using multiple overlays to communicate different ideas.

Film/VHS/DVD

In certain situations, the most effective way to communicate your message is with a film, video, or DVD. Films are rarely used because videotapes and DVDs are more convenient and more readily available. In a speech on tornadoes, showing a video of the damage done by a tornado is likely to be quite impressive. Showing snippets of a press conference or showing a movie clip to illustrate or emphasize a particular point can also be interesting and effective.

The novice speaker giving a five-minute speech may not edit the video carefully enough, however. The result may be four minutes of video and one minute to speak. If you choose an audio or video clip, practice with them, plan how to use them, and know how to operate the equipment. Know what to do if the equipment fails.

It is also possible to be upstaged by your video clip. Your visual presentation—rather than your speech—may hold center stage. To avoid this, carefully prepare an introduction to support the video clip. Point your listeners to specific parts so they focus on what you want rather than on what happens to catch their interest. After the visual, continue your speech, and build on its content with the impact of your own delivery.

When thinking about using any of the above projected images, do not forget to allow for sufficient set-up time. Check the equipment to make sure you can operate it and that it is in good working order. Remember also, a darkened room can disrupt your presentation if you need to refer to detailed notes, and if you want students to take notes, the room may be too dark.

PowerPoint Slides

Not all classrooms are technology-enhanced, but soon they will be. In April 2006, Microsoft estimated that it had 400 million PowerPoint customers worldwide. It claims that PowerPoint can improve the way "you create, present, and collaborate on presentations" (office.microsoft.com).

We agree that PowerPoint slides can be used effectively within the public speaking environment, but we will also provide some guidelines. Not everything is meant for a slide presentation. Imagine what the Gettysburg Address might have looked like when accompanied by PowerPoint as shown in figure 7.15.

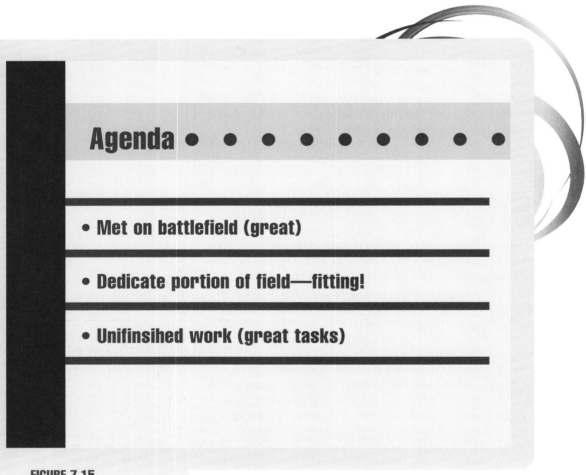

FIGURE 7.15
Not every speech is meant to be accompanied by a PowerPoint presentation.

"We have come to dedicate a portion of that field, as a final resting place for those who here gave their lives that that nation might live. It is altogether fitting and proper that we should do this. But, in a larger sense, we can not dedicate —we can not consecrate—we can not hallow—this ground. The brave men, living and dead, who struggled here, have consecrated it, far above our poor power to add or detract. The world will little note, nor long remember what we say here, but it can never forget what they did here. It is for us the living, rather, to be dedicated here to the unfinished work which they who fought here have thus far so nobly advanced. It is rather for us to be here dedicated to the great task remaining before us…"

Peter Norvig, current Director of Research at Google, provides the example above as a parody, but he argues that a slide presentation may reduce the speaker's effectiveness, because "it makes it harder to have an open exchange between presenter and audience to convey ideas that do not readily fit into outline format" (Norvig, 2003, 343).

Presentation specialist Dave Parodi (2004) urges people to "awaken themselves to the power of a well-designed, well-structured, well-delivered presentation, and work as hard as they can to make it happen." Author of the article "Scoring Power Points," Jamie McKenzie (2000) notes that in the best case, PowerPoint "enhances and communicates a larger and deeper body of work and thought"; however, in the worst case, "students will devote more attention to special effects than they will spend on the issues being studied".

Similarly, in *Wired* magazine, presentation graphics guru Edward R. Tufte (July 2006), notes that PowerPoint is a competent slide manager and projector but bemoans the fact that speakers often use PowerPoint to substitute rather than supplement a presentation. He argues, "Such misuse ignores the most important rule of speaking: Respect your audience".

For those in the public speaking arena, these words have great instructional value. The speaker needs to act with the listener in mind. This is true in terms of designing and using presentational aids as well as the development and delivery of the speech.

FIGURE 7.16
Dilbert causes a PowerPoint tragedy.
© *Scott Adams/Dist. by United Feature Syndicate, Inc.*

PowerPoint Guidelines

In newspapers across the country, the Dilbert cartoon from August 16, 2000 depicted a co-worker collapsing from "PowerPoint poisoning" when he heard Dilbert announce "slide 397" (figure 7.16). Many of you can relate to this cartoon. You probably learned how to create a PowerPoint presentation well before you reached college. By now, you have probably seen a hundred, if not a thousand, PowerPoint presentations.

Indeed, effective computer-generated graphics can have a great impact on your listeners. But the opposite is true, also. "Some of the world's most satisfying naps, deepest day dreams, and most elaborate notebook doodles are inspired by the following phrase, 'I'll just queue up this PowerPoint presentation,'" states Josh Shaffer, staff writer for the Raleigh, North Carolina *News & Observer* (April 27, 2006).

Given the ubiquitous nature of computer-generated graphics along with the fact that careful audience analysis is crucial, the following guidelines are offered. Although these relate to computer-generated graphics, much of the following information applies to most presentational aids.

1. ***Make sure the presentational aid fits your purpose, the occasion, and your audience.*** Developing a specific purpose early on in the speech process is not just an exercise to keep you busy. Katherine Murray, author of more than forty computer books, offers the suggestion, "Start with the end in mind" (www.microsoft.com). Think about your speech from beginning to end. Make sure you are clear on the purpose of your speech. Do this before deciding on any presentational aid. Knowing what you are trying to accomplish should guide you in designing your PowerPoint presentation.

   In addition to choosing a presentational aid that suits your purpose, you should also choose aids that are appropriate for the occasion. Certain situations are more serious or formal than others. Displaying a cartoon with little content or merit during a congressional hearing on the problems of the DC-10 aircraft diminishes the credibility of the speaker.

   As you determine your purpose, ask yourself whether the visual support is right for your listeners, considering their age, socioeconomic backgrounds, knowledge, and attitudes toward your subject. Consider their sensibilities, as some listeners are offended by visuals that are too graphic. Pictures of abused children, for example, can be offensive to an audience not prepared for what they will see. If you have doubts about the appropriateness of a visual, leave it out of your presentation.

2. ***Emphasize only relevant points.*** Do not be "PowerPointless," a word coined by Barb Jenkins of the South Australia Department of Education Training and Employment, meaning, avoid "any fancy transitions, sounds, and other effects that have no discernible purpose, use, or benefit" (www.wordspy.com). The bells and whistles may be fun, but they can be annoying, or worse, distracting.

   We have all seen PowerPointless presentations. One slide has the words "The facts" on it...and that is all. A second slide says "The causes," and a third slide says "The solution." Maybe each slide contains a cute picture, or perhaps there is an elaborate template. Lacking content, they were unnecessary.

   In your desire to create an attractive, professional slide presentation, do not forget the message. It is easy to find tips on general design, the number of words per slide, number of slides, images, transitions, color, and so on. But after you select the presentational aid that meets your purpose most effectively, think about what information needs to be on each slide.

Link only the most important points in your speech with a presentational aid. Focus on your thesis statement and main points and decide what words or concepts need to be highlighted graphically.

3. *Implement the "Rule of Six."* Use no more than six words per line, and no more than six lines per slide. Avoid using full sentences. This is an outline, not an essay. Make the text easy to read. Words need to be large enough, and do not think that using CAPITALIZED words will help. In addition to being a symbol for yelling when instant-messaging, it actually takes more effort to read words that are all capitalized. Try using 24-point type or larger. If the audience cannot read your slide, the message is lost.

Compare figure 7.17A with figure 7.17B. Similarities include the title, points covered, and organization. However, figure 7.17A violates many rules of effective PowerPoint, including too many icons (too busy), full sentences, and small font size. Figure 7.17B is clear, simple, and professional. The template used would be appropriate for all slides used for a presentation on traveling abroad.

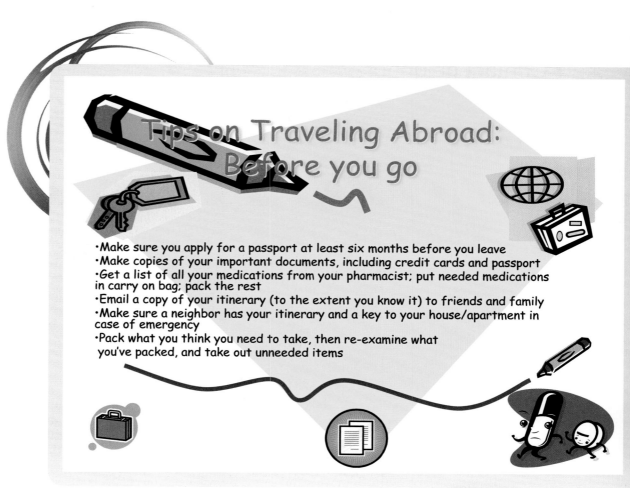

FIGURE 7.17A
What features make this an ineffective PowerPoint slide?

Tips on Traveling Abroad: Before you Go

- Apply for passport
- Copy important documents
- Visit pharmacy
- Email itinerary
- Contact neighbor
- Pack; Re-pack

FIGURE 7.17B
What features make this an
effective PowerPoint slide?

4. *Select appropriate design features.* Decisions need to be made regarding template, type of font, and color. The template, which provides color, style, and decorative accents may be distracting to your audience if you change it regularly. Use one template consistently. One can fritter away many minutes trying to determine what font-type (typeface) to use. In general, select something simple. While font-types may look fun, cute, or dramatic, they may also be hard to read, or distracting. Remember, keep your audience focused on the message; they may be distracted from the text if you have moving animations, and slides filled with "special effects."

Make sure the font-type and font-color complement the template. Rely on strong, bold colors that make your message stand out even in a large auditorium. In their article "About choosing fonts for presentations", Microsoft Office Online suggests, "To ensure readability, choose font colors that stand out sharply against the background" (Microsoft Office PowerPoint 2003). The words you place on the slide should not melt into the background color. Aim for contrast but keep in mind that the contrast you see on your computer screen may not exist on the projected screen.

The color wheel in figure 7.18 will help you choose contrasting colors. You will achieve the strongest contrasts by using colors opposite one another. When these complements are combined, they produce distinct images.

Blue and orange make an effective visual combination as do red and green, and so on. Colors opposite each other on this wheel provide the most striking contrasts for visual displays.

5. *Do not let your visual upstage you.* Keep in mind that your audience has come to hear you, not to see your presentational aids. If you create a situation in which the visual support is more important than the speaker or the purpose of the speech, you will have defeated your purpose.

With some exceptions, you will want to avoid using any presentational aid for the first few minutes. After you have set the tone of your speech and introduced your main idea you can turn to your first aid. Do not use a presentational aid to end your speech. Doing so eliminates the person-to-person contact you have built to that point by shifting the focus away from you.

6. *Preview and practice.* After creating your PowerPoint slides, run through them. Make sure slides are in the correct order, and that font-type, font-color, and font-size are consistent. Proofread and run spell check. Make printouts of your slides. Then practice the speech using your slides. According to a survey conducted by Dave Parodi (2003 (needs to be checked), the most annoying aspect of the PowerPoint presentation was when "The speaker read the slides to us." (Need more info. for references and need the page number after the quote here.)

One way to avoid sounding as though you are reading to the audience is through practice. Adding some type of presentational aid makes practicing even more important because you do not want to disrupt the flow of your speech.

During your practice session, focus on your audience, not your presentational aid. Many speakers turn their backs on the audience. They talk to the projection screen or poster instead of looking at the audience. To avoid this tendency, become familiar with your aid so that you have little need to look at it during your talk.

Color Wheel

Yellow-Green · Yellow · Yellow-Orange · Green · Orange · Blue-Green · Red-Orange · Blue · Red · Blue-Violet · Violet · Red-Violet

FIGURE 7.18

Colors opposite each other on this wheel provide the most striking contrast for visual displays. Using an overhead projector during your speech gives you greater flexibility than many other visual aids.

Summary

Presentational aids serve many different functions in a speech. They help to create interest in your subject; they make complex ideas clear and abstract ideas concrete. They help make your message memorable; they help to organize you.

Presentational aids fall into four general categories including actual objects, three-dimensional models, two-dimensional reproductions, and technology-based visual aids. Two-dimensional reproductions include photographs, diagrams and drawing, maps, tables, and charts. Two-dimensional visual aids can be mounted on poster board and displayed on an easel or displayed on a flip chart, or on repositional note pads. Technology-based visual aids include slides, film, videotape and audiotape, overhead projections, and computer-generated images.

Effective presentational aids are simple; they use bold, contrasting colors and they are large enough for everyone to read with ease. To present effective aids, choose the points in your speech that need visual support; set up your presentation in advance; never let your presentational aids upstage you. Use multimedia presentations only if they are well planned and rehearsed. Avoid repeating what your audience sees in the visual and learn to display each aid only when you are talking about it. Focus on your audience, not your visual. Display your visual, then pause before talking, although you need to avoid long pauses during demonstrations. Do not circulate your presentational aids around the room. Choose visuals appropriate for the audience and occasion and rehearse your presentation.

 ## Questions for Study and Discussion

1. What are the functions of presentational aids?
2. What are the different types of presentational aids?
3. What are the general criteria for using presentational aids?
4. What criteria must be met when thinking about particular presentational aids?
5. What should you know about displaying presentational aids?
6. What should you keep in mind as you design and develop a PowerPoint presentation?

 ## Activities

1. Plan to use presentational aids in your next speech. Spend enough time designing and preparing the visuals so they will have the impact you want.
2. Contact several business or professional speakers in your campus community or hometown. Based on what you have learned in this chapter, interview them about using visual aids in their presentations. Report your findings to your class, paying special attention to the similarities and differences in their approaches.
3. Locate individuals on your campus or in your community who produce presentational aids for speeches. Interview these specialists to learn the information they need to design effective aids and how much they cost. Consider both two-dimensional and technology-based visual aids and write a report on your findings.

References

Berg, K. and A. Gilman 1989. Get to the point: How to say what you mean and get what you want. New York: Bantam.

McKenzie, J. 2000. "Scoring PowerPoints", From *Now On, The Educational Technology Journal*, Vol. 10, No. 1

Molotsky, I. "No more than 1 in 5 athletes graduating at many schools," *New York Times*, September 10, 1989, A1 and 46.

Norvig, P. Accessed August 12, 2007. "PowerPoint: Shot with its own bullets," *The Lancet*, Vol. 362, No. 9381, pages 343–344.

Vogel, D. R., G. W. Dickson, and J. A. Lehman. 1986. "Persuasion and the role of visual presentation support: the UM/3M study," commissioned by Visual Systems Division of 3M.

"Let our advance worrying become advance thinking and planning."

Winston Churchill

Organizing and Outlining Your Ideas

The **organization of ideas** in public speaking refers to the placement of lines of reasoning and supporting materials in a pattern that helps to achieve your specific purpose. Following a consistent pattern of organization helps listeners pay attention to your message. An organized speech with connected main points helps you maintain a clear focus that leads listeners to a logical conclusion. An organized speech flows smoothly and clearly, from introduction through body to conclusion.

Your introduction and conclusion support the body of your speech. The **introduction** should capture your audience's attention and indicate your intent, and the **conclusion** reinforces your message and brings your speech to a close. The **body** includes your main points and supporting material that supports your specific purpose and thesis statement. The introduction and conclusion are important, but audiences expect you to spend the most time and effort amplifying your main points.

It is easy to detect disorganized speakers. Their presentations ramble from topic to topic as they struggle to connect ideas. As a listener, you may be confused about what the speaker is trying to communicate. In the following example, a disorganized speaker addresses an audience on the topic of addictions:

> We are a nation of addicts. Not only are we addicted to drugs and alcohol—the substances usually associated with addiction—millions of us are also addicted to gambling, shopping, promiscuous sex, overeating, relationships that tear down our self-esteem, and even shoes.
>
> Before I explain how researchers view these addictions, I want to say something about the thousands of self-help groups that have sprung up across the nation to save addicts from themselves—groups like Debtors Anonymous, Women Who Love Too Much, and Neurotics Anonymous. Well, maybe I should start with a discussion of what an addiction is. According to Florida State University researcher Alan Lang, quoted in *U.S. News & World Report*, "There is no single characteristic or constellation of traits that is inevitably associated with addiction." There are about 2,000 addiction groups that hold meetings each week, up twenty percent from a year ago.
>
> Now let's get back to the concept of addiction. Can someone really be addicted to soap operas in the same way they are addicted to cocaine? According to Harvey Milkman, professor of psychology at Metropolitan State College in Denver and co-author of *Craving for Ecstasy*, "The disease concept may be applied to the entire spectrum of compulsive problem behaviors" (*US News & World Report* 1990, 62–63).

Listening to this speech is like watching a ping-pong ball bounce aimlessly across a table. You never know where the speaker will land next or what direction the speech will take. If your ideas are organized, however, you will help your audience follow and understand your message.

Organizing the Body of Your Speech

The body of your speech should flow from your introduction. Therefore, reflect first on your specific purpose and thesis statement. Since your specific purpose is a statement of intent and your **thesis statement** identifies the main ideas of your speech, referring to them as you determine your main points will help prevent misdirection. For example, consider a speech discussing how family pets help children with psychological problems. You might develop the following:

> Specific purpose: *To explain to my class how pets can provide unexpected psychological benefits for children with emotional problems by helping to bolster their self-esteem.*
>
> Thesis statement: *A close relationship with a family pet can help children with emotional problems feel better about themselves, help therapists build rapport with difficult-to-reach patients, and encourage the development of important social skills.*

Your thesis statement indicates your speech will address self-esteem, rapport with therapists, and the development of social skills. This suggests that there are many peripheral topics you will *exclude*, such as the type of pet, pet grooming tips, medical advances in the treatment of feline leukemia, how to choose a kennel when you go on vacation, and so on.

1. Select Your Main Points

Organizing the body of your speech involves a *four-step process: selecting the main points, supporting the main points, choosing the best organizational pattern, and creating unity throughout the speech.* Before you think about organizing your speech, you need to decide which points are essential. They must relate to your specific purpose and thesis statement. An audience analysis should help direct you in terms of what points you need to make and the extent to which you need to support them.

Usually you should limit your main points to no fewer than two and not more than five. If you add more, you are likely to confuse your listeners.

Generate and Cluster Ideas

With your specific purpose and thesis statement clearly in mind, your next step is to generate a list of ideas consistent with the goals of your speech without critical evaluation initially. This stage is commonly known as **brainstorming**. Based on your research, write down ideas as they occur to you, using phrases or sentences. For purposes of illustration, consider the following:

> Specific Purpose: *To describe to my class the causes, symptoms, and treatment of shyness.*
>
> Thesis Statement: *Shyness, which is an anxiety response in social situations that limits social interactions, may respond to appropriate treatment.*

Based on your research, spend some time brainstorming to generate ideas for your speech.
© Leach-Anne Thompson, 2008. Under license from Shutterstock, Inc.

Your brainstorming process for the topic of shyness might result in a list of possible main points that include, but are clearly not limited to, the following: symptoms of shyness, shyness and heredity, shyness as an anxiety response, physical and psychological indications of shyness, number of people affected by shyness, shyness and self-esteem, how to handle a job interview if you are shy, treatment for shyness, and what to do when your date is shy.

Upon reflection, you may realize that several of these points overlap, and others do not relate as much to your thesis statement and should be discarded. So, you make the following list of six possible important points: Symptoms of shyness, causes of shyness, treatment for shyness, number of people affected by shyness, shyness as an anxiety response, and shyness and self-esteem.

With six being too many main points to develop, you decide that "shyness as an anxiety response" describes a symptom of shyness and that "shyness and self-esteem" describes a cause. You decide that a discussion of the number of people affected by shyness belongs in your introduction. Your final list of main points may look like this: symptoms of shyness, causes of shyness, treatment for shyness.

Through this process, you transformed a random list into a focused list of idea clusters reflecting broad areas of your speech. Your main points should be mutually exclusive; each point should be distinct. In addition, each point should be important in expressing your thesis statement.

 ## 2. Support Your Main Points

After selecting your main points, use the supporting material you gathered to strengthen each main point. Fitting each piece of research into its appropriate place may seem like completing a complex jigsaw puzzle. Patterns must be matched, rational links must be formed, and common sense must prevail. When you finish, each subpoint should be an extension of the point it supports. If the connection seems forced, reconsider the match. Here, for example, is one way to develop the three main points of the speech on shyness. As you sit at your computer, you can expand phrases into sentences. So for now, you can begin to think in terms of the language of your speech.

Main Point 1: *The symptoms of shyness fall into two categories: those that can be seen and those that are felt.*
- Objective symptoms (symptoms that can be seen) make it apparent to others that you are suffering from shyness. These include blushing, dry mouth, cold clammy hands, trembling hands and knocking knees, excessive sweating, an unsettled stomach, and belligerence.
- According to psychologist Philip Zimbardo, many shy people never develop the social skills necessary to deal with difficult situations (symptoms that are felt).
- They may experience embarrassment, feelings of inferiority or inadequacy, feelings of self-consciousnes, a desire to flee, and generalized anxiety. They overreact by becoming argumentative.
- Internal symptoms make the experience horrible for the sufferer.

Main Point 2: *Recent research has focused on three potential causes of shyness.*

• Heredity seems to play a large part.
• Psychologists at Yale and Harvard have found that ten to fifteen percent of all children are shy from birth.—Dr. Jerome Kagan of Harvard found that shy children are wary and withdrawn even with people they know.
• Shyness is also the result of faulty learning that lowers self-esteem instead of boosting self-confidence.
  • When parents criticize a child's ability or appearance or fail to praise the child's success, they plant the seeds of shyness by lowering self-esteem.
  • Older siblings may destroy a child's self-image through bullying and belittlement.
• Shyness is also attributable to poor social skills, due to never having learned how to interact with others, which leaves shy people in an uncomfortable position.

Main Point 3: *Shyness is not necessarily a life sentence; treatment is possible and so is change.*

• In a survey of 10,000 adults, Stanford University researchers found that forty percent said that they had been shy in the past but no longer suffered from the problem.
• People who are extremely shy may benefit from professional therapy offered by psychiatrists and psychologists.

As you weave together your main points and support, your speech should grow in substance and strength. It will be clear to your listeners that you have something to say and that you are saying it in an organized way.

3. Choose the Best Pattern for Organizing Your Main Points

The way you organize your main points depends on your specific purpose and thesis statement, the type of material you are presenting, and the needs of your audience. As you develop your main points, you need to consider what you want to emphasize. Assuming you have established three main points, you need to choose your emphasis. You have three options. First, you may choose the **equality pattern**, which involves giving equal time to each point. This means that you will spend approximately the same time on each point as you deliver your speech. If the body of your speech was nine minutes long, each point would take about three minutes to develop.

A second option is to use a **progressive pattern**, which involves using your least important point first and your most important point last. If you choose to emphasize one point over another, the nine minutes of the body might be broken up into approximately one and a half minutes on the first point, three minutes on the second point, and four and a half minutes on the third point.

Your third option is to follow the **strongest point pattern**. In this case, your first point would take about four and a half minutes, the second point would be given about three minutes, and your final point would take approximately one and a half minutes.

The pattern you choose depends on your topic and audience. The equality pattern makes sense if you have three main points you think are equally strong and important. Some people believe that the progressive pattern is most effective, suggesting it is the first point listeners will be most likely to remember. This concept is known as the **primacy effect.** Others believe in the strongest point pattern, suggesting it is your last point listeners will remember most. This is the **recency effect.** There is general agreement, however, that your strongest argument, or the aspect you want to emphasize most strongly does *not* go in the middle of your main points.

In addition to organizing your main points by emphasis, it is important to have an overall organizational framework. A speaker has many choices in terms of how to organize his or her speech, but based on the specific purpose statement, one pattern of organization is generally more appropriate than the others. The five effective patterns of organization we will cover are chronological, topic, spatial, causal, and problem-solution.

Chronological Organization

In a chronological speech, information is focused on relationships in time. Events are presented in the order in which they occur. When developing your speech chronologically, you can choose to organize your ideas by starting at the beginning and moving to the present, then looking to the future, or going step-by-step.

To show how different organizational patterns affect the content and emphasis of a speech, we will choose a topic, establish different purposes for speaking, and show how the presentation differs when the organizational pattern is changed.

In an informative speech on civil rights, you would likely include information about Rosa Parks' contributions to the cause.
© *Reuters/Corbis.*

Topic: *The civil rights movement.*
Specific Purpose: *To inform my audience of college students about certain crucial events that occurred in the civil rights movement between 1954 and 2007.*
Thesis statement: *The civil rights movement made dramatic progress from 1954 to 2007 as can be seen in events that occurred, legislature passed, and political involvement of African Americans.*

In an informative speech on the civil rights movement, the speaker could include the following events:

1. The 1954 U.S. Supreme Court decision (Brown vs. Board of Education) made school segregation unconstitutional.
2. In 1955, Rosa Parks refused to give her seat to a white rider on a bus in Montgomery, Alabama. African Americans boycotted city buses for a year, and the courts ruled bus segregation unconstitutional.
3. In 1964, Congress passed sweeping civil rights law.
4. In 1984, the Reverend Jesse Jackson ran for president and became of powerful spokesperson at the Democratic National Convention.
5. In 2005, Edgar Ray Killen, member of the KKK and the ringleader of murdering civil rights activists Goodman, Chaney, and Swerner is convicted of manslaughter on the forty-first anniversary of the crimes.

6. In 2007, U.S. Senator Barack Obama easily became a leading contender for the Democratic nomination as a candidate for the presidency.

To be consistent, every event you analyze must be woven into the existing chronological outline.

Past-Present-Future

Chronological order can also be used to construct a past-present-future organizational pattern. For example, if you were talking about the women's movement, you might have three points. First, you note that before the movement for women's equality, women's opportunities in the workplace were limited. Then you purport that today, greater opportunity is a reality, but women must cope with the dual responsibilities of career and home. Finally, you point out that you look forward to greater awareness from corporate America of women's dual roles and to accommodations that make the lives of working women easier. Using a past-present-future order allows a speaker to provide perspective for a topic or issue that has relevant history and future direction or potential.

Step-by-Step

Chronological patterns can be used to describe the steps in a process. Here is a step-by-step description of how college texts are produced. Like the other patterns, the process shows a movement in time:

Step 1: *The author, having gathered permissions for use of copyrighted material, delivers a manuscript to the publisher.*
Step 2: *The manuscript is edited, a design and cover are chosen, photos are selected, and illustrations are drawn.*
Step 3: *The edited manuscript is sent to a compositor for typesetting and set in galley and page proof form.*
Step 4: *The final proof stage is released to the printing plant where the book is printed and bound.*

Spatial Organization

In speeches organized according to a spatial pattern, the sequence of ideas moves from one physical point to another—from London to Istanbul, from basement to attic, from end zone to end zone. To be effective, your speech must follow a consistent directional path. If you are presenting a new marketing strategy to the company sales force, you can arrange your presentation by geographic regions—first the East, then the South, then the Midwest, and finally, the West. If, after completing the pattern, you begin talking about your plans for Boston, your listeners will be confused.

Using space as the organizational key, our speech on civil rights takes the following form. Although the central topic is the same, the pattern of organization is tied to a different specific purpose and core idea:

Specific Purpose: *To inform my audience of college students how the civil rights movement spread across the nation.*

Thesis Statement: *The civil rights movement spread from the cities and rural areas of the South to the inner-city ghettos of the North and West.*

1. In places like Selma and Montgomery, AL and Nashville, TN, white brutality led to civil rights boycotts and protests.
2. Angry African Americans, pent up and hopeless in inner-city ghettos, rioted in Harlem, Newark, Chicago, and Detroit.
3. Riots took place in the Los Angeles ghetto of Watts, resulting in many deaths, far more arrests, and enormous losses from arson and looting.
4. In our 21st century we can easily see that African-Americans have become highly visible leaders in business, politics, education and religion, but the civil rights movement is still active, addressing issues of inequality and violence against minorities.

Cause and Effect

You may find that the most logical and effective way to organize is to arrange your main points into causes and effects. Here are the main points of our speech on civil rights arranged in a cause and effect pattern:

Specific Purpose: *To inform my audience of college students how the suffering experienced by African Americans in the 1950s and 1960s created the environment for social change.*

Thesis Statement: *Racial discrimination in America during the 1950s and 1960s made sweeping social change inevitable.*

Through the 1950s and early 1960s, discrimination prevented African Americans from using public accommodations, being educated with whites, riding in the front of buses, exercising their constitutional right to vote, being hired by corporations, and working for equal pay.

This pattern of discrimination resulted in landmark Supreme Court cases such as Brown vs. Board of Education, which declared separate but equal schools unconstitutional; the hugely successful march on Washington in 1963; and the passage in 1964 of the Civil Rights Act. With the cause and effect organizational pattern, the speaker can focus specifically on why something happened and what the consequences of the event or action were.

Problem-Solution Organization

A common strategy, especially in persuasive speeches, is to present an audience with a problem and then examine one or more likely solutions. For example, in a classroom speech, one student described a serious safety problem for women students walking alone on campus after dark.

Persuasive speeches often present an audience with a problem and examine potential solutions.© *Corbis.*

He cited incidents in which women were attacked and robbed and described unlit areas along campus walkways where the attacks had taken place. Next, he turned to a series of proposals to eliminate, or at least minimize, the problem. His proposals included a new escort service, sponsored and maintained by various campus organizations, the installation of halogen lights along dark campus walks, and the trimming of bushes where muggers could hide.

Occasionally, speakers choose to present the solution before the problem. Had this student done so, he would have identified how to provide effective security before he explained why these solutions were necessary. Many audiences have trouble with this type of reversal because they find it hard to accept solutions when they are not familiar with the problems that brought them about.

Let us turn, once again, to our speech on civil rights, this time arranging the material in a problem-solution pattern.

Specific Purpose: *To persuade my audience of college students that, although the civil rights movement has reduced racial discrimination in many areas, the movement must continue to press for equality in education and employment.*
Thesis Statement: *The civil rights movement in America must remain strong and active because discriminatory patterns still exist in education and employment.*

Problem: Discrimination in education and employment has perpetuated a culture of poverty and joblessness for millions of African Americans who remain second-class citizens despite the gains of the civil rights movement.

Solution: Joblessness, and the poverty that results from it, must be addressed through job training programs and by continuing to pressure corporations to hire minorities through affirmative action programs.

Here, the goal is to persuade an audience that a problem still exists and to have listeners agree about how it can be effectively handled.

Topical Organization

The most frequently used organizational system is not tied to time or space, problem or solution, or cause or effect, but, instead, to the unique needs of your topic. The nature and scope of your topic dictate the pattern of your approach.

Working within the confines of your topic, you determine a workable pattern. If you are delivering an after-dinner humorous speech on the responses of children to their first week of preschool, you can arrange your topics according to their level of humor. For example:

1. The *school supplies* preschoolers think are necessary to survive at school.
2. The *behavior of youngsters at school* when they do not get their own way.
3. Children's stories of *their lives at home.*
4. *The reasons children believe their parents send them to school.*

These topics relate to children and their first week at school, but there is no identifiable chronological pattern, so topical order makes sense. When organizing topically, think about how to link and order topics. Transitions can help the audience understand the connections and will be discussed in the following section.

The following example shows how a speech on the civil rights movement might be treated using a topical organizational pattern.

Specific Purpose: *To inform my audience of college students about how the emergence of African American leaders in American politics and government influences the struggle for civil rights in our county.*

Thesis Statement: *The movement for civil rights is being waged from within the political establishment, and African Americans are achieving key positions in politics and in government.*

- Jesse Jackson became a leader in the Democratic party and succeeded in working within the system to register tens of thousands of African Americans to vote.
- Clarence Dinkins served as Mayor of New York City from 1990–1993.
- Clarence Thomas was appointed to the U.S. Supreme Court by President George H. W. Bush in 1991, and in 2004 President George W. Bush appointed Condoleezza Rice to be secretary of state for the United States.

Jesse Jackson's key role as a leader in the Democratic party could be a main point in a topical organizational pattern speech on civil rights. © *Reuters/Corbis.*

4. Create Unity Through Connections

Without connections, your main points may be difficult to follow. Your audience may wonder what you are trying to say and why you have tried to connect ideas that do not seem to have any relationship with each other. To establish the necessary connections, use transitions, internal previews, and internal summaries.

Transitions

Transitions are the verbal bridges between ideas. They are words, phrases, or sentences that tell your audience how ideas relate. Transitions are critical because they clarify the direction of your speech by giving your audience a means to follow your organization. With only one opportunity to hear your remarks, listeners depend on transitions to make sense of your ideas.

It helps to think of transitions as verbal signposts that signal the organization and structure of your speech. Here are several examples:

"The first proposal I would like to discuss…"
This tells listeners that several more ideas will follow.
"Now that we've finished looking at the past, let's move to the future."
These words indicate a movement in time.
"Next, I'll turn from a discussion of the problems to a discussion of the solutions."
This tells your listeners that you are following a problem-solution approach.
"On the other hand, many people believe…
Here you signal an opposing viewpoint.

The following is a list of common transitional words and the speaker's purpose in using them.

Speaker's Purpose	Suggested Transitional Words
1. To define:	*that is to say; according to; in other words*
2. To explain:	*for example; specifically*
3. To add:	*furthermore; also; in addition; likewise*
4. To change direction:	*although; on the other hand; conversely*
5. To show both sides:	*nevertheless; equally*
6. To contrast:	*but; still; on the contrary*
7. To indicate cause:	*because; for this reason; since; on account of*
8. To summarize:	*recapping; finally; in retrospect; summing up*
9. To conclude:	*in conclusion; therefore; and so; finally*

(Makay and Fetzger 1984, 68)

Internal Previews and Summaries

Internal previews are extended transitions that tell the audience, in general terms, what you will say next. These are frequently used in the body of the speech to outline in advance the details of a main point. Here are two examples:

- I am going to talk about the orientation you can expect to receive during your first few days on the job, including a tour of the plant, a one-on-one meeting with your supervisor, and a second meeting with the personnel director, who will explain the benefits and responsibilities of working for our corporation.
- Now that I've shown you that "junk" is the appropriate word to describe junk bonds, we will turn to an analysis of three secure financial instruments: bank certificates of deposit, Treasury bonds, and high quality corporate paper.

In the second example, the speaker combines a transition linking the material previously examined with the material to come with an internal preview. Previews are especially helpful when your main point is long and complex. They give listeners a set of expectations for what they will hear next. Use them whenever it is necessary to set the stage for your ideas (Turner 1970, 24–39).

Internal summaries follow a main point and act as reminders. Summaries are especially useful if you are trying to clarify or emphasize what you have just said, as is shown in the following two examples:

- In short, the American family today is not what it was forty years ago. As we have seen, with the majority of women working outside the home and with divorce and remarriage bringing stepchildren into the family picture, the traditional family—made up of a working father, a nonworking mother, and 2.3 kids—may be a thing of the past.
- In sum, the job market seems to be easing for health care professionals, including nurses, aides, medical technicians, physical therapists, and hospital administrators.

When summaries are combined with previews, they emphasize your previous point and make connections to the point to follow:

> In sum, it is my view that cigarette advertising should not be targeted specifically at minority communities. As we have seen, R. J. Reynolds test-marketed a cigarette for African Americans known as ``Uptown,'' only to see it come under a barrage of criticism. What is fair advertising for cigarette makers? We will discuss that next.

Organization plays an important role in effective communication. The principles rhetoricians developed five centuries ago about the internal arrangement of ideas in public speaking have been tested by time and continue to be valid. Internal previews and summaries help the speaker create meaning with the audience by reinforcing the message and identifying what is coming next. Keep in mind that audience members do not have the opportunity to replay or to stop for clarification. Using transitions, previews, and internal summaries are tools a speaker can use to facilitate understanding and reduce the potential for misunderstanding (Clarke 1963, 23–27; Daniels and Whitman 1981, 147–160).

Constructing an Outline and Speaker's Notes

Presenting your ideas in an organized way requires a carefully constructed planning outline and a key-word outline to be used as speaker's notes. Both forms are critical to your success as an extemporaneous speaker—one who relies on notes rather than a written manuscript. Your outline is your diagram connecting the information you want to communicate in a rational, consistent way. It enables you to assemble the pieces of the information so that the puzzle makes sense to you and communicates your intended meaning to your audience. Think of outlining as a process of layering ideas on paper so that every statement supports your thesis. It is a time-consuming process, but one that will pay off in a skillful, confident presentation (Sprague and Stuart 1992, 92).

Be familiar with the criteria for each speech assignment. Each instructor has his or her own requirements. Some may want to see your planning outline and speaker's notes while others may not. Instead of a planning outline, your instructor may ask you to turn in a full-sentence outline that includes points, subpoints, source citation, and reference page, but excludes statements about transitions or speech flow. The following discussion is designed to help you develop and, by extension, deliver, an effective speech. Your instructor will have specific ideas about the outline and note cards.

What information would you include in your planning outline? © *Laurence Gough, 2008. Under license from Shutterstock, Inc.*

The Planning Outline

The planning outline, also known as the full-content outline, includes most of the information you will present in your speech. It does not include every word you plan to say, but gives you the flexibility required in extemporaneous speaking.

When developing a planning outline, it is important to use a traditional outline format that allows you to see the interconnections among ideas—how some points are subordinate to others and how main ideas connect. In a traditional outline, roman numerals label the speech's main ideas. Subordinate points are labeled with letters and numbers.

The proper positioning of the main and subordinate points with reference to the left margin is critical, for it provides a visual picture of the way your speech is organized. Be consistent with your indentation. The main points are along the left margin, and each sub-point is indented. Each sub-sub-point is indented under the sub-point. This visual image presents a hierarchy that expresses the internal logic of your ideas.

The outline labels (introduction, body, conclusion) remind the speaker to give each section appropriate attention, focusing on the objectives of each section. These labels should be written in the left-hand margin of your outline.

The following "boilerplate" suggests the format for a speech.

Name:
Specific purpose:
Thesis statement:

Title of Speech

Introduction
I.   Capture attention and focus on topic
II.   Set tone and establish credibility
III. Preview main points

Body
I.   First main point
   A. First subordinate (sub-) point to explain first main point
      1. First sub-point/supporting material for first sub-point
         a. Sub-point that provides greater details or explanations
         b. Sub-point that provides more details, examples, or explanations to clarify and explain
      2. Second sub-point/supporting material for first sub-point
   B. Second subordinate (sub-) point to explain first main point
      1. First sub-point/supporting material for second sub-point
      2. Second sub-point/supporting material for second sub-point
         a. Sub-point that provides greater details or explanations
         b. Sub-point that provides more details, examples, or explanations to clarify and explain

II. Second main point
   A. First subordinate (sub-) point to explain second main point
      1. First sub-point/supporting material for first sub-point
         a. Sub-point that provides greater details or explanations
         b. Sub-point that provides more details, examples, or explanations to clarify and explain
      2. Second sub-point/supporting material for first sub-point
   B. Second subordinate (sub-) point to explain second main point
      1. First sub-point/supporting material for second sub-point
      2. Second sub-point/supporting material for second sub-point

III. Third main point
    A. First subordinate (sub-) point to explain third main point
    B. Second subordinate point to explain third main point
       1. First sub-point/supporting material for second sub-point
       2. Second subpoint/supporting material for second sub-point

Conclusion
I.   Summary of main points
II. Relate to audience
III. Provide closure/final thought
References (on separate sheet)

Notice the particulars:

1. Your name, the specific purpose, thesis statement, and title of your speech are all found at the top of the page.
2. Each section (introduction, body, and conclusion) is labeled.
3. Each section begins with the Roman numeral "I."
4. Each level has at least two points. So if you have "I," minimally, you will see a "II." If you have an "A," minimally, you will see a "B." You should never have just one point or sub-point.
5. Each point is not developed identically. In some cases, there are sub-points and sub-sub-points. One point may need more development than another point.

A well-constructed planning outline ensures a coherent, well-thought-out speech. Using full sentences defines your ideas and guides your choice of language. Phrases and incomplete sentences will not state your points fluently, nor will they help you think in terms of the subtle interrelationships among ideas, transitions, and word choice.

Check with your instructor to see if you should have a regular planning outline or a full-sentence outline. A full-sentence outline requires that each point have one full-sentence. This means no sentence fragments, and no more than one sentence per point.

Include at the end of your planning outline a reference page listing all the sources used to prepare your speech, including books, magazines, journals, newspaper articles, videos, speeches, and interviews. If you are unfamiliar with documentation requirements, check the style guide preferred by your instructor, such as the *American Psychological Association (APA) Publication Manual* (online access at www.apastyle.apa.org), and the *Modern Literature Association (MLA) Handbook for Writers of Research Papers* (online access at www.mla.org).

Check with your instructor to see how detailed your source citation should be in the outline. Check to see if you should include last name, credentials, type of book (or magazine, journal, web page, etc.), year/date of publication?

Transitional sentences are valuable additions to your planning outline. They are needed when you move from the introduction to the body to the conclusion of the speech. They also link various main points within the body and serve as internal previews and summaries. Put these sentences in parentheses between the points being linked and try to use the language you may actually speak. When appropriate, include internal summaries and previews of material yet to come.

Here is an example of a planning outline that includes transitional sentences.

Speaker's name: *Jim Doe*
Specific Purpose: *To provide a solution to the problem that marriageable young men outnumber marriageable young women.*
Thesis Statement: *Because there are far more unmarried men in their twenties than there are women in the same age group, young men often find it harder to meet eligible partners.*

Title of Speech: *Young women take control of the marriage pool*

Introduction
I.   It wasn't that long ago that sociologists were telling us that there were far more women of marriageable age than men.
  A. A report issued by the University of California at Berkeley told us that if we tried to match each woman born in 1950 with a man three years older, we would have millions of women left over.
  B. Neil G. Bennett, Patricia H. Craig, and David E. Bloom, researchers at Yale, predicted a lifetime of singlehood for college-educated women who postponed marriage into their thirties and forties.
II. New data from the U.S. Census Bureau suggests this trend has reversed itself for people in their twenties.
  A. For every five single young women in their twenties, there are now six single young men.
  B. Young women now have the advantage.

(Transition): Since I already see the men in my audience squirming and the women smiling, you must realize that the implications of this demographic shift are enormous. Because there are far more unmarried men in their twenties than there are women in the same age group, young men today find it harder to meet eligible partners.

We will look at the problem men face from a number of different perspectives, including loneliness, pressure from corporations to marry, and the growing rivalry between older and younger men for the same women. At the end of the speech, we will examine some possible solutions.

Body

I.   Before we begin, let's take a closer look at the hard data from the Bureau of Census.
  A. About twenty years ago there were 19.9 million men and 20.4 million women in their early twenties.
  B. However, there also were about 2.3 million more unmarried men in their twenties than unmarried women in the same age group.
    1. In part, this statistic is explained by the fact that women tend to marry older men, thus removing themselves from the marriage pool.
    2. Since the number of births in the United States fell by an average of 1.7 percent a year between 1957 and 1975, the men born in any given year outnumber the women born in the years that follow, making it even more difficult for men to find a mate.

II. The result is that an increasing number of young men find themselves without a date on Saturday night.
   A. These men are lonely.
   B. Young male college graduates also feel the pressure to marry in order to get the right job in corporate America.
      1. According to career consultants, many corporations view unmarried men in their thirties as oddballs.
      2. Corporations expect their young male managers to marry by the age of thirty.
   C. Young men resent older men who date younger women.
      1. According to William Beer, the deputy chairman of the sociology department at New York's Brooklyn College, young men feel that these older men are "poaching."
      2. Older men claim they are just following a traditional pattern.

(Transition): Why are younger women attracted to older men, especially with a glut of younger men to choose from?

III. Older men are perceived as more sophisticated.
   A. They have had more time to explore the world and their personal interests.
   B. "The older men that I have met have done so much after college … that I haven't done," said Martha Catherine Dagenhart, then a senior at the University of North Carolina at Chapel Hill.

IV. Older men have more money.
   A. A thirty-year-old man may have worked eight years longer than a twenty-two-year-old college graduate.
   B. Many older men have money in the bank.

V. Older men are perceived as more powerful.
   A. An attractive woman in her twenties may be willing to have a relationship with a man in his forties if he's achieved a certain status in society.
      1. Often an executive will marry an assistant who sees him as a powerful person.
      2. Film stars and other major celebrities or prominence find themselves with women much younger then they are because of the power or status that goes with being a famous entertainer.
   B. Many older men cultivate an image of power and influence.

(Transition:) Now that we've examined the extent and implications of this phenomenon and looked at the reasons young women are attracted to older men, let's look at what eligible bachelors in their twenties can do.

Conclusion
I. One solution to this problem is that young men in their twenties date older women.
   A. Unmarried women over thirty still outnumber men in the same age group.
   B. Women have traditionally dated older men, so demographic realities may force men to consider doing the same.

II. Men can be less selective in their choice of mates.
  A. An "I'm not willing to settle" attitude may leave many men without a companion.
  B. Turning to the Internet is currently popular, in part because of the difficulty men may have in initiating a relationship with someone they do not know.

III. Men must learn to accept the fact that they no longer have a ready supply of eligible partners—a fact older women have struggled with for years.

References

Bradsher, K. *For every five young women, six young men. New York Times, (1990, January 17), pp. C1 and C10.*

Bradsher, K. *Young men pressed to wed for success. New York Times, (1989, December 13), pp. C1 and C12.*

Too late for Prince Charming? (1986, June 2). Newsweek, June 2, 54–61.

A Brief Analysis of the Planning Outline

When applying a real topic to the boilerplate provided earlier, it is easy to see how the process unfolds. Note how transitions work, moving the speaker from the introduction of the speech to the body, from one main point to the next and, finally, from the body of the speech to the conclusion.

Remember, although the word "transition" appears in the outline, it is not stated in your speech. Transitions help connect listeners in a personal way to the subject being discussed. It also provides the thesis statement and previews the main points of the speech.

Notice that quotes are written word for word in the outline. Also, note the preview that is included at the end of the transition from introduction to body. Once stated, the audience will know the main ideas you will present.

As the outline proceeds from the first- to the second- to the third-level headings, the specificity of details increase. The planning outline moves from the general to the specific.

Speaker's Notes

Speaker's notes are an abbreviated key-word outline, lacking much of the detail of the planning outline. They function as a reminder of what you plan to say and the order in which you plan to say it. Speaker's notes follow exactly the pattern of your planning outline, but in a condensed format.

Follow the same indentation pattern you used in your planning outline to indicate your points and subpoints. Include notations for the introduction, body, and conclusion and indicate transitions. It is helpful to include suggestions for an effective delivery. Remind yourself to slow down, gesture, pause, use visual aids, and so on. This will be helpful during your speech, especially if you experience speech tension.

Include only the necessary information in your speaker's notes to remind you of your planned points.
© *Lawrence Gough, 2008. Under license from Shutterstock, Inc.*

Guidelines for Constructing Speaker's Notes

1. *Avoid overloading your outline.* Many speakers feel that the more information they have in front of them, the better prepared they will be to deliver their speech. The opposite is usually true. Speakers who load themselves with too many details are torn between focusing on their audience and focusing on their notes. Too often, as they bob their heads up and down, they lose their place.

2. *Include only necessary information.* You need just enough information to remind you of your planned points. At times, of course, you must be certain of your facts and your words, such as when you quote an authority or present complex statistical data. In these cases, include all the information you need in your speaker's notes. Long quotes or lists of statistics can be placed on separate index cards or sheets of paper.

3. *Reduce your sentences to key phrases.* Instead of writing: "The American Medical Association, an interest group for doctors, has lobbied against socialized medicine;" write: "The AMA and socialized medicine." Your notes should serve as a stimulus for what you are going to say. If you only need a few words to remind you, then use them. For example, a speaker who had directed several high school musicals planned to discuss the various aspects of directing a high school musical. Her speaker's notes could include the key words "casting," "blocking," "choreography," "singing," and "acting." Little else would be needed, since she can define and/or describe these aspects of directing. However, under the key word "casting," she might include "when to cast," and "how to cast." Relevant quotes or perhaps a reference to a dramatic story would be included in the notes as well.

4. *Include transitions, but in an abbreviated form.* If you included each transition, your notes would be too long, and you would have too much written on them. Look at one of the transitions from the previous speech about men and marriage:

   > *(Transition):* Since I already see the men in my audience squirming and the women smiling, you must realize that the implications of this demographic shift are enormous. Because there are far more unmarried men in their twenties than there are women in the same age group, young men today find it harder to meet eligible partners.
   >
   > We will look at the problem men face from a number of different perspectives, including loneliness, pressure to marry from corporations, and the growing rivalry between older and younger men for the same women. At the end of the speech, we will examine some possible solutions.

   Instead of these two paragraphs, your speaker's notes might look like this:

   Men squirming/women smiling
   More unmarried men than women
   Problems: loneliness, pressure to marry, growing rivalry

   If you practice your speech, these words should suffice as notes. Abbreviate in a way that makes sense to you. Each person will have his or her own version of shorthand.

5. *Notes must be legible.* Your notes are useless if you cannot read them. Because you will be looking up and down at your notes as you speak, you must be able to find your place with ease at any point. Do not reduce your planning outline to 8-point and paste it to note cards. If you can type your notes, make sure they eare 14-point or larger. If you write your notes, take the time to write legibly. Think about this: You may have spent several hours researching, preparing, and organizing your speech. Why take the chance of reducing the impact of your speech by writing your notes at the last minute?

Following is an example of a set of speaker's notes. The transformation from planning outline to key-word outline is noticeable in terms of length and detail. Transitions, delivery hints, and the parts of the outline are emboldened.

Sample speakers' notes from the speech,

Young Women Take Control of the Marriage Pool

(Introduction)

I. Sociology and the male/female dating ratio.
   A. Berkeley study: 3 million women born in 1950 will never have a mate
   B. Yale study

II. New Census Bureau data
   A. Ratio five single women to six single men in their twenties
   B. Advantage: women

(Look around room. Make eye contact. Slow down.)

(Men are finding it hard to meet mates. We will examine the problem and its implications.)

(Body)
(Slow down)

I. Closer look at data
   A. 19.9 million men, 20.4 million women in their twenties
   B. However, 2.3 million more unmarried men
      1. Women marry older men
      2. How declining birth rate affects pool of marriageable singles

II. Result for men: No dates
   A. Loneliness
   B. Pressure to marry from corporate America
      1. Unmarried "oddballs"
      2. Climb the corporate ladder: marry by thirty
   C. Young and old fight for same women
      1. William Beer, Brooklyn College sociologist: "Older men are poaching."
      2. Men are following tradition

(Why are younger women drawn to older men?)
III. More sophisticated.
    A. Time to explore interests and the world.
    B. *"The older men that I have met have done so much after college that I haven't done."* (Martha Catherine Dagenhart, senior at U. of NC at Chapel Hill.)

IV. More money
    A. Working longer
    B. Money in the bank

V. More powerful.
    A. Relationships based on status of man
        1. E.g., administrative assistant marries boss
        2. Stereotype: May–September marriages
    B. Older men cultivate the image of power

(Conclusion)
(Make eye contact during list)
I. Date older women
    A. Plenty of women over thirty
    B. Women have always dated older men

II. Be less picky
    A. "I'm not willing to settle."
    B. Try to meet someone through the Internet

III. Accept and adjust

A Brief Analysis of Speaker's Notes

Including your specific purpose and thesis statement in your speaker's notes is unnecessary. Speaker's notes follow exactly the pattern of the planning outline so you maintain the organizational structure and flow of your speech. The introduction, body, and conclusion are labeled, although it is possible you might only need the initial letters "I," "B," and "C" to note these divisions. Nonessential words are eliminated, although some facts are included in the speaker's notes to avoid misstatement. Delivery instructions help emphasize that your speech has implications to your listeners and can help personalize the message.

The more experience you have as a speaker, the more you will come to rely on both your planning outline and speaker's notes, as both are indispensable to a successful presentation.

Summary

The first step in organizing your speech is to determine your main points. Organize your efforts around your specific purpose and thesis statement, then brainstorm to generate specific ideas, and finally, group similar ideas.

Your second step is to use supporting material to develop each main point. In step three, choose an organizational pattern. Arrange your ideas in chronological order, use a spatial organizational pattern, follow a pattern of cause and effect, look at a problem and its solutions, or choose a topical pattern. Your final step is to connect your main ideas through transitions, internal previews, and internal summaries.

As you develop your speech, your primary organizational tool is the planning outline, which includes most of the information you will present. The outline uses a traditional outline format, which establishes a hierarchy of ideas. The number of main points developed in your speech should be between two and five. The planning outline also uses complete sentences, labels transitions, and includes a reference list.

Speakers' notes, the notes you use during your presentation in an extemporaneous speech, are less detailed than the planning outline. They serve as brief reminders of what you want to say and the order in which you say it. They may include complete quotations and statistical data as well as important delivery suggestions. Speakers' notes are organized around phrases, not sentences, and they use the same format as the planning outline.

Questions for Study and Discussion

1. Match five speech topics with five different organizational patterns. Which pattern did you choose for each topic, and on what basis did you make your choice?
2. In public speaking, what functions are served by transitions and summaries? Can you think of several effective transitional statements to develop the speech topics from question number one?
3. Review the essential requirements for planning and key-word outlines. Why is it necessary to develop both outline forms, and why are both equally important in extemporaneous speaking? Explain the role each plays in different phases of a speech.

Activities

1. Read a speech from *Vital Speeches of the Day* or from another collection. Outline the speech, identifying the specific organizational pattern or patterns the speaker has chosen. Write a paragraph examining whether the pattern chosen effectively communicates the core idea.
2. Write a specific purpose statement for a speech, then use three different organizational patterns to organize the speech.

3. Select a video from your library that contains a speech. Then listen to the speech to identify the organizational pattern. List the previews, transition, and summaries. Identify the core idea and its placement in the speech.

References

Clarke, M. L. 1963. *Rhetoric at Rome: Historical survey.* New York: Barnes & Noble.

Daniels, T. D., and Witman, R. F. 1981. The effects of message structure in verbal organizing ability upon learning information. *Human communication research*, Winter, 147–60.

Makay, J., and R. C. Fetzger. 1984. *Business communication skills: Principles and practice (2nd ed.).* Englewood Cliffs, NJ: Prentice-Hall.

Sprague, J., and Stuart, D. 1992. *The speaker's handbook, 3rd ed.* San Diego, CA: Harcourt Brace Jovanovich.

Turner Jr., F. H. 1970. The effects of speech summaries on audience comprehension. *Central States Speech Journal*, Spring, 24–39.

"The first ninety seconds:
They're absolutely crucial."

Ron Hoff, public speaking consultant

© Corbis.

Introducing and Concluding Your Speech

Introductions

Functions of Introductions

Focus Attention on Topic and Speaker

Personal Greeting

Capture and Focus Attention

Set the Appropriate Tone and Mood

Provide a Motive to Listen

Enhance Credibility

Preview Your Message and Organization

Ten Techniques of Introductions

1. Startling Facts/Intriguing Statements
2. Dramatic Story/Build Suspense
3. Quotation and/or Literature Reference
4. Humor
5. Rhetorical Question
6. Illustrations, Examples, and Anecdotes
7. Physically Involve the Audience
8. Relate Personal Experience
9. Use a Visual or Media Aid
10. Refer to the Situation

Five Guidelines and Suggestions for Introductions

1. Prepare After Body of Speech
2. Make It Easy to Follow and Be Creative
3. Practice and Communicate High Energy
4. Engage Audience Nonverbally Before You Start
5. Consider Time Constraints and Mood

Conclusions

Functions of Conclusions

Summarizing Important Information

Motivating Listeners

Creating Closure

Concluding Techniques

Thanking as Transition

Call to Action

Use a Dramatic Illustration

Close with a Quotation

Conclude with a Metaphor That Broadens the Meaning of Your Speech

Conclude with Humor

Encourage Thought with a Rhetorical Question

Refer to Your Introduction

Summary

Questions for Study and Discussion

Activities

References

Imagine your classmate is about to give a persuasive speech on intercultural communication, and is mulling over an almost unlimited number of ways to start. Consider the following three possibilities:

- Bonjour! Parce que ma presentation s'agit d'une question de la communication interculturelle, j'ai decidé de presenter completement en francais! D'accord? Bien. La communication interculturelle est un grand probleme dans l' Etats Unis et d'autres nations ont beaucoup souffert. In other words, intercultural communication, or rather, lack thereof, is a huge problem that has plagued America as well as other foreign countries across the world....
- How many of you have finished your foreign language requirement for college graduation? How many of you feel that you are fluent in another language? Do you realize that it's not unusual for our European counterparts to speak four different languages? Intercultural communication, or rather, lack thereof, is a huge problem that has plagued America as well as foreign countries across the world....
- Intercultural communication, or rather, lack thereof, is a huge problem that has plagued America as well as foreign countries across the world...

Which beginning do you find most creative? Least creative? Most engaging? Least engaging? Which one would be the easiest to develop? The most difficult?

As you look at the above examples, a final question comes to mind. Are all three examples acceptable ways to begin a speech? The answer may certainly be "yes," but you need to keep in mind that the way you begin and end your speech is critical to your overall success. Expending effort on your introduction is time well spent.

This chapter approaches introductions and conclusions in relation to how your speech can make a lasting impression. Two topics will be considered: how to engage your audience at the beginning of your speech so they will be motivated to listen to the rest of it, and how to remind your audience at the end of what you said and why it was relevant.

The **primacy/recency effect** sheds light on the importance of effective speech beginnings and endings. According to this theory, we tend to recall more vividly the beginning and ending, and less so the middle, of an event. When a series of candidates are interviewing for a job, the first and last candidates have an advantage because the interviewer is most likely to recall more about these two than the others. This theory also holds true for speeches; your audience will have greater recall of how you began and ended your speech.

The familiar speaker adage: "Tell them what you are going to say, say it, and then tell them what you said" addresses this truth. Beginning and ending a speech well helps your audience to recall and later, to use, the ideas you present. Let us begin with a closer look at introductions.

Introductions

Why pay so much attention to an introduction? If done well, an introduction can help your audience make a smooth transition to the main points of your speech, create a positive first impression, and set an appropriate tone and mood for your talk. If done poorly, your audience may prejudge your topic as unimportant or dull and stop listening.

Consider the following example. As part of a conference for a group of business executives, business consultant Edith Weiner was scheduled to deliver a speech on the unequal distribution of world resources—admittedly, a topic with the potential to put her listeners to sleep. She was experienced enough as a speaker, though, to realize that the last thing her listeners wanted to hear at the beginning was a long list of statistics comparing the bounty of North America to the failures of other parts of the world. Her speech would never recover from such a dull start. The challenge she faced was to capture the audience's attention at the outset.

Arriving at the auditorium early on the morning of her speech, Weiner marked off different size sections of the hall to represent, proportionately, the various continents. She allotted coffee, cake, and chairs according to the availability of food and income in each. Then she assigned audience members to these areas according to actual world population ratios.

What happened was quite memorable. While thirty people in the area representing Africa had to divide three cups of coffee, two pastries, and two chairs, the seventeen people assigned to North America had more coffee and cake than they could eat in a week, surrounded by forty chairs. As participants took their seats (with those in Asia and Africa standing most of the morning), they did so with a new perspective on world hunger and poverty, and with a desire to listen to whatever Weiner had to say. She began:

A good introduction can help you set an appropriate tone for your speech. *© Rohit Seth, 2008. Under license from Shutterstock, Inc.*

> I wanted to speak with you today at this prestigious conference about a topic most people tire of, but you, being so important to the financial community, cannot ignore.

> I know that some of you are now hungry and some of you are stuffed, and I want you to take the next few minutes to look around you and observe the obvious.

> Hunger and poverty aren't comfortable, are they? Neither is bounty when you realize the waste and mismatch of people and resources.

> This is only a game, but it demonstrates what numbers, charts, and speeches cannot. The world's population is forced to live every day with overabundance and scarcity—realities that cost millions their lives as U.S. farmers and consumers throw away food and disposables.

> Can you, as a business, do anything to resolve these inequities and, ultimately, profit from your role? I intend to explore several options during the rest of my speech. (Based on an interview with Edith Weiner, October 10, 1989.)

Edith Weiner's risky introduction grabbed the attention of all audience members in a powerful way.

Functions of Introductions

The emphasis on strong opening comments has long been held as important. In the first century A.D. Roman philosopher Quintillion noted that for a speech to be effective, an introduction must do four things. It must:

INTRO MUST DO 4 things

- Focus attention on the topic and speaker
- Provide a motive for your audience to care about your speech
- Enhance your credibility as a speaker
- Preview your message and organization

Edith Weiner's introduction was effective because it accomplished each of these objectives, as we shall see.

Focus Attention on Topic and Speaker

INTRO

Your introduction should first offer a personal greeting, capture and focus attention on your topic, and set an appropriate tone and mood.

Personal Greeting

An introduction should contain a personalized greeting, which is usually your first words and might be considered a preamble to your introduction. A personal greeting at the start of your speech tells your listeners that you see the speech as an opportunity to communicate your point of view. When Martin Luther King Jr. looked out over the sea of faces on the Washington Mall on August 28, 1963, he began by telling his audience, "I am happy to join with you today in what will go down in history as the greatest demonstration for freedom in the history of our nation." Then he delivered his "I Have a Dream" speech—his powerful and memorable civil rights address (King, in Johannesen, Allen, and Linkugel, 1988, 30). Personal greetings make the audience feel welcome and set the stage for the introduction that follows.

Martin Luther King, Jr. incorporated personal greetings into his introductions to make the audience feel welcome. © *Flip Schulke/Corbis.*

Capture and Focus Attention

Every experienced speaker knows that the first few minutes are critical to the success of the entire speech. It is within these minutes that your listeners decide whether they care enough to continue listening. You want your listeners to say to themselves, "Hey, this is interesting," or "I didn't know that," or "I never thought of it in quite that way," or "That was really funny." The common denominator in each of these responses is piqued audience interest. Weiner explains: "I know if I'm successful when I start a speech. I try to establish a rapport with the audience and sail from there. If you wait till the end to deliver the 'Big Bang,' you've already lost most of your audience—and there's no getting them back. I always start with some kind of hook, and from there on, the audience is in the palm of my hand" (Weiner 1989). We do not expect beginning speakers to have the audience "in the palm of their hands," but the importance of capturing attention cannot be understated.

Set the Appropriate Tone and Mood

Imagine observing the following scenario: Angela stood behind the podium beside the closed casket as she delivered the eulogy to tearful faces. Her sentimental message of grief was appropriate in every way except that she delivered it with a smile. The whole speech! The disconnect between her words and facial expressions was a bit unsettling to say the least. When asked about it later, Angela was surprised. She confessed that the smile was her trying to communicate that she was glad to be there and happy to be performing such an important family duty. Unfortunately, Angela did not create an appropriate tone and mood in her introduction.

The mood of a speech refers to the overall feeling you hope to engender in your audience. Tone is the emotional disposition of the speaker as the speech is being delivered. Tone is created verbally by the words and ideas you select and nonverbally by the emotions you communicate. As during most funerals, the mood was of sadness and solidarity. Yet Angela's tone was upbeat and happy. Consider the desired mood and adjust your tone appropriately in the introduction. In this way, you ensure that your tone matches your reason for speaking and that your speech helps to create the desired mood in your audience.

Provide a Motive to Listen

An effective speaker will quickly establish a reason for audience members to listen. Edith Weiner's introduction helped build that critical relationship with her public speaking audience. She wanted her listeners to care about her message. She wanted them to decide from the outset that what she was saying had meaning and importance. Although the introduction also helped to make her point with its physical demonstration of world food problems, its primary purpose was to build a psychological bridge that would last throughout the speech. Her well-designed demonstration forced her audience to care about her topic because Weiner had effectively related the topic of her speech to something the audience cared about, their own hunger.

The introduction should seek to establish common ground with the audience. By focusing on something you and your audience can share and announcing it early, you will help people identify with your topic. When people perceive that your message is meant for them and really is relevant to their lives, they will listen attentively.

Enhance Credibility

During your introduction, your listeners make important decisions about you. They decide whether they like you and whether you are credible. Your credibility as a speaker is judged, in large part, on the basis of what you say during your introduction and how you say it.

Edith Weiner became a credible speaker by demonstrating, in a participatory way, that she understood the problems of world food distribution and that she cared enough about her audience—and topic—to come up with a creative way to present her ideas. Credibility also increases as you describe, early on, what qualifies you to speak about a topic. Weiner might have said, "I want to talk to you about world resources because for several years I have studied how your investments overseas can have important impacts on your future economic well-being." In this case, she may not have established her credibility to the extent her actual introduction accomplished.

Your introduction is an ideal place to enhance your credibility. © *Corbis*.

Audiences may have an initial sense of your credibility even before you speak. Your introduction is an ideal place to enhance that impression. As we will discuss later in the text, you can think of your credibility in terms of your perceived competence, concern for your audience, dynamism, and personal ethics. Put another way, if you know your subject, care about your audience, offer an enthusiastic delivery, and communicate a sense of ethical integrity, your audience's impression of your credibility will likely be positive. The content and delivery of your introduction must maximize these four aspects if you want your audience to listen attentively throughout your speech.

Preview Your Message and Organization

Finally, Weiner used her introduction to tell her audience what she would talk about during the rest of her speech. In a sentence, she previewed her focus. ("I intend to explore several options [for maximizing your role and gain] during the rest of my speech.") This simple statement helped her listeners make the intellectual connections they needed to follow her speech. Instead of wondering, "What will she talk about?" or "What is her point of view?" they were ready for her speech to unfold.

As we said in the opening of this chapter, your audience will recall your message more fully if you tell them what you are going to say, say it, and then tell them what you said. Repeating key ideas helps us recall important information. But the first part of that, telling them what you are going to say, also serves to provide a preview of the organization you intend to use. If your audience knows the main points you intend to develop in your speech, they are less likely to be confused and distracted. So, an effective introduction might offer a preview statement similar to "Today it is important that we better understand the nature of world hunger, explore creative solutions to this problem, and finally, see if some of these solutions might also be profitable to your business." In this example, the audience now knows that there will be three main points to the message.

Here is how John E. Jacob, president and chief executive officer of the National Urban League, previewed a speech delivered to the Congressional Clearinghouse of the Future:

> Today I want to begin by briefly sketching what the Urban League is, and going on from there, to discuss the plight of black citizens. Along the way, I'd like to look back at some of the things America has done to deal with its racial problems. And I'd like to look ahead as well, to suggest some of the things we can do to secure the future for black people and for all Americans (1988, 616).

If you preview your message, the audience will listen and understand with increased clarity. © *Corbis*.

When Jacob finished this statement, his audience had no doubt what his speech would cover. When you preview your message, your audience will listen and understand with increased clarity and will remember more of your message later.

How to Introduce the Same Speech in Different Ways

Many topics lend themselves to different types of introductions. A startling statement, a dramatic anecdote, a quotation, or a humorous story may each serve as an effective introduction to the same speech. Here, for example, is the same speech introduced in three different ways:

Startling Statement

Microwave cooking can be hazardous to your child's health. Children have been burned by opening bags of microwave-heated popcorn too close to their faces. Their throats have been scalded by jelly donuts that feel cool to the touch, but are hot enough inside to burn the esophagus. These and other hazards can transform your microwave into an oven of destruction in the hands of a child. What I would like to talk about today is how dangerous microwaves can be to young children and how you can safeguard your family from accidents.

Dramatic Story

Nine-year-old Jenny was one of those kids who managed quite well on her own. Every day she got home from school at 3:30 while her parents were still at work and made herself a snack in the microwave. She had been using the microwave since she was five, and her parents never questioned its safety—that is, not until Jenny had her accident.

It began innocently enough. Jenny heated a bag of microwave popcorn in the oven and opened it inches from her face. The bag was cool to the touch, hiding the danger within. Hot vapors blasted Jenny's face, leaving her with second and third-degree-burns.

What I would like to talk about today is how dangerous microwaves can be to young children and how you can safeguard your family from accidents.

Quotation

Three out of every four American homes have microwave ovens and with them a potential for danger. Louis Slesin, editor of "Microwave News," a health and safety newsletter, explains how this common kitchen appliance can present potential hazards for young children:

"On a rainy day," says Slesin, "a kid could climb up on a stool, put his face to the door and watch something cook for a long time. It's mesmerizing, like watching a fish tank, but his eye will be at the point of maximum microwave leakage. We don't know the threshold for cataract formation—the industry says you need tons of exposure, but some litigation and literature say you don't need much [for damage to occur]. Children younger than 10 or 12 shouldn't use the oven unsupervised. It's not a toy. It's a sophisticated, serious, adult appliance, and it shouldn't be marketed for kids" (Shapiro 1990, 56).

I agree with Slesin, and what I want to talk about today is how dangerous the microwave can be to a young child.

Ten Techniques of Introductions

There are many ways to accomplish Quintillion's four functions of an introduction. Following are ten different techniques often used in introductions. You might consider using one or combining several to provide the initial impact you want. This is one area where a little creativity can go a long way. Keep your audience in mind. A few of these techniques may be more appropriate or attention-getting for your specific audience and specific purpose.

1. Startling Facts/Intriguing Statements

Some introductions seem to force listeners to pay attention. They make it difficult to think of other things because of the impact of what is being said. The effectiveness of these introductions in part, comes from the audience's feeling that the speaker's message is directed at them.

Here is how Thomas K. Hearn Jr., president of Wake Forest University, caught the attention of his audience of college football coaches:

> Your profession—college football coaching—is at risk. Paradoxically, the risk arises from the very success and influence of college football. Successful people in your profession

are being given generous doses of the three most dangerous and addictive drugs known: fame, wealth, and power. Big time sports have made football coaches into entertainment celebrities. The question is whether the pursuit of the rewards of victory will destroy the comfortable houses your game has made for you. 'Impossible,' you say? You are one scandal away (1988, 20).

Hearn's audience was captivated by the drug addiction metaphor and the provocative comment, "You are one scandal away." Startling statements often challenge common misconceptions. Instead of revealing the expected, the speaker takes a slightly—or perhaps even a radically—different turn.

2. Dramatic Story/Build Suspense

Closely related to the startling statement is the dramatic story, which involves listeners in a tale from beginning to end. Shortly after returning from a winter vacation break, Shannon delivered a speech to her classmates that began this way:

My friends and I were driving home from a day at the ski slopes when suddenly, without warning, a pair of headlights appeared directly in front of our car. To avoid a collision, I swerved sharply to the right, forcing our car off the road into a snow-filled ditch.

It's funny what comes into your mind at moments like this. All I could think of was how New York Yankee manager Billy Martin had died in a ditch a few years ago after his car skidded off an icy road. I thought I was going to die too, just because of another driver's stupidity and carelessness.

Obviously, I didn't die or even suffer any serious injuries. And my friends are safe too, although my car was totaled. I'm convinced that we are all here today because we were locked into place by our seat belts. Billy Martin might have been here too had he bothered to buckle up.

Introduce your speech with an opener that will capture peoples' attention. © Corbis.

Everyone in the audience knew what it was like to be driving home with friends—feeling safe and secure—only to be shocked into the realization that they were vulnerable to tragedy. Audience attention was riveted on the speaker as she launched into her speech on seat belt use.

3. Quotation and/or Literature Reference

You can capture audience attention by citing the words of others. If you use an appropriate poem, the words themselves may be compelling enough to engage your listeners. E. Grady Bogue, chancellor of Louisiana State University, opened the commencement address he delivered at Memphis State University with the following quotation:

> They deem me mad because I will not sell my days for gold;
> And I deem them mad because they think my days have a price
> (1988, 615).

As Bogue continued, he celebrated the "nobility" of a career in teaching:

> Teaching is a journey of the heart, an opportunity to touch a life forever. It is an unselfish investment in the dignity and potential of one's student. The life of the master teacher honors all that is good and noble in mankind (615).

Introducing a speech with a quote is also appropriate when you cite the words of a well-known individual or a recognized authority whose reputation enhances your topic. Here, for example, is how Tisha Oehmen, a student at Lane Community College, began her speech to capture the attention of her audience. Quoting a knowledgeable public figure, she began:

> Each day the Columbia River dumps in the Pacific Ocean 90 billion gallons of fresh water. That is 3.7 billion gallons an hour, 61 million gallons a minute, and 1 million gallons a second. This is wasteful and sinful.' These are the words of Los Angeles County Supervisor Kenneth Hahn, as quoted in *The Washington Post*, May 20, 1990. This is how Hahn prepared his Board of Supervisors for his proposal to siphon water out of the Columbia River to quench the thirst of his drought-stricken city. If he succeeds in building this aqueduct, the life and the environment in the Pacific Northwest and all who depend on its resources may be changed. The Columbia's diversion would not only scar the landscape, but the proposed diversion would slow shipping, cripple irrigation, harm the fragile salmon runs, and reduce the available electricity (1991, 96).

In similar fashion, Andy Wood, studying at St. Petersburg Junior College, captured his audience's attention when speaking about the nation's trauma centers by stating:

> If a criminal has a right to an attorney, don't you have a right to a doctor?' Democrat Harris Woffard used this slogan last year to win the Pennsylvania senate race. *The Washington Post*, November 24, 1991, reports that Woffard also sent an alarming wakeup call to President Bush and Congress to get serious about health care in America (1992, 8).

4. Humor

At the beginning of a speech, humor helps break down the psychological barriers that exist between speaker and audience. Here is how Karen used humor at the start of a classroom speech on the problem of divorce in America:

> Janet and Lauren had been college roommates, but had not seen each other in the ten years since graduation. They were thrilled when they ran into each other at a college reunion and had a chance to talk.
>
> "Tell me," asked Janet, "has your husband lived up to the promises he made when he was dating you in college?"
>
> "He certainly has!" said Lauren. "He told me then that he wasn't good enough for me and he's proven it ever since."

The class laughed, Karen waited, then:

> I laughed too when I heard that story. But the fact remains that about half the marriages in our country end in divorce and one of the major reasons for these failures is that one partner can't live up to the expectations of the other.

Humor works in this introduction for two reasons. First, the story is genuinely funny; we chuckle when we hear the punch line. And, second, the humor is tied directly to the subject of the speech; it is appropriate for the topic and the occasion. It also provides an effective transition into the speech body.

5. Rhetorical Question

When you ask your audience, "How many of you ate breakfast this morning?" you expect to see people raise their hands. When you ask a rhetorical question, however, you do not expect an answer. What you hope is that your question will cause your listeners to start thinking about the subject of your speech. This was the plan of Paula Pankow (1991), a student at the Eau Claire campus of the University of Wisconsin, when she began her speech about sleep deprivation:

> Do you ever go through the day feeling like you're missing something? Well, what would you do if I said each one of you probably suffers directly from a deficit every day that you might not even realize? A loss that, according to the May 15, 2006 issue of the *New York Times*, affects 100 million Americans and 200 billion dollars a year in lost creativity and business productivity, industrial and vehicular accidents, and medical costs.

The speaker linked these rhetorical questions and startling statistics firmly to her audience of students by connecting them with the lifestyle familiar to residential college students and to her thesis statement and to a preview of the main points in her speech:

> This loss is not our deprivation of national dollars, but a loss concerning deprivation of sleep. Now granted, we're in an academic setting and getting a full night's rest isn't as important to adults as getting our work done. Free from

the nagging voices of parents who may order a nine o'clock bedtime, we now enjoy the freedom of going to bed when we want and sometimes where we want, whether it be 10 p.m., 1 a.m., or even 6 a.m. after pulling an all-nighter! Of course, a mild loss of sleep once in awhile won't do that much harm to a person, but most of us would be more good-humored, productive, and satisfied with life in general if we got a full complement of sleep each night. Instead, what we're finding in society today is that sleep deprivation is becoming chronic and extensive, leading to serious consequences. So today I'd like to address the problem of sleep deprivation by explaining its nature and consequences, exploring why we don't get enough sleep and, finally, offering some things we can do to better our chances for a full night's rest (123).

The best rhetorical questions are probing in a personal way. They mean something to every listener and encourage active participation throughout your speech.

6. Illustrations, Examples, and Anecdotes

Speakers often begin with an interesting comment about the immediate surroundings or some recent or historical event. These openings are even more powerful when the speaker carefully plans these comments. Through the skillful use of illustrations ("In the short time I will be talking with you, 150 violent crimes will have been committed in our nation…"), examples ("Lisa was a young woman from our community who's life was forever altered on January 18th…"), and anecdotes ("Once, while traveling on the subway, I noticed a shifty looking man carefully watching each passenger enter and leave the car…"), speakers gather our attention to them and their message.

7. Physically Involve the Audience

Recall from the opening of this chapter how Edith Weiner began her speech by getting her audience physically involved in her message. Some went hungry while others had too much. Another example of this technique frequently occurs at sales seminars, where the speaker offers a gift, usually money, to the first person in the audience who will simply leave his/her seat and come to the front to get it. Eventually some brave soul approaches, takes the money, and returns to his/her seat. Then everyone else in the audience realizes they could have had the gift themselves if they had only been willing to act instead of sitting passively.

How can you get your audience involved in your presentation? © *Corbis*.

8. Relate Personal Experience

Sharing a story or several examples from your past with your listeners can be an effective start. Be sure your personal experiences will not hurt your credibility and that they relate directly to your topic. Recently, a student giving a speech supporting gun control caught the attention of his audience by retelling an event he had witnessed–an angry driver brandishing a gun at another driver at a stop light. Although the gun was not fired, the story caught the audience's attention and introduced the idea that there is potential harm associated with widespread and unregulated gun ownership. Because he saw the event, we considered the speaker to have more credibility in his speech about gun control.

9. Use a Visual or Media Aid

Before the President of the United States speaks, the broadcast feed from the White House shows the presidential seal. This is no accident; it helps to draw attention to the upcoming speech and also helps reinforce the president's credibility. But you do not have to be the President to use this technique. Beginning your speech with an interesting sound recording, visual, or prop is guaranteed to draw attention to the beginning of your speech, too.

10. Refer to the Situation

Skilled public speakers often begin with a positive comment related to the occasion, the person who spoke before them, the audience, the date, or even the physical location. Each of these may be more appropriate at one time than at another. For example, a commencement speaker at her alma mater might start with, "It's hard for me to believe that twenty-five years ago I sat in those seats listening to the commencement speaker..." Or, if an audience was waiting outside in the rain to hear a Democratic candidate who was late, the candidate might start with, "I bet there isn't a more committed group of voters than those of you here who have been standing in the rain waiting for me..." When you are planning a speech, ask yourself if referencing the event, a prior speaker, the audience or the significance of this date in history would create interest and gather attention.

Each of these ten options is a possible opening for a speech. Keep in mind that your attention-gaining device must relate in some way to your topic or you run the risk of confusing your audience. Your choice should be guided by several other factors. First, consider the mood you are attempting to create. Second, consider your audience's expectations of you and the occasion. Third, consider how much time and resources each approach will require. Finally, consider your strengths and weaknesses—you may not be as strong at joke telling as recalling a powerful story.

Five Guidelines and Suggestions for Introductions

As you focus on crafting your introduction for your next speech, consider how you can create a strong and effective message. Remember, as in any recipe, no ingredient stands on its own. Attention to each part of the process leads to an excellent final product. After choosing the most appropriate beginning, consider these general guidelines as you prepare and deliver your introduction.

1. Prepare After Body of Speech

Your introduction will take form more easily after you have created an outline of the body of your speech. When speakers attempt to create the introduction first, they inevitably rewrite it several times as they continue to change the body of their message.

2. Make It Easy to Follow and Be Creative

Whether you are offering a startling statistic or asking a question, be sure to keep things simple. When you offer your thesis and even when you preview your main points for your audience, look for ways to keep things concise and straight-forward. Recently, a student beginning his persuasive speech started with his arms open in a pleading gesture, zealously urging the class, "Please! Please I beg of you—stop washing your hands!" He then briefly noted the dangers of too much cleansing and stated his thesis. His enthusiastic approach and startling plea made for a creative introduction that was simple and easy to understand.

Consider your introduction as an opportunity for you to be creative. The more creative your introduction, the more likely your audience will listen to the entire message.

3. Practice and Communicate High Energy

The most important part of your speech to practice thoroughly is the introduction, followed by the conclusion, and then the body. The first impression created by a well-practiced introduction lays the foundation for your ultimate success. So be sure to rehearse it many times. Your introduction should be enthusiastically delivered. Since introductions are relatively short, put your heart, mind, and energy into it. If you are truly engaged in the introduction, your audience is much more likely also to become involved in your message.

It is difficult to communicate high energy if you are dependent on notes. You should be able to speak to the audience for at least fifteen seconds without looking at your notes.

4. Engage Audience Nonverbally Before You Start

Poise counts! Recall that your speech actually begins as you rise to speak. Approach with confidence, once there, pause, catch and hold your audience's eye contact for a moment, and take a deep breath. Each of these measures is critical to beginning your speech effectively. You want your audience to know you are interested in the speech and that you want them to be part of the experience.

5. Consider Time Constraints and Mood

When giving a five-minute speech, telling a protracted, dramatic story would be inappropriate. The same is true of showing a one-minute video clip. Alternately, when delivering a forty-five-minute lecture, such a beginning would be wholly acceptable. The mood you are hoping to create in your audience is related to your tone, and vice versa. The introduction is your best chance to establish your tone and alter the mood of your audience.

TTYL (Talk to Your Listener)
Ten Common Pitfalls of Introductions

As they say, you never get a second chance at a first impression. Here is a list of problematic approaches to avoid during your introduction.

1. Beginning with an apology

Do not use your introduction to apologize for mistakes you are likely to make, for inadequate visual aids, being ill-prepared or even just plain ill. Apologies set a negative tone that is hard to overcome.

2. Being too brief or too long

Do not jump into the body of the speech or spend too much time setting up the speech. Your introduction should take between ten and twenty percent of your total allotted speaking time. Not adhering to this guideline means violating an audience expectation and potentially annoying them.

3. Giving too much away

While the introduction should provide a road map for your speech, you do not want to give the substance of your speech in your preview. Instead, use general terms to tell your audience what you intend to cover.

4. Reading

We have advised you to rehearse your introduction thoroughly. Do not read your introductory remarks to your audience. Your script becomes a barrier between you and your audience. Worse yet, you will likely sound more like a reader than a public speaker. Avoid reading extensively in the introduction.

5. Relying on shock tactics

Your victory will be short-lived if you capture audience attention by screaming at the top of your lungs, pounding the table, telling a bawdy joke, or using material that has nothing to do with your speech. Your audience will trust you less because of the way you manipulated their attention. Using an innovative approach is effective as long as it is tied directly to the topic of your speech.

6. Promising too much

Some speakers, fearful that their speech says too little, promise more than they can deliver, in the hope that the promise alone will satisfy their listeners. It rarely does. Once you set expectations in the introduction, the body of your speech has to deliver or you will lose credibility.

7. Using unnecessary prefatory remarks

Resist the urge to begin with: "I'm so nervous," "I can't believe I have to do this speech," or "Okay, deep breath, here we go." Even if you feel these things, such verbal adaptors are likely to make you even more nervous and are also likely to hurt your credibility. Instead, begin with your planned opening statement. And avoid having the first word you say be "uh."

8. Using long-winded poems, quotations, and prose

We understand that for full effect, an entire piece of prose or poetry should be read. We also know that editing a poem or piece of prose may not be easy. However, it is possible to find an appropriate nugget embedded within the piece that is perfect for your speech. Consider paraphrasing or moving the longer passage to the body of your speech.

9. Becoming someone else

Because your initial credibility is being established in the introduction, you will want to present a rational view of yourself to your audience. Avoid histrionics and melodrama if you hope to earn the respect of your listeners.

10. Overusing some techniques

Often overused are simple questions, rhetorical questions, and startling, catastrophic stories. This is made worse by relying on trite phrases. Spend some time thinking about how to begin your speech. Think about what might be most effective with your particular audience. Seek to be original and creative.

Conclusions

Think of your conclusion as the pinnacle of your speech—the words you want your listeners to remember as they leave the room. Too often, speakers waste the opportunity with endings like, "That's it," "I guess I'm finished now," or "I'm through. Any questions?" Or they simply stop talking, giving the audience no indication that they have finished their speech. Just as an introduction sets a first impression, a well-delivered conclusion leaves a lasting mark on your audience.

A conclusion should not be viewed as an afterthought. Understand that the conclusion is your last opportunity to have an impact. Just as the introduction should be clear and flow smoothly to the body of the speech, the body should flow smoothly to the conclusion. Following are three functions of conclusions to consider as you think about the transition from the body to the conclusion and determine how to create the greatest effect on your audience.

Functions of Conclusions

Strong endings to speeches summarize important information, motivate listeners, and create a sense of closure. After talking about the rebuilding and the reconciliation that took place at the end of World War II, and why the American Rangers risked their lives at Normandy, Peggy Noonan (1990) concluded the Pointe du Hoc speech with these words:

> We in America have learned the bitter lessons of two world wars: that it is better to be here and ready to preserve and protect the peace than to take blind shelter in our homes across the sea, rushing to respond only after freedom has been threatened. We have learned that isolationism never was and never will be an acceptable response to tyrannical governments with expansionist intent.

> Let our actions say to them the words for which Matthew Ridgway listened: "I will not fail thee nor forsake thee." Strengthened by their courage, heartened by their valor and borne by their memory, let us continue to stand for the ideals for which they lived and died (85–86).

Summarizing Important Information

The transition from the body to the conclusion is pivotal in signaling the impending end of your speech. Your instructor and your own personal preference may help you decide how you want to tell your audience you are ending. Whether you use a formal "In conclusion…" or prefer something less formal, such as "Now, to wrap this up today…" you want your audience to be clear that you are about to finish. Audiences know that when you give them that signal, they are about to get an important recap of your key ideas.

In the process of ending, an effective conclusion also reinforces the main idea of the speech. The conclusion of the Pointe du Hoc speech, for example, reinforced President Reagan's message that the liberties we fought for in World War II are the liberties we are still committed to today.

Depending upon the length and complexity of your speech, your summary may be brief or more extended. Your review can be as simple as this:

> I would like to conclude by stating once more that our schools have done a dismal job teaching math and science. As we have seen, the results of standardized tests show that our high school and college students are well behind their counterparts in Japan and Western Europe. And, as we have also seen, the demands of businesses for skilled scientists and mathematicians are growing along with the complexity of technology.

An effective summary helps reinforce the main points of your speech. © *Corbis.*

The hard truth is that businesses need many more students trained in math and science than our educational system is now producing. Generally, I don't like to make predictions, but I can say for certain that we face a crisis.

Many speakers believe that the best way to hammer home their point is to tell their audience what they are going to say in their introduction, say it in the body of their speech, and then remind their listeners of what they told them in the conclusion. According to speech communication professor John E. Baird Jr. (1974), "Summaries may be effective when presented at the conclusion of a speech [because] they provide the audience with a general structure under which to subsume the more specific points of the speech" (119–127). Research indicates that in some instances summaries are not essential, but if your audience is unfamiliar with the content of your speech, or if the speech is long or complex, a summary will help reinforce your main points.

Motivating Listeners

Great speakers do more than summarize in their conclusions; they motivate their audiences. Relate your topic to your listeners. Your speech will achieve the greatest success if your listeners feel that you have helped them in some concrete way. Consider making this connection in your conclusion. When Sarah Weddington, the lawyer who successfully argued *Roe v. Wade* before the Supreme Court in 1973—a case that guaranteed American women the right to abortion—spoke to students at Mercer University in Macon, Georgia, she used the conclusion of her speech to broaden her discussion to the lives of her listeners. At the May 10, 1989 commencement ceremony, Weddington (1989) said:

> I appreciate your willingness—at such a busy time—to give me some minutes to talk about the legal issue of *Roe v. Wade* and its implications. Obviously, many of you will not choose this issue to be your key issue, but I hope when you leave Mercer, you will pick some issue that you care about and that you will be involved in as a leader in deciding the path that society will travel.

Communicate a feeling. Perhaps more importantly, the conclusion sets the psychological mood listeners carry with them from the hall. A student speaking against aspartame noted at the beginning of her speech that she believed aspartame contributed to her previous depression and weight gain. She ended her speech by noting that eliminating aspartame from her diet lifted her depression and led to significant weight loss. Her passion about the topic and the relief she feels were clearly communicated.

Broaden your message. Finally, the conclusion can be used to connect your topic to a broader context. If in your speech you talk about the responsibility of every adult to vote on election day, you can use your conclusion to tie the vote to the continuation of our democratic system. If your speech focuses on caring for aging parents, you can conclude with a plea to value rather than discard the wisdom of the elderly.

Creating Closure

Good conclusions create a sense of closure for the speech. The audience needs to find a sense of completeness as listeners. If you are having dinner with others the dessert often provides a tasty completeness to the dining experience. So, when speaking, it is not enough to simply stop with a comment: "Well, that's it, I guess I can see if anyone has a question." leaving the audience without a sense of closure. An effective conclusion tells your listeners your speech has ended. There are several techniques speakers use to create a sense of psychological closure.

Concluding Techniques

Thanking as Transition

Although saying thank you at the end of the speech indicates that you are finished, it is no substitute for a statement that brings your discussion to a close. You can, however, use the thank you statement as a transition into your concluding remarks. For example:

> And so, in summary, women certainly have more opportunity today than they ever had, but they also have more responsibility. Thank you for giving me the honor of being your keynote speaker.

> Sociologist Sylvia Ann Hewlett has described the gains of the women's liberation movement as a myth. She tells women that they have a "lesser life" than men—despite their considerable strides. She may be right today, but let's all do what we can to make sure she is wrong tomorrow.

Call to Action

As you wrap up your speech, you can make a direct appeal to your listeners, urging them to take a specific action or to change their attitudes. In a persuasive speech, the conclusion is where you make your most forcible and most memorable plea to persuade.

Living in an age of mass media, we are bombarded by calls to action every time we turn on the television. Advertisers plead with us to drop everything and buy their products. We see 1-800 numbers flash across the screen, urging us to order knives or DVDs or diet aids. Televangelists urge us to contribute to their mission. The fact that we are all accustomed to these messages makes them a natural conclusion to a speech.

Realizing this, Thomas K. Hearn Jr. (1988), concluded his speech to the College Football Association with these remarks:

> If there are values acquired by a life devoted to a game, even a game as violent as football, then those of you who coach this sport should be examples of the sport's ethical possibilities. Does playing football build ingredients of character? Does it make young men better? Whether team sports are good for people, people at any age, is always a question of coaching leadership. Your game has a noble heritage. All of you are guardians of your sport….

> If football belongs in the university where young minds and character are being formed, and if being called "coach" is a title of honor among all coaches, football can lead the movement of reform, beginning today with all of us (22).

Hearn is challenging his listeners to think and act in a more ethical way. A call to action is an especially appropriate way to conclude a persuasive speech, but it can also be an effective end to an informative speech. Here is how a professor might conclude a lecture:

> I have explained my thoughts on the implications of the changes that are now taking place in Eastern Europe. As you review them, keep this in mind: What we are witnessing is nothing less than a change in world politics. In the days ahead, think about this change and about how it will affect each and every one of us in the free and communist worlds.

In a persuasive speech, conclude with your most forcible and memorable plea. © *Corbis*.

Use a Dramatic Illustration

Ending your speech with a dramatic story connected to your speech's main theme reinforces the theme in your listeners' minds. It is the last message of your speech the audience will hear and, as a story, it is the most likely to be remembered. Investigative reporter Dale Van Atta (1989) concluded a speech on international terrorism with the following story about the struggle for freedom:

> There was a woman in Laos who I will never forget. I was in the refugee camps along the border of the Mekong River. I was meeting with her and an interpreter and I asked her what happened when she escaped [from Laos]; she had come out about a week before.

> She said she was coming to the Mekong River with a group of about forty Laos citizens trying to flee from the communists. They were in the woods and began to hear the patrol and feared they would be caught. She had a four- or five-month-old baby who began to cry. As is common with the Lao

people, they use opium for medicinal purposes. They always have some—they are not addicted; they use it like an herbal medicine. She decided that the only way she could silence the child and save the forty others was to blow a little of this opium into the child's nose so it would become very quiet. And it worked.

And then she began to cry and the interpreter and the head of the camp did not know what had happened. He turned to me—the head of the camp—and said to me, "She doesn't have a baby with her." So I asked her what happened. She said by the time they got to the other side of the river, she found her baby was dead. She had blown too much opium into the baby's nose.

And then there was a long pause as we were all in tears. And I asked her, "If you had to do it again, would you do it again?" And she said, "Yes. To come to America for freedom—for the sake of my other children."

We have a country that is so much [the country described by the] kindergarten child who got the Pledge of Allegiance wrong: "I pledge of allegiance to the flag of the United States of a miracle." He got it right.

Thank you very much.

Close with a Quotation

Closing a speech with the words of others is an effective and memorable way to end your presentation. Here is how Charles Parnell (1989) concluded his remarks on speech writing to a group of business executives:

> In conclusion, let me refer to some words of Dr. E. C. Nance, quoted in *Vital Speeches* more than thirty years ago:

> Words can change the face of a city, build churches, schools, playgrounds, boys' clubs, scout troops, civic forums, civic clubs, little theaters, civic music organizations, garden clubs, and better local governments.

> We need words that will make us laugh, wonder, work, think, aspire, and hope. We need words that will leap and sing in our souls. We need words that will cause us to face up to life with a fighting faith and contend for those ideals that have made this the greatest nation on earth.

> Ladies and gentlemen, with all the problems and challenges facing business, our country, and the world, we are going to need words that can inspire us to do all these things. You the communicators are the people who will give us these words (210).

One of the most famous moments in oratory was the conclusion of President Ronald Reagan's eulogy to the crew of the space shuttle *Challenger*.

The crew of the space shuttle *Challenger* honored us by the manner in which they lived their lives. We will never forget them, nor the last time we saw them—this morning, as they prepared for their journey, and waved good-bye, and "slipped the surly bonds of earth" to "touch the face of God." (President Ronald Reagan's address to the nation on the Challenger disaster from the Oval Office, January 28, 1986.)

As in this example, quotations can be interwoven into the fabric of the speech without telling your listeners that you are speaking the words of others. If you use this technique, it is important that you use the quote exactly and attribute it to the writer.

How to Conclude the Same Speech in Different Ways

Just as many topics lend themselves to different types of introductions, they also lend themselves to various methods of conclusion. Here three different techniques are used to conclude a speech on learning to deal more compassionately with the elderly:

A Quotation That Personalizes Your Message

In 1878, in a poem entitled, "Somebody's Mother," poet Mary Dow Brine wrote these words:

> She's somebody's mother, boys, you know,
> For all she's aged and poor and slow.

Most of us are likely to be somebody's mother—or father—before we die. And further down the road, we're likely to be grandparents, sitting in a rocking chair, hoping that our children have figured out a more humane way to treat us than we have treated our elderly relatives.

A Dramatic Story That Also Serves as a Metaphor

Not too long ago, I had a conversation with a doctor who had recently hospitalized an 82-year-old woman with pneumonia. A widow and the mother of three grown children, the woman had spent the last seven years of her life in a nursing home.

The doctor was called three times a day by these children. At first their calls seemed appropriate. They wanted to be sure their mother was getting the best possible medical care. Then, their tone changed. Their requests became demands; they were pushy and intrusive.

After several days of this, the doctor asked one of the children—a son—when he had last visited his mother before she was admitted to the hospital. He hesitated for a moment and then admitted that he had not seen her for two years.

I'm telling you this story to demonstrate that we can't act like these grown children and throw our elderly away only to feel guilty about them when they are in crisis.

Somehow we have to achieve a balance between our own needs and the needs of our frail and needy parents—one that places reasonable demands on ourselves and on the system that supports the elderly.

Rhetorical Questions

Imagine yourself old and sick, worried that your money will run out and that your family will no longer want you. You feel a pain in your chest. What could it be? You ask yourself whether your daughter will be able to leave work to take you to the hospital—whether your grandchildren will visit you there—whether your medical insurance will cover your bills—whether anyone will care if you live or die.

Imagine asking yourself these questions and then imagine the pain of not knowing the answers. We owe our elderly better than that.

Conclude with a Metaphor That Broadens the Meaning of Your Speech

You may want to broaden the meaning of your speech through the use of an appropriate metaphor—a symbol that tells your listeners that you are saying more. President Reagan used this technique several times at the conclusion of his State of the Union address by citing the heroism of a select group of individuals who were invited to sit in the balcony of the House of Representatives while the speech was being delivered. Here are Reagan's words:

> Tonight I have spoken of great plans and great dreams. They are dreams we can make come true. Two hundred years of American history should have taught us that nothing is impossible.
>
> Ten years ago a young girl left Vietnam with her family, part of the exodus that followed the fall of Saigon. They came to the United States with no possessions, and not knowing a word of English. The young girl studied hard, learned English, and finished high school in the top of her class. This May is a big date on her calendar. Just ten years from the time she left Vietnam, she'll graduate from the United States Military Academy at West Point. I thought you might want to meet an American hero named Jean Nguyen.

(The young woman stood and bowed to the applause.)

> There's someone else here tonight. Born seventy-nine years ago, she lives in the inner city where she cares for infants born to mothers who are heroin addicts. The children, born in withdrawal, are sometimes even dropped at her doorstep. She heals them with love. Go to her house some night and maybe you'll see her silhouette against the window, as she walks the floor talking softly, soothing a child in her arms. Mother Hale of Harlem—she, too, is an American hero.

(Mrs. Hale stood to acknowledge the applause.)

> Your lives tell us that the oldest American saying is new again: Anything is possible in America if we have the faith, the will, and the heart. History is asking us, once again, to be a force for good in the world. Let us begin, in unity, with justice, and love (Noonan 1990, 198–99).

Presidential speechwriter Peggy Noonan explains the symbolic impact of Reagan's conclusion: "The 'heroes in the balcony' was a metaphor for all the everyday heroism that never gets acknowledged. It was for kids, to show them what courage is" (198).

Conclude with Humor

If you leave your listeners with a humorous story, you will leave them laughing and with a reservoir of good feelings about you and your speech. To be effective, of course, the humor must be tied to your core idea.

A Hollywood screenwriter, invited to speak to students in a college writing course about the job of transforming a successful novel into a screenplay, concluded her speech with the following story:

> Two goats who often visited the set of a movie company found some discarded film next to where a camera crew was working. One of the goats began munching on the film.
>
> "How's it taste?" asked the other goat, trying to decide whether to start chomping himself.
>
> "Not so great," said the first goat. "I liked the book better."

The audience laughed in appreciation of the humor. When the room settled down, the speaker concluded her speech:

> I hope in my case the goat isn't right and that you've enjoyed the films I've written even more than the books on which they were based.
>
> Thank you for inviting me to speak.

Encourage Thought with a Rhetorical Question

Rhetorical questions encourage thought. At the end of a speech, they leave listeners with a responsibility to think about the questions raised after your speech is over. Your question can be as simple as, "Can our community afford to take the step of hiring fifty new police officers? Perhaps a better question is, can we afford not to?" Rhetorical questions have the power to sway an audience with their emotional impact.

Refer to Your Introduction

In your conclusion, you can refer to an opening story or quotation or answer the rhetorical questions you raised. Here is how Shannon closed her speech on seat belt safety:

> One thing I didn't tell you at the beginning of my speech about my accident was that for years I resisted wearing my belt. I used to fight with my parents. I felt it was such a personal decision. How could they—or the state government, for that matter—dare tell me what to do?

Thank goodness I had the sense to buckle up that day. And you can be sure that I will never get into a car without wrapping myself securely with my belt of life. I hope that my experience will be enough to convince you to buckle up too.

Like matching bookends, closing your speech with a reference to your introduction provides intellectual and emotional symmetry to your remarks.

Talk to Your Listener
Ten Common Pitfalls of Conclusions

Knowing what *not* to do is almost as important as knowing *what* to do. Here is a list of approaches to avoid during your conclusion.

1. Don't use your conclusion to introduce a new topic.

Develop your main and subordinate points in the body of your speech, not in the conclusion.

2. Don't apologize.

Even if you are unhappy with your performance, do not apologize for your shortcomings when you reach the conclusion. Remarks like, "Well, I guess I didn't have that much to say," or "I'm sorry for taking so much of your time," are unnecessary and usually turn off the audience.

3. Don't end abruptly.

Just because you have made all your points does not mean that your speech is over. Your audience has no way of knowing you are finished unless you provide closure. A one-sentence conclusion is not sufficient closure.

4. Don't change the mood or tone.

If your speech was serious, do not shift moods at the end. A humorous conclusion would be inappropriate and lessen the impact of your speech.

5. Don't use the phrases, "in summary" or "in conclusion," except when you are actually at the end of your speech.

Some speakers use these phrases at various points in their speech, confusing listeners who expect an ending rather than a transition to another point.

6. Don't ask for questions.

Never risk asking, "Any questions?" Think about it, if there are no questions, you will be creating an awkward silence—hardly the climactic conclusion you were hoping for. Also, most speech days in class are designed to have a number of speakers fill the class period. Answering questions or taking comments may interfere with the instructor's schedule.

If there is to be a question and answer session, consider it as a separate event from the speech. Complete your entire conclusion, receive your well-earned applause, and *then* field any questions.

7. Don't ignore applause.

Graciously accept the praise of your audience by looking around the room and saying thank you.

8. Don't forget to thank your audience and host.

Part of your lasting positive impression will come from a sincere thanks offered to both your audience for their attention and your host for allowing you the opportunity to speak. This is true in many speaking situations, but does not apply to the general public speaking class.

9. Don't run away.

Remember to keep your poise as you confidently make your retreat from the speaking platform. Being in too big a rush to sit down gives the appearance that you are glad it is over. You may be ready to leave, but stifle the urge to flee the podium.

10. Don't read it.

Just as with the introduction, the delivery of the conclusion is very important. Practice it enough that you are not dependent on your speaker's notes. Eye contact with your audience as you wrap up your message will reinforce your perceived credibility as well as your message's importance.

Summary

The primacy/recency effect underscores the importance of strong introductions and conclusions. Introductions serve several functions: they focus attention, provide a motive for the audience to listen, build speaker credibility, and preview the topic of your speech.

Several techniques can be used to capture audience attention in the introduction. Among these are startling statements, dramatic stories, quotations, humor, rhetorical questions, illustrations, examples, anecdotes, audience involvement, using personal experiences and visual aids, and making reference to your speaking situation. Your introduction will be successful if you follow established guidelines (such as making it clear and easy to follow), and practicing it as many times as needed, and by avoiding the common pitfalls.

The conclusion of your speech should summarize, motivate, and communicate closure. An effective conclusion reinforces your message, acts as a summary, relates your message to your listeners' lives, and connects your message to a broader context.

Among the techniques you can use to conclude your speech are a call to action, a dramatic story, a closing quotation, a metaphor that broadens meaning, humor, rhetorical questions, and a reference to the introduction.

Questions for Study and Discussion

1. What alternatives are available for capturing audience attention in an introduction? What alternatives are available for bringing closure to a speech?
2. What is the relationship between the effectiveness of a speech's introduction and conclusion and speaker credibility?
3. What mistakes do speakers commonly make in preparing the introduction and conclusion of a speech?
4. How do effective introductions and conclusions help meet the psychological needs of the audience?

Activities

1. Write a thesis statement for a speech, then use different techniques to draft three distinct introductions and conclusions.
2. Examine the transcripts of two speeches in *Vital Speeches of the Day*, *Representative American Speeches*, or a similar collection. Analyze and assess the effectiveness of the speeches' introductions and conclusions. Consider the appropriateness of each for the topic, the audience, and the occasion.
3. Prepare a short persuasive speech with two different introductions and conclusions. Then deliver it in both forms to a small group. Ask the group which introduction and conclusion worked best. Find out how the choice influences your speech's specific purpose.

References

Baird, Jr., J. E. Summer, 1974. The effects of speech summaries upon audience comprehension of expository speeches of varying quality and complexity. *Central States Speech Journal*, 119–127.

Bogue, E. G. May 7, 1988. A friend of mine: Notes on the gift of teaching, Speech delivered as commencement address, Memphis State University. Reprinted in *Vital speeches of the day*, August 1, 1988, 615.

Hearn, Jr., T. K. June 5, 1988. Sports and ethics: The university response, Speech delivered to the College Football Association, Dallas, TX. Reprinted in *Vital Speeches of the Day*, October 15, 1988, 20.

Jacob, J. E. May 30, 1988. The future of black America: The doomed generation, Speech delivered before the members of Congressional Clearinghouse on the Future. Reprinted in *Vital speeches of the day*, August 1, 1988, 616.

King, Jr., M. L. August 28, 1963, I have a dream, Speech delivered Washington, D.C. Reprinted in Johannesen, R. L., R.R. Allen, and W. A. Linkugel. 1988. *Contemporary American speeches (6th ed.)*. Dubuque, IA: Kendall/Hunt Publishing Company.

Noonan, P. 1990. *What I saw at the revolution: A political life in the Reagan era.* New York: Random House.

Oehmen, T. R. 1991. Not a drop to drink, *Winning orations of the interstate oratorical association*. Mankato State University, MN: The Interstate Oratorical Association.

Pankow, P. K. 1991. Hours before I go to sleep, *Winning Orations,* 1991, 123.

Shapiro, L. February 26, 1990. "The Zap Generation," *Newsweek,* 56.

Wood, A. 1992. America's trauma crisis, *Winning orations of the interstate oratorical association*. Mankato State University, MN: The Interstate Oratorical Association.

CHAPTER 1

"*I define conciseness the same way you do. Using no more words than necessary to express an idea well. It just happens that it takes more words to express an idea well in an article.*"

Jerry Tarver, "Words in Time: Some Reflections on the Language of Speech"

© Corbis.

Language, Style, and Humor

How old were you when you realized that your parents were just trying to be helpful when they said, "Sticks and stones may break your bones but words will never hurt you?" We are sure your parents were not intending to mislead you, but we know that while bones mend, words can sting forever. As we write this chapter, Muslims around the world are offended by words the Pope said just recently regarding Islam. Every time a politician speaks, he or she risks losing voters because of word choice. One of your authors still cringes at the memory of her high school principal announcing, "You done good," over the intercom the day after a successful football game. Language matters.

Your language will, in large part, determine the success of your speech. Through words, you create the vivid images that remain in the minds of your audience after your speech is over. Your choice of words and style of language influence your credibility as a speaker. By choosing language that appeals to your audience—by moving your audience intellectually and emotionally through the images of speech—you create a bond that encourages continued listening.

In this chapter, we identify characteristics of spoken language and provide guidelines for using spoken language more effectively. We also address pitfalls, aspects of language that a speaker should avoid. Finally, humor is discussed. Although much of the language you use in public speaking will be extemporaneous, it is important to train yourself to think about how words affect your listeners.

Characteristics of Spoken Language

Having written a paper on a certain topic, using said paper for a speech is expedient. We understand that it certainly saves time and effort. But do not do it. A written report can be used as a speech, but not without major adjustments. The needs of written language and spoken language are different because listeners process information differently from the way readers do. Listen to your instructor speak for a minute. Then imagine what it would be like if that person were reading his remarks from a manuscript; it would be remarkably boring. The spoken and written language differ in many ways, including word order, rhythm, and signals.

Word Order

The first characteristic of spoken language is word order, which relates to the order in which ideas should be arranged in a sentence. In general, the last idea presented is the most powerful. Consider this famous line spoken by John F. Kennedy at his inauguration: "Ask not what your country can do for you, ask what you can do for your country." Inverted, the sentence loses its power: "Ask what you can do for your country, ask not what your country can do for you." Because speech is slower than silent reading, individual words take on more importance, especially those appearing at the end of the sentence.

How long could you pay attention if your instructor read all his comments from a manuscript during class? © *Chad McDermott, 2008. Under license from Shutterstock, Inc.*

Rhythm

The second characteristic of spoken language is rhythm. Rhythm in music and poetry distinguishes these genres from others. The rhythm of a piece of music creates different moods. We may want to listen and reflect or dance like a maniac. Rhythm is important in spoken language, also. It is the speech flow or pattern that is created in many ways, including variations in sentence length, the use of parallel structure, and the expression of images in groups of three.

Read aloud Patrick Henry's famous line, "Give me liberty or give me death," to illustrate the importance of rhythm (Tarver 1988):

> *I know not what course*
> *Others may take.*
> *But as for me,*
> *Give me liberty*
> *Or death.*

Now read the original, and notice the greater impact:

> *I know not what course*
> *Others may take.*
> *But as for me,*
> *Give me liberty*
> *Or give me death.*

By taking out one of the repetitive "give me" phrases, the rhythm—and impact—of the sentence changes. As you develop your speech, consider the following ways you can use rhythm to reinforce your ideas and to maintain audience attention.

Vary sentence length.   First, create rhythm by varying sentence length. The rhythm of speech is affected by how well you combine sentences of varying lengths. Long sentences can be confusing and short sentences boring, but a combination of long and short sentences adds rhythmic interest. On June 1, 1997, Mary Schmich, columnist for the *Chicago Tribune*, wrote an essay, described as a commencement speech, called, "Wear Sunscreen." Rhythm is a critical element of her speech, as can be seen in the following excerpt:

> Wear sunscreen. If I could offer you only one tip for the future, sunscreen would be it…Don't worry about the future.
>
> Schmich continues her speech by discussing all the things in life that are "wasted" on those who are young, and how the things that people typically concern themselves with are never the things that ultimately end up happening. The back-and-forth rhythm of her words holds your attention as you move along with her message.

Schmich's commencement speech is filled with humor and advice, but its impact is due, in part, to the variation in sentence structure. As you probably noticed, the rhythm of this speech was engaging; so much so that two song versions were developed, one by Baz Luhrmann, "Everybody's Free (to Wear Sunscreen)" and one by John Safran, "Not the Sunscreen Song."

Use parallel structure. Second, create rhythm by using parallel structure. Parallelism involves the arrangement of a series of words, phrases, or sentences in a similar form. In his inaugural speech, President John F. Kennedy stated, "If a free society cannot help the many who are poor, it cannot save the few who are rich." Also using parallel structure, in his first inaugural speech, President Richard M. Nixon stated, "Where peace is unknown, make it welcome; where peace is fragile, make it strong; where peace is temporary, make it permanent" (Detz 1984, 69). Parallel structure emphasizes the rhythm of speech. When used effectively, it adds harmony and balance to a speech that can verge on the poetic.

President Richard M. Nixon used parallel structure in his language to make his inaugural speech memorable. © *Wally McNamee/Corbis.*

Use three as a magic number. (Detz 1984, 67–68) Third (yes, we intentionally provided three points!), rhythm can be created by referring to ideas in groups of three. Winston Churchill once said, "If you have an important point to make, don't try to be subtle or clever. Use a pile driver. Hit the point once. Then come back and hit it again. Then hit it a third time—a tremendous whack." Experienced speakers know that saying things three times gets their point across in a way saying it once cannot—not simply because of repetition, but because of the rhythmic effect of the repetition. Many presidents use this device during important speeches. You can hear the emotional impact of Abraham Lincoln's words in his Gettysburg address when he said, "We can not dedicate, we can not consecrate, we can not hallow this ground." Franklin Roosevelt's words created an impact during his second inaugural address when he observed, "I see one-third of a nation, ill-housed, ill-clad, ill-nourished." In his speech "The American Promise" given to Congress in 1965, Lyndon B. Johnson included the following line: "Our mission is at once the oldest and the most basic of this country: to right wrong, to do justice, to serve man" (Detz 1984, 68–69).

Try this device in your classroom speeches. In a speech of tribute, you might say, "I am here to honor, to praise, and to congratulate the members of the campus volunteer fire department."

Signals

A third specific characteristic of spoken language involves using signals. You may reread an important passage in a book to appreciate its meaning, but your audience hears your message only once—a fact that may make it necessary to signal critical passages in your speech. The following signals tell your listeners to pay close attention:

- This cannot be overemphasized…
- Let me get to the heart of the matter…
- I want to summarize…
- My five main points are…

Although all speakers hope to capture and hold listeners' attention throughout their speech, you must draw people back to your message at critical points. Signals are more necessary in spoken language than in print.

Guidelines for Language and Style

As you strive to be precise, clear, and understandable, keep in mind the difference between denotative and connotative definitions. A dictionary provides the literal, objective, **denotative** definition of the word. **Connotation** is the meaning we apply to words as they are framed by our personal experiences. These often lie in the realm of our subjective, emotional responses. For example, the American flag can be described denotatively by its color and design, but connotatively, the meaning varies around the world. Americans, in general, see the flag as a symbol of freedom and democracy, whereas other cultures may view our flag as a symbol of greed and hegemony. Whether the audience favors or disfavors your view, you should ensure that they understand what you mean and what you believe to be the facts that support your ideas. This next section provides six guidelines for effective use of language.

Be Concrete

On a continuum, words range from the most concrete to the most abstract. Concrete language is rooted in real-life experience—things we see, hear, taste, touch, and feel—while abstract language tells us little about what we experience, relying instead on more symbolic references. Compare the following:

Abstract	*Concrete*
Bad weather	Hail the size of golf balls
Nervousness	Trembling hands; knocking knees
An interesting professor	When she started throwing paper airplanes around the room to teach us how air currents affect lift, I knew she was a winner.

Concrete words and phrases create pictures in listeners' minds and can turn a "ho-hum" speech into one that captures listener attention. Winston Churchill understood this premise when he said, during World War II, "We shall fight them on the beaches," instead of "Hostilities will be engaged on the coastal perimeter" (Kleinfeld 1990).Consider the differences between these two paragraphs:

American citizens interpret the flag as a symbol of freedom and democracy.
© *Wellford Tiller, 2008.*
Under license from
Shutterstock, Inc.

Version 1

On-the-job accidents take thousands of lives a year. Particularly hard hit are agricultural workers who suffer approximately 1,500 deaths and 140,000 disabling injuries a year. One-fifth of all agricultural fatalities are children. These statistics make us wonder how safe farms are.

Version 2

Farmers who want to get their children interested in agriculture often take them on tractors for a ride. About 150 children are killed each year when they fall off tractors and are crushed underneath. These children represent about half the children killed in farm accidents each year—a statistic that tells us that farms can be deadly. About 1,500 people die each year on farms, and an additional 140,000 are injured seriously enough so they can no longer work.

In Version 2 the images and language are more concrete. Instead of wondering "how safe farms are," Version 2 declares that "farms can be deadly." Instead of talking about "disabling injuries," it tells us that workers "are injured seriously enough so they can no longer work." More concrete language produces an emotional response in listeners that is likely to stay with them long after a speech is over.

Complete Your Thoughts and Sentences

Focus on completing every sentence you start. This may seem like common sense, but many people do not follow this advice when speaking before groups. Although we accept the fact that many sentences trail off in conversational speech, we lose confidence in a speaker who has this habit. From the mouth of a public speaker, this language is disconcerting:

> In many states, your signature on your driver's license makes you a potential organ donor. If you are killed… . According to the laws in these states, if you are killed in an auto accident, the state has the right… . Your organs can be used to help people in need of organ transplants. There are sick people out there who need the kidneys, corneas, and even the hearts of people killed. Think about it. When you are dead, you can still give the gift of life.

On the other hand, we encourage you to *violate* this rule by incorporating sentence fragments, where relevant. Keep in mind that carefully chosen sentence fragments can contribute to clear communication. Here is an example:

> Is Christmas too commercial? Well, maybe. It wasn't that long ago when the holiday season began after Thanksgiving. Now the first Christmas catalogs reach shoppers in September. Before summer is over. Before the temperature has dropped below 90 degrees. Even before Labor Day.

Do not confuse sentence fragments with the incomplete thoughts and sentences we discussed earlier. In the case above, the fragments are intentional and are used effectively to enhance meaning.

Use the Active Voice and Follow the Rules of Written English—Most of the Time

Rules of grammar and style operate for the spoken language as well as the written language. One rule to follow involves using the active voice. A direct speaking style involves the use of the active rather than passive voice as often as possible. The following example demonstrates the difference between the passive and active voice:

Version 1: Passive voice

Students in an English class at Long Beach Community College were asked by their teacher to stand in line. After a few minutes, the line was broken by a student from Japan who walked a few yards away. The behavior demonstrated by the student shows how cultural differences can affect even the simple act of waiting in line. In this case, the need for greater personal space was felt by the student who considered it impolite to stand so close.

Version 2: Active voice

An English teacher at Long Beach Community College asked the class to stand in line. After a few minutes, a Japanese student broke the line and walked a few yards away. The student's behavior demonstrated how cultural differences affect even the simple act of waiting in line. In this case, the student felt the need for more personal space because the Japanese culture considers it impolite to stand so close.

The same sentences rephrased in the active voice show the subject of the sentence in action. In addition to using fewer words, the active voice is more direct, easier to follow, and more vigorous. We encourage the use of the active voice.

Use Language to Create a Theme

A key word or phrase can reappear throughout your speech to reinforce your theme. Each time the image is repeated, it becomes more powerful and is likely to stay with your listeners after your speech is over. The chairman of a real estate investment company developed the "Amber Light Theory of Real Estate Investment" and used this metaphor as the theme of his speeches. His point was that the real estate market rarely gives investors strong signals to proceed or stop. Instead, its signal is always one of caution. By referring to the amber light image several times in his speech, the speaker delivered a message that was effective and memorable (Berg and Gilman 1989).

Use a tone that appropriately projects the type of impression you wish to convey. © *Corbis.*

Use Language That Fits Your Personality and Position

If you are delivering a speech on advances in microsurgery, a casual, flippant tone is inappropriate, though it might work for a speech on naming the family dog. Audiences are perceptive. They know very quickly whether you are comfortable with your speaking style or whether you are trying to be something or someone you are not. It is hard to fake an emotional presentation if you are a cool, nonemotional person. If you are naturally restrained, it is difficult to appear daring and impulsive. The language you choose mirrors who you are, so choose carefully to reflect what you want others to know about you.

Vary Language Techniques to Engage Listeners

A carpenter uses a saw, a hammer, and nails to construct a building. A speaker uses language to construct a speech. Words are literally the tools of a speaker's trade. When used effectively, they can move an audience to action or to tears. They can change minds or cement opinions. Words can create a bond between you and your listeners or they can destroy a relationship. A speaker has numerous tools to choose from when building a speech.

When constructing your speech, consider using a variety of language techniques to enhance **imagery**. Imagery involves creating a vivid description through the use of one or more of our five senses. Using imagery can create a great impact and lasting memory. Mental images can be created using many devices, including metaphors, similes, and figures of speech.

Metaphors

Metaphors state that something *is* something else. Through metaphors we can understand and experience one idea in terms of another. For example, if you ask a friend how a test went, and the friend responded, "I scored a home run," you would know that your friend felt good about the test. In his "Sinews of Peace" speech to Westminster College in Fulton, Missouri, Prime Minister Winston Churchill used the following metaphor on March 5, 1946: "An iron curtain has descended across the continent." During his inaugural address, President Bill Clinton said, "Our democracy must not only be the envy of the world but also the engine of our own renewal."

Similes

Similes also create images as they compare the characteristics of two different things using the words "like" or "as." Here are two examples Ann Beattie uses in her novel, *Picturing Will*: "Falling snow looked as solid as pearls. Tar could look like satin"; and "Wayne reacted like someone whose cat has proudly brought home a dead mouse." (Beattie 1989) Both metaphors and similes rely on concrete images. Although these can enliven your speech, guard against using images that are trite or too familiar.

Figures of Speech

Figures of speech connect sentences by emphasizing the relationship among ideas and by repeating key sounds to establish a pleasing rhythm. Among the most popular figures of speech are anaphora, epistrophe, alliteration, and antithesis.

Anaphora. Anaphora is the repetition of the same word or phrase at the *beginning* of successive clauses or sentences. In the following example, Georgie

Anne Geyer (1989), foreign correspondent and syndicated columnist, uses this technique as she addresses students at Saint Mary-of-the-Woods College in Indiana.

> There is only one thing that I know to tell you graduates—only one thing—and that is to follow what you love! Follow it intellectually! Follow it sensuously! Follow it with generosity and nobility toward your fellow man! Don't deign to ask what "they" are looking for out there. Ask what you have inside.

Epistrophe. Epistrophe is the repetition of a word or expression at the *end* of phrases, clauses, or sentences. Lincoln used this device in the phrase, "of the people, by the people, for the people." It is an effective technique for emphasis.

Alliteration. Alliteration is the repetition of the initial consonant or initial sounds in series of words. Tongue twisters such as "Peter Piper picked a peck of pickled peppers" are based on alliteration. With "Peter Piper," the "P" sound is repeated multiple times. Alliteration can be used effectively in speeches, such as in Martin Luther King's 1963 *I have a dream* speech when he said, "We have come to our nation's capital to cash a check." Alliteration occurs with the repetition of "C" in "Capital to cash a check."

Antithesis. Antithesis is the use of contrast, within a parallel grammatical structure, to make a rhetorical point. Jesse Jackson told an audience of young African Americans: "We cannot be what we ought to be if we push dope in our veins, rather than hope in our brains." Later, in the same speech, he told his listeners, "You are not a man because you can kill somebody. You are a man because you can heal somebody" (Gustainis 1987, 218.)

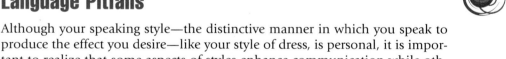

Language Pitfalls

Although your speaking style—the distinctive manner in which you speak to produce the effect you desire—like your style of dress, is personal, it is important to realize that some aspects of styles enhance communication while others detract. You may have a great sense of humor, but some may be put off by your lack of seriousness. You may be very bright and reflective, but your quiet tone may bore your audience. You have read several language guidelines for creating an effective speech. Following are five language pitfalls to avoid.

Long and Unnecessary Words

Using long and unnecessary words violates the first principle of language usage, which is to be simple and concrete. As noted earlier, when you read on your own, you have the opportunity to reread something or to look up a word you do not understand. In a speech, you do not have the rewind option, and if the audience does not understand, they will lose interest.

When Mark Twain wrote popular fiction, he was often paid by the word, a fee schedule that led him to this humorous observation:

By hard, honest labor, I've dug all the large words out of my vocabulary … I never write *metropolis* for seven cents because I can get the same price for *city*. I never write *policeman* because I can get the same price for *cop*.

The best speakers realize that attempting to impress an audience by using four- or five-syllable words usually backfires. When Franklin D. Roosevelt was given this sentence by a speechwriter—"We are endeavoring to construct a more inclusive society"—he simplified it to this: "We are going to make a country in which no one is left out" (Detz 1984, 50–53).

Here are a few multisyllabic words and their simpler alternatives.

Words to Impress	*Words to Communicate*
Periodical	Magazine
Utilize	Use
Reiterate	Repeat
Commence	Begin
Discourse	Talk

Franklin D. Roosevelt simplified his language to make his message more accessible. © *Bettmann/ Corbis*

Unnecessary words can be as problematic as long words. Spoken language requires some redundancy, but when people are forced to listen to a barrage of unnecessary words, they find it difficult to tell the difference between the important and the trivial. When the listening process becomes too difficult, they stop paying attention. Here is an example of unfocused rambling:

> Let me tell you what I did on my summer vacation. I drove down to Memphis in my car to take part in the dozens of memorial ceremonies marking the anniversary of the death of Elvis Presley. There were about 40,000 or 50,000 other people at the ceremony along with me.
>
> I took a tour of the mansion Elvis lived in before his death, known as Graceland, and I visited the new museum dedicated solely to his cars. The museum holds twenty different vehicles, including the favorite of Elvis's mother: a pink 1955 Cadillac Fleetwood.

Here is something less verbose:

> During summer vacation, I drove to Memphis to celebrate the anniversary of Elvis Presley's death. With about 40,000 or 50,000 other people, I toured Graceland, Elvis' home, and visited the museum dedicated to his twenty vehicles, including his mother's favorite, a pink 1955 Cadillac Fleetwood.

Not only does the second version eliminate almost half of the words, it also sharpens the message and helps listeners focus on the important points.

Lack of Content, Masking Meaning, or Using Euphemisms

As a speaker, you want to be clear and to provide something meaningful for your audience. You want to avoid sentences that lack content, mask meaning, or include euphemisms. Sentences that say nothing or, worse yet, mask meaning or use euphemisms damage a speaker's credibility. Listeners wonder what to believe, and begin to question the speaker's competence. By the time listeners start asking these questions, the speech has almost certainly failed.

Speech tension, lack of preparation, or ill-intentions can cause or contribute to this language pitfall. If you do not know as much as you should about your topic or if you are trying not to reveal your intentions, you may fall into this language trap.

Language that masks or muddies rather than clarifies meaning is the downfall of many speakers. Former Secretary of State Alexander Haig combined the language of the military with the language of diplomacy to create phrases like these:

saddle myself with a statistical fence
caveat my response
epistemologicallywise
careful caution
definitizing an answer (Rackleff 1987, 312)

Although few speakers go as far as Haig in using incomprehensible language, we do find speakers using **euphemisms,** which are words or phrases substituted for more direct language. Consider, for instance, the number of ways corporate spokespersons refer to firing employees:

Euphemism: We are engaged in downsizing our operation.

Meaning: We are firing 5,000 employees.

Euphemism: We are offering employees over the age of fifty-five early retirement.

Meaning: If these older employees don't accept the deal, we'll fire them.

Euphemism: We are suggesting a career redirection.

Meaning: You no longer have a job here, so we suggest you find another type of work.

Although euphemisms like these serve a purpose (they make it easier for speakers to deal with unpleasant topics), they can make it difficult, sometimes impossible, for listeners to understand what is being said.

Jargon, Slang, and Profanity

Jargon is the technical terminology unique to a special activity or group. For example, the jargon of the publishing business includes such terms as "specs," "page proofs," "dummy stage," and ``halftones." Although these terms are not five syllables long, they are difficult to understand if you are unfamiliar with publishing.

A special kind of jargon involves the use of acronyms—the alphabet soup of an organization or profession. Instead of saturating your speech with references to the FDA, PACs, or ACLI on the assumption that everyone knows what the acronyms mean, define these abbreviations the first time they are used. Tell your listeners that the FDA refers to the Food and Drug Administration; PACs, political action committees; and the ACLI, the American Council of Life Insurance.

Jargon can be used effectively when you are *sure* that everyone in your audience understands the reference. Therefore, if you are the editor-in-chief of a publishing company addressing your editorial and production staffs, publishing jargon requires no definition. However, if you deliver a speech about the publishing business to a group of college seniors, definitions are needed.

Listeners almost always expect a degree of decorum in a formal speech, requiring that certain language be avoided. Profanity, of course, is the most obvious offender, but using the vernacular or slang can also be inappropriate. Terms like "ain't," and "you guys" should be used *only* for specific effect. In public discourse, they can violate an audience's sense of appropriateness—or propriety.

Jargon is safe to use only if you're certain everyone will understand it. © *Corbis.*

Exaggeration and Clichés

Exaggerations are statements made to impress, not aiming for accuracy. Instead of telling your classmates that you "always" exercise an hour a day, tell them that you exercise an hour a day "as often" as you can. Some of your classmates may know you well enough to realize that "always" is a stretching the truth. Instead of saying that you would "never" consider double parking, tell your listeners that you would consider it "only as a last resort in an emergency." Obvious exaggerations diminish your credibility as a speaker.

Clichés, according to communication professors Eugene Ehrlich and Gene R. Hawes (1984), are the "enemies of lively speech." They explain:

> They are deadwood: the shiny suits of your word wardrobe, the torn sandals, the frayed collars, the scuffed shoes, the bobby socks, the fur pieces, the Nehru jackets, the miniskirts—yesterday's chewing gum (48).

Clichés can lull your listeners into a state of boredom as they suggest that both your vocabulary and imagination are limited. Here is a section of a speech filled with slang and clichés, which have been emboldened:

> Two years ago, the real estate market was weak. **At that point in time** I would **guesstimate** that there were 400 more houses on the market than there are today. For us, it was time to **hustle. We toughed it out and held onto the ball**. The **game plan** we should follow from now on is to convince potential buyers that we **have a good thing going** in this commu-

nity—good schools, good libraries, a good transportation system. We should also convince them that we're a **community with a heart**. We're here to help each other when we're **down and out**.

Imagine listening to this entire speech. Even if the speaker has something valuable to say, it is virtually impossible to hear it through the clichés. Clichés are unimaginative and add unnecessary words to your speech.

Phrases That Communicate Uncertainty

Speakers should avoid phrases that communicate uncertainty. Language can communicate a sense of mastery of your subject, or it can communicate uncertainty. Compare the following paragraphs:

Version 1

It seems to me that too many students choose a career solely on the basis of how much they are likely to earn. In my estimation, they forget that they also have to enjoy what they are going to spend the rest of their work lives doing.

Version 2

Too many students choose a career solely on the basis of how much they are likely to earn. They forget that they also have to enjoy what they are going to spend the rest of their work lives doing.

Version 1 contains weakening phrases: ``it seems to me'' and ``in my estimation,'' which add nothing but uncertainty to the speaker's message. If you have a position, state it directly without crutch words that signal your timidity to the audience.

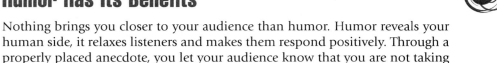

Humor Has Its Benefits

Nothing brings you closer to your audience than humor. Humor reveals your human side, it relaxes listeners and makes them respond positively. Through a properly placed anecdote, you let your audience know that you are not taking yourself—or your subject—too seriously. Even in a serious speech, humor can be an effective tool to emphasize an important point.

Research has shown the favorable impact humor can have on an audience. In particular, humor accomplishes two things. First, according to Charles R. Gruner (1985), a communication professor and recognized expert on the use of humor in public speaking, when appropriate humor is used in informative speaking, the humor enhances the speaker's image by improving the audience's perception of the speaker's character. Second, research has also shown that humor can make a speech more memorable over a longer period of time. In one study, two groups of subjects were asked to recall lectures they heard six weeks earlier. The group who heard the lecture presented humorously had higher recall than the group who heard the same lecture delivered without humor (Kaplan and Pascoe 1977).

In another experiment, students who took a statistics course given by an instructor who used humor in class lectures scored fifteen percent higher on objective exams than did students who were taught the same material by an instructor who did not (Ziv 1982).

Humor works only if it is carefully used and only if it is connected to the theme of your speech. Here are five guidelines for the effective use of humor in a speech.

Use Humor Only If You Can Be Funny

Some speakers do not know how to be funny in front of an audience. On a one-on-one basis they may be funny, but in front of a group, their humor vanishes. They stumble over punch lines and their timing is bad. These people should limit themselves to serious speeches or "safe" humor. For example, former Maine senator Ed Muskie made his audience laugh by describing the shortest will in Maine legal history—a will that was only ten words long: "Being of sound mind and memory, I spent it all" (Rackleff 1987, 313).

Laugh at Yourself, Not at Others

Former California governor George Deukmajian sometimes used the following line to break the ice with his audience:

> I understand that you have been searching for a speaker who can dazzle you with his charm, wit, and personality. I'm pleased to be filling in while the search continues (Robinson 1989, 68).

Research has shown that speakers who make themselves the object of their own humor often endear themselves to their listeners. In one study, students heard brief speeches from a "psychologist" and an "economist," both of whom explained the benefits of their professions. While half the speeches were read with mildly self-deprecating humor directed at the profession being discussed, the other half were read without humor. Students rated the speakers with the self-deprecating humor higher on a scale of "wittiness" and "sense of humor," and no damage was done to the perceived character or authoritativeness of the speaker (Chang and Gruner 1981).

It can be effective to tell a joke at your own expense, but it is in poor taste to tell a joke at the expense of others. Racial, ethnic, or sexist jokes are rarely acceptable, nor are jokes that poke fun at the personal characteristics of others. Although stand-up comics like Dane Cook, Jeff Foxworthy, and Chris Rock may get away with such humor, public speakers cannot.

Chris Rock's typical comedy routine should not be emulated by public speakers. © *Reuters/Corbis.*

Understated Anecdotes Can Be Effective

An economist speaking before a group of peers starts with the following anecdote:

> I am constantly reminded by those who use our services that we often turn out a ton of material on the subject but we do not always give our clients something of value. A balloonist high above the earth found his balloon leaking and managed to land on the edge of a green pasture. He saw a man in a business suit approaching, and very happily said: "How good it is to see you. Could you tell me where I am?"
>
> The well-dressed man replied: "You are standing in a wicker basket in the middle of a pasture." "Well," said the balloonist, "You must be an economist." The man was startled. "Yes, I am, but how did you know that?"
>
> "That's easy," said the balloonist, "because the information you gave me was very accurate—and absolutely useless" (Valenti 1982, 80–81).

This anecdote is funny in an understated way. It works because it is relevant to the audience. Its humor comes from the recognition that the speaker knows—and shares—the foibles of the audience.

Find Humor in Your Own Experiences

The best humor comes from your own experiences. In general, avoid books of jokes and stories from the Internet. Humor is all around you. You might want to start now to record humorous stories for your speeches so that you will have material when the need arises. If you decide to use someone else's material, you have the ethical responsibility to give the source credit. You might start with, "As Jerry Seinfeld would say…"This gives appropriate source citation and makes clear that line or story is meant as a joke. Usually you will get bigger laughs by citing their names than if you tried to convince your audience that the humor was original.

Avoid Being *NOT* Funny

We use the double negative to make a point. When humor works and the audience responds with a spontaneous burst of applause or laughter, there is little that will make you feel better—or more relaxed—as a speaker. Its effect is almost magical. However, when the humor is distasteful to the audience or highly inappropriate, a speaker may find no one is laughing. On April 30, 2006, Stephen Colbert of *The Colbert Report* spoke at the White House Correspondents' Association dinner where the President was in attendance. Although his speech became the number one download on iTunes, he received a very lukewarm reception during his speech because of his critique of the President, which included the following:

The greatest thing about this man is he's steady. You know where he stands. He believes the same thing Wednesday that he believed on Monday, no matter what happened Tuesday. Events can change, this man's beliefs never will. (Transcript of speech available at www.dailykos.com.)

Many of us may find this quite humorous, but it was not funny to many attending. As a result, for the 2007 White House Correspondents Association dinner, Rich Little, a comedian who rose to fame in the 1970s with his Richard Nixon impression, was the after-dinner entertainment. His tamer, less edgy speech was well-received.

It is important to keep in mind that humor is criticism. We laugh at things people do, what they say, how they react, and so on. In fulfilling our ethical responsibilities, however, we need to remember that while someone or some event is being mocked, the speaker needs to do so with taste and appropriateness.

So, to avoid being *not* funny, audience analysis is vital. As a beginning public speaker, we urge you to err on the side of caution. It is better to avoid humor than to fail at it. While most humor is risky, there are certain things you can be fairly sure your audience will find funny. Stick with those, and try riskier humor as you gain confidence and experience. You might also check with a friend or classmate if you have any question about the humor of a line or story.

Summary

Spoken language differs from written language in several important ways. In many cases, spoken language requires redundancy; it affects the order of ideas, and requires that the speaker pay attention to rhythm. Spoken language may also require that you signal your audience before you present important material.

The most effective language is simple, clear, and direct. Use short, common words instead of long, unusual ones; avoid euphemisms and jargon; eliminate unnecessary words that pad your speech; be direct and concrete and avoid exaggeration.To improve your speaking style, avoid clichés, complete your thoughts, and use sentence fragments for specific effect. Avoid profanity, slang, and jargon, as well as sentences that say nothing. Because certain phrases communicate uncertainty, avoid using them during your presentation.

Try to engage the imagination of your listeners through the use of metaphors and similes that paint memorable word pictures. Use language to create a theme. Regardless of the choices you make, be certain your language fits your personality, position, and the needs of your audience.The effective use of humor requires that you have confidence in your ability to make people laugh. Do not use humor if you have never been funny. Laugh at yourself, not others. Use understated anecdotes. And remember, humor is everywhere. Find humor in your own experiences. Seriously!

Questions for Study and Discussion

1. How is spoken language different from written language?
2. How can language contribute to or detract from the effectiveness of your speech?
3. Why must language fit the needs of the speaker, audience, occasion, and message?
4. What do you need to consider when choosing proper language in a speech?
5. What language techniques can you employ when you speak?
6. What are some of the language pitfalls that reduce the effectiveness of your speech?
7. Why is humor important in public speaking?
8. How does humor affect the speaker-audience relationship?

Activities

1. Read aloud a written report you wrote for another class, then analyze whether the report's language is appropriate as a speech. Analyze the changes necessary to transform the report into an effective oral presentation.
2. Select a speech from *Vital Speeches of the Day* or from another collection in your library. Study the language of the speech and write an assessment of its effectiveness, strengths, and weaknesses. Because the language was intended to be spoken, you might have to read the speech aloud during your evaluation.
3. Begin collecting humorous ideas, stories, and incidents for your next speech. As you develop your ideas, blend the humor into the speech, remembering to practice your delivery with a tape recorder.

References

Beattie, A. 1989. *Picturing will*. New York: Bantam Books.

Berg, K., and A. Gilman. 1989. *Get to the point: How to say what you mean and get what you want*. New York: Random House.

Chang, M. and C. R. Gruner. 1981. Audience reaction to self-disparaging humor. *Southern Speech Communication Journal*, 46: 419–26. Reported in Gruner, Advice to the beginning speaker, 142–47. (Listed below.)

Detz, J. 1984. *How to write and give a speech*. New York: St. Martin's Press.

Ehrlich, E., and G. R. Hawes. 1984. *Speak for success*. New York: Bantam Books.

Geyer, G. A. May 7, 1989. Joy in our times: I am responsible for my own fight. Speech delivered as commencement address at Saint Mary-of-the-Woods College. Reprinted in *Vital Speeches of the Day*, August 15, 1989, 668.

Gruner, C. R. April, 1985. Advice to the beginning speaker on using humor— What the research tells us. *Communication Education* 34:142.

Gustainis, J. J. 1987. Jesse Louis Jackson, in B. K. Duffy and H. R. Ryan, Eds., *American orators of the twentieth century: Critical studies and sources*. New York: Greenwood Press.

Kaplan, R. M., and G. C. Pascoe. 1977. Humorous lectures and humorous examples: Some effects upon comprehension and retentions. *Journal of Educational Psychology*, 69: 61–65.

Kleinfeld, N. R. March 11, 1990. "Teaching the 'Sir Winston' method," *New York Times*, 7.

Rackleff, R. B. September 26, 1987. The art of speech writing: A dramatic event. Speech delivered to the National Association of Bar Executives Section on Communication and Public Relations. Reprinted in *Vital Speeches of the Day*, March 1, 1988.

Robinson, J. W. 1989. *Better speeches in ten simple steps*. Rocklin, CA: Prima Publishing and Communications.

Schmich, M. June 1, 1997. Advice, like youth, probably just wasted on the young. *Chicago Tribune*. Retrieved June 10, 2007 on www.chicagotribune.com.

Tarver, J. March 2, 1988. Words in time: Some reflections on the language of speech. Speech delivered to the Chicago Speech Writer's Forum. Reprinted in *Vital Speeches of the Day*, April 15, 1988, 410–12.

Valenti, J. 1982. *Speak up with confidence*. New York: William Morrow and Company, Inc.

Ziv, A. 1982. Cognitive results of using humor in teaching. Paper presented at the Third International Conference on Humor, Washington, D. C. Cited in Gruner, Advice to the beginning speaker, 144. (Listed above.)

CHAPTER

11

Your ability to communicate information, persuade, and entertain is influenced by the manner in which you present yourself to your audience.

Delivery

Methods of Delivery
Memorization
Using a Manuscript
Extemporaneous Speaking
Impromptu Speaking

Aspects of Vocal Delivery
Articulation
Pronunciation
Volume
Rate
Pitch
Pauses
Emphasis
Eliminating Non-fluencies

Aspects of Physical Delivery
Gestures
Actions That Inhibit Gesturing
Using Note Cards
Common Problems Using Note Cards
Using a Legal Pad
Physical Movement
Eye Contact
Appearance

Summary

Questions for Study and Discussion

Activities

References

What do you remember after a speaker is finished? Although you may walk away with the speaker's ideas buzzing through your mind, it is often the quality of the performance that remains with you long after you have forgotten the content of the message. That is to say, the *how* of public speaking—the speaker's style of delivery—often makes the most lasting impression.

Words alone are not enough to make audiences want to listen to a speech. Many brilliant people—scientists, lawyers, politicians, engineers, environmentalists—never connect with their listeners, not for lack of trying, but for problems with the delivery of their speech. Maybe they are too stiff or appear uninvolved. Worse, they may try to imitate other speakers and be something they are not.

Delivery affects your credibility as a speaker. Your ability to communicate information, persuade, and entertain is influenced by the manner in which you present yourself to your audience. An effective delivery works *for* you, an ineffective delivery against you—even when the content of your message is strong.

Methods of Delivery

The following section identifies four different methods of delivery. You may find comfort in one style more than the other, but hopefully, you will have an opportunity to explore different methods of delivery during your public speaking course. Each of the four methods is appropriate in certain situations. As a speaker, you need to be aware of your audience and the occasion when choosing the method of delivery that is most appropriate and effective. Performance guidelines accompany each method of delivery. These are aspects to consider as you plan to deliver the speech. Your four choices are to memorize your speech, speak from a manuscript, use carefully prepared notes and speak extemporaneously, or give an impromptu, spur-of-the-moment speech.

Memorization

It is every speaker's nightmare: You are in the middle of a ten-minute speech and you cannot remember the next word. Because you memorized the speech (or so you thought), you have no note cards to help you through the crisis. This nightmare becomes reality on a regular basis in public speaking classes. Nervous students who have memorized their speeches find themselves without a clue as to what to say next. Even those who spend hours preparing for the presentation may forget everything when facing an audience. This situation is made worse if you are part of a group presentation because other people depend on you.

While memorization is unnecessary in many situations, there are times when having your speech memorized is preferable. For example, when you know you will be receiving an award or recognition, memorization may be a useful delivery tool. Special occasions, such as toasting the bride and groom or delivering a *brief* commencement address, are also opportunities for delivering a memorized speech. Memorization enables you to write the exact words you will speak without being forced to read them. It also makes it easier to establish eye contact with your audience and to deliver your speech skillfully. If you find yourself in a situation where memorization is necessary, consider the following four performance guidelines.

Start memorizing the speech as soon as possible. You do not want to delay the process so that you are under a severe time constraint. (Such as the night before!) Make sure you have ample time to work on the memorization aspect of your delivery. Even experienced professional speakers have to work hard to remember their lines.

Memorize small sections of your speech at a time. Do not allow yourself to become overwhelmed with the task. Memorizing small sections of your speech at a time will help minimize the chance that you will forget your speech during the delivery. Remember that some people can memorize speeches more easily than others, so work at your own pace and do not compare yourself to the classmate who memorized her speech in a very short period of time.

Memorize small sections of your speech at a time.
© *JupiterImages Corporation.*

Determine where you need pauses, emphasis, and vocal variety. You want to convey the appropriate tone for your speech—enthusiasm, excitement, anger, bewilderment. You can achieve this by emphasizing certain words, speaking faster or more slowly, and increasing or lowering your volume and/or pitch. More about vocal aspects of delivery will be discussed shortly.

Avoid looking like you are trying to remember the speech. As instructors, sometimes we feel as though we can *see* the speaker trying to remember the words, as though the speaker has a disk in his/her head, and he/she is trying to access the right file. The speaker might look up, look to the side, or simply look pensive as he/she tries to "retrieve" the information.

Overall, delivering a memorized speech can be very effective, but it is also a gamble. In addition to the actual task of memorization, students need to make sure they work on vocal variety, so they can connect with their audience. For the student in the basic public speaking class, a memorized speech is seldom what an instructor wants to hear.

Using a Manuscript

Manuscript reading involves writing your speech out word for word and then reading it. A manuscript speech may be considered in formal occasions when the speech is distributed beforehand or if it is archived. Many presidential speeches are manuscript speeches. The president is expected to follow a teleprompter, which is frequently used. On occasion, scholars give speeches that are then printed in the "proceedings" of a conference. On other occasions, the speaker may be addressing an international conference, and the manuscript is translated into one or more languages. Having a manuscript speech minimizes the temptation to add remarks during the speech.

If an issue or occasion is controversial or sensitive, a speaker may choose to rely on a manuscript. Having a carefully crafted statement may help avoid misstating a position. You may also choose to read from a manuscript when addressing a hostile audience because you know your listeners are ready—and waiting—to attack your statement. You want to be sure your communication is exact.

For those who are not professional speakers, a manuscript may be troublesome. If the font size is too small, it may be difficult to read. Each time you look up and then back down, it is possible to lose your place in the manuscript. Some people tend to sound as though they are reading rather than speaking when working from a manuscript. We encourage students to avoid writing out their speeches verbatim, but recognize that there are occasions when manuscript speaking is appropriate. If you find yourself involved in one of these occasions, we offer four performance guidelines.

Pay special attention to preparing the written text. If you cannot read what you have written, your delivery will falter. Avoid using a handwritten manuscript. Make sure you choose a large enough font to see without squinting, and have the lines spaced well enough that you do not lose your place.

Practice. The key to successful manuscript speaking is practice and more practice. One run through is not sufficient.

Express yourself naturally and communicate your personality. You do not want to look frozen in time. Think about what you want to emphasize and vary the pitch of your voice to avoid being monotone. Pronounce words as you would in normal speech and be conscious of speaking too quickly or too slowly.

Make eye contact with your audience. Glance back and forth between your manuscript and your audience. Take care not to bob your head in the process. When a speech is memorized, this is not an issue. However, when you are dependent on a manuscript, you need to make sure it does not *sound* like you are reading to the audience. Looking up from the manuscript and making eye contact with members of your audience are important aspects of manuscript delivery.

Expressing yourself naturally helps you connect with your audience.
© *JupiterImages Corporation.*

A big mistake students make is typing the entire speech on the required number of note cards (even though they have been warned not to do this). A five- to eight-minute speech is typed on three to five note cards. The outcome is not pretty. Students find themselves unable to read the cards—font size is six, and twelve lines of type are on each note card. They cannot read, they lose their place, they stumble as they try to decipher the words, and even worse, because they are concentrating so hard on reading the notes, they forget about the vocal aspects of delivery! The lesson learned? Use a manuscript *only* when the occasion suggests it.

Extemporaneous Speaking

The most appropriate mode of delivery for students of public speaking is **extemporaneous speaking,** a method of delivery that involves using carefully prepared notes to guide the presentation.

Extemporaneous speaking has many advantages. In particular, speakers can maintain a personal connection with their listeners and can respond to their feedback. The most effective public speaking is often described as the speaker's response to the listener's reaction. This takes shape in the communication transaction. The extemporaneous mode of delivery allows this interaction to occur as you adjust your choice of words and decide what to include—or exclude—in your speech. You can shorten a speech (you may want to follow the advice of the Reverend William Sloane Coffin (1988) who said about the length of an effective sermon, "No souls are saved after twenty minutes") or go into greater detail than you originally planned. This mode of speaking provides flexibility.

Extemporaneous speaking allows you to move freely and emphasize points with gestures. © *JupiterImages Corporation.*

Speaking extemporaneously means that your word choice is *fresh.* Although you know the intent of your message in advance, you choose your words as you are delivering your speech. The result is a spontaneous, conversational tone that puts you and your audience at ease. This is not to say that as you practice your speech, key words or phrases will not remain with you. On the contrary, the more you practice, the more likely you are to commit a particularly fitting word or phrase to memory. Extemporaneous speaking gives you the freedom to gesture as you would in conversational speech. With both hands free, (you can gesture with note cards in one hand) you can move about and emphasize key points with forceful gestures. Consider the following guidelines as you prepare for your extemporaneous speech.

Prepare carefully. In terms of preparation, use the same care you would use when preparing a written report. Choose your purpose, develop your core idea, research your topic, organize your ideas, and select the language and presentation style that is most appropriate for your audience.

Prepare both a full content and key-word speaker's outline. Recently, a student gave his own eulogy as a special occasion speech. He worked from a very brief outline. His speech was too short, and he seemed to have a lapse of memory. Had he used a more fully-developed outline, these problems would have been eliminated.

Develop an outline containing main points and subpoints, then create a key-word outline that can be transferred to index cards of the appropriate size. Cards should be large enough to accommodate information from your key-word outline, yet small enough to be unobtrusive. Cards may be held or placed on a lectern.

Place detailed information on separate note cards. Facts, figures, and quotations may be written on separate note cards for easy reference. Always remember your ethical responsibility not to misrepresent facts or opinions that require careful and precise explanations. Rather than take the chance of misquoting people or facts, it may help to have the information written on separate cards.

Write legibly. Your notes are useless if you cannot read them, so print your words boldly and consider highlighting critical ideas. If typing, use an appropriate font size. Remember, too, that your visual aids can serve as notes to some extent.

Use your notes as a prompter. Notes enable you to keep your ideas in mind without committing every word to memory. Notes also make it possible to maintain eye contact with your listeners. You can glance around the room, looking occasionally at your cards, without giving anyone the impression that you are reading your speech.

Impromptu Speaking

Impromptu speaking term involves little to no preparation time. This means using no notes or just a few. In your lifetime, there may be many occasions when you are asked to speak briefly without any advanced notice. For example, you may be a principal of a high school attending a local school board meeting, and someone on the school board asks you to comment on the recent basketball victory. Or, at that same meeting, a school board member may decide it is the right moment to recognize the accomplishments of a retiring teacher. During other occasions, you may be asked to "say a few words" about a newlywed couple, the dearly-departed, or a scholarship you just received.

In a public speaking class, many instructors include impromptu speaking opportunities throughout the semester. In particular, it is helpful for students to give a brief impromptu speech at the beginning of the semester just to get on their feet and face the audience. Instructors generally feel that the more opportunities we give students to present, the more comfortable students will feel in the speaking environment. You may have an activity in class where you introduce yourself or someone in the class. You may be called upon to give an impromptu speech on "my proudest moment," or "my favorite vacation spot."

Not everyone has the ability of Marcus Garvey, African American nationalist leader, to speak on the spur of the moment. Dorothy L. Pennington, an expert in the rhetoric of African Americans, describes Garvey's oratorical style:

> He often spoke impromptu, gleaning his topic and remarks from something that had occurred during the earlier portion of the program. For example, in speaking before the conference of the Universal Negro Improvement Association in August 1937, Garvey showed how his theme emerged: "I came as usual without a subject, to pick the same from the surroundings, the environment, and I got one from the sing-

Be sure to develop an outline that contains main points and subpoints before moving on to keywords only. © *JupiterImages Corporation.*

ing of the hymn `Faith of our Fathers.' I shall talk to you on that as a theme for my discourse." This type of adaptation allowed Garvey to tap into the main artery of what an audience was thinking and feeling (Duffy and Ryan 1987, 170).

Impromptu speaking forces you to think on your feet. With no opportunity to prepare, you must rely on what you know. Here are several suggestions that will help you organize your ideas:

Focus your remarks on the audience and occasion. Remind your listeners of the occasion, or purpose of the meeting: ("We have assembled to protest the rise in parking fines from $10 to $25.") When unexpectedly called to speak, talk about the people who are present and the accomplishments of the group. You can praise the group leader ("She's done so much to solve the campus parking problem"), the preceding speaker, or the group as a whole. You may want to refer to something a previous speaker said, whether you agree or disagree: ("The suggestion to organize a petition protesting the fine increase is a good one.") The remarks give you a beginning point, and a brief moment to think and organize your comments.

Use examples. Be as concrete as possible. ("I decided to become active in this organization after I heard about a student who was threatened with expulsion from school after accumulating $500 in unpaid parking fines.") Keep in mind that as an impromptu speaker, you are not expected to make a polished, professional speech--everyone knows you have not prepared. But you are expected to deliver your remarks in a clear, cogent manner.

Do not try to say too much and do not apologize. Instead of jumping from point to point in a vague manner, focus on your specific purpose. When you complete the mission of your speech, turn the platform over to another speaker. Never apologize. Your audience is already aware it is an impromptu moment, apologizing for the informality of your address is unnecessary. You do not need to say anything that will lessen your audience's expectations of your speech.

Who knows when you'll be called upon to give a toast to someone celebrating a special occasion?
© *JupiterImages Corporation.*

Aspects of Vocal Delivery

The speaker should never forget about the needs of the audience, and this applies to vocal delivery, also. It is always beneficial to speak clearly. A German friend of ours once said, "Americans speak as though they have hot potatoes in their mouths." Indeed, many of us mumble, leave off the endings of our words, and fail to pronounce words correctly. When presenting in public, consider the following aspects of vocal delivery: articulation, pronunciation, volume, rate, pitch, pauses, and emphasis.

Articulation

A person who articulates well is someone who speaks clearly and intelligibly. **Articulation** refers to the production of sound and how precisely we form our words. The more formal the situation, the more precise our articulation needs to be. The more casual the situation, the more likely we are to be relaxed in our speech. Thus, when you are giving a speech in front of an audience, the sloppy or careless pronunciation patterns you use with your friends and family should not find their way into your presentation.

Words should be crisp and clear. The listener should be able to distinguish between sounds and not be confused. The popular phrase, "Da Bears" shows how we mainstream some of our inarticulation. Leaving off the "g" in going, driving, shopping, etc. is common in American culture. Saying "I wanna," "I coulda," and "I hafta" are other examples of sloppy articulation which is perfectly acceptable in informal situations, but not so in a formal context.

The informal, careless speech you use when talking with friends is not polished enough for a presentation.
© *JupiterImages Corporation.*

Remember to adapt to your audience. In a formal setting, such as a commencement speech or an awards ceremony, you want to be as articulate as possible. In an informal setting, articulation is not as big of an issue, but it is *always* important to be understood.

Work to eliminate bad habits. Reflect a moment about how you articulate. Do you speak clearly? Do you mumble? Do you have certain words that you mispronounce? Do you leave the endings off of words? You should make a conscious effort to think about articulation. Following are several tongue twisters. You might want to see how well you do.

> Betty Botter had some butter,
> "But," she said, "this butter's bitter.
> If I bake this bitter butter,
> it would make my batter bitter.
> But a bit of better butter—
> *that* would make my batter better."
>
> So she bought a bit of butter,
> better than her bitter butter,
> and she baked it in her batter,
> and the batter was not bitter.
> So 'twas better Betty Botter
> bought a bit of better butter.
>
> A big black bug bit a big black bear,
> made the big black bear bleed blood.
>
> Toy boat. Toy boat. Toy boat.

Pronunciation

In contrast to articulation problems, mispronunciation is not knowing how to say a word and, as a result, saying it incorrectly. Sometimes speakers simply do not know the word and mispronounce it; other times, a word is mispronounced because of dialect differences among speakers. For example, you may have heard President George W. Bush leave off the "g" in "recognize," so the words sounds like "reconize." Politicians or their detractors sometimes talk about "physical" responsibility, instead of the two-syllable word, "fiscal" responsibility. People also present "satistics" instead of "statistics," and talk about the "I-talians" and the people from "I-raq."

One of your authors lives in Illinois, near a town called Mattoon. Residents of the area can tell when someone is not from the area, because at first, they say, "Ma-toon" instead of "Mat-toon." Are you someone whose name is always mispronounced? If so, you know it can be annoying.

Check pronunciation of unfamiliar words. Part of the ethical responsibility of a speaker is to check his or her pronunciation. The speaker should know how to pronounce all words in his or her speech, including the names of people and places and foreign terms.

Do not comment on your pronunciation. Do not say, "or however you pronounce that" or "I cannot pronounce that." While we are likely to forgive regional differences, our credibility will be reduced if our listeners see we have made little or no effort to determine the correct pronunciation.

Practice the pronunciation of difficult words. You do not want to stumble or draw attention away from the point you are making.

Volume

If your audience cannot hear you, your speech serves little purpose. The loudness of your voice is controlled by how forcefully air is expelled through the trachea onto the vocal folds. This exhalation is controlled by the contraction of the abdominal muscles. The more forcefully you use these muscles to exhale, the greater the force of the air, and the louder your voice.

Do not mistake shouting for projection. Shouting involves forcing the voice from the vocal folds, which is irritating to the folds, instead of projecting the sound from the abdominal area. Straining your voice will only make you hoarse. Instead, work on your posture and breathing from the diaphragm.

Use volume to add interest and variety to your speech. Maybe you want to add a bit of humor to your introduction of a speaker. Using a "stage whisper," you could say something like, "And if we all clap very loudly, we can coax him on to the stage…." On his television show, Dr. Phil uses volume effectively by getting loud when he thinks people should be annoyed by what is happening and speaking softly when he is showing amazement or shares a startling fact.

Do not talk to the podium. If you have your notes on the podium and your head is bent, the audience will not be able to hear.

Rate

During the first week of teaching at the University of Arkansas at Little Rock, a student said to Dr. Mason, "You are not from around here, are you?" When asked what gave it away, the student replied that it was the rate of speech. In the United States, Southerners generally speak more slowly than Northerners. Overall, the average rate of speech for Americans is between 120 and 160 words per minute.

Nervousness may affect your normal pattern. When practicing alone, you may be relieved when you find that in timing your speech you are just over the minimum time required. However, under the pressure of giving a speech, you may find yourself speeding up ("The faster I talk, the faster I'll finish") or slowing down. Rate is also affected by mode of delivery. If you read a manuscript rather than speak extemporaneously, you may find yourself running a verbal road race.

Choose an appropriate rate. Your rate of speech should be consistent with the ideas being expressed and for the context. For example, it makes sense that a sportscaster announcing a basketball game speaks faster than a sportscaster at a golf match.

Vary your rate of speech. By changing your rate, you can express different thoughts and feelings. You may want to speak slowly to emphasize an important point or to communicate a serious or somber mood. A faster pace is appropriate when you are telling your audience something it already knows (many speeches include background information that sets the scene) or to express surprise, happiness, or fear.

Pitch

Pitch refers to your vocal range or key, the highness or lowness of your voice produced by the tightening and loosening of your vocal folds. The range of most people's voices is less than two octaves. Pitch is a problem when your voice is too high-pitched; in men a high-pitched voice may sound immature, and in women it may sound screechy.

Vary your pitch. Variety adds interest to your presentation. Avoid a monotone. When you do not vary the pitch of your voice, you risk putting your listeners to sleep.

Use your voice potential. Take advantage of the fact that our voices have incredible range. To add color, lower the pitch of a word or phrase you want to emphasize. Resist the temptation to raise your voice too much at key points.

Pauses

Some speakers talk nonstop until, literally, they run out of breath. Others pause every three or four words in a kind of nervous verbal chop. Still others, particularly those who read their speeches, pause at the wrong times—perhaps in the middle of an important idea—making it difficult for their listeners to follow.

Pauses add color, expression, and feeling to a speech. They should be used deliberately to achieve a desired effect. If used effectively, pauses also can add power and control to your speech. They may get you into trouble when it seems like you have lost your place or forgotten what you were going to say. This may suggest you are unprepared and have not practiced sufficiently.

Pauses serve multiple purposes. First, they communicate self-confidence. Pauses deliver the nonverbal message that you are relaxed enough to stop talking for a moment. Second, they help listeners digest what you are saying and anticipate what you will say next. Third, a significant pause also helps you move from one topic to the next without actually telling your listeners what you are doing. Fourth, a pause signals *pay attention*. (This is especially true for long pauses lasting two or three seconds.) According to Don Hewitt, producer of *60 Minutes*, "It's the intonation, the pauses, that tell the story. They are as important to us as commas and periods are to the *New York Times*" (in Fletcher 1990, 15).

In 1993, Nelson Mandela, then President of the African National Congress, received the Nobel Peace Prize. The following is an excerpt from his acceptance speech:

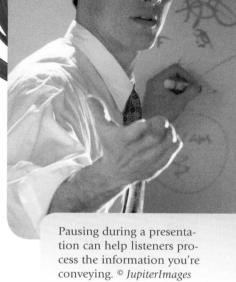

Pausing during a presentation can help listeners process the information you're conveying. © *JupiterImages Corporation.*

> We speak here of the challenge of the dichotomies of war and peace, violence and non-violence, racism and human dignity, oppression and repression and liberty and human rights, poverty and freedom from want.
>
> We stand here today as nothing more than a representative of the millions of our people who dared to rise up against a social system whose very essence is war, violence, racism, oppression, repression and the impoverishment of an entire people.
>
> I am also here today as a representative of the millions of people across the globe, the anti-apartheid movement, the governments and organizations that joined with us, not to fight against South Africa as a country or any of its peoples, but to oppose an inhuman system and sue for a speedy end to the apartheid crime against humanity.
>
> Copyright © 1993 by Nelson Mandela Foundation and Nobel Foundation. Reprinted by permission.

Try reading the excerpt aloud, using pauses where you find commas. Try using pauses of different lengths. While his words are powerful, they gain greater impact as he pauses before or after key words or phrases.

Pause when you introduce a new idea or term. This gives your listeners time to absorb what you are saying. It helps listeners keep up with you.

Tie your pauses to verbal phrasing. To a speaker, a phrase has a different meaning than it does to a writer. It is a unit you speak in one breath in order to express a single idea. Each pause tells your listeners you are moving from one thought to the next.

Use pauses to change the pace and add verbal variety. Pauses can be an effective tool speakers use to keep attention or to draw attention to a particular thought or emotion. Pause just before you speed up or pause just before you slow down. In both cases, the pause indicates to the audience that something is going to happen.

Extend pauses when displaying a visual. This tactic enables your audience to read the information on the visual without missing your next thought. It is important to pause after the display, not before it. Try pausing for two or three seconds.

Pause for two or three seconds when displaying a visual to let your audience read it without missing your next comment.
© JupiterImages Corporation.

Emphasis

A speaker uses emphasis to draw attention to a specific word or phrase. It involves stressing certain words or phrases. It can add weight to what you say, and make a particular word or phrase more noticeable or prominent. An emotion can be highlighted through the use of emphasis. Emphasis is a nonverbal way of saying, "Listen to this!"

Think about how many ways you can say "Come in." Depending on how they are said and how they are accented by nonverbal behavior, these words can be:

A *friendly invitation*	(from one friend to another)
A *command*	(from a supervisor to an employee)
An *angry growl*	(from a mother with a headache to her teenage son who has already interrupted her five times)
A *nondescript response*	(to a knock at your office door)

These changes give meaning to a word or phrase. By singling out a few words for special attention, you add color to your speech and avoid monotony. Emphasis can be achieved by using different techniques.

Change your volume and pitch. Whether you choose to speak more loudly or more quietly, you draw attention to your speech through contrast. A quieter approach is often a more effective attention-grabber. When you speak in a monotone, you tell your listeners you have nothing to emphasize. When you vary the pitch of your voice, you let them know that what you are saying is important.

Pause when changing your speaking rate. A change of pace—speeding up or slowing down—draws attention to what will come next: Pausing can do the same.

Use emotion. Emphasis comes naturally when you speak from the heart. When you have deep feelings about a subject—drug abuse, for example, or the need to protect the environment from pollution—you will express your feelings emphatically. Anything other than an impassioned delivery may seem inadequate.

Work with the previous excerpt from Nelson Mandela's acceptance speech. Read it aloud. The first time, do not emphasize anything. Read it in a monotone, just as you would a telephone book. It is hard to get involved, is it not? Now, underscore the words or phrases that, if emphasized, would add meaning to the speech. Then read it a second time, adding the emphasis and emotion you think appropriate. You may find that the words seem to take a life of their own as they demand attention.

Eliminating Non-fluencies

Non-fluencies are meaningless words that interrupt the flow of our speech. We may use them unintentionally, but we need to work consciously to avoid them. Non-fluencies are also known as filled pauses or vocal fillers. While pauses can work *for* you, non-fluencies distract your listeners. These include: "you know," "uh," "um," "so," and "okay." If your economics professor says "okay" after every concept presented, or your history professor adds "uh" or "um" after every thought, it can cause you to lose focus. A sociology professor told us his students once kept track of his non-fluencies, and reported to him after class that that he said "you know" thirty-two times during the fifty-minute period. Non-fluencies are verbal debris; they add nothing to the content of your speech, and they also annoy an audience. Avoid them.

Throw out other types of speaking debris as well: giggling, throat clearing, lip smacking, and sighing. These interrupt the flow of speech and can also be annoying to the audience. As you give speeches during this term, think about any habits you have that may distract your audience. We do not expect you to be perfect, but striving to improve your speaking ability is a realistic goal.

Be aware of your speech patterns Many people do not realize they use fillers. If you have been videotaped, listen for them as you watch your speech. Or, you can record your own phone conversation on a tape recorder. You can also ask friends to identify them when they hear you use fillers, or ask your teacher or classmates to keep track of non-fluencies.

Train yourself to be silent. Work actively to rid your speech of non-fluencies. Pause for a second or so after completing a phrase or other unit of thought. Because fillers indicate, in part, a discomfort with silence, this approach will help you realize that pauses are an acceptable part of communication.

What are the two central themes throughout this discussion of vocal delivery? *To practice and use vocal variety.* It is important to practice your speech so it flows smoothly. Practice pronouncing unfamiliar words so they come easily to you when you give your speech. Try varying pitch, rate, and volume to keep the audience's attention. Create interest in your speech, and stress key words, phrases, and thoughts. You have something relevant to share with your audience. You want to make it easy for them to understand you, and you want to keep them interested in what you have to say.

Aspects of Physical Delivery

Your physical delivery may convey professionalism or lack thereof. It can convey self-confidence or nervousness. Your delivery communicates enthusiasm or lack of interest. The ways you gesture, move, look at people, and dress say a great deal about you. More importantly, these elements leave a lasting impression that affects the speaker-audience connection. Although mastering the art of nonverbal communication will not guarantee your speaking success, it will help you convince your audience to pay attention.

Gestures

Gestures involve using your arms and hands to illustrate, emphasize, or provide a visual experience that accompanies your thoughts. Before we discuss the importance of gestures, body movement, and eye contact, we have a story about Katie, a non-traditional student who returned to school after five years of working for the loan department of a bank. She gave a speech adapted specifically to her audience. Her specific purpose was to explain how recent college graduates abuse credit cards and wind up owing thousands of dollars. She began:

> When you receive your first credit card, think of it as a loaded gun. If you don't use it properly you may wind up killing your credit for up to ten years.
>
> That means that no one will loan you money to buy a car, a plasma TV, or a house. You may not get the job you want because your credit is bad (prospective employers check applicants' credit ratings). And you'll go through a lot of torment while this is going on.
>
> Take my word for it. I've seen it happen dozens of times to people just like you.

Making a connection between a credit card and a loaded gun is a great attention-getter. Also, college students are usually fairly new to using credit cards, so the message is an important one to the audience. Although Katie's message was effective, her delivery was stiff and uncomfortable. She grasped the lectern for dear life, as if she were afraid to move from her spot. She was a talking statue, and her listeners responded by becoming restless and uncomfortable themselves. During the post-speech criticism, one audience member explained what he was feeling: "You looked so wooden that I had trouble listening to what you were saying, which is amazing since I'm already in credit card trouble."

Katie's problem was a lack of gestures and body movement, which her audience could not ignore despite the inherent interest of her speech. Gestures tell an audience that you are comfortable and self-confident. As an outlet for nervous energy, they actually help you feel more at ease. Gestures encourage an enthusiastic presentation. If you put your body into your speech through movement and gestures, it is difficult to present a stilted speech. Gestures also have a positive effect on breathing, helping you relax the muscles that affect the quality of the voice.

Gestures are especially important when you are speaking to a large audience. People in the back rows may not be able to see the changes in your facial expressions, and gestures may be their only way of seeing your involvement with your speech.

You can tell if your gestures are effective by checking where your listeners are looking. If they are focusing on the movement of your arms and hands instead of your face, your gestures are a distraction rather than a help. If this situation occurs, reduce the amount of gestures during the rest of your speech. Think about the following three guidelines as your practice using gestures.

Use natural gestures. Your gestures should reinforce both the ideas in the message and your own personality. Stand straight, with your arms bent at the waist and your hands relaxed, so you are ready to gesture. Pay attention to the position of your elbows. If they hang stiffly at your sides, your gestures will look shortened and artificial. To move your hands and forearms freely, make sure there is plenty of room between your elbows and your body.

When speaking to a large audience, gestures play a key part in reinforcing the ideas in your message.
© *JupiterImages Corporation*.

Gesture purposefully. Gestures should be meaningful and enhance your message. They should not appear random. For example, if you were trying to persuade people to donate blood, you might want to give your audience three reasons for doing so. When you say, "three reasons," you can hold up three fingers. When you say, "First," hold up one finger, and then when you say, "Second," hold up two fingers. You get the picture. These gestures are meaningful because they serve as an organizational guide. They tell your audience where you are in your speech. The same thing is true if you were giving an after-dinner speech in which you were trying to convince your audience to stop complaining. You could put up one or both hands in the "stop" position when you say, "Stop complaining" to your audience. This is meaningful because it emphasizes your assertion.

Gesture appropriately. Gestures should be timely. You do not want to hold three fingers up before or after you say "three reasons," but *as* you are saying it. You do not want arms flailing around as you speak; they should match what you are saying. Appropriate gestures are timely, and they should make sense within the context of your message. If you are speaking before a large audience, gestures are bigger and, generally, more dramatic. Those same gestures may look awkward and exaggerated in a smaller environment.

Actions That Inhibit Gesturing

The preceding three guidelines are designed to help you gesture effectively. Your authors have over seventy years of combined experience grading student speeches, and we have noticed several actions that reduce the overall effectiveness of a student's speech and/or distract the audience. As you deliver your speech, try to avoid the following:

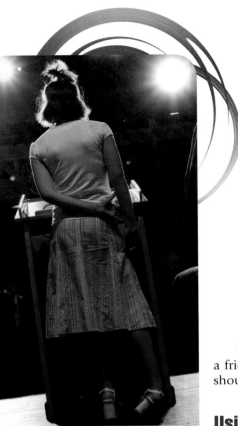

Clasping your hands together.	It makes gesturing impossible except if you are willing to raise both hands at once.
Hugging your body.	It makes you look as though you are trying to protect yourself from assault.
Clasping your hands in the "fig leaf" stance.	Holding your hands together at your crotch is another protective position, and it may be distracting.
Locking your hands behind your back.	That position may encourage you to rock back and forth. This "at ease" military stance is not appropriate for the classroom.
Putting your hands in your pocket.	This restricts movement and may encourage you to play with change in your pocket or something else that will make sound and distract your audience.
Grasping and leaning into the lectern.	Some students do this for support when they are nervous. You can touch the lectern; just do not hold it in a death grip. Free your hands so you can gesture. Release your energy through your movement.

For your next speech, work to make your gestures appear more natural. Ask a friend or colleague to comment on your movement and gestures. Gestures should *not* draw attention to themselves and away from the ideas.

If you hold your hands behind your back, you won't be able to gesture.
© *JupiterImages Corporation.*

Using Note Cards

Many instructors restrict the number and size of the note cards you may use during your speech. Follow their instructions, and consider the following:

- View your note cards as an extension of your arm, gesturing as you would without the note cards.
- Cards should fit into your hand comfortably.
- Generally, 4" x 6" cards are going to be easier to read than 3" x 5" cards.
- Number your note cards so you are able to keep them in order as you write them, transport them, and use them when you deliver your speech.
- Check to see that they are in sequence before speaking.
- Never staple your note cards.

Common Problems Using Note Cards

Using note cards effectively is not as easy as it seems. Sometimes, students wait until the last moment to create their note cards. Just like every other aspect of speaking, students should practice their speech using note cards, and consider the following pitfalls.

Holding note cards with both hands. Holding on to note cards with both hands may be distracting to the audience because cards are relatively small pieces of paper that do not need the support of both hands. Holding on with both hands restricts your movement, also.

Putting too much on the note cards. You only need enough information on your note cards to trigger your thoughts. If you have practiced enough, you do not need many notes. Also, if you have most of your speech on your note cards, you may end up sounding like you are reading to the audience.

Having too many note cards. Teachers sometimes swap stories about how many note cards a particular student used. The assignment may call for three note cards, and a student has a quarter-inch pile of note cards—sometimes as many as twenty for a four- to six-minute speech. This is not necessary if you have practiced your speech!

Writing on both sides of the card. Sometimes students misinterpret the "three cards rule" and use three note cards, but write on both sides. It is easy to lose your place when you have written on both sides, and it can be distracting to the audience ("Hey! She used bright pink ink for her notes!"), and it usually means that you are relying too heavily on your notes. Practice!

Using a Legal Pad

Traditionally, public speaking instructors wince at the notion of allowing students to use something other than note cards. Our professors taught us to use note cards, and we teach our students the same. In reality, not every occasion calls for small note cards. It is certainly not uncommon to see speakers using note pads or legal pads of some kind in the corporate world. Long and detailed presentations may be better served by using a note pad instead.

Your instructor may allow the use of a note pad in your class, or you may be in a situation where having a pad of paper makes sense. Once you have your notes on something larger than your hand, it may be more distracting when you gesture. You do not want a pad of paper waving around in the air. It should *not* be used as an extension of your arm. Hold the pad in one hand, at a distance from your eyes that allows you to see your notes but not covering your face. Gesture with your free hand.

Physical Movement

Remember the second problem related to Katie's delivery? She appeared glued to the lectern. After a while, her listeners got tired of watching her. Katie's mistake is typical. Like many speakers, she failed to realize that an active speaker can encourage an active response from an audience, but an immobile speaker can leave listeners listless. When you move from one place to another while you speak, your listeners are more likely to keep their eyes on you. Movement has an additional advantage of helping to reduce your nervous energy. It can work against you, however, if you look like a moving target or if your movement has no purpose. Think about the following three guidelines as you prepare your speech.

Move naturally. Relax and use movement reasonably. Do not pace back and forth like a caged lion or make small darting movements that return you to the safety of the lectern.

CAUTION

Holding a piece of paper is different than holding a note card. If you are nervous, the audience is more likely to see a full-sized piece of paper shake than a smaller, sturdier note card.

Tie your movements to your use of visual aids. Walk over to the visual as you are presenting it and point to its relevant parts. Walk back to the lectern when you are through. Make sure the movement is fluid.

Be prepared. Your instructor and the speaking environment will influence the opportunities for physical movement. Your instructor may allow or prohibit you from speaking behind a lectern or podium. In informal situations, it may be appropriate to walk through the aisles as you talk. In a small room, you can walk around without a microphone and still be heard. In a large room, you may need the help of a wireless microphone. Be prepared to adapt to your instructor's rules and the speaking environment. Remember that movement is a way to connect with the audience, get them involved, and keep their attention.

Eye Contact

No other aspect of nonverbal behavior is as important as eye contact, which is the connection you form with listeners through your gaze. You engage your audience by drawing them in through eye contact. Sustained eye contact can communicate confidence, openness, and honesty. It suggests you are a person of conviction, you care what your listeners are thinking, and you are eager for their feedback. Making eye contact with your audience is a way for you to express nonverbally, "I want you to understand me."

When your eye contact is poor, you may be sending unintentional messages that the audience interprets as nervousness, hostility, being uncomfortable, or lack of interest. The audience may think you have something to hide or that you are not prepared.

In the process of writing this text, one of the authors attended a recognition ceremony where several honorees gave brief speeches. One speaker began by looking at her notes, then made eye contact with the audience, looked back at her notes, and then appeared to look at something on the wall to her right. She repeated these behaviors throughout her speech. Audience members were observed looking up at the same spot. The speaker admitted to being nervous before her speech. Clearly, this nervous tic distracted her audience.

Sometimes students only look at the instructor during their speech. Do not do this! It makes teachers uncomfortable and you are excluding the rest of the audience. Also, some student speakers ignore half the class by looking at the right side or the left side of the class only.

When you turn on the nightly news, you see the anchor looking straight at you. As a result of television, eye-to-eye contact is what you expect from every speaker; it is the norm. When a speaker looks away, we sense that something is wrong. We offer the following four performance guidelines for reflection.

When you don't make eye contact with your audience, it may be interpreted as a lack of interest in your subject. © *JupiterImages Corporation.*

Distribute your gaze evenly. Work on sustained eye contact with different members in the audience. Avoid darting your eyes around or sweeping the room with your eyes. Instead, try maintaining eye contact with a single person for a single thought. This may be measured in a phrase or a sentence. It may help to think of your audience as divided into several physical sectors. Focus on a different person in each sector, rotating your gaze among the people and the sectors as you speak.

Glance only briefly and occasionally at your notes. Do not keep your eyes glued to your notes. You may know your speech well, but when you are nervous, it may feel safer to keep looking at your notes. However, this is counterproductive.

Do not look just above the heads of your listeners. Although this advice is often given to speakers who are nervous, it will be obvious to everyone that you are gazing into the air.

Appearance

Standards for appearance are influenced by culture and context. Americans visiting the Vatican will find that shoulders and knees should be covered in order to gain entry. It is okay for students to wear baseball caps outside, but some in some contexts, it may be offensive to keep one on inside. In high school, you may have violated the student conduct code by wearing something that was deemed inappropriate. Most school districts have clearly-stated standards related to appearance. However, these standards differ from one district to another.

An effective speaker is aware of the norms and expectations for appearance as he or she moves from one culture to another. In a 1989 summit between Soviet President Mikhail Gorbachev and Chinese leader Deng Xiaoping, Gorbachev made a nearly fatal blunder: He wore a pair of beige loafers with his formal suit, a choice that offended the Chinese who believed that "holiday shoes" should not be worn on such a special occasion. Gorbachev's advisors failed to provide him with such relevant information.

We do not have to move from one country to another to experience differences in perspectives on appearance. Some businesses allow more casual attire; others expect trendy, tailored clothing. As rhetorical theorist Kenneth Burke (1969, 119) reminds us, your clothes make a rhetorical statement of their own by contributing to your spoken message.

Your choice of shoes, suits, dresses, jewelry, tattoos, hair style, and body piercings should not isolate you from your listeners. If that occurs, the intent of your speech is lost. We offer the following guidelines for appearance, but the bottom line is, *do nothing to distract from the message.*

Your appearance should be in harmony with your message. Communication professor Leon Fletcher (1990) describes a city council meeting addressed by college students pleading for a clean-up of the local beaches. Although the speeches were clearly organized, well-supported, and effectively presented, the unkempt physical appearance of the speakers conflicted with their message. They wore torn jeans, T-shirts and sloppy sandals. Their hair looked ungroomed. The city council decided to take no action. Several months later, the same issue was brought before the council by a second group of students, all of whom wore ties and sport jackets—symbols of the neatness they wanted for the beaches. This time the proposal was accepted (14).

Although no one would tell you that wearing a certain suit or dress will make your listeners agree with your point of view, the image you create is undoubtedly important. Research on employment interviews suggests that "physical appearance and grooming habits are factors in the hiring process" (Shannon and Stark 2003, 613).

Be clean and appropriately dressed and groomed. In your public speaking class, your shoe choice is not likely to create a stir. However, your audience expects that you will be clean and appropriately groomed. Your instructor may provide you with specific guidelines regarding your appearance on the day you speak. A general guideline is to be modest and slightly more formal than your audience.

Avoid clothing that detracts from your message. If the audience focuses on your appearance, your speech loses effectiveness. Wearing a cap is usually frowned upon. The audience wants to see your eyes, and you should not ignore the possibility that your instructor views caps as outdoor, not indoor, wear.

Avoid shirts that have writing on them. It is probably not wise to give a persuasive speech on the day you wear a t-shirt with "I make stuff up" on it. One of our female students held her poster in front of her, with the word "Hooters" showing on her t-shirt, just above the visual aid. Whether what is written on your t-shirt is witty or offensive, it takes focus off the message.

Some students may need the following gentle reminder: Your instructors, and probably many of your classmates are not interested in seeing your belly or *any* type of cleavage. And a note to the females—if you wear a tight shirt or a short skirt, and you tug or pull on it, you draw attention to yourself, not what you are trying to say.

Summary

The four methods of speech delivery are memorization, manuscript speaking, extemporaneous speaking, and impromtu speaking. Each method is appropriate in varying circumstances. Following the guidelines for the method you choose will enhance the effectiveness of your speech. In this chapter we focus on extemporaneous speaking, a method in which you prepare the content of your speech in advance, but speak from a key-word outline. Impromptu speaking involves speaking without preparation.

Nonverbal communication is an important part of delivery. Your vocal and physical delivery affect your presentation. Aspects of vocal delivery include articulation, pronunciation, volume, rate, pitch, pauses, and emphasis. Guidelines for effective vocal delivery are provided. In addition, an effective speaker has relatively few non-fluencies. Aspects of physical delivery include gestures, physical movement, eye contact, and appearance. A good speaker will use nonverbal delivery to capture and maintain the attention of the listeners.

Questions for Study and Discussion

1. Why is extemporaneous speaking generally the most appropriate form of delivery? Under what circumstances is manuscript reading, memorization, and impromptu speaking appropriate?
2. How do your movements, gestures, eye contact, and clothing influence your relationship with your audience and the communication of your message?
3. What do you need to remember about using note cards during your speech?

Activities

1. Select a CD/DVD/Video that contains a complete speech. With your class-mates, study the speaker's delivery style, examining strengths and weaknesses.
2. Prepare a two- to three-page report on a public speaker's delivery style. Assess how the speaker's delivery contributes to or diminishes his or her power as a speaker.
3. Record your own speech and make a written inventory of your strengths and weaknesses. Then describe what you must do to improve your delivery.
4. Write twenty to thirty different speech topics, each on a different piece of paper. Fold the papers and place them in a bowl. In small groups of three or four, each person then pulls a topic from the bowl and delivers an impromptu speech lasting one and a half to two minutes. Try to make your presentation as clear, organized, and fluent as possible.
5. Try a group speech. Five classmates stand in front of the class, and decide on a topic. The first person starts, and as soon as that person uses a non-fluency, the next person takes over. See how long each person can speak without using vocal fillers.

References

Burke, K. 1969. *A rhetoric of motives.* Berkeley, CA: University of California Press.

Duffy, B., and H. Ryan, eds. 1987. *American Orators of the Twentieth Century: Critical Studies and Sources.* New York: Greenwood Press.

Fletcher, L. 1990. Polishing your silent languages. *The Toastmaster* (March), 14.

Shannon, M.L. and Stark, C.P. 2003. The influence of physical appearance on personnel selection. *Social Behavior and Personality,* 31(6), 613–124.

Sloane Coffin, W. 1988. How to wow 'em when you speak. *Changing Times,* August, 30.

Types of Public Speaking

When you deliver an informative speech, your intent is to enlighten your audience—to increase understanding or awareness and, perhaps, to create a new perspective.

© *Stanislav Mikhalev, 2008. Under license from Shutterstock, Inc.*

Speaking to Inform

Informative Speaking

When you deliver an **informative speech,** your goal is *to communicate information and ideas in a way that your audience will understand and remember.* Whether you are a nurse conducting CPR training for new parents at the local community center, a museum curator delivering a speech on impressionist art, or an auto repair shop manager lecturing to workers about the implications of a recent manufacturer's recall notice, you want your audience to gain understanding of your topic. An important caveat for students of public speaking to remember is that the audience should hear *new* knowledge, not facts they already know. For example, the nurse conducting CPR training for new parents would approach the topic differently than if the audience was comprised of individuals from various fields working on their yearly recertification. New parents may have never had CPR training, whereas the others receive training at least once a year.

In this chapter, we first distinguish an informative speech from a persuasive one. The different types of informative speeches are identified, and goals and strategies for informative speaking are presented.

Informative Versus Persuasive Intent

When you deliver an informative speech, your intent is to enlighten your audience—to increase understanding or awareness and, perhaps, to create a new perspective. In contrast, when you deliver a persuasive speech, your intent is to influence your audience to agree with your point of view—to change attitudes or beliefs or to bring about a specific, desired action. In theory, these two forms are distinctly different. In practice, as we noted earlier, this may not be the case.

For example, if during an informative speech on the ramifications of calling off a marriage you suggest to the engaged couples in your audience that safeguards may have to be taken to prevent emotional or financial damage, you are being persuasive implicitly. If you suggest to the men in your audience that they obtain a written statement from their fiancées pledging the return of the engagement ring if the relationship ends, you are asking for explicit action, and you have blurred the line between information and persuasion.

The key to informative speaking is intent. If your goal is to expand understanding, your speech is informational. If, in the process, you also want your audience to share or agree with your point of view, you may also be persuasive. In describing the different kinds of assault rifles available to criminals, you may persuade your audience to support measures for stricter gun control. Some of your listeners may write to Congress while others may send contributions to lobbying organizations that promote the passage of stricter gun control legislation. Although your speech brought about these actions, it is still informational because your intent was educational.

To make sure your speech is informational rather than persuasive, start with a clear specific purpose signifying your intent. Compare the following two specific purpose statements:

Is your goal to expand the audience's understanding of a topic? If this doctor is outlining the latest advances in neurosurgery, he is giving an informational speech.
© *JupiterImages Corporation.*

Specific purpose statement #1 (SPS#1) To inform my listeners about the significance of the bankruptcy of the leading American energy company, Enron Corporation

Specific purpose statement #2 (SPS#2) To inform my listeners why the investment firm Drexel Burnham Lambert was a symbol of Wall Street greed, power, and the corruption that marked the decade of the 1980s

While the intent of the first statement is informational, the intent of the second is persuasive. The speaker in SPS#1 is likely to discuss the fallout of Enron's bankruptcy, such as decrease in consumer confidence, changes in federal securities laws, and how employees were affected. The speaker in SPS#2 uses subjective words such as "greed, power, and corruption." Most likely this speech would focus more on the unethical practices that resulted in employees and investors losing their life savings, children's college funds, and pensions when Enron collapsed.

Types of Informative Speaking

Although all informative speeches seek to help audiences understand, there are three distinct types of informative speeches. A speech of **description** helps an audience understand *what* something is. When the speaker wants to help us understand *why* something is so, they are offering a speech of **explanation.** Finally, when the focus is on *how* something is done, it is a speech of **demonstration.** Each of these will be discussed in more detail.

Speeches of Description

Describing the circus to a group of youngsters, describing the effects of an earthquake, and describing the buying habits of teenagers are all examples of informative speeches of description. These speeches paint a clear picture of an event, person, object, place, situation, or concept. The goal is to create images in the minds of listeners about your topic or to describe a concept in concrete detail. Here, for example, is a section of a speech describing a reenactment of the 1965 civil rights march in Selma, Alabama. We begin with the specific purpose and thesis statement:

Specific purpose. To have my audience learn of the important connections between the civil rights marches in Selma, Alabama in 1965 and 2005.

Thesis statement. Civil rights marchers returned to Selma, Alabama, in 2005 to commemorate the violence-marred march forty years earlier.

Thousands of civil rights marchers came together in Selma, Alabama, to walk slowly across the Edmund Pettus Bridge. The year was 2005 and the reason for the march was to commemorate the brutal and violent march that took place in Selma forty years earlier. The first march awakened the country to the need to protect the civil liberties of African

Americans, but this one was a time of celebration and rededication to the cause of civil rights.

The 2005 march was peaceful. Only sound effects reminded participants of the billy club-wielding state troopers, of the screams and clomping horse hoofs, of the beatings and the inhumanity (Smothers, 1990).

In this excerpt, the speaker is making a contrast between two similar events that occurred forty years apart. Audience members are provided with images of what was named "Bloody Sunday," in 1965, and they can picture the peaceful, even celebratory, mood of the similar event forty years later. Specific, concrete language conveys the information through vivid word pictures.

Speeches of Explanation

Speeches of explanation deal with more **abstract** topics (ideas, theories, principles, and beliefs) than speeches of description or demonstration. They also involve attempts to simplify complex topics. The goal of these speeches is audience understanding. A psychologist addressing parents about the moral development of children or a cabinet official explaining U.S. farm policy are examples of speeches of explanation.

To be effective, speeches of explanation must be designed specifically to achieve audience understanding of the theory or principle. Avoid abstractions, too much jargon, or technical terms by using verbal pictures that define and explain. Here, for example, a speaker explains the concept of depression by telling listeners how patients describe it.

Serious depression, a patient once said, is "like being in quicksand surrounded by a sense of doom, of sadness." Author William Styron described his own depression as "a veritable howling tempest in the brain" that took him down a hole so deep that he nearly committed suicide.

Veteran and senior CBS correspondent Mike Wallace reached a point in his life where he found himself unable to sleep, losing weight, and experiencing phantom pains in his arms and legs. "Depression is palpable," explained Wallace. "You begin to feel like a fake and a fraud. You second guess yourself about everything" (1990, 48–55).

Compare this vivid description with the following, more abstract version:

Severe depression involves dramatic psychological changes that can be triggered by heredity or environmental stress. Depression is intense and long lasting and may result in hospitalization. The disease may manifest itself in agitation or lethargy.

If the second is presented alone, listeners are limited in their ability to anchor the concept to something they understand. The second explanation is much more effective when combined with the first.

Speeches of explanation may come from a corporate officer outlining business policy to people in the company. © *JupiterImages Corporation.*

Speeches of explanation may involve policies: statements of intent or purpose that guide or drive future decisions. The president may announce a new arms control policy. A school superintendent may implement a new inclusion policy. The director of human resources of a major corporation may discuss the firm's new flextime policy.

A speech that explains a policy should focus on the questions that are likely to arise from an audience. For example, prior to a speech to teachers and parents before school starts, the superintendent of a school district implementing a new inclusion policy needs to anticipate what the listeners will probably want to know—when the policy change will be implemented, to what extent it will be implemented, when it will be evaluated, and how problems will be monitored, among other issues. When organized logically, these and other questions form the basis of the presentation. As in all informative speeches, your purpose is not to persuade your listeners to support the policy, but to inform them about the policy.

Speeches of Demonstration

Speeches of demonstration focus on a process by describing the gradual changes that lead to a particular result. These speeches often involve two different approaches, one is "how," and the other is a "how to" approach. Here are four examples of specific purposes for speeches of demonstration:

- To inform my audience *how* college admissions committees choose the most qualified applicants
- To inform my audience *how* diabetes threatens health
- To inform my audience *how to* sell an item on Ebay
- To inform my audience *how to* play the Internet game Bespelled

Speeches that take a "how" approach have audience understanding as their goal. They create understanding by explaining how a process functions without teaching the specific skills needed to complete a task. After listening to a speech on college admissions, for example, you may understand the process but may not be prepared to take a seat on an admissions committee.

Let us look more closely at a small section of a "how" speech.

> How are shows selected by the networks to be placed in prime time for an upcoming television season? The answer to this question describes a complex process involving a host of people ranging from developers with an idea to advertising executives responsible for deciding whether or not to sponsor a program. When the proposed television programs are presented to advertisers, the process engaged is one which can allow advertisers to have some influence over the content of programs they choose to sponsor. Before this sort of influence takes effect, the network officials and advertising executives go through what is called "speculation season." In early spring those involved in the decision-making process may consider about 100 hours' worth of programs. Usually no more than 23 to 25 hours of airtime eventually make it. The networks may develop 30 to 40 projects, while many more do not get past a one-page plot outline (Carter 1992).

Although this sample begins to explain how television programs are selected for the fall season, its primary goal is understanding, not application.

In contrast, *"how to"* speeches try to communicate specific skills, such as selling an item on Ebay, changing a tire, or making a lemon shake-up. Compare the previous "how" example discussing network television show selection with the following "how to" presentation on "how to" make a lemon shake-up.

In front of me are all the ingredients for a lemon shake-up: lemons, water, sugar, a knife, and two cups. First, cut the lemons into quarters. If you love the tart taste of lemons...

The main object of Bespelled is to win points by connecting letters or "tiles" on a board to spell words that are at least three letters long. After downloading the game from msn.com and pressing "play," look at the board. Seven rows of seven letters are arranged randomly, and to the left of the board, you'll see a wizard and a score box. Look for words arranged in any fashion. One letter of a word must be connected to the next letter. You use the mouse to highlight each letter, and then click when you have finished the word.

Points are based on two things: the length of the word, and value of the letters. A second object is to keep letters or "tiles" that catch on fire from reaching the bottom of the board. The game is over when a burning tile ignites the whole board. So, you need to put out the fire by creating a word that incorporates the burning letter. If you avoid one burning tile, more will appear. Each burns the tile beneath them, and at some point, the board goes up in flames...

At the end of this speech of demonstration, the listener should know the ingredients and how to make a lemon shake-up.

One clear difference between the speech of demonstration and the speeches of presentation and explanation is that the *speech of demonstration benefits from presentational aids.* When your goal is to demonstrate a process, you may choose to complete the entire process—or a part of it—in front of your audience. The nature of your demonstration and the constraints of time determine your choice. If you are giving CPR training, a partial demonstration will not give your listeners the information they need to save a life. If you are demonstrating how to cook a stew, however, your audience does not need to watch you chop onions; prepare in advance to maintain audience interest and save time.

After a speech of demonstration about how to plan an Internet game, you should know the object of the game and be able to play it. © *JupiterImages Corporation.*

Goals and Strategies of Informative Speaking

Although the overarching goal of an informative speech is to communicate information and ideas in a way that the audience will understand, there are other goals that will help you create the most effective informative speech. Whether you are giving a speech to explain, describe, or demonstrate, the following five goals are relevant: **be accurate, objective, clear, meaningful, and memorable**. After each goal, two specific strategies for achieving that goal are presented.

1. Be Accurate

Facts must be correct and current. Research is crucial to attaining this goal. Do not rely solely on your own opinion; find support from other sources. Information that is not current may be inaccurate or misleading. Informative speakers strive to present the truth. They understand the importance of careful research for verifying information they present. Offering an incorrect fact or taking a faulty position may hurt speaker credibility and cause people to stop listening. The following two strategies will help speakers present accurate information.

Question the source of information. Is the source a nationally recognized magazine or reputable newspaper, or is it from someone's post on a random blog? Source verification is important. Virtually anyone can post to the Internet. Check to see if your source has appropriate credentials, which may include education, work experience, or verifiable personal experience.

Research is crucial to attain correct information to present in your speech.
© JupiterImages Corporation.

Consider the timeliness of the information. Information can become dated. There is no hard and fast rule about when something violates timeliness, but you can apply some common sense to avoid problems. Your instructor may take this decision-making out of your hands by requiring sources from the last several years or so. If not, the issue of timeliness relates directly to the topic. If you wanted to inform the class about the heart transplant process, relying on sources more than a few years old would be misleading because scientific developments occur continuously.

2. Be Objective

Present information that is fair and is unbiased. Purposely leaving out critical information or "stacking the facts" to create a misleading picture violates the rule of objectivity. The following two strategies should help you maintain objectivity.

Take into account all perspectives. Combining perspectives creates a more complete picture. Avoiding other perspectives creates bias, and may turn an informative speech into a persuasive one. The chief negotiator for a union may have a completely different perspective than the administration's chief negotiator on how current contract negotiations are proceeding. They may be using the same facts and statistics, but interpreting them differently. An impartial third party trying to determine how the process is progressing needs to listen to both sides and attempt to remove obvious bias.

Show trends. Trends put individual facts in perspective as they clarify ideas within a larger context. The whole—the connection among ideas—gives each detail greater meaning. If a speaker tries to explain how the stock market works, it makes sense to talk about the stock market in relation to what it was a year ago, five years ago, ten years ago, or even longer, rather than focus on today or last week. Trends also suggest what the future will look like.

3. Be Clear

To be successful, your informative speech must communicate your ideas without confusion. When a message is not organized clearly, audiences can become frustrated and confused and, ultimately, they will miss your ideas. Conducting careful audience analysis helps you understand what your audience already knows about your topic and allows you to offer a clear, targeted message at their level of understanding. The following five strategies are designed to increase the clarity of your speech.

Carefully organize your message. Find an organizational pattern that makes the most sense for your specific purpose. Descriptive speeches, speeches of demonstration, and speeches of explanation have different goals. Therefore, you must consider the most effective way to organize your message. *Descriptive speeches* are often arranged in spatial, topical, and chronological patterns. *Speeches of demonstration* often use spatial, chronological, and cause-and-effect or problem-solution patterns. *Speeches of explanation* are frequently arranged chronologically, or topically, or according to cause-and-effect or problem-solution.

Define unfamiliar words and concepts. Unfamiliar words, especially technical jargon, can defeat your purpose of informing your audience. When introducing a new word, define it in a way your listeners can understand. Because you are so close to your material, knowing what to define can be your hardest task. The best advice is to put yourself in the position of a listener who knows less about your topic than you do or ask a friend or colleague's opinion. In addition to explaining the dictionary definition of a concept or term, a speaker may rely on two common forms of definitions: operational and through example.

Operational definitions specify procedures for observing and measuring concepts. We use operational definitions to tell us who is "smart," based on a person's score on IQ test. The government tells us who is "poor" based on a specified income level, and communication researchers can determine if a person has high communication apprehension based on his or her score on McCroskey's Personal Report of Communication Apprehension.

Definition through example helps the audience understand a complex concept by giving the audience a "for instance." In an effort to explain what is meant by the term, "white-collar criminal," a speaker could provide several examples, such as Jeff Skilling, (former Enron executive convicted on federal felony charges relating to the company's financial collapse), George Ryan (former Illinois governor indicted on federal racketeering, fraud, and conspiracy charges), and Duke Cunningham (former congressional representative from California, convicted of various bribery and fraud charges).

4. Be Meaningful

A meaningful, informative message focuses on what matters to the audience as well as to the speaker. Relate your material to the interests, needs, and concerns of your audience. A speech explaining the differences between public and private schools delivered to the parents of students in elementary and secondary school would not be as meaningful in a small town where no choice exists as it would be in a large city where numerous options are available. Here are two strategies to help you develop a meaningful speech:

The setting makes a difference as to what information is important to people, and you should plan your focus accordingly.
© *JupiterImages Corporation.*

Consider the setting. The setting may tell you about audience goals. Informative speeches are given in many places, including classrooms, community seminars, and business forums. Audiences may attend these speeches because of an interest in the topic or because attendance is required. Settings tell you the specific reasons your audience has gathered. A group of middle-aged women attending a lifesaving lecture at a local YMCA may be concerned about saving their husbands' lives in the event of a heart attack, while a group of nursing students listening to the same lecture in a college classroom may be doing so to fulfill a graduation requirement.

Avoid information overload. When you are excited about your subject and you want your audience to know about it, you can find yourself trying to say too much in too short a time. You throw fact after fact at your listeners until you literally force them to stop listening. Saying too much is like touring London in a day--it cannot be done if you expect to remember anything.

Information overload can be frustrating and annoying because the listener experiences difficulty in processing so much information. Your job as an informative speaker is to know how much to say and, just as importantly, what to say. Long lists of statistics are mind-numbing. Be conscious of the relationship among time, purpose, and your audience's ability to absorb information. Tie key points to anecdotes and humor. Your goal is not to "get it all in" but to communicate your message as effectively as possible.

5. Be Memorable

Speakers who are enthusiastic, genuine, and creative and who can communicate their excitement to their listeners deliver memorable speeches. Engaging examples, dramatic stories, and tasteful humor applied to your key ideas in a genuine manner will make a long-lasting impact.

Speakers who are enthusiastic, genuine, and creative make a long-lasting and favorable impression upon their audience.
© *JupiterImages Corporation.*

Use examples and humor. Nothing elicits interest more than a good example, and humorous stories are effective in helping the audience remember the material. When Sarah Weddington (1990), winning attorney in the Roe v. Wade Supreme Court case, talks about the history of discriminatory practices in this country, she provides a personal example of how a bank required her husband's signature on a loan even though she was working and he was in school. She also mentions playing "girls" basketball in school and being limited to three dribbles (boys could dribble the ball as many times as they wanted). While these stories stimulate interest and make the audience laugh, they also communicate the message that sex discrimination was pervasive when Weddington was younger.

Physically involve your audience. Ask for audience response to a question: "Raise your hand if you have…" Seek help with your demonstration. Ask some audience members to take part in an experiment that you conduct to prove a point. For example, hand out several headsets to volunteers and ask them to set the volume level where they usually listen to music. Then show how volume can affect hearing.

Guidelines for Effective Informative Speeches

Regardless of the type of informative speech you plan to give, there are characteristics of effective informative speeches that cross all categories. As you research, develop, and present your speech, keep the following nine characteristics in mind.

The best informative speakers know what their audiences want to learn from their message.
© *JupiterImages Corporation.*

Consider Your Audience's Needs and Goals

Considering your audience is the theme of the book, but it is always worth repeating. The best informative speakers know what their listeners want to learn from their speech. A group of Weight Watchers members may be motivated to attend a lecture on dieting to learn how to lose weight, while nutritionists drawn to the same speech may need the information to help clients. Audience goals are also linked to knowledge. Those who lack knowledge about a topic may be more motivated to listen and learn than those who feel they already know the topic. However, it is possible that technology has changed, new information has surfaced, or new ways to think about or do something have emerged. The speaker needs to find a way to engage those who are less motivated.

Make connections between your subject and your audience's daily needs, desires, and interests. For example, some audience members might have no interest in a speech on the effectiveness of half-way houses until you tell them how much money is being spent on prisons locally, or better yet, how much each listener is spending per year. Now the topic is more relevant. People care about money, safety, prestige, family and friends, community, and their own growth and progress, among other things. Show how your topic influences one or more of these and you will have an audience motivated to listen.

Consider Your Audience's Knowledge Level

If you wanted to describe how to use eSnipe when participating in Ebay auctions, you may be speaking to students who have never heard of it. To be safe, however, you might develop a brief pre-speech questionnaire to pass out to your class. Or you can select several individuals at random and ask what they know. You do not want to bore the class with mundane minutia, but you do not want to confuse them with information that is too advanced for their knowledge level. Consider this example:

> As the golf champion of your district, you decide to give your informative speech on the game. You begin by holding up a golf club and saying, "This is a golf club. They come in many sizes and styles." Then you hold up a golf ball. "This is a golf ball. Golf balls are all the same size, but they come in many colors. Most golf balls are white. When you first start playing golf, you need a lot of golf balls. So, you need a golf club and a golf ball to play golf."

Expect your listeners to yawn in this situation. They do not want to hear what they already know. Although your presentation may be effective for an audience of children who have never seen a golf club or ball, your presentation has started out too simplistic even for people who have some knowledge of the game.

Capture Attention and Interest Immediately

As an informative speaker, your goal is to communicate information about a specific topic in a way that is understandable to your listeners. In your introduction, you must first convince your audience that your topic is interesting and relevant. For example, if you are delivering a speech on white-collar crime, you might begin like this:

> Imagine taking part of your paycheck and handing it to a criminal. In an indirect way, that's what we all do to pay for white-collar crime. Part of the tax dollars you give the federal government goes into the hands of unscrupulous business executives who pad their expenses and over-charge the government by millions of dollars. For example, General Dynamics, the third-largest military supplier, tacked on at least $75 million to the government's bill for such "overhead" expenses as country-club fees and personal travel for corporate executives...

This approach is more likely to capture audience attention than a list of white-collar crimes or criminals.

Sustain Audience Attention and Interest by Being Creative, Vivid, and Enthusiastic

Try something different. Change your pace to bring attention or emphasis to a point. Say the following phrase at a regular rate, and then slow down and emphasize each word: "We must work together!" Slowing down to emphasize each word gives the sentence much greater impact. Varying rate of speech can be an effective way to sustain audience attention.

Also, show some excitement! Talking about accounting principles, water filters, or changes in planet designations with spirit and energy will keep people listening. Delivery can make a difference. Enthusiasm is infectious, even to those who have no particular interest in your subject. It is no accident that advertising campaigns are built around slogans, jingles, and other memorable language that people are likely to remember after a commercial is over. We are more likely to remember vivid language than dull language.

Show some excitement regardless of your topic!
© *Corbis.*

Cite Your Oral Sources Accurately

Anytime you offer facts, statistics, opinions, and ideas that you found in research, you should provide your audience with the source. In doing this, you enhance your own credibility. Your audience appreciates your depth of research on the topic, and you avoid accusations of plagiarism. However, your audience needs enough information in order to judge the credibility of your sources. If you are describing how the HBO show *Deadwood* became an acclaimed yet controversial drama, it is not sufficient to say, "Ashley Smith states…" because Ashley Smith's qualification to comment on this show may be based on the fact that she watches television regularly. If the speaker said, "Ashley Smith, television critic for the Chicago Tribune, states…" then we know she has some expertise in the area.

Signpost Main Ideas

Your audience may need help keeping track of the information in your speech. Separating one idea from another may be difficult for listeners when trying to learn all the information at once. You can help your audience understand the structure of your speech by creating oral lists. Simple "First, second, third, fourth…" or "one, two, three, four…" help the audience focus on your sequence of points. Here is an example of signposting:

> Having a motorized scooter in college instead of a car is preferred for two reasons. The first reason is a financial one. A scooter gets at least 80 miles per gallon. Over a period of four years, significant savings could occur. The second reason a scooter is preferred in college is convenience. Parking problems are virtually eliminated. No longer do you have to worry about being late to class, because you can park in the motorcycle parking area. They're all around us…

Signposting at the beginning of a speech tells the audience how many points you have or how many ideas you intend to support. Signposting during the speech keeps the audience informed as to where you are in the speech.

Relate the New with the Familiar

Informative speeches should introduce new information in terms of what the audience already knows. Analogies can be useful. Here is an example:

> A cooling-off period in labor management negotiations is like a parentally-imposed time-out. When we were children, our parents would send us to our rooms to think over what we had done. We were forbidden to come out for at least an hour in the hope that by the time we were released our tempers had cooled. Similarly, by law, the President can impose an 80-day cooling-off period if a strike threatens to imperil the nation's health or safety.

Most of us can relate to the "time out" concept referred to in this example, so providing the analogy helps us understand the cooling-off period if a strike is possible. References to the familiar help listeners assimilate new information.

Use Repetition

Repetition is important when presenting new facts and ideas. You help your listeners by reinforcing your main points through summaries and paraphrasing. For example, if you were trying to persuade your classmates to purchase a scooter instead of a car, you might have three points: (1) A scooter is cheaper than a car; (2) A scooter gets better gas mileage than a car; and (3) You can always find a nearby parking spot for your scooter. For your first point, you mention purchase price, insurance, and maintenance cost. As you finish your first point, you could say, "So a scooter is cheaper than a car in at least three ways, purchase price, insurance, and maintenance." You have already mentioned these three sub-points, but noting them as an internal summary before your second main point will help reinforce the idea that scooters are cheaper than cars.

Offer Interesting Visuals

Using pictures, charts, models, PowerPoint slides, and other presentational aids helps maintain audience interest. Jo Sprague and Douglas Stuart, (1988) explain:

> "Your message will be clearer if you send it through several channels. As you describe a process with words, also use your hands, a visual aid, a chart, a recording. Appeal to as many senses as possible to reinforce the message…If a point is very important or very difficult, always use one other channel besides the spoken word to get it across" (299).

Use effective presentational aids in your informative speech to hold your audience's attention. © *Corbis*.

Use humorous visuals to display statistics, if appropriate. Demonstrate the physics of air travel by throwing paper airplanes across the room. With ever-increasing computer accessibility and WiFi in the classroom, using computer-generated graphics to enhance and underscore your main points and illustrations is a convenient and valuable way to help you inform your audience effectively.

Ethics of Informative Speaking

Think about the advertising you see on television and the warning labels on certain products you purchase. Listening to a commercial about a new weight-loss tablet, you think you have just found a solution to get rid of those extra twenty pounds you carry with you. Several happy people testify about how wonderful the drug is, and how it worked miracles for them. At the end of the commercial, you hear a speaker say, "This drug is not for children under 16. It may cause diarrhea, restlessness, sleeplessness, nausea, and stomach cramps. It can lead to heat strokes and heart attacks. Those with high blood pressure, epilepsy, diabetes, or heart disease should not take this medicine..." After listening to the warnings, the drug may not sound so miraculous. We have government regulations to make sure consumers make informed choices.

As an individual speaker, *you need to regulate yourself.* A speaker has ethical responsibilities, no matter what type of speech he or she prepares and delivers. The informative speeches you deliver in class and those you listen to on campus are not nearly as likely to affect the course of history as those delivered by high-ranking public officials in a time of war or national political campaigns. *Even so, the principles of ethical responsibility are similar for every speaker.*

The President of the United States, the president of your school, and the president of any organization to which you belong all have an obligation to inform their constituencies (audiences) in non-manipulative ways and to provide them with information they need and have a right to know. Professors, doctors, police officers, and others engaged in informative speaking ought to tell the truth as they know it, and not withhold information to serve personal gain. You, like others, should always rely on credible sources and avoid what political scientists label as "calculated ambiguity." **Calculated ambiguity** is a speaker's planned effort to be vague, sketchy, and considerably abstract.

You have many choices to make as you prepare for an informative speech. Applying reasonable ethical standards will help with your decision-making. An informative speech requires you to assemble accurate, sound, and pertinent information that will enable you to tell your audience what you believe to be the truth. Relying on outdated information, not giving the audience enough information about your sources, omitting relevant information, being vague intentionally, and taking information out of context are all violations of ethical principles.

 # Summary

Informative speeches fall into three categories. Speeches of description paint a picture of an event, person, object, place, situation, or concept; speeches of explanation deal with such abstractions as ideas, theories, principles, and beliefs; and speeches of demonstration focus on a process, describing the gradual changes that lead to a particular result.

A somewhat blurry line exists between informative and persuasive speaking. Remember that in an informative speech your goal is to communicate information and ideas in a way that your audience will understand and remember. The key determinant in whether a speech is informative is speaker intent.

As an informative speaker, you should strive to be accurate, objective, clear, meaningful, and memorable. Preparing and delivering an effective informative speech involves applying the strategies identified in this chapter. In order to increase accuracy, make sure you question the source of information, consider the timeliness, and accurately cite your sources orally. Being objective includes taking into account all perspectives and showing trends. Crucial to any speech is clarity. To aid your audience, carefully organize your message, define unfamiliar words and concepts, signpost main ideas, relate the new with the familiar, and use repetition.

Audience members have gathered for different reasons. No matter what the reason, you want your speech to be meaningful to all listeners. In doing so, consider the setting, your audience's needs and goals and knowledge level, and try to avoid information overload. An informative speaker also wants people to remember his or her speech. In order to meet that goal, try to capture attention and interest immediately, sustain audience attention and interest by being creative, vivid, and enthusiastic, use examples and humor, offer interesting visuals, and physically involve your audience.

As you prepare your informative speech, make sure the choices you make are based on a reasonable ethical standard. You have an obligation to be truthful, and we presented many ways to accomplish this as you prepare your speech as well as when you deliver it.

TTYL (Talk to Your Listener)

In an informative speech, you are likely to encounter questions, comments, and interruptions while you speak. Here are some tips to cope with these unpredictable events.

Decide whether you want questions during your presentation or at the end. If you prefer they wait, tell your audience early in your speech or at the first hand raised something like, "I ask that you hold all questions to the end of this presentation, where I have built in some time for them."

When fielding questions, develop the habit of doing four things in this order: thank the questioner, paraphrase the question in your own words (for the people who may not have heard the question), answer the question briefly, and then ask the questioner if you answered their question.

Note that the second step in answering questions is to paraphrase the question in your own words. This provides you with the opportunity to point questions in desirable directions or away from areas you are not willing to go. Paraphrasing allows the speaker to stay in control of the situation.

For any question, you have five options: (1) answer it, and remember "I do not know" is an answer; (2) bounce it back to the questioner, "Well, that is very interesting. How might you answer that question?"; (3) Bounce it to the audience, "I see, does anyone have any helpful thoughts about this?"; (4) Defer the question until later, "Now you and I would find this interesting, but it is outside the scope of my message today. I'd love to chat with you individually about this in a moment"; (5) Promise more answer later, "I would really like to look further into that. May I get back to you later?" Effective speakers know and use all five as strategies to keep their question-and-answer period productive and on track.

When random interruptions occur, do not ignore them. Call attention to the distraction. This allows your audience to get it out and then return their attention to you. One speaker was interrupted when a window washer suspended outside the building dropped into view, ropes and all. The speaker paused, looked at the dangling distraction and announced, "Spiderman!" Everyone laughed, and he then returned to his speech. At a banquet, a speaker was interrupted by the crash of shattering dishes from the direction of the kitchen. She quipped, "Sounds like someone lost a contact lens." Whether humorous or not, calling attention to distractions is key to maintaining control.

The heckler is a special kind of distraction that requires prompt attention. If you notice a man in the audience making comments for others to hear that undercut your message, first, assume he is trying to be helpful. Ask him to share his comments for all to hear. This will usually stop the heckler. If it does not, ask him his name, and use it as often as you can in your message. This usually works because oftentimes the heckler simply wants more attention. When all else fails, enlist the assistance of your audience. Ask if anyone wants to hear what you have to say more than what the heckler is say-ing. (Your audience will indicate they do.) Then ask if there is a volunteer, preferably a big one, who can help us all out. The combination of humiliation and the implied threat should do the trick.

Questions for Study and Discussion

1. How does speaker intent differentiate informative from persuasive speaking?
2. How do the three types of informative speeches differ?
3. What are the characteristics of an effective informative speech?
4. What is the purpose of providing five goals for informative speeches?
5. How can effective visuals enhance an informative speech?
6. What role do ethics play in informative speaking?

Activities

1. Attend an informative lecture on campus (not a class lecture). Assess whether the lecture was strictly informative or whether it was also persua-sive. Describe and explain your findings in a written report.
2. Prepare a five-to-six minute informative speech that is primarily a descrip-tion, an explanation, or a demonstration. Develop a planning and key-word outline, and practice the speech aloud.
3. Attend another informative lecture in your community. Take notes on the effectiveness of the speaker's message. Describe the techniques the speaker used to improve communication. Evaluate the speech on the message and the presentation.

References

Beating depression. 1990. *U.S. News & World Report*, March 5, 48–55.

Carter, B. 1992. Right of spring in assessing the next season's hopefuls. *New York Times*, May 11, C6.

Crime in the suites. 1985. *Time*, June 10, 56–7; Stealing $200 billion 'the respectable' way. 1985. *U.S. News & World Report*, May 20, 83–85; Making punishment fit white-collar crime. 1987. *Business Week*, June 15, 84–85.

Smothers, R. 1990. A Selma march relives those first steps of '65, *New York Times*, March 5, B6.

Sprague, J., and D. Stuart. 1988. *The speaker's handbook (2nd ed.)*. San Diego, CA: Harcourt Brace Jovanovich.

"In a sense, persuasion is not a field a person might go into, or a 'subject' he may decide to 'take up' or not. Rather it is a part of living, the most sanctioned means by which one tries to influence others."

Professor Wallace C. Fotheningham

Speaking to Persuade

Q: Defind ethos, and how it used in persausive speech?

Q: State two guidlenes of small group presentation and why are they important?

Sharing your opinion on something even as simple as where you will go to eat lunch involves persuasion skills. © *JupiterImages Corporation.*

Individuals engage in persuasive speaking at all levels of communication. Interpersonally, we try to convince people to share our opinions or attitudes about very small things ("Burger King fries are better than McDonald's fries") and very significant things ("We shouldn't have children until we've been married for ten years"). We also engage in persuasive discourse at a societal level ("Homosexuals should be allowed to marry"). The ability to express one's self is a cornerstone of our democracy. The power of free speech is most clearly realized in speeches to persuade. Here is one example.

After the defeat of the "Clinton health care program" in the fall of 1994, Hillary Clinton stepped up the efforts to bring a more universalized system of healthcare to the American public. Her steadfast belief in this cause resulted in extensive worldwide campaigning, which led to her giving a speech before the World Health Organization (WHO) on September 5, 1995.

> At long last, people and their governments everywhere are beginning to understand that investing in the health of women and girls is as important to the prosperity of nations as investing in the development of open markets and trade... (Remarks to the World Health Organization Forum on Women and Health Security. Delivered in Beijing, China.)

Clinton's speech stressed the need to come together as a worldwide community with the goal of bettering the health and well-being of all women and families so the new century would open with marked improvement in the lives of women.

Clinton continued by outlining the basic needs that women have not had access to in the past. Women have lived without the necessities that help anyone look forward to a full life of health and productivity. These necessities include medical care, education, legal protection, the chance to better their economic position, and human rights. There are many places in the world where womens' health is in jeopardy because health care is not available or does not do enough to adequately meet needs. Often health care is simply too expensive for those who need it. Even the most basic needs, such as good, clean drinking water and good nutrition are not readily available. Moreover, many women are the victims of sexual abuse and ignorance of health concerns.

Too many women have been suffering for too long, Clinton proclaimed. She said the state of their health is one of continuous pain. The women who are suffering could be any woman in the world or any girl in the world. You could be looking in the mirror at that woman. Or it could be another person very close to you...your friend, your sister, your child, your neighbor.

In her speech, Clinton quoted compelling statistics about how many women in the world die or nearly die because of serious difficulties during childbirth. She expanded the information about reproductive issues, citing statistics about women who do not use any family planning methods due to a lack of education, no access to such services, or just because of their poverty. Because of this, Clinton stated that millions of women end up having abortions that are unsafe and ultimately result in lifelong medical problems or even death. More women are facing unplanned, unwanted pregnancies when they themselves can scarcely be called women, as young as they are. Good opportunities available for those babies born to very young mothers are few and far between. Mother and child both suffer in so many ways.

Another topic Clinton spoke out against was violence, saying that women not only suffer because of violence, but they also die. Violence takes many forms against women, whether it takes place within the home or outside the home. She said that violence, too, is an issue of health.

Breast cancer statistics also served as startling reminders to show the numbers of women throughout the world who suffer from this disease and who ultimately die because of it. Clinton even mentioned how many women would have died in the amount of time it took for her to deliver her speech that day.

Clinton remarked that using tobacco products kills as well and it is a killer that can be prevented. Even though it is not one of those things that people immediately think of as being deadly, it is one that causes horrible suffering to those who are affected by it. Along with such diseases as AIDS, there needs to be a focus on this killer as well. There is much that can be done to prevent those deaths that are caused by tobacco use.

Clinton closed her speech with a plea for all the nations who had representatives present that day to make every effort to ensure that the childbearing years of womens' lives should be a healthy and safe time. She implored every nation to do everything possible to make health care accessible and affordable for all women. She made a call for action on the issue.

Although retrospectives of Clinton's stay as First Lady often point to the failure of the "Clinton health care plan," her remarks before the WHO led to a substantial change in the healthcare of both women and their children.

Elements of Persuasion

Hillary Clinton's speech embodies the critical elements of persuasion that have been defined by generations of rhetorical scholars, starting with Aristotle. Persuasion is intended to influence choice through appeals to the audience's sense of ethics, reasoning, and emotion, Aristotle's views on the use of what he termed ethos, pathos, and logos provide the underpinnings of our modern study of persuasion.

Ethos and the Power of the Speaker's Credibility

Aristotle believed that **ethos,** which refers to speaker credibility, makes speakers worthy of belief. Audiences trust speakers they perceive as honest, especially "on points outside the realm of exact knowledge, where opinion is divided." In this regard, he believed, "we trust [credible speakers] absolutely. . . ."(Cooper 1960, 8). Hillary Clinton appealed to her audience through her own credibility as First Lady of the United States and as Chairwoman of the Task Force on National Health Care Reform. Due to her experiences with health and healthcare, Clinton was viewed as a credible source on several dimensions.

Dimensions of Speaker Credibility

What your audience knows about you before you speak and what they learn about your position during your speech may influence your ability to persuade them. Credibility can be measured according to four dimensions: perceived competence, concern for the audience, dynamism, and ethics.

Perceived competence. In many cases, your audience will decide your message's value based on perceived speaker competence. Your listeners will first ask themselves whether you have the background to speak. If the topic is crime, an audience is more likely to be persuaded by the Atlanta chief of police than by a postal worker delivering his personal opinions. Second, your audience will consider whether the content of your speech has firm support. When it is clear that speakers have not researched their topic, their ability to persuade diminishes. Finally, audiences will determine whether you communicate confidence and control of your subject matter through your delivery.

Concern for audience. Persuasion is also influenced by concern for your audience. Communication Professor Richard L. Johannesen (1974) differentiates between speakers who engage in "dialogue" and those who engage in "monologue." A **dialogue** takes into account the welfare of the audience; a **monologue** focuses only on the speaker's self-interest (95). Audiences sense a speaker's concern by first analyzing the actions a speaker has taken before the speech. If the group has formed to protest the location of a highway through a residential community, the audience will consider what the speaker has already done to convince highway officials to change their minds. Second, audiences listen carefully to the strength and conviction of the speaker's message. For instance, does the speaker promise to fly to Washington, D.C., if necessary, to convince federal officials to withhold funds until a new site is chosen? Persuasive speakers are able to convince their audiences that they are on their side.

Persuasive speakers have the ability to convey to listeners that you are on their side. © *JupiterImages Corporation.*

Dynamism. Your credibility and, therefore, your ability to persuade are also influenced by the audience's perception of you as a dynamic spokesperson. A person who is dynamic is lively, active, vigorous, and vibrant. Your listeners will ask themselves whether you have the reputation for being someone who gets the job done. They will listen for an energetic style that communicates commitment to your point of view, and for ideas that build upon one another in a convincing, logical way.

Ethics. Finally, your ability to persuade is influenced by the audience's perception of your ethical standards. If you come to the lectern with a reputation for dishonesty, few people will be persuaded to trust what you say. If your message is biased and you make little attempt to be fair or to concede the strength of your opponent's point of view, your listeners may question your integrity. They may have the same questions if you appear manipulative (Sprague and Stuart 1988, 208–10).

If you analyze Hillary Clinton's speech to the WHO, all four dimensions of speaker credibility can be seen. *Perceived competence* is illustrated by her official positions (First Lady and Chair of the Task Force on National Health Care Reform) and her research. She cites several statistics related to childbirth complications, violence against women, breast cancer, and tobacco usage. *Concern for audience* is found in her topic selection and approach. Her target audience is members of the World Heath Organization, so the variety of health-related topics addressed by Hillary Clinton is appropriate. Also, she shares information rather than lectures, and approaches the topics as issues "we" need to address rather than what "you" need to be concerned about. *Dynamism* is shown through her articulate and energetic presentation, and the straight-forward approach. Known concern for women's health issues and use of statistics suggest a solid set of *ethics*.

Does credibility make a difference in your ability to persuade? Researchers have found that, in many cases, the most credible speakers are also the most persuasive (Aronson, Turner, and Carlsmith 1963). One powerful way speakers enhance their credibility is by creating a strong sense of identification in their audiences.

The Strategy of Identification: Seeking Common Ground

Your credibility and your ability to persuade may increase if you convince your audience that you share "common ground." In his classic work, *Public Speaking*, published in 1915, James A. Winans introduced the concept of "common ground." "To convince or persuade a man," he writes, "is largely a matter of identifying the opinion or course of action which you wish him to adopt with one or more of his fixed opinions or customary courses of action. When his mind is satisfied of the identity, then doubts vanish" (Day 1959).

Labor leader Cesar Chavez forged a common bond with his audience after a twenty-day fast in 1968 to call attention to the plight of California farm workers by proclaiming that the end of his fast was not the true reason for the gathering. Rather, people had come to observe that, "we are a family bound together in a common struggle for justice. We are a Union family celebrating our unity and the nonviolent nature of our movement." Chavez explained why he had fasted: "My heart was filled with grief and pain for the suffering of farm workers. The Fast was first for me and then for all of us in this Union. It was a Fast for nonviolence and a call to sacrifice." Chavez concluded with, "We have something the rich do not own. We have our own bodies and spirits and the justice of our cause as our weapons. It is how we use our lives that determines what kind of men we are. . . . I am convinced that the truest act of courage, the

Cesar Chavez established a common ground with his audience and effectively used emotional arguments.
© *Farrell Grehan/Corbis.*

strongest act of manliness is to sacrifice ourselves for others in a totally non-violent struggle for justice. To be a man is to suffer for others. God help us to be men" (Hammerback and Jensen 1987, 57).

In this instance, Chavez establishes a common ground through identifying with his audience and provoking them to identify with him. Moreover, Chavez also makes effective use of emotional arguments, which Aristotle referred to as *pathos*.

Pathos and the Power of Emotion

Aristotle believed in the power of speakers to persuade through emotional appeals. He explained, "Persuasion is effected through the audience, when they are brought by the speech into a state of emotion; for we give very different decisions under the sway of pain or joy, and liking or hatred. . . ."(Cooper 1960, 9). Hillary Clinton appealed to the emotions of her listeners with the words, "In too many places, the status of women's health is a picture of human suffering and pain. The faces in that picture are of girls and women who, but for the grace of God or the accident of birth, could be us or one of our sisters, mothers, or daughters." This call to visualize harm to one's own family members served as a powerful example of utilizing emotion to appeal to the sensibilities of her audience members.

Appeal to Audience Emotion

Emotional appeals have the power to elicit happiness, joy, pride, patriotism, fear, hate, anger, guilt, despair, hope, hopelessness, bitterness, and other feelings. George Kennedy (1991), a scholar of classical rhetoric, tells us, "Emotions in Aristotle's sense are moods, temporary states of mind (123–4). But according to persuasion theorists Martha Cooper and William Nothstine (1992), "modern research into motivation and the passions moved beyond Aristotle's emphasis on the emotions themselves and moved extensively into broader theories of human psychology" (74). The persuader, they advise us, can influence his or her audience by using appeals to create an emotional, as well as a cognitive, state of imbalance in listeners, which arouses feelings that something is wrong and something must be done. By taking the essential needs of an audience into consideration, the persuader can develop lines of reasoning that respond to pertinent needs. Yes, human needs can be described in terms of logic or what makes sense to a listener, but needs are immersed in emotions of the individual as well.

Psychologist Abraham Maslow classified human needs according to the hierarchy pictured in figure 13.1. An analysis of these needs will help you understand audience motivation as you attempt to persuade. Maslow believed that our most basic needs—those at the bottom of the hierarchy—must be satisfied before we can consider those on the next levels. In effect, these higher level needs are put on "hold" and have little effect on our actions until the lower level needs are met.

Physiological needs. At the bottom of the hierarchy are our biological needs for food, water, oxygen, rest, and release from stress. If you were delivering a speech in favor of a proposed new reservoir to a community experiencing problems with its water supply, it would be appropriate to appeal to the need for safe and abundant water.

Safety needs. Safety needs include the need for security, freedom from fear and attack, a home that offers tranquility and comfort, and a means of earning a living. If you are delivering the same speech to a group of unemployed construction workers, you might link the reservoir project to jobs and a steady family income.

Belongingness and love needs. These needs refer to our needs for affiliation, friendship, and love. When appealing to the need for social belonging, you may choose to emphasize the camaraderie that will emerge from the community effort to bring the reservoir from the planning stage to completion.

Esteem needs. Esteem needs include the need to be seen as worthy and competent and to have the respect of others. In this case, an effective approach would be to praise community members for their initiative in helping to make the reservoir project a reality.

FIGURE 13.1
Maslow's Hierarchy of Needs

Self-actualization needs. People who reach the top of the hierarchy seek to fulfill their highest potential through personal growth, creativity, self-awareness and knowledge, social responsibility, and responsiveness to challenge. Addressing this audience, you might emphasize the long-range environmental and ecological implications of the reservoir. Your appeal may include the need to safeguard the water supply for future generations.

Maslow's Hierarchy of Needs can guide you in preparing a persuasive speech when you think about the feelings of your audience and how you can reach them in combination with the factors of credibility and sound argument. Understanding the basis for Maslow's hierarchy is critical to your success as a persuasive speaker, for if you approach your listeners at an inappropriate level of need, you will find them unable or unwilling to respond.

Our emotions are powerful ingredients in our human composition. You accept an ethical responsibility when you use emotional appeals. *The ethically responsible speaker does not distort, delete, or exaggerate information for the sole purpose of emotionally charging an audience in order to manipulate their feelings for self-centered ends.*

Everyone has attachment needs and can identify with appeals for friendship and camaraderie.
© *JupiterImages Corporation.*

Yet, emotional appeals are often the most persuasive type of appeal because they provide the motivation listeners need to change their minds or take action. Instead of simply listing the reasons high fat foods are unhealthy, a more effective approach is to tie these foods to frightening consequences:

> Jim thought nothing could ever happen to him. He was healthy as an ox—or so he thought. His world fell apart one sunny May morning when he suffered a massive heart attack. He survived, but his doctors told him that his coronary arteries were blocked and that he needed bypass surgery. "Why me?" he asked. "I'm only 42 years old." The answer, he was told, had a lot to do with the high fat diet he had eaten since childhood.

Some subjects are more emotionally powerful than others and lend themselves to emotional appeals. Stories such as personal health crises, children in need, or experiences with crime and deprivation engage the emotions of listeners. Delivery also has an impact. Your audience can tell if you are speaking from the heart or just mouthing words. They respond to the loudness of your voice, the pace and rhythm of your speech, and to your verbal cues. Finally, the placement of the appeal is important. Corporate speech consultant James Humes suggests using an emotional ending to motivate an audience to action. In his view, the same emotions that stir people in their private lives motivate audiences. He explains, "CEOs tell me, 'Listen, Jim, I'm not trying to save England, I'm just trying to get a message across to the company.' Well, you still want to ask the employees to join you in something. End on an emotional pitch. Work that audience up" (Kleinfeld 1990).

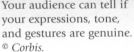

Your audience can tell if your expressions, tone, and gestures are genuine.
© *Corbis.*

Because of their power, emotional appeals can be tools of manipulation in the hands of unscrupulous speakers who attempt to arouse audiences through emotion rather than logic. These speakers realize that fear and other negative emotions can be more powerful persuaders than reason when the audience is receptive to their emotional message.

Logos and the Power of Logical Appeals and Arguments

In addition to ethical (ethos) and emotional (pathos) appeals and arguments, logos or logical appeals and arguments are critical to the persuasive process. A logical appeal is rational and reasonable based on evidence provided. For example, if a friend tried to convince you *not* to buy a new car by pointing out that you are in college, have no savings account, and are currently unemployed, that friend would be making a logical argument. Aristotle saw the power of persuasion relying on logical arguments and sound reasoning. Clinton appealed to her audience's reasoning by constructing an inequality of healthcare as evidenced by the positions of doctors, scientists, and nurses.

Reasoning refers to the sequence of interlinking claims and arguments that, together, establish the content and force of your position. Although we believe the treatment of public speaking throughout this book promotes being reasonable, *no aspect of our book is more instrumental in guiding you to improve your critical thinking than reasoning as logical appeal.* Logical thought as critical thinking is intended to increase your ability to *assess, analyze,* and *advocate* ideas. As a persuasive speaker you will reason logically either through induction or deduction. Your responsibility is to reason by offering your audience factual or judgmental statements based on sound inferences drawn from unambiguous statements of knowledge or belief (Freeley 1993, 2).

To construct a sound, reasonable statement as a logical appeal for your audience you need to distill the essential parts of an argument:

1. The evidence in support of an idea you advocate;
2. A statement or contention the audience is urged to accept; and,
3. The inference linking the evidence with the statement.

Of the three parts to an argument, the most difficult part to understand is often the inference. It may be an assumption that justifies using evidence as a basis for making a claim or drawing a conclusion. For example, suppose you take a big bite out of food you have taken for dinner in your cafeteria or apartment and claim, "This is the worst piece of meat I have ever put in my mouth." With this claim you are making a statement that you *infer* from tasting the meat.

What is the evidence? The meat before you. The statement or contention is, "The meat is awful." The relation of the evidence to the claim is made by an inference, which may be an *unstated belief* that spoiled, old, or poorly prepared meat will taste bad. Stephen Toulmin, the British philosopher acknowledged as an expert on argument, speaks of the inferential link between evidence and claim as the *warrant.* Toulmin points out that a warrant is the part of the argument that states or *implies* an inference (Vancil 1993, 120–24).

When you reason with your audience by trying to persuade the listeners with an argument you want them to accept and act upon, you must use evidence, inferences, and statements as contentions the audience can understand and accept. Sound reasoning is especially important when your audience is skeptical. Faced with the task of trying to convince people to change their minds or do something they might not otherwise be inclined to do, your arguments must be impressive.

Supporters in an audience may require arguments in the form of reinforcement. You may have to remind a sympathetic crowd of the reasons your shared point of view is correct. This reminder is especially important if your goal is audience action. If you want a group of sympathetic parents to attend a board of trustees meeting to protest tuition increases, you must persuade them that a large turnout is necessary. It is up to you, through the presentation of an effective argument, to make action the most attractive course.

In persuasion, ethical and emotional appeals may be powerful factors, but reasoning or logical appeal can be your most effective tool. Well-developed reasons stated without exaggeration tell your listeners that you trust them to evaluate the facts on their merit rather than emotional appeal. Through the framework of a logical appeal, we piece together important elements to persuade listeners to accept our position and respond to a call to action. The

You must have strong evidence and show that you've carefully supported your points to convince your audience that your claim has merit. © *Corbis.*

framework for logical appeal is based on inductive and deductive modes of reasoning, in particular reasoning by analogy, reasoning from cause, and reasoning from sign.

To persuade your audience that a claim or conclusion is highly probable, you must have strong evidence and show that you have carefully reasoned the support of your points. Only when strong probability is established can you ask your listeners to make the inductive leap from specific cases to a general conclusion, or to take the deductive move from statements as premises to a conclusion you want them to accept. We will look more closely now at inductive and deductive reasoning.

Inductive Reasoning

Aristotle spoke of inductive reasoning in his *Rhetoric* (Cooper 1960, 10). Through inductive reasoning, we generalize from specific examples and draw conclusions from what we observe. Inductive reasoning moves us from the specific to the general in an orderly, logical fashion.

When you argue on the basis of example, the inference step in the argument holds that what is true of specific cases can be generalized to other cases of the same class, or of the class as a whole. Suppose you are trying to persuade your audience that the disappearance of downtown merchants in your town is a problem that can be solved with an effective plan you are about to present. You may infer that what has worked to solve a similar problem in a number of highly similar towns is likely to work in the town that is the subject of your speech.

One problem associated with inductive reasoning is that individual cases do not *always* add up to a correct conclusion. Sometimes a speaker's list of examples is too small, leading his/her audience to an incorrect conclusion based on limited information. Here, as in all other cases of inductive reasoning, you can never be sure that your conclusions are absolutely accurate. Because you are only looking at a sample, you must persuade your audience to accept a conclusion that is probable, or maybe even just possible.

Reasoning by Analogy

Analogies establish common links between similar and not-so-similar concepts. They are effective tools of persuasion when you can convince your audience that the characteristics of one case are similar enough to the characteristics of the second case that your argument about the first also applies to the second.

As noted in Chapter Six, a **figurative analogy** draws a comparison between things that are distinctly different, such as "Eating fresh marshmallows is like floating on a cloud." Figurative analogies can be used to persuade, but they must be supported with relevant facts, statistics, and testimony that link the dissimilar concepts you are comparing.

Although figurative analogies can provide valuable illustrations, they will not prove your point. For example, before the United States entered World War II, President Franklin D. Roosevelt used the analogy of a "garden hose" to support his position that the United States should help England, France, and other European countries already involved in the war. In urging the passage of the Lend-Lease Bill, he compared U.S. aid to the act of lending a garden hose to a neighbor whose house was on fire. Although this analogy supplied ethical and emotional proof, it did not prove the point on logical grounds. It is vastly different to lend a garden hose to a neighbor than it is to lend billions of dollars in foreign aid to nations at war (Freeley 1993, 119).

Whereas a figurative analogy compares things that are distinctly different and supply useful illustrations, a literal analogy compares things with similar characteristics and, therefore, requires less explanatory support. One speaker in our class compared the addictive power of tobacco products, especially cigarettes, with the power of alcoholic beverages consumed on a regular basis. His line of reasoning was that both are consumed for pleasure, relaxation, and often as relief for stress. While his use of logical argument was obvious, the listener ultimately assesses whether or not these two things—alcohol and tobacco are sufficiently similar. It may be that their differences diminish the strength of the speaker's argument. The distinction between literal and figurative analogies is important because only literal analogies are sufficient to establish a logical proof. The degree to which an analogy works depends on the answers to the following questions:

1. Are the cases being compared similar?
   Only if you convince your listeners of significant points of similarity will the analogy be persuasive.
2. Are the similarities critical to the success of the comparison?
   The fact that similarities exist may not be enough to prove your point. Persuasion occurs when the similarities are tied to critical points of the comparison.
3. Are the differences relatively small?
   In an analogy, you compare similar, not identical, cases. Differences can always be found between the items you are comparing. It is up to you as an advocate for your position to decide how critical the differences are.
4. Can you point to other similar cases?
   You have a better chance of convincing people if you can point to other successful cases. If you can show that the similarities between your position and these additional cases are legitimate, you will help sway audience opinion (Freely 1993, 119–20).

Reasoning from Cause

When you are reasoning from cause the inference step is that an event of one kind contributes to or brings about an event of another kind. The presence of a cat in a room when you are allergic to cats is likely to bring about a series of sneezes until the cat is removed. As the preceding example demonstrated, causal reasoning focuses on the cause-and-effect relationship between ideas.

Cause: inaccurate count of the homeless for the 2000 census

Effect: less money will be spent aiding the homeless

An advocate for the homeless delivered the following message to a group of supporters:

> We all know that money is allocated by the federal government, in part, according to the numbers of people in need. The census, conducted every ten years, is supposed to tell us how many farmers we have, how many blacks and Hispanics, how many homeless.
>
> Unfortunately, in the 2000 census, many of the homeless were not counted. The government told us census takers would go into the streets, into bus and train station waiting rooms, and into the shelters to count every homeless person. As advocates for the homeless, people in my organization know this was not done. Shelters were never visited. Hundreds and maybe thousands of homeless were ignored in this city alone. A serious undercount is inevitable. This undercount will cause fewer federal dollars to be spent aiding those who need our help the most.

When used correctly, causal reasoning can be an effective persuasive tool. You must be sure that the cause-and-effect relationship is sound enough to stand up to scrutiny and criticism. To test the validity of your reasoning, ask yourself the following questions:

1. Do the cause and effect you describe have anything to do with one another?
   Some statements establish a cause-and-effect relationship between ideas when the relationship is, at best, questionable. Ask yourself whether other factors contributed to the change. You may be attributing cause and effect where there is only coincidence.
2. Is the cause acting alone or is it one of many producing the effect?
   Even if the connection you draw is valid, it may be only one of several contributing factors that bring about an effect. To isolate it as solely responsible for an effect is to leave listeners with the wrong impression.
3. Is the effect really the effect of another cause?
   To use a medical example, although fatigue and depression often occur simultaneously, it may be a mistake to conclude that depression causes fatigue when other factors may also be involved. Both conditions may be symptoms of other illnesses such as mononucleosis, or the result of stress.
4. Are you describing a continuum of causes and effects?
   When you are dealing with an interrelated chain of causes and effects, it is wise to point out that you are looking at only one part of a broader picture.
5. Are the cause and effect related but inconsequential?
   Ask yourself whether the cause you are presenting is sufficient to bring about the effect you claim.
6. Is your claim and evidence accurate?
   To be an effective persuasive tool, causal reasoning must convince listeners that the link you claim is accurate. Your listeners should be able to judge probability based on your supporting evidence. They will ask themselves if your examples prove the point and if you explain or minimize conflicting claims (Sprague and Stuart 1988, 165–66).

Causal reasoning is effective if your argument can withstand scrutiny.
© *JupiterImages Corporation.*

To be effective, causal reasoning should never overstate. By using phrases like, "This is one of several causes," or "The evidence suggests there is a cause-and-effect link," you are giving your audience a reasonable picture of a complex situation. Public speakers could learn from medical researchers who are reluctant to say flatly that one thing causes another. More often than not, researchers indicate that cause-and-effect relationships are not always clear and that links may not be as simple as they seem.

Reasoning from Sign

In the argument from sign, the inference step is that the presence of an attribute can be taken as the presence of some larger condition or situation of which the attribute is a part. As you step outside in the early morning to begin jogging, the gray clouds and moist air can be interpreted as signs that the weather conditions are likely to result in a rainy day. Argumentation Professor David Vancil (1993) tells us that, "arguments from sign are based on our understanding of the way things are associated or related to each other in the world with them, [so] we conclude that the thing is present if its signs are present. The claim of a sign argument is invariably a statement that something is or is not the case" (149).

The public speaker who reasons from sign must do so with caution. Certainly, there are signs all around us to interpret in making sense of the world, but signs are easy to misinterpret. Therefore, the responsible speaker must carefully test any argument before using it to persuade an audience.

Deductive Reasoning

Aristotle also spoke of deduction as a form of reasoning in persuasive argument. Through deductive reasoning, we draw conclusions based on the connections between statements that serve as premises. Rather than introducing new facts, deductions enable us to rearrange the facts we already know, putting them in a form that will make our point. Deductive reasoning is the basis of police work and scientific research, enabling investigators to draw relationships between seemingly unrelated pieces of information.

At the heart of deductive reasoning is the syllogism, a pattern of reasoning involving a major and a minor premise and a conclusion. Syllogisms take this form:

a = b

b = c

c = a

Here is an example:

1. All basketball players can dribble the ball.
2. Anthony is a basketball player.
3. Anthony can dribble the ball.

Using this pattern of logic, the conclusion that Anthony can dribble the ball is inescapable. If your listeners accept your premise, they are likely to accept your conclusion. The major premise in this case is statement (1) "All basketball players can dribble the ball," while the minor premise is statement (2) "Anthony is a basketball player." Whether the deductive reasoning is stated in part or not, it leads us down an inescapable logical path. By knowing how two concepts relate to a third concept, we can say how they relate to each other.

Recognizing that people do not usually state every aspect of a syllogism as they reason deductively, Aristotle identified the **enthymeme** as the deductive reasoning used in persuasion. Because speakers and listeners often share similar assumptions, the entire argument may not be explicitly stated, even when the elements of a syllogism are all present. This truncated, or shortened, form of deductive reasoning is the enthymeme. The inference step in reasoning with an enthymeme is that the audience, out of its judgment and values, must supply and accept the missing premises or conclusions. If a classmate in a persuasive speech makes the claim that a newly elected congressional representative will probably take unnecessary trips costly to the taxpayers, your classmate's claim is drawn from the major premise (unspoken) that most, if not all, congressional representatives engage in unnecessary and costly travel.

The interrelationships in a syllogism can be established in a series of deductive steps:

1. **Step One:** Define the relationship between two terms.
   Major premise: Plagiarism is a form of ethical abuse.
2. **Step Two:** Define a condition or special characteristic of one of the terms.
   Minor premise: Plagiarism involves using the words of another author without quotations or footnotes as well as improper footnoting.
3. **Step Three:** Show how a conclusion about the other term necessarily follows (Sprague and Stuart 1988, 160).
   Conclusion: Students who use the words of another, but fail to use quotations or footnotes to indicate this, or who intentionally use incorrect footnotes, are guilty of an ethical abuse.

Your ability to convince your listeners depends on their acceptance of your original premise and the conclusion you draw from it. The burden of proof rests with your evidence. Your goal is to convince your listeners through the strength of your supporting material to grant your premises and, by extension, your conclusion. Considering persuasion from the vantage point of such outcomes will be considered next.

Outcomes and the Power of Goals, Aims, and Claims

Since Aristotle, scholars have focused on the elements of ethos, pathos, and logos as the primary aspects of persuasion. Some researchers have added to these principles an emphasis on outcomes. Gary Woodward and Robert Denton, Jr. (1992), explain: "Persuasion is the process of preparing and delivering messages through verbal and nonverbal symbols to individuals or groups in order to alter, strengthen, or maintain attitudes, beliefs, values, or behaviors" (18–19). Careful consideration of the goals of persuasion, the aims of your speech, and the type of claim you are making will help your message achieve the influence that will allow you to advance your agenda.

Goals of Persuasion

Critical to the success of any persuasive effort is a clear sense of what you are trying to accomplish. As a speaker, you must define for yourself your overall persuasive goals and the narrower persuasive aims. The two overall goals of persuasion are **to address attitudes** and **to move an audience to action.**

Speeches that focus on attitudes. In this type of speech, your goal is to convince an audience to share your views on a topic (e.g., "The tuition at this college is too high" or "too few Americans bother to vote"). The way you approach your goal depends on the nature of your audience.

When dealing with a negative audience, you face the challenge of trying to change your listeners' opinions. The more change you hope to achieve the harder your persuasive task. In other words, asking listeners to agree that U.S. automakers need the support of U.S. consumers to survive in the world market is easier than asking the same audience to agree that every American who buys a foreign car should be penalized through a special tax.

By contrast, when you address an audience that shares your point of view, your job is to reinforce existing attitudes (e.g., "U.S. automakers deserve our support"). When your audience has not yet formed an opinion, your message must be geared to presenting persuasive evidence. You may want to explain to your audience, for example, the economic necessity of buying U.S. products.

Speeches that require action. Here your goal is to bring about actual change. You ask your listeners to make a purchase, sign a petition, attend a rally, write to Congress, attend a lecture, and so on. The effectiveness of your message is defined by the actions your audience takes.

Motivating your listeners to act is perhaps the hardest goal you face as a speaker, since it requires attention to the connection between attitudes and behavior. Studies have shown that what people feel is not necessarily what they do. That is, little consistency exists between attitudes and actions (Wicker 1969, 41–70). Even if you convince your audience that you are the best candidate for student body president, they may not bother to vote. Similarly, even if you persuade them of the dangers of smoking, confirmed smokers will probably continue to smoke. Researchers have found several explanations for this behavior.

First, people say one thing and do another because of situational forces. If support for your position is strong immediately after your speech, it may dissipate or even disappear in the context in which the behavior takes place. For example, even if you convince listeners to work for your political campaign, if their friends ridicule that choice, they are unlikely to show up at campaign headquarters.

Even if you convince a group that you are the best candidate, they may not bother to vote in the election. © *JupiterImages Corporation.*

Researchers have found that an attitude is likely to predict behavior when the attitude involves a specific intention to change behavior, when specific attitudes and behaviors are involved, and when the listener's attitude is influenced by firsthand experience (Zimbardo 1988, 618–19). Firsthand experience is a powerful motivator. If you know a sun worshipper dying from melanoma, you are more likely to heed the speaker's advice to wear sun block than if you have no such acquaintance. An experiment by D. T. Regan and R. Fazio (1977) proves the point:

A field study on the Cornell University campus was conducted after a housing shortage had forced some of the incoming freshmen to sleep on cots in the dorm lounges. All freshmen were asked about their attitudes toward the housing crisis and were then given an opportunity to take some related actions (such as signing a petition or joining a committee of dorm residents). While all of the respondents expressed the same attitude about the crisis, those who had had more direct experience with it (were actually sleeping in a lounge) showed a greater consistency between their expressed attitudes and their subsequent behavioral attempts to alleviate the problem (28–45).

Therefore, if you were a leader on this campus trying to persuade freshmen to sign a petition or join a protest march, you would have had greater persuasive success with listeners who had been forced to sleep in the dorm lounges. Once you establish your overall persuasive goals, you must then decide on your persuasive aims.

Persuasive Aims

The aims of persuasion, or the type and direction of the change you seek, is the important next consideration. You must define the narrower aims of your speech. Four persuasive aims define the nature of your overall persuasive goal.

Adoption. When you want your audience to start doing something, your persuasive goal is to urge the audience to adopt a particular idea or plan. As a spokesperson for the American Cancer Society, you may deliver the following message: "I urge every woman over the age of forty to get a regular mammogram."

Continuance. Sometimes your listeners are already doing the thing you want them to do. In this case, your goal is to urge continuance. For example, the same spokesperson might say:

> I am delighted to be speaking to this organization because of the commitment of every member to stop smoking. I urge all of you to maintain your commitment to be smoke free for the rest of your life.

Speeches which urge continuance are necessary when the group is under pressure to change. In this case, the spokesperson realized that many reformed smokers constantly fight the urge to begin smoking again.

Discontinuance. You attempt to persuade your listeners to stop doing something:

> I can tell by looking around that many people in this room spend hours sitting in the sun. I want to share with you a grim fact. The evidence is unmistakable that there is a direct connection between exposure to the sun and the deadliest of all skin cancers—malignant melanoma.

Deterrence. In this case, your goal is avoidance. You want to convince your listeners not to start something, as in the following example:

> We have found that exposure to asbestos can cause cancer twenty or thirty years later. If you have flaking asbestos insulation in your home, don't remove it yourself. Call in experts who have the knowledge and equipment to remove the insulation, protecting themselves as well as you and your family. Be sure you are not going to deal with an unscrupulous contractor who is likely to send in unqualified and unprotected workers likely to do a shoddy job.

Speeches that focus on deterrence are responses to problems that can be avoided. These messages are delivered when a persuasive speaker determines that an audience possesses something which the speaker sees as highly threatening or likely to result in disaster. The speaker may try to bring about some sort of effective block or barrier to minimize, if not eliminate, the threat or danger. New homeowners, for example, may find themselves listening to persuasive presentations about the purchase of a home security system. The thrust of such a persuasive speech is the need to prevent burglary through use of an effective and economical security system.

Types of Persuasive Claims

Within the context of these persuasive goals and aims, you must decide the type of persuasive message you want to deliver. Are you dealing with a question of fact, value, or policy? To decide, look at your thesis statement which expresses your judgment or point of view. In persuasive speeches, the thesis statement is phrased as a proposition that must be proved.

For example, if your thesis statement was, "All college students should be required to take a one-credit Physical Education course each year," you would be working with a proposition of policy. If instead, your thesis statement was, "Taking a Physical Education course each year will benefit all college students," this would be a proposition of value.

Propositions are necessary because persuasion always involves more than one point of view. If yours were the only way of thinking, persuasion would be unnecessary. Because your audience is faced with differing opinions, your goal is to present your opinion in the most effective way. The three major types of propositions are those of *fact*, *value*, and *policy*.

Proposition of fact. Because facts, like beauty, are often in the eye of the beholder, you may have to persuade your listeners that your interpretation of a situation, event, or concept is accurate. Like a lawyer in a courtroom, you have to convince people to accept your version of the truth. Here are two examples of facts which would require proof:

1. Water fluoridation can lead to health problems.
2. American corporations are losing their hold on many world markets.

When dealing with propositions of fact, you must convince your audience that your evaluation is based on widely accepted standards. For example, if you are trying to prove that water fluoridation can lead to health problems, you might point to a research article that cites the Environmental Protection

Agency (EPA) warning that long-term exposure to excessive fluoridation can lead to joint stiffness and pain and weak bones. You may also support your proposition by citing another research study that reports that children who are exposed to too much fluoridation may end up having teeth that are pitted and/or permanently stained.

Informative speakers become persuasive speakers when they cross the line from presenting facts to presenting facts within the context of a point of view. The informative speaker lets listeners decide on a position based on their own analysis of the facts. By contrast, the persuasive speaker draws the conclusion for them.

Proposition of value. Values are deep-seated beliefs that determine what we consider good or bad, moral or immoral, satisfying or unsatisfying, proper or improper, wise or foolish, valuable or invaluable, and so on. Persuasive speeches that deal with propositions of value are assertions based on these beliefs. The speaker's goal is to prove the worth of an evaluative statement, as in the following examples:

1. It is *wrong* for men to leave all the housework and childcare to their working wives.
2. Plagiarism is terribly *dishonest* for anyone who engages in it to complete an assignment.

When you use words that can be considered judgments or evaluations, such as those italicized above, you are making a proposition of value.

Proposition of policy. Propositions of policy are easily recognizable by their use of the word "should":

1. Campus safety should be the number one priority of the college.
2. Student-athletes should adhere to the same academic standards as other students.

In a policy speech, speakers convince listeners of both the need for change and what that change should be. They also give people reasons to continue listening and, in the end, to agree with their position and to take action.

A speaker's persuasive appeal, in summary, derives from the audience's sense of the speaker's credibility as well as from appeals to an audience's emotion and logic. At times, one persuasive element may be more important than others may. Many speakers try to convince audiences based primarily on logical appeal, some use mainly emotional appeals, and others rely on their image and credibility as a speaker. The most effective speakers consider their intended outcomes and appropriately combine all persuasive elements to meet a variety of audience needs and achieve their ultimate persuasive ends. Now we will turn our attention to a powerfully influential sequence of steps often used to organize persuasive messages.

Monroe's Motivated Sequence

As emphasized throughout this text, communication is a process connecting both speaker and audience. This awareness is particularly important in speeches to persuade, for without taking into account the mental stages your audience passes through, your persuasion may not succeed. The *motivated sequence*, a widely used method for organizing persuasive speeches developed by the late communication professor Alan H. Monroe (1965), is rooted in traditional rhetoric and shaped by modern psychology.

The method focuses on five steps to motivate your audience to act, and as Monroe would tell his students, they follow the normal pattern of human thought from attention to action. The motivated sequence clearly serves the goal of action if all five steps are followed. When the goal is to move your audience to act, each of the following five steps would be needed.

If someone wants only to persuade the audience there is a problem, then only the first two steps are necessary. If the audience is keenly aware of a problem, then a speaker may focus only on a solution.

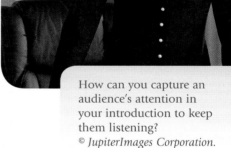

Attention. Persuasion is impossible without attention. Your first step is to capture your listeners' attention in your introduction and convince them that you have something to say that is of genuine importance to them. You have several possibilities, including making a startling statement, using an anecdote, and asking a rhetorical question. For example, in addressing the problem of injuries and deaths in youth baseball, Cherie Spurling (1992) began her speech by saying:

> Take me out to the ball game. Take me out to the crowd. Buy me some peanuts and Cracker Jack. I don't care if I ever get back …" Have you ever thought you might go to a ball game and never get back? Neither did nine-year-old Ryan Wojic. As his mother drove him to the ball field one day Ryan announced, "I am going to steal two bases, Mom …" His mother replied: "Ryan, you don't have to steal two bases; just do the best you can." We'll never know whether Ryan would have stolen two bases or done the best he could, because his first time up to bat was his last time up to bat. He sustained a lethal injury, and Ryan Wojic never got back.

How can you capture an audience's attention in your introduction to keep them listening?
© *JupiterImages Corporation.*

Need. In the *need step*, you describe the problem you will address in your speech. You hint or suggest at a need in your introduction, then state it in a way that accurately reflects your specific purpose. Your aim in the need step is to motivate your listeners to care about the problem by making it clear the problem affects them. You can illustrate the need by using examples, intensifying it through the use of carefully selected additional supporting material, and *linking* it directly to the audience. Too often the inexperienced speaker who uses the motivated sequence will pass through the need step too quickly in haste to get to the third step, the satisfaction step. Let us look at how Ms. Spurling described part of the need to recognize and eliminate a serious problem she asked her audience to face.

Ryan Wojic was killed when one of these speeding balls struck his chest. His heart went into immediate cardiac arrhythmia and paramedics could not revive him. And Ryan is not alone, as I mentioned previously. A Consumer Product Safety Commission Report stated that in a single ten-year period 51 children have died from baseball injuries. Of these, 23 were caused by the impact of the ball to the chest. The players at greatest risk are the pitchers and batters, and every kid bats at some point.

The same holds true for the risk of head and facial injuries. Take the case of Daniel Schwartz for instance, as reported by ABC's Stone Phillips. Thirteen-year-old Daniel went up to bat. The first ball was pitched low; the second to the inside. The third nailed Daniel in the face, shattering his cheekbone and nearly destroying his left eye. According to the April 1988 issue of *American Health*, each year baseball produces thousands of stories like Daniel's.

Satisfaction. The *satisfaction step* presents a solution to the problem you have just described. You offer a proposal in the form of an attitude, belief, or action you want your audience to adopt and act upon. Explanations in the form of statistics, testimony, examples, and other types of support ensure that your audience understands exactly what you mean. You clearly state what you want your audience to adopt and then explain your proposal. You have to show your audience how your proposal meets the need you presented. To be sure everyone understands what you mean, you may wish to use several different forms of support accompanied by visuals or audiovisual aids. An audience is usually impressed if you can show where and how a similar proposal has worked elsewhere. Before you move to the fourth step, you need to meet objections that you predict some listeners may hold. We are all familiar with the persuader who attempts to sell us a product or service and wants us to believe it is well worth the price and within our budget. In fact, a considerable amount of sales appeal today aims at selling us a payment we can afford as a means to purchasing the product, whether it is an automobile, a vacation, or some other attractive item. If we can afford the monthly payment, a major objection has been met. Here is how Ms. Spurling wanted to solve the problem she addressed:

Well, "some sort" of protection has been developed. *American Health* reports that Home Safe, Inc. has found an all-star solution. Teams like the Atlee Little Leaguers in Mechanicsville, Virginia, have solved many of their safety problems by wearing face shields like this one [shown]. This molded plastic shield snaps onto the earflaps of the standard batter's helmet, which incidentally, was invented in 1959 by none other than Creighton Hale. Most youth teams require the use of a batter's helmet, but with this shield they could add complete facial protection, including the eyes, for a cost of under $15 per shield. Daniel Schwartz's injuries have cost $23,000 so far.

Players could also be protected from chest impact death by wearing one of these padded vests [shown]. The vest may be a bit of a hindrance, that's true, but had Ryan Wojic been wearing one he would probably be stealing bases today.

Visualization. The *visualization step* encourages listeners to picture themselves benefiting from the adoption of your proposal. It focuses on a vision of the future if your proposal is adopted and, just as important, if it is rejected. It may also contrast these two visions, strengthening the attractiveness of your proposal by showing what will happen if no action is taken.

Positive visualization is specific and concrete. Your goal is to help listeners see themselves under the conditions you describe. You want them to experience enjoyment and satisfaction. In contrast, negative visualization focuses on what will happen without your plan. Here you encourage discomfort with conditions that would exist. Whichever method you choose, make your listeners feel part of the future. Ms. Spurling's speech did not include the visualization step but rather moved from satisfying the need to calling for action. Before moving to her strong call for audience action she could have added persuasive appeal to this important message. She might have said:

> Imagine yourself on a quiet and lazy summer afternoon watching your own child, a niece, a nephew, a cousin or a neighborhood friend up to bat in an exciting youth-league baseball game. Think about the comfort you will experience when you see that she or he has the proper safety equipment on so that there is no possibility that a speeding baseball will take his or her life, or result in any permanent disability. See for a moment the face and the form of a child enthusiastically awaiting the pitch and see as well this child effectively shielded from impact that could come from a missed pitch.

Action. The *action step* acts as the conclusion of your speech. Here you tell your listeners what you want them to do or, if action is not necessary, the point of view you want them to share. You may have to explain the specific actions you want and the timing for these actions. This step is most effective when immediate action is sought.

Many students find the call to action a difficult part of the persuasive speech. They are reluctant to make an explicit request for action. Can you imagine a politician failing to ask people for their vote? Such a candidate would surely lose an election. When sales representatives have difficulty in closing a deal because they are unable to ask consumers to buy their products, they do not last long in sales. Persuasion is more likely to result when direction is clear and action is the goal. Ms. Spurling concluded her speech by asking her audience:

> We must realize, however, that it may be awhile before this equipment scores a home run, so now it is your turn up to bat. If you are personally interested in protecting these young ball players, spread the word about these injuries, especially to businesses that sponsor youth teams. Encourage them to

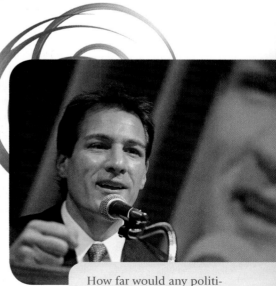

How far would any politician get if he/she failed to directly ask people to vote for him? © *Corbis.*

purchase safety equipment for the teams and then to sponsor them only on the condition that the equipment be used.

You can also write to Little League of America or any other youth league, requesting that they take their members' safety more seriously. And yes, do write to your congressional representative, because he or she may have a child or grandchild who plays on a youth team. Finally, if you happen to have a few extra dollars in your pocket, you could purchase some of this equipment and donate it to a local team as I'll do with this [equipment shown].

Ms. Spurling provided effective closure to her persuasive speech and call for action when she told her audience:

Now that we have discovered how children are being seriously injured and even killed while playing baseball, I know that you agree that given the children's lack of skill, we need to mandate the use of face shields, padded vests, and safer balls. So take them out to the ball game, but make it one that children can play safely, because children may be dying to play baseball, but they should never die because of it.

In review, remember the five-step pattern if you want to lead your audience from attention to action. The motivated sequence is effective, and like all tools of persuasion, can be misused. The line between use and abuse of persuasive tools warrants further examination.

Ethics and Persuasive Speaking

Do you want to be lied to—by anyone? Even when the truth hurts, we prefer it to deception. Telling the truth is the paramount ethical standard for the persuasive speaker. The importance of ethics in public speaking is stressed both implicitly and explicitly throughout this book. Ethics provide standards for conduct that guides us. Persuasive speaking requires asking others to accept and act on ideas we believe to be accurate and true. The ethics of persuasion merit particular consideration in our plans for persuasion.

Think for a few moments about rhetoric as persuasive speaking. Rhetoric is framed and expressed in language and presents ideas within a range of choice. As a speaker, when you make choices, some degree of value is involved in your choosing, whether you speak about the quality of the environment or television programs to select. When choice is involved, ethics are involved. Rhetoric and ethics are bound together.

As a speaker, you must decide not only what to tell your audience, but also what you should avoid saying. In a persuasive speech, you are asking listeners to think or act in ways needed to achieve your specific purpose, a desired response. Emotional appeals entail ethical responsibility, and this responsibility extends to other appeals as well. Consider the four habits discussed earlier in Chapter Three as applied to ethical persuasion:

1. **The habit of search**, in which we look for information to confirm or contradict a point of view, demands that we express genuine knowledge of our subject and an awareness of its issues and implications. As a persuasive

speaker, you know that controversy exists in matters requiring persuasion. Your task, within the time constraints you face and resources you utilize, is to develop sound and good reasons for the response you desire from an audience. This task is centered in a careful search for the truth.

2. **The habit of justice** asks that you be fair in your search, selection, and presentation of facts for the audience to consider and accept. You should not distort ideas or hide information that an audience needs to properly evaluate your speech, neither should you use loaded language or guilt-by-association tactics.

3. **The habit of preferring public to private motivation** stems from the fact that when you are involved in public speaking, you act as public persons. As such, you have a responsibility to disclose any special bias, prejudice, and private motivations in your sources and in your own motives. There are times in our society when political, religious, or economic spokespersons will articulate a public position that clearly indicates motives in the public interest when, in fact, their persuasive message is actually rooted in a private agenda that is self-serving.

4. **The habit of respect for dissent** requires that, as a persuasive speaker, you must recognize the legitimate diversity of positions that differ from yours. As a persuader, you are not compelled to sacrifice principle but, as Karl Wallace (1955) puts it, you should "prefer facing conflict to accepting appeasement" (9). Leaders who serve as spokespersons, from local community centers to the centers of power in Washington, DC, are constantly being challenged about their opinions, policies, and actions. As a persuasive speaker, you can ask with respect for dissent: "Can I freely admit the force of opposing evidence and argument and still advocate a position that represents my convictions?"

The ethics of persuasion call for honesty, care, thoroughness, openness, and a concern for the audience without manipulative intent. The end does *not* justify the means at all costs. In a society as complex as ours, one marked in part by unethical as well as ethical persuaders, the moral imperative is to speak ethically.

Summary

Your credibility as a speaker is determined by the way the audience perceives you. Credibility is measured in terms of perceived competence, concern for the audience, dynamism, and ethics. According to rhetorical theorist Kenneth Burke, you can increase your credibility and ability to persuade if you convince your audience that you share "common ground" by identifying with your listeners.

Emotional appeals (pathos) can be powerful because they provide the motivation for action and attitude change. Through emotional appeals you can elicit the full range of human feelings in your listeners. To strengthen your appeal, use concrete detail and emotional language, and concentrate on delivering your speech effectively. Persuasive speaking also invites ethical responsibility (ethos). As a persuasive speaker, you should be conscious of ethical standards and what the implications are of the choice you are asking your audience to make. The audience needs to be treated to the truth, without manipulative intent.

Understanding Abraham Maslow's hierarchy of human needs is helpful to persuasive speakers. The five levels of Maslow's hierarchy form a pyramid, with the basic levels forming the base. From bottom to top, these needs are physiological, safety, belongingness and love, esteem, and self-actualization. If you approach your listeners at an appropriate level of need, you will find them more able or willing to respond.

When making logical arguments (logos), one can take an inductive or deductive approach. Inductive reasoning enables you to generalize from specific instances and draw a conclusion from your observations. Deductive reasoning draws a conclusion based on the connections between statements. Depending on your purpose for persuasion, you may choose to reason from examples, analogies, causal relations, or with enthymemes. Choosing the right amount of support, the most persuasive kind of evidence, and then reasoning carefully are essential for successful persuasion.

The two overall persuasive goals are to address audience attitudes and to move an audience to action. Four specific persuasive aims define the focus of your speech. These aims include adoption, continuance, discontinuance, and deterrence. Your point of view, or thesis statement, is expressed in the form of a proposition that must be proved. Propositions take three basic forms: fact, value, and policy.

An effective method for organizing a persuasive speech is Monroe's Motivated Sequence that includes five steps designed to motivate the audience to action: attention, need, satisfaction, visualization, and action. The motivated sequence is a widely used method for organizing persuasive speeches which follows the normal pattern of human thought from attention to action.

 ## Questions for Study and Discussion

1. What are the dimensions of credibility, and how important is credibility to the overall effectiveness of a persuasive speech?
2. How would you define persuasion, persuasive goals, and persuasive aims? Illustrate your definitions with specific examples.
3. Why is the motivated sequence audience-centered? How does the motivated sequence relate to Maslow's hierarchy of needs?
4. What are ethical, logical, and emotional appeals? How are these appeals distinct, yet interrelated?
5. After choosing a specific purpose for a persuasive speech, decide on the kind of reasoning that will provide the strongest arguments. Why did you choose this reasoning form?
6. How important is evidence in a persuasive speech? How important are ethics in persuasive speaking? Does the importance depend on the audience and its shared needs and expectations? Is there a relationship among evidence, emotions, and credibility, or is evidence simply a matter a presenting the facts?

Activities

1. List three people you recognize as spokespersons on important public issues. In a written analysis, describe the *ethos* of each speaker.
2. Select a persuasive political speech and analyze the reasoning used in the speech. Present an oral analysis to the class.
3. Find transcripts, excerpts, or detailed news accounts of a well-known courtroom trial. Write a 500- to 750-word essay on the role of persuasive appeals in the attorneys' opening and closing arguments. Your focus should be on the strengths and weaknesses of the attorneys' persuasive appeals.
4. Prepare a five- to six-minute persuasive speech, organizing it according to the motivated sequence. Prepare a written analysis of why the speech fits the requirements of the sequence. Then deliver the speech to your class.
5. Look through an anthology of speeches, such as *Vital Speeches of the Day*, or a video collection, to find an effective persuasive speech. Evaluate the persuasion used in the speech according to what you learned in this chapter.

References

Aronson, E., J. A. Turner, and J. M. Carlsmith. 1963. Communicator credibility and communication discrepancy as determinants of opinion change. *Journal of Abnormal and Social Psychology, 67*: 31–36.

Cooper, L. 1960. *The rhetoric of Aristotle.* New York: Appleton-Century-Crofts.

Cooper, M. D., and W. L. Nothstine. 1992. *Power persuasion moving from an ancient art into the media age.* Greenwood, IN: The Educational Video Group.

Day, G. D. 1959. Persuasion and the concept of identification. Paper delivered at the SAA Convention, Washington, DC.

Freeley, A. J. 1993. *Argumentation and debate: Critical thinking for reasonable decision-making (8th ed.).* Belmont, CA: Wadsworth Publishing.

Hammerback, J. C., and R. J. Jensen. 1987. Cesar Estrada Chavez, in B.K. Duffy and H. R. Ryan (Eds.), *American orators of the twentieth century: Critical studies and sources* New York: Greenwood Press.

Johannesen, R. L. Summer 1974. Attitude of speaker toward audience: A significant concept for contemporary rhetorical theory and criticism. *Central States Speech Journal*, 95.

Kennedy, G. A. (Trans.). 1991. *Aristotle's on rhetoric—A theory of civic discourse.* New York: Oxford Press.

Kleinfield, N. R. March 11, 1990. "Teaching the 'Sir Winston' method," *New York Times*, Section 3, 7.

Monroe, A. H. 1965. Monroe first explained the motivated sequence to the author in a 1965 seminar on "The Psychology of Speech" at Purdue University. See also Gronbeck, B. E.,

German, K., Ehninger, D. and Monroe, A. H. *Principles of speech communication (11th brief ed.)* New York: Harper Collins, 263–272.

Regan, D. T., and R. Fazio. 1977. On the consistency between attitudes and behavior: Look to the method of attitude formation. *Journal of Experimental Social Psychology,* 13: 28–45. Cited in Zimbardo, 618. (Listed below.)

Sprague, J., and D. Stuart. 1988. *Speaker's handbook (2nd ed.).* San Diego, CA: Harcourt Brace Jovanovich.

Spurling, C. 1992. Batter up—Batter down. *Winning orations of the interstate oratorical association.* Mankato State University: The Interstate Oratorical Association.

Vancil, D. L. 1993. *Rhetoric and argumentation.* Boston: Allyn and Bacon.

Wicker, A. W. 1969. Attitudes versus actions. The relationship of verbal and overt behavioral responses to attitude objects. *Journal of Social Sciences* 25, no. 4, 41–78.

Wallace, K. R. January 1955. An ethical basis of communication. *The Speech Teacher*: 9.

Woodward, G., and R. Denton, Jr. 1992. *Persuasion and influence in American life (2nd ed.)*, Prospect Heights, IL: Waveland Press.

Zimbardo, P. G. 1988. *Psychology and life (12th ed.).* Glenview, IL: Scott, Foresman and Company.

CHAPTER

14

The words you choose to mark the occasion should remind people of the event they are commemorating. The more you say about the people and the occasion, the more intimate and fitting your speech becomes.

Speeches for Special Occasions

General Guidelines for Special Occasion Speeches

1. Make Sure Your Speech Meets Expectations
2. Tailor Your Remarks to the Audience/Occasion
3. Use Personal Anecdotes and Appropriate Humor
4. Avoid Clichés
5. Be Aware That You Are Speaking for Others as Well
6. Be Sincere but Humble
7. Be Accurate

Speeches of Introduction

Specific Guidelines for Speeches of Introduction

1. Set the Tone and Be Brief but Personal
2. Create Realistic Expectations
3. Avoid Summarizing the Speaker's Intended Remarks
4. Be Willing to Be Spontaneous

Speeches of Presentation

Specific Guidelines for Speeches of Presentation

1. State the Importance of the Award
2. Explain the Selection Process
3. Note the Honoree's Qualifications
4. Be Brief

Speeches of Acceptance

1. Be Sincere
2. Describe How You Reached This Point of Achievement
3. Use Anecdotes

Commemorative Speeches

Toasts

Commencement Speeches

Eulogies

Keynote Speech

1. Remember That Your Speech Sets the Tone for the Event
2. Select Your Topic and Language After Analyzing the Audience and Occasion
3. Time Is Still a Factor

After-dinner Speeches

1. Focus on the Specific Purpose, to Entertain
2. Use the Opportunity to Inspire

Summary

Questions for Study and Discussion

Activities

References

Like all other forms of public speaking, a speech delivered on a special occasion can rise to the level of the extraordinary. Certainly the college student, few ceremonies are likely to be more important than your commencement ceremony. In his commencement address, Curt Smith, former speechwriter for the President of the United States, expressed his feelings to his State University of New York Geneseo audience by saying:

> …let me thank all of you for your generous welcome. And say that to address these commencement ceremonies is, of course, among the greatest privileges of my life. Mark Twain once wrote: "In Boston, they ask, 'How much does he know?' In Philadelphia, 'Who were his parents?' In New York, 'How much is he worth?'" Well, from my perspective, you couldn't put a price tag on this morning. It is an honor to join you—especially my soon-to-be-fellow graduates. Sixteen years ago, I sat where you do, as undergraduates, about to receive my degree (May 20, 1989)

Like all good ceremonial speeches, the speech expressed Smith's most sincere feelings about the event and his audience. He used graciousness and humor to set an appropriate tone, and he established common ground through their shared experience of higher learning.

General Guidelines for Special Occasion Speeches

It is likely you will be called upon to give a special occasion speech at least once in your lifetime. You may have already given one. Perhaps you were chosen to speak at your high school graduation ceremony. Maybe you were asked to speak after receiving an award such as "Athlete of the Year." Or maybe, as president of a high school organization, you introduced a featured speaker or an award-winner.

Special occasion speeches, while aptly named, occur every day. In order to prepare you to give an impromptu toast or say a few words of praise or thanks, this chapter provides some general suggestions for special occasion speaking, and then offers guidelines for several of the most common situations wherein a brief speech is appropriate.

Whether you are introducing a guest speaker at your church, presenting an award honoring the volunteer of the year, or toasting the marriage of your sister, the following guidelines will help you decide what to say and how best to say it. Although there are differences among the types of special occasion speeches, as addressed later in this chapter, these guidelines apply in most cases.

1. Make Sure Your Speech Meets Expectations

Ceremonies and the speeches that mark them are surrounded by sets of expectations. Mourners listening to a eulogy, graduates listening to a commencement address, and members of a wedding party toasting the new couple expect certain words, gestures, and acts. Do not disappoint them. The words you choose to mark the occasion should remind people of the event they are commemorating. Even if you are sure everyone realizes the reason for your speech, explain it anyway. For example, it is difficult to imagine an awards presentation speech that did not mention the background and purpose of the award and the reason the recipient was chosen. Similarly, a speech of acceptance that failed to say thank you would be less than appropriate.

2. Tailor Your Remarks to the Audience/ Occasion

Saying what people expect is not the same as delivering a generic speech that could be given before any audience on a similar occasion. It is not enough to change a few facts here and there and give the same speech of introduction no matter who the audience is. For example, introducing a candidate at a fundraiser comprised of close friends and colleagues will sound different than introducing that same candidate before a group of citizens gathered for a candidate's forum. In the first situation, the audience knows the candidate and supports his or her positions on issues. In the second situation, the audience may not know the candidate, and may be unclear as to his or her stance on various positions.

The words you choose should include an explanation of the reason for the occasion you are commemorating. © JupiterImages Corporation.

3. Use Personal Anecdotes and Appropriate Humor

The more you say about the people and the occasion, the more intimate and fitting your speech becomes. Personal anecdotes—especially humorous ones—help create the feeling that the speech was written for that event and no other. On May 20, 2004, Jon Stewart, host of the popular *Daily Show*, spoke to the graduates of his alma mater, William and Mary.

Stewart begins his speech by explaining that he wanted to share some of his experiences at the college. He discusses the fact that William and Mary probably wasn't an obvious choice as the college he would attend. He also alludes to the fact that, as a freshman, he was awkward and obnoxious and was generally annoying to everyone who had the misfortune of being around him for any length of time. He explains that anyone who knew him as he was then would understandably be shocked and appalled that he would deliver the commencement speech years later.

Stewart continues explaining how physically unattractive and socially inept he was when he arrived in Williamsburg:

> Less than five feet tall, yet my head was the same size it is now…I looked like a Peanuts character.

Not every occasion is one in which humor is anticipated or expected; especially the self-deprecating humor shown by Jon Stewart in his remarks.

4. Avoid Clichés

Although speeches for special occasions should follow a predictable form, they should not be trite. To avoid delivering yet another tired introductory, presentation, acceptance, or commemorative speech, dodge the clichés that seem to be part of every speaker's vocabulary. These include:

"And now ladies and gentlemen …"
Use this line only if you are introducing Jay Leno or David Letterman. Simply avoid saying "ladies and gentlemen." Try saying something like, "And now it gives me great pleasure," or make reference to the occasion.

"Without further ado …"

How many times have you heard this expression in ordinary conversation?

We do not use the word "ado," so try "Finally," or "And now."

"I don't know what to say."

An alternative might be to express a statement of feeling, such as "I'm stunned!" or "How *wonderful* this is."

"My friends, we are truly honored tonight."

Is the audience filled with personal friends?

Instead, it makes more sense to say, "I'm very honored tonight…"

Avoid using trite clichés when presenting to make the occasion more meaningful. © *JupiterImages Corporation.*

"Ladies and gentlemen, here is a speaker who needs no introduction"

why we should avoid saying this statement

Then why bother speaking? Just eliminate the phrase. Everyone needs an introduction. Find something else to say about the speaker, occasion, or award.

Instead of a cliché, Paul Henmueller (1989), as a senior at the University of Illinois at Chicago, used the following metaphor of diamonds of hope in his commencement address:

Buried deep within the earth lie vast deposits of diamonds, the world's most precious gem. Although these stones are tremendously valuable, until they are mined they remain useless—glimmering pebbles hidden beneath the surface. Some day these jewels will be unearthed and the world will marvel at their brilliance.

Just as there is a great storehouse of wealth hidden in the vaults of the earth, so is there tremendous wealth buried deep within the mind and soul of each individual. This wealth may be in the form of intelligence, personality, honor, or a myriad of other abilities and attributes which comprise the spectrum of the human spirit.

This passage illustrates how public speaking is a creative process as well as an art. Rather than relying on worn phrases, Henmueller creates a vivid image that the audience will remember.

5. Be Aware That You Are Speaking for Others as Well

Whether you are presenting a gold watch to commemorate a vice-president's twenty-fifth year of employment or toasting the conference championship of your college football team, you are speaking as a representative of the group. Although your words are your own, your purpose is to echo the sentiments of those who have asked you to speak. In this capacity, you are the group spokesperson. It is acceptable to make "we" statements when you are referencing events and experiences shared by the audience and honoree. But remember, for the most part, it is not about you.

6. Be Sincere but Humble

You cannot fake sincerity. If you have been asked to give an award or to introduce a person you have never met, do not pretend an intimate relationship. Instead of saying, "I've seen what Jim can do when he puts his mind to it," tell your listeners, "I've spoken to the people who know Jim best—his supervisors and co-workers. They told me how, single-handedly, he helped two-dozen of his co-workers escape a fire-filled office and how he refused medical attention until he was certain everyone was safe. I'm proud to honor Jim as our employee of the year."

Being humble is also important. Even when you are accepting an award or being honored as person of the year, resist the temptation to tell everyone how great you are. It is in poor taste. Be appropriately humble, remembering that your audience is aware of your accomplishments. When Phillip Seymour Hoffman won Best Actor in a Leading Role for his portrayal of Truman Capote in *Capote* at the March 2005 Academy Awards, he started his acceptance speech with these words:

When accepting an award, remember that the audience is aware of your accomplishment and remain humble in your remarks. © *JupiterImages Corporation.*

> Wow, I'm in a category with some great, great, great actors. Fantastic actors, and I'm overwhelmed. I'm really overwhelmed. I'd like to thank Bill Vince and Caroline Baron. And Danny Rosett, the film wouldn't have happened without them. I'd like to thank Sarah Fargo, I'd like to thank Sara Murphy. I'd like to thank Emily Ziff, my friends, my friends, my friends. I'd like to thank Bennett Miller, and Danny Futterman, who I love, I love, I love, I love. You know, the Van Morrison song, I love, I love, I love, and he keeps repeating it like that. And I'd like to thank Tom Bernard, and Michael Barker. Thank you so much. And my mom's name is Marilyn O'Connor, and she's here tonight. And I'd like if you see her tonight to congratulate her, because she brought up four kids alone, and she deserves a congratulations for that.

It was not necessary to attend the ceremony to experience Huffman's enthusiasm and gratitude. He avoids bragging, and even requests that his mother be congratulated.

7. Be Accurate

Avoid embarrassing yourself with factual mistakes. If you are introducing a guest speaker, find out everything you need to know before the presentation by talking with the person or reading his or her resumé. If you are giving a commencement address, learn the names of the people who must be acknowledged at the start of your talk as well as the correct pronunciation of the names. If you are toasting an employee for years of dedicated service, make sure you get the number of years right!

You do not want to give people higher or lower rank (Captain/Lieutenant), or state incorrect marital status (Ms./Mrs./Miss), or give incorrect information about children, current and past employment, or education.

The guidelines we provided above will fit almost any special occasion speech. As we have mentioned throughout the book, the speech should be audience-centered. Clearly, the communication element "occasion" is the other crucial element. While all special occasion speeches should follow general guidelines, we will now turn to some of the specific types of special occasion speeches to see how these general guidelines apply and how other, more specific, rules help define these speech forms.

Speeches of Introduction

The purpose of a speech of introduction is to **introduce the person who will give an important address**. Keynote speakers are introduced, as are commencement speakers and speakers delivering inaugural remarks. When you deliver this type of speech, think of yourself as the conduit through which the audience learns something about the speaker. Research has shown that this speech is important because of its power to enhance the speaker's credibility.

It is your job to heighten the anticipation and to prepare your audience for a positive experience. You can accomplish these goals by describing the speaker's accomplishments in an appropriate way. Tell your listeners about the speaker's background and why he or she was invited to address the gathering. This can be accomplished in a brief, but effective, manner as is demonstrated in the following speech of introduction:

We all know Rosita Hernandez as president of the Hispanic students' organization on campus, and as the president of our college's chapter of Students Against Drunk Driving. What few of you may know about Rosita is her untiring commitment to working with abused children. Rosita spends every Saturday afternoon at the Department of Social Service's

Ask yourself what you can do to heighten the anticipation and prepare your audience for a positive experience when you introduce a speaker. © *Corbis.*

shelter, playing games with and reading to children who are desperately in need of love. Please join me in welcoming Rosita Hernandez who will talk about how volunteering has changed her life (Daniels and Whitman 1981).

Specific Guidelines for Speeches of Introduction

The following four guidelines will help you prepare appropriate introductory remarks:

1. Set the Tone and Be Brief but Personal

If you are going to err in an introductory speech, err on the side of brevity and personalization. Also, realize that it is your responsibility to set the tone of the speech. Recently, we heard a speech introducing a congressman at a U.S. Naval retirement ceremony. The speaker went into great detail introducing the man, detailing his education, military service, activities in community service organizations, campaigns for Congress, and so on. This introductory speech was too long, it was not personal, and the speaker failed to set the appropriate tone for the featured speaker. As a result of this information overload, members of the audience shifted restlessly, coughed, yawned, and even dozed off. In this situation, the main speaker began his speech at a disadvantage.

2. Create Realistic Expectations

By telling the audience, "This is the funniest speech you'll ever hear," or "This woman is known for being a brilliant communicator," you are making it difficult for the speaker to succeed. Few speakers can match these expectations.

As you prepare your introductory speech, remember to keep it brief and set the proper tone for the upcoming message. © *JupiterImages Corporation.*

3. Avoid Summarizing the Speaker's Intended Remarks

Your job is to provide an enticement to listen, not a summary of the remarks to follow. If you have any questions, share your proposed comments with the main speaker before your presentation.

4. Be Willing to Be Spontaneous

Spontaneous introductions are sometimes appropriate. An unexpected guest who you want to acknowledge may be in the audience. Something may have happened to the speaker, in the audience, or in the world just before the introductory speech, making the planned introduction less effective. For example, when actor Dustin Hoffman was taking his curtain calls after completing a performance of a Shakespearean play on Broadway, he noticed that Arthur Miller, well-known playwright, was seated in the audience. Hoffman raised his hands, asked for quiet, and said:

> When we were doing the play in London, we had the pleasure of playing one night to an audience that included Dame Peggy Ashcroft, who was introduced from the stage. We do not have knights in America, but there is someone special in the audience tonight. He is one of the greatest voices and influences in the American theater—Mr. Arthur Miller (Heller Anderson 1990).

Hoffman's impromptu introduction demonstrated that brevity and grace are the hallmarks of an effective introduction.

Speeches of Presentation

Each year, the nation honors five distinguished performing artists as recipients of the Kennedy Center Honors. In an award ceremony, each honoree receives a gold medallion. Actor Gregory Peck, who presented the awards, later admitted that his was an enviable job. "It's easy to throw roses at people," said Peck (Gamarekian 1989).

Throwing roses is an apt description for the presentation speech, which is delivered as part of a ceremony *to recognize an individual or group chosen for special honors.* Our personal and professional lives are marked, in part, by attendance at, or participation in, awards ceremonies to recognize personal achievement.

We also witness these presentations in the public forum. Each of these ceremonies includes one or more presentation speeches. Some occasions for presentation speeches include commencements (high school, college, and graduate school) where special presentations are made to students with exceptional academic and community service records, and corporate awards ceremonies where employees are honored for their years of service or exemplary performance. Televised ceremonies involve award presentations such as the Academy Awards, the Emmy Awards, and Country Music Awards. Other ceremonies recognize achievement in a sport, such as the Heisman Memorial Trophy, presented each year to the nation's most outstanding college football player.

Specific Guidelines for Speeches of Presentation

Every speech of presentation should accomplish several goals. A speech marking the presentation of the "Reporter of the Year" award for a student newspaper is provided in excerpts to illustrate four specific guidelines for speeches of presentation.

1. State the Importance of the Award

Many departmental scholarships and awards are available in college to qualified students. A scholarship may be significant because the selection criteria include finding the individual with the most outstanding academic achievement. Other scholarships may have been established to help single mothers, residents of the town, or students who engage in significant community service. Some awards are established in the names of people living and deceased.

The award may be worth $100 or it may be $5,000. Regardless of the monetary value, the audience needs to know why the award is important. You may need to describe the achievements of the individual or individuals for whom the award has been established.

Here is the beginning of a speech of presentation, as Tom speaks about his fellow reporter, Kathryn Remm.

> I am pleased to have been asked by our editorial staff to present the "Reporter of the Year" award—the college's highest journalistic honor. This award was established six years ago by a group of alumni who place great value on maintaining our newspaper's high standard of journalism.

In this example, Tom clearly states the importance of the award when he mentions that it is the college's highest journalistic honor.

2. Explain the Selection Process

The selection process may involve peers, students, teachers, or a standard committee. The audience needs to know that the award was not given arbitrarily or based on random criteria. Explaining the criteria and selection process may help to further establish the significance of the award. If the award is competitive, you may wish to mention the nature of the competition, but do not overemphasize the struggle for victory at the expense of the other candidates.

The following passage illustrates how this guideline can be followed effectively.

> The award selection process is long and arduous. It starts when the paper's editorial staff calls for nominations and then reviews and evaluates dozens of writing samples. The staff sends its recommendations to a selection committee made up of two alumni sponsors and two local journalists. It is this group of four who determines the winner.

Explaining the criteria and selection process when presenting an award helps establish the significance of the award. © *JupiterImages Corporation.*

3. Note the Honoree's Qualifications

Many organizations honor their members and employees. For example, Midas Auto Service recognizes various dealers at their annual conference, including the "South Central Regional Dealer of the Year." The awards are based on criteria such as regional retail sales, overall retail image, and customer satisfaction. Edward Jones chooses employees for the Partner's Award, which is based on sales and service efforts over the past year. The nature of the award will suggest what you should say about the honoree. The example below shows why the reporter is being recognized.

This year's honoree is Kathryn Remm, the community affairs reporter on the paper. Almost single-handedly, Kathryn reached out to non-college community residents and established channels of communication that have never been open. In a series of articles, she told students about the need for literacy volunteers at the community library and for "Big Brothers" at the local Boys Club.

4. Be Brief

Like speeches of introduction, the key to a successful presentation speech is brevity. Choose your words with care so that the power of your message is not diminished by unnecessary detail. Within this limited context, try to humanize the award recipient through a personal—perhaps humorous—anecdote.

As a final note about speeches of presentation, occasionally it is appropriate to ask past recipients of the award to stand up and receive applause. This decision should be based, in part, on your conviction that this acknowledgement will magnify the value of the award to the current recipient as well as to the audience.

Speeches of Acceptance

The main purpose of an acceptance speech is to *express gratitude for the award*. It is personal, gracious, and sincere. Most speakers start out with something like, "I am genuinely grateful for this award, and I want to express my sincere thanks to everyone here." It also makes sense to tell your audience what receiving the award means to you.

Most acceptance speeches are brief. In many instances, such as an awards night in high school and departmental recognition in college, several individuals are recognized for their achievements. If acceptance speeches are long, the event will seem interminable. However, in some cases, such as the Nobel Peace Prize ceremony, recipients are asked to do more than express gratitude. These speeches fit within the category of "Keynote Speeches," which are discussed later in this chapter. Following are three guidelines for the successful speech of acceptance:

Build your acceptance speech around the theme of "thank you" to show your sincere appreciation.
© Corbis.

1. Be Sincere

An acceptance speech is built around the theme of "thank you." You thank the person, group, or organization bestowing the award. You recognize the people who helped you gain it. Your acceptance should be sincere and heartfelt. The audience wants to feel that the individuals bestowing the award have made the right choice.

So if you know you will be asked to give a brief acceptance speech, think about who deserves recognition. It is not necessary to give a long list of all the individuals who have influenced you in your life time, but you want to acknowledge those who have had an impact on you in some way

that relates to your accomplishing this goal. A well-developed and delivered acceptance speech allows the listeners to be part of the moment and share the recipient's joy or amazement.

2. Describe How You Reached This Point of Achievement

As you are thanking people, you can mention how you reached this point of recognition. If you are a gymnast, you can talk about your training and gymnastic meets. If you are a pianist, you can talk about practice and recitals. The audience wants to know that you worked for this award, and that you deserve it.

3. Use Anecdotes

As you express gratitude and explain how you have reached this point of achievement, select with care the events you want to mention to avoid an endless chronology of your life. Stories about your life, or personal anecdotes, give people a lasting impression of your achievement. Instead of simply telling your listeners, "I am grateful to everyone who supported me in this project," provide your audience with a personal anecdote. For example, when Joanne received an award for being the Most Valuable Player on her soccer team, she provided this story as part of her acceptance speech:

> Three events contributed to my success on the soccer field. The first occurred on Christmas four years ago when I found a soccer ball under the tree and a completed registration form to a soccer camp held in my hometown.
>
> The second event was our final game during my senior year in high school when we won the city championship and I was fortunate enough to score the winning goal. I cannot tell you the great sense of satisfaction I felt when my kick took the ball past the goal tender and into the net.
>
> The third event was the call I received from our coach inviting me to be part of this college team with its winning tradition and offering me an athletic scholarship.

Commemorative Speeches

When we commemorate an event, we mark it through observation and ceremony. Public or private, these ceremonies are often punctuated by speeches appropriate for the occasion. Commencement speeches at college graduation, eulogies at the funeral of a loved one, speeches to celebrate the spirit of a special event or a national holiday like the Fourth of July, congratulatory toasts at a wedding or the birth of a baby or a business deal, inaugural speeches, and farewell addresses all fit into this category.

Although commemorative speeches may inform, their specific purpose is not informational. Although they may persuade, their purpose is not persuasive. They are *inspirational messages designed to stir emotions* and make listeners reflect on the message through the use of rich language that lifts them to a higher emotional plain. More than in any other special occasion speech, your choice of words in the commemorative address will determine your success.

Many commemorative speeches express the speaker's most profound thoughts. As you talk about what it means to graduate from college, be inaugurated to office, or lose a family member, your goal is to leave a lasting impression on your audience. Although many commemorative speeches are short, they often contain memorable quotations that add strength and validity to the speaker's own emotion-filled message.

Commemorative speeches can vary significantly, but what they have in common is that they are inspirational. The next section will cover three forms of commemorative speeches. These include toasts, commencement speeches, and eulogies.

Toasts

It is thought that the custom of toasting began when the Norsemen, Vikings, and Greeks lifted their glasses in honor of the gods. But the newer "toast" derives from the seventeenth century British custom of placing toasted bits of bread in glasses to improve the taste of the drink. As the concept of the toast evolved, so did the customs surrounding it. In England, those proposing the toast got down on "bended" knee. In France, elaborate bows were required. In Scotland, the toast maker stood with one foot on a chair, the other on a table. Today, Western tradition dictates the clinking of glasses (Bayless 1988).

You are more likely to be asked to deliver a toast than any other form of commemorative speech. Toasts are given at engagements, weddings, graduations, confirmations, births, the sealing of business deals, at dinner parties, and so on. They are *brief messages of good will and congratulations.*

Remember that a toast should be a brief message of good will and congratulations. © *JupiterImages Corporation.*

Following are three guidelines to help you deliver a memorable toast:

Prepare a short, inspirational message and memorize it. If you are the best man at your brother's wedding, the mother of the new college graduate at his graduation dinner, a close associate of an executive just promoted to company president, you may be asked in advance to prepare a toast to celebrate the occasion. Even though most toasts are generally no more than a few sentences long, do not assume that you will be able to think of something appropriate to say when the glasses are raised. To avoid drawing a blank, write—and memorize—the toast in advance.

Choose words with care that address the audience and occasion. There is a time to be frivolous and a time to be serious. The audience and the occasion will suggest whether it is appropriate to be humorous or serious, inspirational or practical. Here is an example of an appropriate toast to a new law partner:

> Ken has been a tower of strength for all of us. When four partners were sick with the flu at the same time last year, Ken

worked round the clock, seven days a week, to meet our deadlines. Here's to Ken—the best lawyer in town and the newest partner of our law firm.

<u>Be positive and avoid cliché</u>s. A toast is upbeat. Look to the future with hope. It is inappropriate to toast a college graduate saying, "If John does as poorly at work as he did at college, we may all be asked to help pay his rent."

Remember that public speaking is a creative activity. Avoid saying things that could be said by anyone, anywhere. Clichés such as, "Down the hatch," "Here's mud in your eye," and "Cheers," are a waste of the moment. Instead, you can say something simple like, "To Ken's future success," or, as is noted in the previous example, "Here's to Ken—the best lawyer in town and the newest partner of our law firm."

Commencement Speeches

No other speech offers a greater potential to achieve the aims of a ceremonial speech than the commencement address delivered by an honored guest to a graduating class. Here is the commencement speech we referenced at the opening of this chapter delivered by Curt Smith, a former speechwriter for President George Bush, and a successful sportswriter as well as political analyst. Speaking to a graduating class at the State University of New York at Geneseo, his alma mater, Smith's carefully chosen language stirs thoughts, images, and memories. He starts with an *expression of honor:*

> Let me thank all of you for your generous welcome. And say that to address these commencement ceremonies is, of course, among the greatest privileges of my life. Mark Twain once wrote: "In Boston, they ask: 'How much does he know?' In Philadelphia, 'Who were his parents?' In New York, 'How much is he worth?'" Well, from my perspective, you couldn't put a price tag on this morning. It is an honor to join you—especially my soon-to-be fellow graduates. Sixteen years ago, I sat where you do, as undergraduates, about to receive my degree.

At this point, the speaker shifts from the honor of being invited to a *tribute to the college from which he was graduated.* Vivid language conjures up images that have remained with him over the years:

> I loved bonfires, Indian summer, snow-flecked evenings, and the Boston Red Sox. But most of all, I loved tomorrow. Its possibilities were soaring, distant; they lay out ahead of us, like a day right behind the rain....
>
> Yes, rhetoric, like perspective, can often be unclear. But as students in the early 1970s at Geneseo State University, our perspective—for better or worse—was perfectly clear. ...Even then, we inhaled the age's often brooding and quite wonderful songs—"Taxi" and "American Pie" and "Layla" and the classic "Maggie May." And we believed

ours to be what retrospect proclaims it: The most tumultuous freshman class in the history of American education. We entered college in the fall of 1969; our first
months were marked by Woodstock, moratoria, and talk of
"impudent snobs." We left in the spring four years later—
the Viet Nam conflict ending; our prisoners of war at
home; and scandal searing—indelibly, tragically—an epochal
American Presidency. It was a time to begin, of intolerance
and, yet, of idealism—for in the cultural collision, which
marked the early 1970s, the university campus was its spiritual heart.

Then Smith pays *tribute to the college as a place of excellence* marked by
enduring and important values:

Mostly, though, Geneseo thrived in the early 1970s because of
the Geneseo Experience, which is your experience: Excellence
without elitism, Main Street values without facade.

She knew, as you do, that those who burned buses and
bombed buildings were not the voice of America's academic
tradition. She knew that amid the tumult and the shouting,
government at all levels must hear the voices of those who
work and pay their taxes and who speak from conscience:
Americans who ask government not to bless their lives, only
to go their own way—gently, modestly—with the respect and
dignity they deserve.

After his tribute, Smith *offers counsel to the graduating members of his audience*, urging his audience to strive for themselves and others. He concludes on
a *congratulatory* note:

In coming years, as alumni, you can reaffirm that voice. And
as you do, remember how nearly a half-century ago Churchill
said of a great battle of World War II: "Now this is not the
end. It is not even the beginning of the end. But it is, perhaps,
the end of the beginning."

My friends, in the deepest personal sense, this Commencement
marks the end of your beginning. Cherish the memories of
your time at this university. Understand its joys, worries, and
confessions of the heart. Care intensely, and give intensely of
yourselves. Help spur that unity of purpose, which benefits
the nation as a whole. Your inheritance is America; treasure
it. May your future be worthy of your dreams. And may you
recall the penultimate words of a great film from my college
years, Summer of '42: "Life is made of comings and goings.
And for everything we take with us, we leave a part of us
behind." Good luck, my heartfelt congratulations, and thank
you so very much (1989).

Although Smith's speech lasted only eighteen minutes, the strength of its
emotional appeal endures.

Eulogies

Eulogies are perhaps the most difficult commemorative speeches to make, since they involve paying tribute to a family member, friend, colleague, or community member who died. It is a difficult time for the speaker as well as the audience. A eulogy generally focuses on universal themes such as the preciousness and fragility of life, the importance of family and friends at times of great loss, and the continuity of life. Here are five guidelines that will help you develop and present a eulogy:

Acknowledge the loss and refer to the occasion. Your first words should focus on the family and/or significant others of the deceased. Talk directly to them, taking care to acknowledge by name the spouse, children, parents, and special friends of the deceased. It is safe to assume that all members of the audience feel loss. People come together to mourn because they want to be part of a community; they want to share their grief with others. By using "we" statements of some kind, you acknowledge the community of mourners. For example, you might say, "We all know how much Andrew loved his family," or "I am sure we all agree that Andrew's determination and spirit left their mark."

Celebrate life rather than focusing on loss. Some deaths are anticipated, such as dying from ailments related to old age or after a lengthy illness. Others are shocking and tragic, and those left behind may have unresolved issues. Although it is appropriate to acknowledge shared feelings of sadness and even anger, the eulogy should focus on the unique gift the person brought to the world.

Use quotes, anecdotes, and even humor. Nothing is better than a good story to celebrate the spirit of the deceased. A well-chosen anecdote can comfort as it helps people focus on the memory of the person's life. Fitting anecdotes need not be humorless. On the contrary, according to professor of journalism Melvin Helitzer, euphemisms such as "a loving husband," "a loving father," "a wonderful person" mean far less to people than a humorous account of an incident in the person's life. Helitzer explains: "To say the deceased had a wonderful sense of humor and I remember the time …," helps mourners get through the experience of attending the memorial as they recall pleasant memories and laugh along with you (Helitzer 1990).

Quote others. You may choose to turn to the remarks of noted public figures such as Winston Churchill, John F. Kennedy, and Mark Twain, or you may choose to use words from the deceased, as Senator Edward M. Kennedy did in 1968 at his brother Robert's funeral.

You do not need to rely on writers, poets, famous actors, or politicians. You may choose to include the words of friends and family of the deceased. As part of her eulogy at her mother's funeral, a daughter said the following:

> After reading the cards sent by her many friends, it made sense to include some of what others thought of her. I'd like to share a few of these: "She was so full of enthusiasm and curiosity about everything. Whatever project she took on, she did it with a flair that no one else could match." "A gentle

person who really did make a difference in each life she touched." "A warm vibrant personality and so much courage." "I doubt that anyone has left more happy memories."

The person and occasion of the individual's death should provide guidance in terms of what qualities to highlight and stories to tell. Remember, also, a eulogy can include input from others, so do not hesitate to seek advice from others close to the person being eulogized.

Work to control your emotions. Composure is crucial. If you have any questions about your ability to control your grief, suggest that someone else be chosen. As you offer comfort to others, try not to call undue attention to your own grief. While an expression of loss is appropriate, uncontrolled grief is out of place. If you do not think you can make it through the eulogy without falling apart, have someone else do it or bring someone up to the podium with you who can take over, if necessary.

Be sincere and be brief. Speak from the heart by shunning such clichés as "words cannot express our sorrow," "the family's loss is too much to bear," and "we were all privileged to know him." Rely instead on personal memories, anecdotes, and feelings. Focus also on your delivery for it will affect the sincerity of your message. Eulogies need not be lengthy to be effective. The following is an excerpt from a eulogy a woman gave for her father that indicates how she felt about him.

> Throughout the years, he has been there for my failures and successes, providing me with meaningful advice. His opinion has always been very important to me. My father was a warm and loving man, a man of integrity, a great teacher. I miss him and I love him.

Depending on the wishes of the family, several individuals may be called upon to eulogize the deceased. A brief, sincere speech will be greatly appreciated by those attending the memorial service.

 ## Keynote Speech

A **keynote speaker** is the featured speaker at an event. There may be several people who speak briefly, but the keynote speaker is the focal point of the event. Whatever the setting, whether it is a gathering of members of the American Society of Journalists and Authors or the annual convention of the American Bar Association, the keynote address is usually anticipated as a highlight that has the potential to excite the audience to thought and action. Unlike many special occasion speeches, the keynote speech is not brief. You may be called upon to give a keynote speech at some point. We offer the following guidelines.

1. Remember That Your Speech Sets the Tone for the Event

Think of keynote speakers as cheerleaders and their speeches as the cheers that set the tone for an event. The purpose of the gathering may be to celebrate the group's achievements, to share information with each other, or to give individuals the opportunity to interact with people who are in similar positions or situations. The keynote speaker is there to excite people, to stimulate thought and action.

Keynote addresses at political conventions are known for their hard-hitting approach and language. When he was a candidate for the U.S. Senate in Illinois, Barack Obama delivered the keynote address at the Democratic National Convention in Boston in July, 2004. Following is an excerpt from that speech:

> Tonight, we gather to affirm the greatness of our nation not because of the height of our skyscrapers, or the power of our military, or the size of our economy; our pride is based on a very simple premise, summed up in a declaration made over two hundred years ago: "We hold these truths to be self-evident, that all men are created equal... that they are endowed by their Creator with certain inalienable rights, that among these are life, liberty and the pursuit of happiness."
>
> That is the true genius of America, a faith... a faith in simple dreams, an insistence on small miracles; that we can tuck in our children at night and know that they are fed and clothed and safe from harm; that we can say what we think, write what we think, without hearing a sudden knock on the door; that we can have an idea and start our own business without paying a bribe; that we can participate in the political process without fear of retribution; and that our votes will be counted—or at least, most of the time.
>
> This year, in this election, we are called to reaffirm our values and our commitments, to hold them against a hard reality and see how we are measuring up, to the legacy of our forbearers and the promise of future generations. And fellow Americans, Democrats, Republicans, Independents, I say to you, tonight, we have more work to do...

Copyright © 2004 Barack Obama. Reprinted with permission.

The keynote address is the focal point of the occasion, and is anticipated as an exciting event. © *Corbis*.

Obama's speech makes patriotic references that may stir American's sense of pride in their country. But he also suggests that things could be better. His words clearly set the tone for Democrats at that convention.

2. Select Your Topic and Language After Analyzing the Audience and Occasion

There is a reason you were asked to be the keynote speaker. It may be fame, fortune, or simply achievement based on hard work. You may be provided with some basic guidelines for your speech, such as "motivate them," or "talk about success." How you develop the content of your speech and the words you choose to express yourself should be made after reflecting on the audience and occasion. At the Illini Girls State Conference in 1999, Dr. Melanie Mills, the keynote speaker included the following in her keynote address:

> …I'd like to close with a few words about leadership and what it means. First, it means having a dream or vision and believing it is possible. It is important that you are practical and think things out, but don't be afraid to color outside the lines. Second, it means believing it is necessary. Make a commitment to your commitments and see them through. Make your attitude contagious…Finally, you've got to be hungry. People are critical of leaders. Someone's opinion of you doesn't have to become your reality. Believe in yourself. Be disciplined. Be flexible. Be fair. Be compassionate. Be true to yourself and your values…Make a difference!

The audience for this occasion included high school girls who had been nominated by teachers to participate in this leadership conference. Dr. Mills used the theme of the conference (leadership) as the basis of her speech. Note her approach, and the phrase, "don't be afraid to color outside the lines." Imagine giving the same speech to a different audience, such as a group of newly-appointed managers. It is unlikely this approach would be as effective.

3. Time Is Still a Factor

Yes, people are gathered to hear you. You are the focus of attention. Say what you need to say, but do not waste their time. Think about what has happened in the time before your speech, and what will happen after your speech. Even if you have what seems to be an unlimited amount of time, realize that your audience may have other things to do. Think about the audience's attention span. Have they been in the same room for the last four hours? An audience can be enthralled for some period of time, but there is a limit as to how long they can pay attention. One of your authors attended a ceremony celebrating the university's 100-year anniversary, and slipped out of the room after forty-five minutes of listening to the keynote speaker. (The speech lasted another twenty minutes!) Time is a factor. You do not want to have your audience dreaming of an escape plan.

After-dinner Speeches

If the keynote address is the meat-and-potatoes speech of a conference, the after-dinner speech is the dessert. It is a speech delivered, literally, after the meal is over and after all other substantive business is complete. Its purpose is *to entertain, often with humor, although it may also convey a thoughtful message.* Keep in mind, a more accurate description of this speech would be "after-meal" as an after-dinner speech can occur after any meal.

1. Focus on the Specific Purpose, to Entertain

Do not make the mistake of delivering a ponderous speech filled with statistics and complex data. Talking about the national debt would probably be inappropriate, as would a speech on what to do with the tons of garbage Americans produce each day. You can discuss these topics in a humorous way, however, relating, for example, how handling the national debt has become a growth industry for economists or how families are trying to cope with community rules to separate garbage into various recycling categories.

2. Use the Opportunity to Inspire

As is noted in the definition of the after-dinner speech, you do not have to rely solely on humor. You can also be inspirational, filling your speech with stories from personal experiences that have changed your life. This approach is especially effective if you are well-known or if the events you relate have meaning to others.

Read the words of former Chicago Bears running back Gale Sayers below. He used an inspirational approach in the remarks he delivered at the annual prayer breakfast of the South Carolina Law Enforcement Officers Association. Sayers' reputation as a football player preceded him and made him a credible spokesperson when he began talking about athletic achievement. Although his speech is humorous at times, its intent is inspiration:

> When I was a student at Kansas, I ran track in my sophomore and junior years. My track coach, Bill Easton, was a man who had a profound influence on my life. Bill Easton was the man who taught me about work and discipline. … The first time I went to Coach Easton's office during my sophomore year, I couldn't help but notice a small sign on his desk. It said simply, 'I am third!' Coach Easton had an enviable record of success. He had won a couple of national championships; he always seemed to be winning. You can imagine I found that little sign puzzling at best. Coaches, as a rule, don't even want to know how to spell third. I was kind of shy at this time of my life. I was still trying to get the feel of things at Kansas so I said nothing. Coach Easton challenged me that year and the next.
>
> I remember once we were in a triangular meet. I was in the hurdles and broad jump and that day Easton said, 'Why don't you run the 330-intermediate, too, just to keep in shape and get your wind up and everything?' So I ran it and, I tell you, I [felt like I was about to die]. I finished third—which is last really, but third sounds better. People were laughing at me. The first five hurdles I was ahead, then six got [gesture] that big, and seven got [gesture] that big, and I tried to go under

the last two because I was real tired. I was so tired, and I struggled across the finish line and Easton came up to me and said, 'Way to go, at least you finished the race.' The one point I got finishing that race enabled us to beat out the third-place team by a point.

I never could get that little sign out of my mind, and, finally, after two years I asked Bill Easton about it. He said, 'The Lord is first, my friends are second, and I am third.' The more I thought about his adage the more sense it made and it continues to hold a lot of meaning for me.

I've tried to live by that motto and it is very hard to do. I haven't always been successful in living up to the standards of being third. Like everyone else I have my problems, but whenever I feel like my life is getting out of hand, I think of Bill Easton and 'I am third,' and it helps me get things back in order and it motivates me to try harder (1989).

Helpful Outlines for Special Occasion Speeches

Following are fourteen outlines for you to consider. Each commemorates a different event that you will probably encounter in the future. Each outline spells out both what is expected and the traditional order sequence used.

Speech of Introduction
1. Greeting and reference to the occasion
2. Statement of the name of the person to be introduced
3. Brief description of the person's speech topic/company position/role in the organization, etc. This should generate substantial interest in the speaker and/or message to come.
4. Details about the person's qualifications
5. Enthusiastic closing statement
6. Inviting a warm reception for the next speaker

Speech of Welcome
1. Expression of honor this person's visit brings to the group
2. Description of the person's background and special achievements
3. Statement of the reason for the visit
4. Greeting and welcome to the person

Speech of Dedication
1. Statement of reason for assembling
2. Brief history of efforts that have led to this event
3. Prediction for the future success of the company, organization, group, or person

Anniversary Speech
1. Statement of reason for assembling
2. Sentimental significance of the event
3. Explanation of how this sentiment can be maintained
4. Appeal for encouraging the sentiment to continue in future years

Speech of Presentation
1. Greeting and reference to the occasion
2. History and importance of the award

3. Brief description of the qualifications for the award
4. Reasons for this person receiving the award
5. Announcement of the recipient's name
6. Presentation of the award

Speech of Acceptance
1. Expression of gratitude for the award
2. Brief praise of the appropriate people
3. Statement of appreciation to those giving the award
4. Closing of pleasure and thanks

Speech of Farewell
1. Expression of sorrow about the person's departure
2. Statement of enjoyment for the association with this person
3. Brief description of how the person will be missed
4. Announcement of friendship and best wishes for the future
5. Invitation to return again soon

Speech of Tribute (if honoree is alive) or the Eulogy (if deceased)
1. Expression of respect and love for the honoree
2. Reasons for paying tribute to this person
3. Review of the person's accomplishments and contributions
4. Clarification of how this person has touched the lives of others
5. Closing appeal to emulate the good qualities of this person

Speech of Installation
1. Orientation of the audience to the occasion and the theme of this installation
2. Introduction of the current officers
3. Praise of the current officers for the work they have accomplished
4. Announcement for the new officers to come forward
5. Explanation of the responsibilities for each office
6. Recitation of the organization's installation of officers pledge
7. Declaration of the installation of the new officers

Speech of Inauguration
1. Expression of appreciation for being elected or placed in office
2. Declaration of the theme or problem focus while in office
3. Explanation of policy intentions
4. Announcement of goals to achieve while in office
5. Closing appeal for confidence in a successful future

Keynote Address
1. Orientation of the audience to the mood and theme of the convention
2. Reference to the goals of the organization and their importance
3. Brief description of the convention's major events
4. Closing invitation for active participation in the convention

Commencement Address
1. Greeting to the graduates and the audience
2. Review of the graduates' successful accomplishments
3. Praise to the graduates for reflecting respected values
4. Prediction and discussion of future challenges
5. Closing inspiration for the graduates to meet these new challenges successfully

After-dinner Speech
1. Statement of reference to the audience and the occasion
2. Humorous transition into the central idea or thesis
3. Presentation of major points developed with humorous supporting materials
4. Closing that is witty and memorable

Humorous Speech
1. Humorous attention-getter
2. Preview of the comic theme and intent of the speech
3. Presentation of humorous points and supporting materials that are typical of the audience in terms of events, feelings, experiences, or thoughts
4. Closing that presents a strong punch line. (Harrell 1997)

Summary

At some point in your life, chances are you will give a special occasion speech. You may be called upon to toast a member of your family, a colleague, or a good friend. Perhaps you will introduce a guest speaker, or your alma mater may invite you to address the graduating class. All special occasion speeches have certain characteristics in common. When delivering a speech for a special occasion, make sure it meets audience expectations. Tailor your speech to the honoree and the occasion, use personal anecdotes and appropriate humor, and avoid clichés. Be aware that you are speaking for others as well as yourself, be sincere, be humble, and be accurate.

The purpose of a speech of introduction is to introduce the person who will deliver an important address. Your role is to heighten audience anticipation of the speaker through a brief, personal description of why he or she has been chosen to speak. Speeches of presentation are delivered as part of special recognition ceremonies. These speeches tell the audience why the award is being given and state the importance of the award. Marked by grace and sincerity, speeches of acceptance express gratitude for an award. Commemorative speeches include toasts, commencement speeches, and eulogies. Commemorative speeches are inspirational messages designed to stir emotions and cause listeners to reflect. Keynote speeches often set the tone for an event through the use of direct language. After-dinner speeches are speeches of entertainment and inspiration, generally delivered at the conclusion of substantive business.

Questions for Study and Discussion

1. How would you evaluate Curt Smith's commencement address in light of what you have learned about this speech form?
2. What are the elements of an effective toast?
3. What are the elements of an effective speech of introduction? What should speakers avoid?
4. Why are brevity and gratitude key elements of an effective acceptance speech?

Activities

1. Select a famous person from the past and prepare a three- to four-minute eulogy in his or her honor. Follow the guidelines presented in this chapter, and deliver the eulogy in front of your classmates. A sincere, thoughtful eulogy is difficult to prepare, so spend time developing and practicing your speech.
2. Locate an individual in your community who is known as an effective special occasions speaker. Interview the speaker about how he or she selects materials, meets audience expectations, adapts to the occasion, and uses language and humor to influence the audience.
3. Team up with a classmate for the purpose of presenting and accepting an award. Toss a coin to determine who will present and who will accept the award. Then join with other teams in your class for a round of speeches involving the presentation and acceptance of awards.

References

Bayless, J. 1988. Are you a master of the toast? *The Toastmaster* (November), 11.

Daniels, T., and R. F. Whitman. 1981. The effects of message introduction, message structure, and verbal organizing ability upon learning of message information, *Human Communication Research* (Winter): 147–60.

Finesilver, S. G. May 7, 1989. The tapestry of your life: Don't be afraid to fail. Speech delivered at the Front Range Community College commencement, University of Colorado Events Center, Boulder. Reprinted in *Vital Speeches of the Day*, November 15, 1989, 82.

Gamarekian, B. 1989. "Performing Artists Honored in Words and Music," *New York Times*, December 4, C17.

Harrell, A. 1997. *Speaking beyond the podium: A public speaking handbook (2nd ed.).* Fort Worth: Harcourt Brace College Publishing: Fort Worth.

Heller Anderson, S. 1990. "Chronicle," *New York Times*, January 18, B6. *Interview with Professor Melvin Helitzer, January 17, 1990.*

Henmueller, P. June 11, 1989. Diamonds of hope: The value of a person. Speech delivered at commencement, University of Illinois, Chicago. Reprinted in *Vital Speeches of the Day*, September 1, 1989, 680–81.

Sayers, G. 1989. Remarks of Mr. Gale Sayers. Speech delivered at the South Carolina Law Enforcement Officers Association Annual Prayer Breakfast, February 22, Columbia, South Carolina.

Each person has something to contribute to the group, whether it is in the form of offering specific information, analyzing the issue, or being creative. An active participant contributes to the discussion, shares responsibility for task completion, and works effectively with other group members.

Small Group Presentations

Small Groups in Life

Small groups are a part of life. If you are on the editorial board of your school newspaper or are an organizer of the community blood drive, you are a member of a small group. If you are a member of a church, a musical, athletic, or academic group, you are a member of a small group. Think about how many groups you have participated in, and realize your membership in small groups may increase after you leave college. In business, academic life, government, and civic affairs, tasks are defined and completed through small-group communication. Many of the major decisions affecting your life are made by small groups. College admissions departments, school boards, and zoning boards are a few groups whose policies directly influence behavior.

As a homeowner, you may have an opportunity to present before a governing board. Perhaps you are a budding environmentalist who has noticed that the city has been pruning trees excessively or is making plans to eliminate landmark trees in order to widen streets. You take an opportunity to encourage the city council to approach city growth in a more "green" fashion. As a parent, you speak before the school board to convince them to eliminate vending machine drinks that contain sugar and/or caffeine. You argue that these are not healthy choices for young school children. In these situations, you have asked to speak before some group. As a professional, however, you receive requests to speak before a group because of your expertise. A state senator might talk to the local League of Women Voters about proposed state legislation. An insurance agent presents a bid before the city council or school board. As the chair of a university-funded organization, you present a budget request before the school's Apportionment Board, the group that allocates funds to college organizations.

Small groups are a part of life and you may have opportunities to speak before your city council, school board, or other community groups. © JupiterImages Corporation.

Participating in a Small Group

The most common way to be involved in groups is to participate in a small group. Groups meet for a variety of purposes. Sometimes the purpose of a small group meeting is to discuss a current problem. For example, if your organization is low on funds. You must find a way to raise money. A group of individuals wanting to become a recognized group on campus, needs to think of a strategy for presenting your case to the appropriate governing body. Everyone contributes to the discussion, and usually a designated leader facilitates the discussion. In college, study groups, sororities

Chances are you've been involved in various small groups, such as a study group, during college. © JupiterImages Corporation.

and fraternities, residence halls, honorary societies, academic groups, athletic groups, and church groups are just some of the possible ways you connect with others through small group communication.

Speaking as an Individual Before a Group

A second way to be involved with a small group is by speaking before one. This is considered public speaking and is the focus of this text book. Unlike regular public speaking, however, you may have two audiences, not one. The *primary audience* is the small group, such as a seven-member school board, a five-member city council, or a ten-member Apportionment Board. Your purpose is to provide information, to express a concern, or attempt to persuade. Also in attendance, however, may be a *secondary audience*. This is a collection of individuals who attend the open meeting for any number of reasons, including simply observing its proceedings. It's possible these individuals may have no knowledge or interest in your specific topic, and did not know you were planning to speak.

In a situation involving both primary and secondary audiences, do you construct a message for the primary audience, accepting the fact that the secondary audience may not understand the context, concern or content? Or do you construct a message that takes into account both audiences, knowing that for members of the primary audience, some of the information will be unnecessary or redundant? Complexity of the issue, size of the secondary audience, and time constraint are a few of the factors to consider before developing your message.

Speaking as a Member of a Group Before a Group

Alternatively, you may find yourself in a third speaking situation where you are a member of a small group presenting before another group. This may occur in your business class when you are part of a group presenting a case study, in a psychology class when your group presents results of its research project, or in a public relations class when you are asked, as a group, to present your public relations campaign. There are many instances in college when you work as a group to accomplish a task and report the results to your classmates. In your community, as a health care professional, you may be asked to join a panel with several other health care professionals to discuss the health care crisis before a group of senior citizens. The focus is not just on you, but on your group.

Many contexts are possible with the small group presentation, including being the only person who speaks before a small group or being one of many individuals who speak before a group. In some instances you will find yourself on a panel with individuals you have never met and in others you will partici-

When presenting in small groups, members need to consider which format is most appropriate for the occasion. © *JupiterImages Corporation.*

pate in significant small group interaction before your group presents. Given our interest in helping you become the most effective speaker possible regardless of context, this chapter will focus on (1) working in small groups, and (2) presenting in small groups. In order to work in a small group, it is helpful to know the characteristics of small groups, including purpose, goals, and size. When presenting in small groups, each person should understand his or her role responsibilities, and the members should consider which group format is most appropriate for the purpose and audience. Included in this chapter are suggestions for working in a small group and small group performance guidelines.

Working in a Small Group

In a college classroom, whether or not you were able to choose your "groupmates," the members of your group, these are the individuals with whom you must interact and cooperate. Each person brings to the group his or her own predispositions, attitudes, work ethic, personality, knowledge, and ability. You may find your groupmates friendly, fascinating, frustrating, or infuriating. Likewise, they will have their own perceptions of you and of each other. Regardless, in all but the most dire circumstances, you will traverse the hills and valleys of group work with these people.

Characteristics of Small Groups

We should acknowledge that many academic institutions have semester-long courses devoted to the topic of small group communication, and we could discuss small group characteristics indefinitely. However, for our purposes, three characteristics seem to be most relevant to the public speaking classroom.

Shared purpose. One characteristic of a small group is that group members share a purpose for communication, unlike a collection of individuals who share the same physical space. Seven people waiting in line for tickets to see the Los Angeles Lakers are not considered members of a small group. Neither are five people sharing a taxi from the Dallas-Fort Worth airport or eight people sitting in a dentist's waiting room. They lack a communication purpose. But if the individuals waiting in line for tickets interact with each other to form a cooperative so that only one of the seven individuals will wait in line for tickets at subsequent games, they would then have a shared purpose that would guide communication in all future meetings.

Group-oriented and self-oriented goals. A second characteristic of small groups is that members usually have both group-oriented and self-oriented goals. **Group-oriented** goals center around specific tasks to be performed, whereas **self-oriented** goals relate to the individual's personal needs and ambitions. Say you are a member of a small group charged with the responsibility of determining policies of a new campus radio station. Some of the tasks you face are developing station operating policies, purchasing equipment, and attracting advertisers. As an individual, however, a self-oriented goal may be to emerge as leader of the group in order to demonstrate leadership potential. Self-oriented goals may complement group-oriented goals, or they may provide distracting roadblocks.

Size. A third characteristic of small groups is group size. Scholars agree that a group must have a minimum of three members to be considered a small group. Communication professor Vincent DiSalvo notes that the ideal group size is from five to seven members (DiSalvo 1973, 111–112). According to Philip E. Slater, "These groups are large enough for individuals to express their feelings freely and small enough for members to care about the feelings and needs of other group members" (Slater 1958). However, a three-person group may lose effectiveness if one member is left out or if one member withdraws or chooses not to contribute. Also, groups with even numbers need to have some mechanism in place for solving the problem of a potential tie. As groups grow in numbers, the need for coordination and structure increases.

A group with an even number needs to determine what to do in the event of a tie vote on an issue.
© *Corbis.*

Role Responsibilities

When you become a group member, how you communicate is shaped, in large part, by your role in the group. If you have been appointed leader or have a special expertise that sets you apart from the other members, you may be given more responsibility than the other members.

Roles quickly emerge in small groups. While one group member emerges as the leader, taking the initiative in setting the group's agenda, another is uncommunicative and plays a minor role in group discussions. Still other members of the group may try to dominate the discussion, oppose almost every point raised, and close their minds before the discussion begins (Bales 1953, 111–61).

The role you assume determines how you will communicate in the group and how effective the group will be. Although there are many types of roles, we focus on two broad categories: your role as a group leader and your role as a group member.

Group roles evolve quickly and if you are the appointed leader, you will likely have more responsibility than other members.
© *JupiterImages Corporation.*

Leader Responsibilities

You may be elected or appointed as leader of a group, or you may emerge as leader over time. As leader, you need to be aware of the group's *process and the relationships* among group members. Behaviors that relate to *process* are designed to help the group complete the task. These include *providing direction and purpose, keeping the group on track, and providing clarifying summaries.*

Provide direction and purpose. As part of your responsibility to provide direction and purpose, you may choose to open the meeting with action-directed comments ("We are here to establish whether or not it is feasible to add another organization to our college") or to examine items on an agenda. Once the discussion begins, others will contribute, but it is the leader's role to focus the meeting at the start.

Keeping the group on track. Keeping the group on track simply means making sure the group does not drift too far from the task at hand. If you are talking about offering healthy alternatives in the cafeteria line, it is easy to start talking about favorite foods or incidents that occurred in the cafeteria or people who work or who eat in the cafeteria. While *some* extraneous conversation help build relationships among group members, the leader is responsible for making sure time is not wasted and the group does not get side-tracked on irrelevant issues.

Provide a clarifying summary. Groups, like the individuals who comprise them, can be confused by the information they hear. Warning signs include questions for clarification, puzzled looks, and drifting attention. When you sense confusion, one of the best ways to move forward is to provide a clarifying summary, which recaps what has just occurred. For example, after hearing evidence and testimony at a student disciplinary hearing, the board voted that a student (Martin) was guilty of vandalism. After some time, the group was getting nowhere in terms of determining a punishment. As a leader, you say,

> We've agreed that Martin is guilty of vandalism, and that his actions are worthy of punishment, but we seem to be stuck on the concept of expulsion. We agree that suspension is too lenient, and expulsion is more warranted. The confusion seems to rest on how we are interpreting 'expulsion,' with some thinking the student may never return to our school and others thinking the student may return after a specified period of time, provided certain conditions are met.

With this type of clarifying summary, you have eliminated suspension from further discussion and identified the source of confusion. Clarifying summaries help bring focus back to the meeting.

In addition to facilitating the group's *process*, an effective group leader is concerned with *relationship* aspects, which facilitate communication. An effective leader will draw information from participants, keep group communication from being one-sided, and try to maintain the cohesiveness of the group. Ultimately, the relationship aspects allow the group to accomplish its task.

Draw information from participants. Each person has something to contribute to the group, whether it is in the form of offering specific information, analyzing the issue, or being creative. However, some people are hesitant to speak even when they have something valuable to contribute. Their reasons may range from communication anxiety to uncertainty about their role in the group. As a leader, draw information from participants by directing questions to those who remain silent, asking each group member to speak, and being supportive when a normally quiet member makes a comment in the hope of encouraging additional responses at a later time. Getting everyone to contribute is particularly important when one or more members of the group seem to dominate the discussion. It is up to the group leader to make sure the group benefits from the combined wisdom of all its members.

Try to keep group communication from being one-sided. A leader should try to keep group communication from being one-sided. We often have preconceived ideas of how something should be done. While dissent is healthy, these ideas may be obstacles to group communication if the leader allows the discussion to become one-sided. The leader needs to recognize when one point of view is dominating the discussion. Inviting others into the discussion or providing a varying opinion yourself may open up the discussion for multiple perspectives.

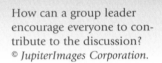

Try to maintain the cohesiveness of the group. As a leader, you should try to maintain the cohesiveness of the group. You want the group to see themselves as a group and function as a group, not as a collection of individuals. Everyone needs to work toward the group goal, while not ignoring his or her personal goals. Nothing is inherently wrong with a heated discussion, especially when the issue is controversial. But when the discussion turns into a shouting match, it is no longer productive. In a conflict situation, the leader should acknowledge the person's point of view but suggest that the problem be analyzed from other perspectives as well. Conflict is healthy, but unproductive conflict is a major obstacle to task completion. Keeping communication flowing effectively and making sure members feel their contributions are valued are important to the overall cohesiveness of the group.

How can a group leader encourage everyone to contribute to the discussion?
© *JupiterImages Corporation.*

Member Responsibilities

Being an active participant is the most important responsibility of each group member. An active participant contributes to the discussion, shares responsibility for task completion, and works effectively with other group members. Some group members believe that their participation is unnecessary because others will pick up their slack. Others view the experience as less important than other college work or activities. Complaining about group members is nothing new. Here are common complaints about other group members:

- Doesn't work or prepare enough
- Others have to nag group members to get work done
- Procrastinates
- Doesn't keep group members informed of content of presentation
- Information in presentation overlaps too much
- Information is excessive or too brief
- Too controlling
- Too apathetic
- Doesn't return calls or email
- Difficult to contact
- Doesn't stay after class to check with group
- Doesn't come to class on group work days
- Doesn't proofread PowerPoint

The previous is only a partial list of complaints we hear about group members. We understand that students take several academic courses. They have a social and/or work life, and priorities differ among students. But once you are part of a group, your actions have an impact on the other people in that group. In a classroom setting, you may not be thrilled with the topic, the assignment, or the other group members. But you do need to work with your group in order to complete the required assignment. Actively working to complete your individual tasks and being available and cooperative will make the situation better for all involved. Fulfill a commitment to the group.

Suggestions for Group Members

The following seven suggestions are designed to create the most effective small group experience within the context of your classroom. Many of these translate easily to experiences outside the college classroom. The suggestions are derived partially from *Speak from Success* by Eugene Ehrlich and Gene R. Hawes (1984, 133).

Know the constraints of the assignment. Read the syllabus or any other material given to you related to the assignment. Make sure everyone agrees as to the constraints of the assignment. The following are some questions that may guide your group:

- When does the group present?
- How much time does the group have to present?
- Does each speaker have the same amount of time?
- What information needs to be included in the presentation?
  - Are presentational aids required?
    - Does each speaker use a set of note cards? Is there a restriction?
      - Is there audience involvement at some point during the group presentation?
        - Can group members interrupt each other to comment or add insight?
          - Is there a paper required? Or an outline?
          - How many and what type of sources are required, and should they be cited during the presentation?
          - Does the group choose its format, or is there a particular format that is required?
        - Are students being graded individually, as a group, or both?
- Will there be any peer evaluations?

When you feel strongly about your position, you can try to convince others that you're correct. Ultimately, though, you need to put the group's goals above your own.
© *JupiterImages Corporation.*

Work to achieve group goals. Instructors understand that each individual is concerned about his or her own grade. However, the purpose of a group assignment is to work collectively and collaboratively. Make group goals your top priority. Making a commitment to the group means making a commitment to achieve group goals at each meeting. When you feel strongly about your position, it is legitimate to try to convince the group you are correct. But if others disagree, it is important that

you listen to their objections and try to find merit in them. You need an objective detachment from your own proposals to enable you to place the group's goals above your own. A group needs a shared image of the group, in which individual aspirations are subsumed under the group umbrella that strives for the common good.

Be responsible for completing your part of the assignment. Group membership brings with it a set of roles and responsibilities. It may not have been your choice to work in a group or to work with that specific group of individuals. The fact is, the assignment is mandatory. Everyone has a life. Everyone has distractions in their lives. You may be very busy, or you may be uninterested, but your group needs your help. If a group member volunteers to make the PowerPoint presentation consistent from speaker to speaker, you need to make sure that person has your slides when they are requested. If you are supposed to make contact with city officials or individuals who may help with a fundraising idea, you need to come to the group with that information. Do not be responsible for the group's progress being delayed, or the task not completed. If you cannot attend a meeting, make sure someone knows. Send your work with someone else. If you do get behind, make sure group members know so they have an opportunity to respond in some way.

Research sufficiently. Most group work involves research of some type. When you are finished researching, you should feel confident that you have ample support or that the topic or issue has been covered in enough depth. Depending on the group's purpose or goal, research may involve surfing the Internet, conducting a library search, looking through the local Yellow Pages, calling different social service agencies in town, or interviewing members of the local city council. If your group sought to determine what Americans consider the most important political issues for the 2008 presidential campaign, locating *one* website or *one* magazine article is not sufficient. If your group wanted to determine which pizza place in town served the best pizza, selecting two from the Yellow Pages is not sufficient, particularly in a city that has ten or more places that sell pizza. If you have been assigned to interview city council members, talking to one person for five minutes is not sufficient.

Communicate effectively and efficiently. Different people bring to a group a wide range of knowledge and views that help complete the task. Group discussion often produces creative approaches that no one would have thought of alone. Group involvement through communication increases the likelihood that the group's decision will be accepted and supported by all group members and by the broader community. Do not waste time and do not monopolize the group discussions or the presentation.

Most group work involves some research so you feel confident that the topic has been covered in enough depth. © *JupiterImages Corporation.*

Antagonistic comments can be permanently damaging and make it impossible for the group to function.
© *Marcin Balcerzak, 2008. Under license from Shutterstock, Inc.*

Avoid personal attacks. Comments like, "You have to be an idiot to believe that will work," or "My six-year-old cousin has better ideas than that," accomplish nothing. On the contrary, these comments are so antagonistic that they make it virtually impossible for people to work together. If you do not like an idea, say so directly by focusing on the idea, not the person, such as "It may be difficult to get funds for that project," or "I don't think parents will want to volunteer their time for that." Try not to make your disagreement too negative. Find areas of agreement, where possible.

Leave personal problems at home. Group conflicts are often the result of personal problems brought to the group meeting. A fight with a family member, a poor test grade, an alarm clock that failed to ring, a near-accident on the highway, or school or work pressure can put you in a bad mood for the meeting and lessen your tolerance for other group members. Although an outburst of anger may make you feel better for the moment, it can destroy the relationships you have with other members of the group.

Reflective Thinking Process

You may be called upon in a college course or in an organization to work with others on a problem-solving task. On campus for example, the Student Senate needs to find ways to get more students involved in campus events , while off campus the local Chamber of Commerce is trying to find ways to entice new businesses to join their organization. Groups are faced with small and large problems on a regular basis. Almost 100 years ago, John Dewey developed a theory of reflective thinking that is now applied to group communication (1910). If you are working on a problem-solving task, consider following the following seven steps:

1. Identify and Define the Problem

The first step of this process is to make sure group members understand and agree on what the problem is. Otherwise, the discussion may scatter into many different directions and time will be misused, for example, a newly elected Student Senate member wants to work with a group to deal with student complaints about residence hall assignments. One problem is that students are not given enough options about where they may live or with whom. A second problem is that the administration does not process complaints effectively. Third, students are unhappy about meal plan options and residence hall rules and contracts. Does the group want to take on all of these problems, or to focus on the complaint process? The first thing the group needs to do is identify the problem.

2. Analyze the Problem

In the process of analyzing the problem, group members need to identify what they know about the problem, what they do not know, and what resources are available to help them acquire more information. In this step, group members should find out what caused the problem, how long the problem has been an issue, and the extent of the problem. If only one student has complained about her residence hall assignment, there is not much of a problem. But if significant staff time is devoted to addressing students' complaints, then the problem is significant. Perhaps the problem started when a new administrator took office. Perhaps the problem is ongoing. This is the information-gathering, sorting, and evaluation stage of the reflective thinking process.

3. Determine Criteria for an Acceptable Solution

Many groups skip this step, whether they are newly formed groups in a college classroom or well-established policy groups in a community. However, it is a mistake to come into the problem-solving process with a firm idea of what you think is the best solution. Whatever solution your group suggests must meet agreed-upon criteria or standards. Criteria will differ vastly from situation to situation. For example, if four students turned in a group paper that was clearly pla- giarized, before determining the punishment, an instructor might consider the following criteria:

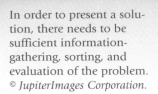

- Is (the punishment) it fair (to the four students and the rest of the class)?
- Is it appropriate (given the nature of the misconduct)?
- Will it deter future misconduct (on the part of the students who cheated as well as other students who might be contemplating misconduct)?

Criteria related to the residence hall complaints issue might include the following:

In order to present a solution, there needs to be sufficient information-gathering, sorting, and evaluation of the problem.
© JupiterImages Corporation.

- Does the solution consider both the needs of students and college administrators?
- Does the solution apply to all students living in residence halls, not just incoming freshmen?
- Does the solution allow students to change residence halls?
- Does the solution recognize that freshmen do not have cars?

Establishing criteria keeps group members from simply proposing their solution. Any solution presented needs to meet the criteria established by group members.

4. Generate Possible Solutions

According to Dewey, suspended judgment is critical at this point in the deci- sion-making process (Ross and Ross 1989, 77). Group members need to identify available options without stifling the process by providing immedi- ate evaluation. **Brainstorming,** which involves generating as many solutions as possible without critical evaluation, may be useful during this step of the reflective thinking process. Be creative. Encourage group members to think "outside the box." Avoid the temptation to say, "that won't work," "that's not possible," or worse, "that's a dumb idea." Instead, generate ideas until you agree you have exhausted the possibilities. If possible, give yourselves time to think about these solutions before evaluating or moving on to the next step. For the teacher who caught the group of students plagiarizing, some of the punishment options include ignoring it, talking to the students, requiring them to give a group presentation on the evils of plagiarism, requiring them to write another paper, lowering their grade on the paper, failing them for the assignment, failing them for the semester, and reporting the students to the Office of Judicial Affairs.

Regarding the problem of residence hall complaints, the group may develop several options, including changing the forms students fill out, suggesting a policy change, providing clearer, more specific information to students, and establishing a committee to hear complaints not resolved between students and administration. The important thing is to *have* alternatives, and not be single-minded in your approach.

5. Choose the Solution That Best Fits the Criteria

Each solution identified in Step Four needs to be evaluated based on the criteria established in Step Three. Ideally, the best solution is one that meets all the established criteria. If that does not happen, the group may need to revisit the possible solutions, and determine if amending one of the solutions might result in it meeting all of the established criteria. The instructor who caught students plagiarizing needs to evaluate her possible options by the criteria she has set. For example, if she ignores the misconduct, is that fair to those in the class who did not plagiarize? Is failing the students for the course an appropriate punishment for the students' misconduct?

In terms of the residence hall complaints, does changing the form students fill out meet both the needs of students and administrators? Will the form address the issue of changing residence hall assignments? Will a committee be formed to hear complaints from all students in residence halls? An option might not meet each of the criteria perfectly, but the point of this step is to choose the solution that best meets the criteria. If multiple options are acceptable, the group needs to determine how it will decide on which solution to implement.

6. Implement the Solution

Implementing the solution means putting it into effect. It is one thing to decide that a car wash will raise the most money; it is another thing to advertise, staff, supply, and conduct the fundraiser. The work involved in implementing the solution will vary according to the problem. For example, an instructor dealing with plagiarism can determine the best solution and then communicate that decision to the students and/or administration. If the group dealing with residence hall complaints decides to form a committee to hear complaints, then implementing the solution entails setting up committee structure, policies and procedures, soliciting membership, and informing students about the committee.

In a public speaking class, your group may be involved in determining a solution and suggesting how it could be implemented, but it is possible the group will not be involved with the actual implementation. For example, your group may be given the task of determining how to get students more involved in their department's activities. Your group could work through Step Five and decide that the best solution is to advertise activities earlier so that students can work them into their schedules. As a group, you may present Steps One through Five to a faculty committee, but Step Six might ultimately be the committee's responsibility.

7. Reassess

Reassessing at some point prevents the group from saying "we're done" after implementing the solution. It is an important part of the process because you evaluate your group's success or lack thereof. Fundraisers are carefully planned and executed, but still may fail. New policies are developed with the best intentions, but may still be ineffective. Do you try the same fundraiser again? Do you keep the new policy? Before you answer "yes" or "no" to these questions, the group needs to answer some other questions. Did the fundraiser fail because it was held at a bad time? Was it advertised sufficiently? Did it ask too much of the people working it or attending the fundraiser? In other words, the group needs to decide what contributed to the lack of success. Similarly, with the ineffective policy, did administration evaluate its effectiveness too soon? Were students inadequately informed? Was administration insufficiently trained? Those engaged in reassessment need to discuss what factors influenced the lack of success. In a sense, this final step can be the beginning step of a new process, if the solution has not been effective.

The seven-step reflective thinking process is one way to help groups move through the problem-solving process. It is certainly not the only way. However, regardless of the approach groups take, it is important that a clear process be established that allows for rational, deliberative discussion of all relevant aspects of the problem. A leader should help the group through this process, and group members should contribute productively throughout the process.

Presenting in Small Groups

Just because you are part of a small group discussion does not mean that you will report your results through some type of oral presentation. Some groups prepare written reports that some administrator, council, or committee will evaluate. Sometimes the results of your deliberation are presented before a group, and in many instances a group presents before another group for other reasons. For example, a group of teachers who attended a workshop on working with gifted students present their observations of the workshop to the group of teachers who were unable to attend. Members of the League of Women Voters who attended the national convention present a summary of their experiences to the rest of the membership. Also, many careers have national conferences where people with similar interests have the opportunity to attend or present seminars and panel presentations.

When speaking in a small group format, you need to be aware of how your message fits in with those of the other group members.
© JupiterImages Corporation.

Whether presenting as a group or as an individual to a group successful public speaking strategies are necessary. So all information presented in this textbook is relevant to this context. Audience analysis is essential. Any presentation you prepare should have a clear introduction, body, and conclusion. Your presentation should be well-research, sufficiently supported, and organized effectively. Your delivery should be engaging and extemporaneous. Be sure you are not too dependent on notes.

Speaking as a member of a group, however, involves additional reflection. First, it is important to find a small group format that best suits your purpose. Second, it is important that the speeches all group members give flow as though they were one coherent speech. The last section of this chapter describes a variety of small group formats concerns that need to be addressed before the group speaks, and makes suggestions for the presentation.

Small Group Formats

Most of your group work in class occurs before the day you present. You spend time defining your purpose, setting goals, distributing the work load, researching your topic/issues, and organizing your research into something meaningful. If in business or civic life, you are already an expert on the topic, your task is to determine what you need to bring to this particular presentation. It is possible that you never meet the other group members until moments before the presentation.

In a public speaking class, your instructor may suggest a particular small group format. In business or civic life, a moderator or facilitator decides how the group should present. It is also possible that you determine your format. Regardless, there are three main small group formats: panel discussion, symposium, and forum.

Most of your group work occurs before you present, as you spend time defining your purpose, researching, and organizing your message. © *JupiterImages Corporation.*

Panel Discussion

In a panel discussion, group members have an informal interchange on the issues in front of an audience. The positive and negative features of issues are debated, just as they were in the closed group meeting, but this time in front of an audience. When you are part of a panel discussion, it is important to keep in mind that you are talking for the benefit of the audience rather than for other group members. Although your responses are spontaneous, they should be thought out in advance, just as in any other public speaking presentation.

Panel discussions are directed by a moderator who attempts to elicit a balanced view of the issues and to involve all group members. The role of the moderator is to encourage the discussion—he or she does not take part in the debate. Moderators coordinate and organize the discussion, ask pertinent questions, summarize conclusions, and keep the discussion moving. Once the discussion is over, the moderator often opens the discussion to audience questions.

As you can tell from the previous description, the critical elements of a panel discussion are: (1) it is an informal discussion moderated or facilitated by someone who is not an active participant, (2) interaction should be distributed equitably among group members with no pre-determined time limit for each group member, and (3) generally, there are no prepared remarks.

Symposium

A symposium is more formal and predictable than a panel discussion. Instead of focusing on the interaction among group members, it centers on prepared speeches on a specified subject given by group members who have expertise on the subject. The topic and speakers are introduced by a moderator. A symposium is structured, and speakers are generally given a time frame for their comments. After the formal presentation, a panel discussion or forum may follow. This allows for interaction among group members, and for the audience to ask questions of individual speakers.

Forum

In a forum, group members respond to audience questions. Someone may provide a prepared statement, but it is also possible to introduce group members and their credentials, and then ask for audience questions. Unlike a panel discussion or the second half of a symposium, a forum does not include interactions among group members. The forum is very audience-centered.

The success of the forum depends on how carefully the audience has thought about the topic (the topic is announced in advance) and the nature of their questions. For example, school boards hold public hearings about their annual budget. In addition to the school board, the superintendent and district financial officer will be present. Generally, there is a presentation by the financial officer, and then anyone present at the meeting may ask questions. Questions could be asked about transportation, food service, athletics, computer equipment, and so on. If several concerned citizens show up with questions in mind, the meeting could last for hours. If no one in the community attends the meeting, then it will be very short.

A forum also needs a moderator. When the League of Women Voters holds a candidates' forum, selected League members collect questions from the audience and give them to the moderator who then addresses questions to the appropriate panelists. A forum is not just a collection of individuals, but a group of people who have been chosen for their interest in the topic/issue or because of their expertise.

Preparing to Present as a Group

When you prepare a speech for class, you are responsible for all aspects of the speech. As an individual, you need to prepare, practice, and present. Once you join a group, however, you need to be prepared, but you also need to be aware of how your speech fits into the other speeches, and the group needs to make sure everyone is viewing the presentation from a similar perspective. With

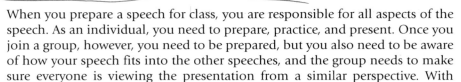

this interest in mind, we present the following aspects of the presentation to consider *before* the group speaks. All group members should know and be in agreement with the following:

1. Speaker order
2. Formality of the presentation
   Can group members interrupt each other?
   Can group members wander from their prepared remarks?
3. Determine where will the group sit/stand?
   Group members need to realize that if they are all in front of the class, whether standing or speaking, audience members will be aware of them, even when they are not speaking.
   Will all sit and then stand up to speak or will all stand throughout the entire presentation?
   Should the group sit to the side and have the speaker stand in the middle of the front of the class?
4. Delivery
   Use note cards? Legal pad? PowerPoint slides?
   Prepare individually—think about eye contact (speak to the group, not the instructor), gestures, and vocal aspects
5. Time constraints for each speech
6. Determine how to signal if someone is speaking too long or if the group is going too long
7. Introduction, body, conclusion
   Who will deliver the group's introduction and conclusion?
   How will each person's introduction and conclusion relate to the group?
   How do you make transitions between speeches so all presentations are connected?
8. Presentational aids
   What is available in the classroom?
   Will they benefit the presentation?
   Who will be responsible for making them and setting them up?

If group members wait until they approach the front of the room to address these concerns, they will appear unprepared. Deciding where to stand, how to signal each other, and what the speaking order is will reduce awkwardness and uncertainty, and should give a more professional, polished look to the presentation.

General Suggestions for Presenting in a Small Group

The following guidelines will help you be a successful participant in a panel discussion, symposium, or forum. Many of the guidelines apply to all three group formats, but others apply just to one.

Limit the number of points you make. Since you will be given some time constraints, limit the number of points you make. Remember that each person has information to present. Your audience cannot process an overload of material. Be brief. Make your point as briefly and clearly as possible and do not confuse your listeners with too many details.

Avoid repetition. Avoid repetition by learning in advance what the other panelists will cover in their speeches. The job of assigning topics should be the responsibility of the presentation organizer. If the organizer is negligent, you may want to get in touch with the other panelists yourself. Keep communication channels open with your group members so you do not find yourself giving the same presentation as the person who spoke before you.

Try to meet in advance. Try to meet your fellow panelists in advance. When group members meet for the first time on stage, there is often an awkwardness in their interchange that comes from not knowing one another. This discomfort may be communicated to the audience.

Restrict your speech to the allotted time. If speakers exceed the time limit, the audience will find it difficult to sit through the entire program, and little opportunity will remain for a panel interchange or a question-and-answer period. In addition, by violating the time constraints, you may cause another speaker to modify his or her speech significantly. Staying within the allotted time frame is a necessary courtesy to the other group members.

Prepare for audience questions. Because the question-and-answer period is often the most important part of the program, spend as much time preparing for the questions as you did for your formal remarks. Anticipate the questions you are likely to be asked and frame your answers. During the question-and-answer period, be willing to speak up and add to someone else's response if none of the questions are being directed to you. When a fellow panel member finishes a response, simply say, "I'd like to make one more point that …" If, on the other hand, a question is directed to you that you think would be better handled by another panel member, say, "I think that considering her background, Therese is better able to answer that question."

Simple visual aids are appropriate for group presentations, as long as you coordinate with other members. © *Yuri Arcus, 2008. Under license from Shutterstock, Inc.*

Consider enhancing your presentation with visual aids. Simple visual aids are as appropriate in group presentations as they are in single-person public speaking. Coordinate the use of visual aids so information is not repeated by multiple speakers. Be consistent and professional. It is inconsistent to allow one group member to use the blackboard when the rest of the group has PowerPoint slides.

Summary

We are all involved in small group activities whether they occur within or outside of the classroom. Opportunities exist for interacting within a group or speaking before a group. As a speaker, consider both primary and secondary audiences. As group members, we share a purpose for communication. Also, group members usually have both group-oriented and self-oriented goals, and group size influences the need for structure and how we communicate.

Each individual has responsibilities within the group setting regardless of the person's role. As leader, you can contribute to the group's process by providing direction and purpose, especially at the beginning of the meeting, keeping the group on track throughout the meeting, and providing a clarifying summary when appropriate. In terms of helping the group communicate effectively, the leader should draw information from participants, try to keep group communication from being one-sided, and try to maintain the cohesiveness of the group.

As a group member, you have several responsibilities, including knowing the constraints of the assignment, working to achieve group goals, being responsible for completing your part of the assignment, researching sufficiently, communicating effectively and efficiently, avoiding personal attacks, and leaving your personal problems at home. Following the seven-step reflective process helps to keep the group organized and focused and helps to make sure that members do not jump to quick solutions without sufficient analysis and deliberation.

When the occasion arises for you to present as a group member before an audience, it is important to determine whether a panel discussion, symposium, or forum best suits your needs and the needs of your audience. Your knowledge of public speaking and your individual skills come into play as you present before the group. However, it is important to meet as a group beforehand to determine such things as speaker order, amount of speaking time allotted for each individual, whether or not presentational aids will be useful, and who will be responsible for preparing such aids. Each person's presentation should cover only a few points. The presentations should not overlap, and group members should be prepared for audience questions. An effective presentation involves preparation on the part of all group members as well as attention to detail regarding content connection, transitions from speaker to speaker, and overall professional performance.

 ## Questions for Study and Discussion

1. What is the difference between being a member of a small group that works together and then presents before another group and being a member of a panel that never meets before it presents before another group?
2. How would your presentation differ if you had a primary audience only or you had both a primary and a secondary audience?
3. When you work with others to accomplish tasks in college, can you usually identify who the leader is? How? What seems to be the most difficult aspect of being a leader in a college classroom project?
4. Can you think of a situation when your fellow group members did not fulfill their group responsibilities? If so, how did you react? How did other group members react?

5. Under what circumstances would it make sense to present as a member of a panel? Of a symposium? When is a forum appropriate?
6. If you were giving advice to a friend who had not participated in a small group presentation, what would you tell your friend about speaking as a member of a group before another group?

Activities

1. Select an actual small group on campus or in your community and obtain permission to observe several meetings. Take notes on what you observe, and write a 500- to 750-word paper connecting your observations to concepts discussed in this chapter. Pay particular attention to how the group approaches problem-solving.
2. Join with three or four other class members to work on a common problem. Use a panel or symposium to present your analysis and recommendations. The group should move through all steps of the reflective thinking process. Present the process and your solution to the class.

References

Bales, R. F. 1953. "The equilibrium problems in small groups" in T. Parson, R. F. Bales and E. A. Shils (Eds.), *Working papers in the theory of action.* Glencoe, IL: Free Press.

Dewey, J. 1910. *How we think.* Boston, MA: D. C. Heath.

DiSalvo, V. 1973. "Small group behavior," in *Explorations in speech communications*, J. J. Makay (Ed.), (111–112). Colombus, OH: Charles E. Merrill Publishing Co.

Ehrlich, E. and Hawes, G. R. 1984. *Speak for success.* New York: Bantam Books.

Ross, R. S. and Ross, J. R. *Small groups in organizational settings.* (Englewood Cliffs, NJ: Prentice-Hall.

Slater, P. E. 1958. "Contrasting correlates of group size," *Sociometry* 21, 129–39.

Glossary

A

Abstract topics
Ideas, theories, principles, and beliefs.

Accurate
Reliable, current, and error-free.

Adoption
When you want your audience to start doing something.

After-dinner speech
Purpose is to entertain, often with humor, although it usually conveys a thoughtful message.

Alliteration
The repetition of the initial consonant or initial sounds in a series of words.

Analogy
Establishes common links between similar and not-so-similar concepts.

Anaphora
The repetition of the same word or phrase at the *beginning* of successive clauses or sentences.

Antithesis
The use of contrast, within a parallel grammatical structure, to make a rhetorical point.

Aristotle
Greek philosopher.

Articulation
The verbalization of distinct sounds and how precisely words are formed.

Attitudes
Predispositions to act in a particular way that influence our response to objects, events, and situations.

Authority
An individual cited or considered to be an expert; power to influence or command thought; credible.

B

Bandwagoning
Unethical speakers may convince listeners to support their point of view by telling them that "everyone else" is already involved.

Beliefs
Represent a mental and emotional acceptance of information. They are judgments about the truth or the probability that a statement is correct.

Body
Includes your main points and supporting material that reinforces your specific purpose and thesis statement.

Brainstorming
Generating a list of ideas consistent with the goals of your speech.

C

Calculated ambiguity
A speaker's planned effort to be vague, sketchy, and considerably abstract.

Captive audience
Those who are required to attend.

Channel
The medium through which the message is sent.

Clear
Communicating ideas without confusion.

Cliché
Trite phrase.

Commemorative speech
An inspirational message designed to stir emotions.

Communication
The creation of shared meaning through symbolic processes.

Conclusion
Supports the body of your speech, reinforces your message and brings your speech to a close.

Connotation
The meaning we apply to words as they are framed by our personal experiences.

Continuance
When your listeners are already doing the thing you want them to do.

Coverage
The depth and breadth of the material.

Critical thinking
The application of the principles of reasoning to your ideas and the ideas of others. Critical thinking enables you to evaluate your world and make choices based upon what you have learned.

Culture
The rules people follow in their relationships with one another; values; the feelings people share about what is right or wrong, good or bad, desirable or undesirable; customs accepted by the community of institutional practices and expressions; institutions; and language.

Currency
The timeliness of the material.

D

Deductive reasoning
Drawing conclusions based on the connections between statements that serve as premises.

Definition through example
Helps the audience understand a complex concept by giving the audience a "for instance."

Denotative
Literal, objective definition provided by a dictionary.

Deterrence
Your goal is to convince your listeners not to start something.

Dialogic communication
Demonstrates an honest concern for the welfare of the listeners.

Dialogue
Takes into account the welfare of the audience.

Discontinuance
An attempt to persuade your listeners to stop doing something.

Dynamic variables
Those things that are subject to change.

Dynamism
A lively, active, vigorous, and vibrant quality.

E

Emphasis
Stressing certain words or phrases to draw attention.

Epistrophe
The repetition of a word or expression at the *end* of phrases, clauses, or sentences.

Equality pattern
Giving equal time to each point.

Ethics
The rules we use to determine good and evil, right and wrong. These rules may be grounded in religious principles, democratic values, codes of conduct, and bases of values derived from a variety of sources.

Ethos
Ethical appeal, makes speakers worthy of belief.

Euphemisms
Words or phrases substituted for more direct language.

Evaluation
Assessing the worth of the speaker's ideas and determine their importance to you.

Examples
Support that helps illustrate a point or claim.

Extemporaneous speaking
A method of delivery that involves using carefully prepared notes to guide the presentation.

Extrinsic ethos
A speaker's image in the mind of the audience.

Eye contact
The connection you form with listeners through your gaze.

F

Facts
Pieces of information that are verifiable and irrefutable.

Feedback
The messages the audience sends back to the speaker.

Figurative analogy
Drawing comparisons between things that are distinctly different in an attempt to clarify a concept or persuade.

Fixed-alternative questions
Limit responses to several choices, yielding valuable information about such demographic factors as age, education, and income.

Flow charts
Used to display the steps, or stages, in a process.

Forum
Group members respond to audience questions.

G

General encyclopedias
Cover a wide range of topics in a broad manner.

General purpose
There are three general purposes for speeches: to inform, to persuade, and to entertain or inspire.

Gestures
Using your arms and hands to illustrate, emphasize, or provide a visual experience that accompanies your thoughts.

Glittering generalities
Rely on audience's emotional responses to values such as home, country, and freedom.

Group-oriented goals
Center around specific tasks to be performed.

H

Habit of justice
Reminds us to select and present facts and opinions openly and fairly.

Habit of preferring public to private motivation
Ethical speakers reveal the sources of their information and opinion, which assists the audience in weighing any special bias, prejudices, and self-centered motivations in source materials.

Habit of respect for dissent
Addresses the necessity for accepting views that differ from our own.

Habit of search
Putting forth effort to learn enough about your topic so you are able to speak knowledgeably and confidently.

Hypothetical examples
A fictional example; the circumstances they describe are often realistic and thus effective.

I

Imagery
Involves creating a vivid description through the use of one or more of our five senses.

Impromptu speaking
Involves little or no preparation time; using no notes or just a few.

Inductive reasoning
Generalizing from specific examples and drawing conclusions from what we observe.

Information absorbtion threshold
The point as which a visual will cease to be useful because it says too much.

Informative speech
Communicates information and ideas in a way that your audience will understand and remember.

Innuendo
Includes hints or remarks that something is what it is not.

Internal previews
Extended transitions that tell the audience, in general terms, what you will say next.

Internal summaries
Follow a main point and act as reminders; useful to clarify or emphasize what you have just said.

Interpretation
Attaching meaning to the speaker's words.

Intrinsic ethos
Ethical appeal found in the actual speech, including such aspects as supporting material, argument flow, and source citation.

Introduction
Supports the body of your speech and should capture your audience's attention and indicate your intent.

J

Jargon
Technical terminology unique to a special activity or group.

K

Keynote speaker
Featured speaker at an event.

Key-word search
A web search that leads you to a list of records which are weighted in order of amount of user access.

L

Line graph
Used to show a trend over time.

Listener
Perceives through sensory levels and interprets, evaluates, and responds to what he or she hears.

Listening
Consists of several identifiable stages: sensing, interpreting, evaluating, and responding.

Literal analogy
Compares like things from similar classes, such as a game of professional football with a game of college football.

Logos
An appeal that is rational and reasonable based on evidence provided.

M

Mean
Calculated by adding all the numbers in a group and dividing by the number of items.

Message
What is communicated by the speaker and perceived by the audience.

Message credibility
The extent to which the speech is considered to be factual and well-supported through documentation.

Mode
The value that occurs most frequently.

Monologic communication

From this perspective, the audience is viewed as an object to be manipulated and, in the process, the speaker displays such qualities as deception, superiority, exploitation, dogmatism, domination, insincerity, pretense, coercion, distrust, and defensiveness.

Monologue

Focuses only on the speaker's self-interest.

Mood

The overall feeling you hope to engender in your audience.

N

Name calling

Linking a person or group with a negative symbol.

Noise

Anything that interferes with the communication process.

Non-fluencies

Meaningless words that interrupt the flow of our speech; also known as filled pauses or vocal fillers.

O

Objective

Information that is fair and unbiased.

Occasion

The time, place, event, and traditions that define the moment.

Open-ended questions

Audience members can respond however they wish.

Operational definitions

Specify procedures for observing and measuring concepts

Opinions

Points of view that may or may not be supported in fact.

Organization of ideas

The placement of lines of reasoning and supporting materials in a pattern that helps to achieve your specific purpose.

Organizational charts

Organized according to official hierarchies that determine the relationships of people as they work.

P

Panel discussion

Group members have an informal interchange on the issues in front of an audience.

Pathos

Persuading through emotional appeals.

Persuasion

Intended to influence choice through appeals to the audience's sense of ethics, reasoning, and emotion.

Pictographs

Most commonly used as a variation of the bar graph. Instead of showing bars of various lengths, comparing items on the graph, the bars are replaced by pictoral representations of the graph's subject.

Pictoral flow charts

Use pictures to display the steps, or stages, in a process.

Pie graph

Also known as circle graphs, show how the parts of an item relate to the whole.

Pitch

Vocal range or key, the highness or lowness of your voice produced by the tightening and loosening of your vocal folds.

Plagiarism

Using other's work, words, or ideas without adequate acknowledgement.

Plain folks

An effort to identify with the audience.

Primacy effect
The belief that it is the first point in your speech that listeners will most likely remember.

Primary sources
Firsthand accounts such as diaries, journals, and letters, as well as statistics, speeches, and interviews. They are records of events as they are first described.

Progressive pattern
Using your least important point first and your most important point last.

Pronunciation
Knowing how to say a word and say it correctly.

Proposition of fact
Persuading your listeners that your interpretation of a situation, event, or concept is accurate.

Proposition of policy
Easily recognizable by their use of the word "should."

Proposition of value
Persuading your listeners based on deep-seated beliefs.

R

Rate
The pace at which you speak.

Reasoning
The process of using known and believed information to explain or prove other statements less well understood or accepted. Refers to the sequence of interlinking claims and arguments that, together, establish the content and force of your position.

Reasoning from cause
The inference step is that an event of one kind contributes to or brings about an event of another kind.

Reasoning from sign
The inference step is that the presence of an attribute can be taken as the presence of some larger condition or situation of which the attribute is a part.

Recency effect
The belief that it is the last point in your speech that listeners will most likely remember.

Research
The raw material that forms the foundation of your speech.

S

Scale questions
A type of fixed-alternative question that ask people to respond to questions set up along a continuum.

Secondary sources
Generally provide an analysis, an explanation, or a restatement of a primary source.

Self-oriented goals
Relate to the individual's personal needs and ambitions.

Sensation
Awareness due to stimulation of a sense organ such as the ear.

Signpost
Create oral lists to help your audience understand the structure of your speech.

Speaker
Person who initiates the message.

Speaker credibility
The extent to which a speaker is perceived as a competent spokesperson.

Specialized encyclopedias
Focus on particular areas of knowledge in more detail.

Specific purpose
The precise response you want from your audience.

Speech of acceptance
Expresses gratitude for the award.

Speech of demonstration
When the focus is on *how* something is done.

Speech of description
Helps an audience understand *what* something is.

Speech of explanation
Helps an audience understand *why* something is so.

Speech of introduction
Introduces the person who will give an important address.

Speech of presentation
Delivered as part of a ceremony to recognize an individual or group chosen for special honors.

Static variables
Those things that remain stable from speaking situation to speaking situation.

Statistics
The collection, analysis, interpretation, and presentation of information in numerical form.

Strongest point pattern
You spend the most time in your speech on the first point; less time on the second point, and even less time on the last point of your speech.

Supporting material
The information used in a particular way to make your case.

Symposium
Centers on prepared speeches on a specified subject given by group members who have expertise on the subject.

T

Testimonials
Statements testifying to benefits received; can be both helpful and destructive.

Testimony
Citing the experience or opinion of others; either directly or through paraphrasing.

Thesis statement
The core idea; identifies the main ideas of your speech.

Toast
Brief message of good will and congratulations.

Tone
The emotional disposition of the speaker as the speech is being delivered.

Transitions
Verbal bridges between ideas; words; phrases, or sentences that tell your audience how ideas relate.

V

Values
Socially shared ideas about what is good, right, and desirable; deep-seated abstract judgments about what is important to us..

Vocal fillers
Words used that add nothing to a speech, such as "you know," "like," "um," "ah," or "er."

Volume
The loudness of your voice, controlled by how forcefully air is expelled through the trachea onto the vocal folds.

Voluntary audience
Those who choose to attend.

Index